TOMMY DOC

TOMMY DOC

The Controversial and Colourful Life
of One of Football's Most
Dominant Personalities

DAVID TOSSELL

MAINSTREAM
PUBLISHING

EDINBURGH AND LONDON

First published in Great Britain in 2013 by

MAINSTREAM PUBLISHING COMPANY

(EDINBURGH) LTD

7 Albany Street

Edinburgh EH1 3UG

ISBN 9781780575841

A catalogue record for this book is available
from the British Library

Printed in Great Britain by
CPI Group (UK) Ltd, Croydon, CR0 4YY

1 3 5 7 9 10 8 6 4 2

ACKNOWLEDGEMENTS

Piecing together the jigsaw of someone's life, even in the instant-research age of the Internet, is impossible without a lot of help. Most importantly, this book has drawn upon interviews with many people, all of whom have my sincere gratitude. The list of those who declined to speak about Tommy Docherty or didn't respond to my requests was, in its own way, almost as revealing. I won't name names, but most readers will be able to work out upon which side of the divide most of the characters in this story sit.

Sadly, one of those I interviewed, Brian Greenhoff, died during the editing stage of this book. I have left his comments in the present tense in order to give a better sense of our conversation.

I have been very lucky that Tommy himself agreed to participate in the project without asking for any control over the end product. For that I have also to thank his wife, Mary, for allowing me to persuade him to be interviewed.

Others who were important to the writing of this book do not appear anywhere except for on the following list: Steve Anglesey, Ted Brack, Stephanie Branston, Garry Bray, David Findlay, Paul Hart, Gary James, Steve Kim, Tom Kundert, Colin Leslie, Tony MacDonald, Paul Mace, Sue McKellar, Jason Morgan, Dermot O'Riordan, Nick Pike, Keir Radnedge, Ian Rigby, Richard Smith, Bruce Talbot, Dan Tolhurst, Richard Whitehead and Ed Wyatt. At Press Association Photos, Laura Wagg was as helpful as ever, while David Shopland kindly allowed me to use one of his photographs.

I am grateful to Birlinn for allowing me to use an extract from Michael Grant and Rob Robertson's book *The Management*. The extract from H. Kingsley-Long and A. McArthur's *No Mean City*, published by Corgi Books, is reprinted by kind permission of the Random House Group Limited.

It is no exaggeration to say that Bill Campbell at Mainstream Publishing changed my life 12 years ago when he phoned to commission an idea I had pitched to him. Suitably buoyed, I have been writing one book or another ever since and I have been fortunate enough to have worked on several further projects with Bill and his talented team, including Graeme Blaikie, Fiona Brownlee and many others. In thanking them for their support and professionalism with this book, I also have to express my regret that the imminent closure of the company means this will be the final time we work together. I know many other authors are sharing the same sense of loss. I sincerely wish the very best to everyone at Mainstream as they write their own new chapters.

My own family might sometimes wish that I was similarly exiting the publishing world. If so, they do a fantastic job of keeping it to themselves and continuing to offer support and patience. This particular book is dedicated to Amy, Sarah, Laura, Karis and my wife, Sara.

CONTENTS

INTRODUCTION

The face, contentedly world-weary, betrays no hint of a smile. The punchlines are delivered with perfect timing, the pause before the pay-off measured immaculately for maximum impact. Les Dawson, the king of the deadpan comedians, couldn't have done this any better. The audience has been warmed up with lines such as 'growing up in the Gorbals in Glasgow, if you wanted a new pair of shoes you went down to the swimming baths on a Saturday morning' and are now roaring their way through a series of clashes with club chairmen and anecdotes about football's most famous names.

This is Tommy Docherty – 'Tommy Doc' to some; to others simply 'The Doc'. Captured on camera during a one-man theatre show in Norwich in the mid-1990s, the figure perched on the centre-stage stool is the embodiment of how many have come to regard one of the sport's most vibrant and divisive characters in the years since his managerial career ran out of last chances. A few gags, an avalanche of name-dropping and a checklist of opinions on the modern game when questions are invited from the auditorium. Job done.

It's a well-rehearsed turn and Docherty appears as comfortable in it as when he sits at home on the edge of the Derbyshire Dales in his slippers. Well into his 80s and into the second decade of the new millennium, the act is still getting a regular airing. But this is not Docherty the football man. It's not the driven and ruthless former Scotland international who arrived at two of the biggest clubs in England wielding an axe that sliced through a forest of veteran players, nurturing exciting young teams and transporting Chelsea and Manchester United from the wretched depths of relegation to the elevated rapture of Wembley appearances and title challenges.

9

The figure on stage is the caricature, the public persona whose jokes, for all the entertainment they offer to folk happy to shell out a few quid, give little insight into the trials and triumphs of a remarkable life. The failures and foul-ups of his managerial career, at places such as Rotherham, Aston Villa and Derby, are merely providers of comedic material. So, too, is the episode when he almost went to prison after admitting to telling lies in court. For many years he even used 'ladies and gentlemen, you're not going to believe this' as the opening line to his speaking engagements. Knowing his public has arrived for gags and giggles, the personal pain of such episodes or analysis of where things went wrong remains hidden behind the one-liners. The stage is no place for self-pity or self-assessment; nor does he use his platform to advance, or even pose, any debate about just how a good a manager he actually was.

'To hear the Doc speak about his career now, it all seems like a bit of a joke,' says author Jim White in *Manchester United: The Biography*. 'To watch him at his prime was to observe a master of the art, charismatic, not fearing of reputation or personal feeling.'

Watching the glib, wisecracking character in full flow it is easy to imagine him among the mud and wintergreen, raising spirits when results were going badly and getting a laugh out of players who really didn't fancy training on a cold, wet winter morning. But you don't see the darker side that clearly existed: the jokes that could frequently be laced with venom, leaving rancour-infested dressing-rooms divided along pro- and anti-Docherty lines. The roadside of his life is strewn with the wreckage of relationships with players, employers and even his family, some of whom have not spoken to him for more than three decades.

Chelsea's rise under his management in the 1960s was accompanied by the rhythm of players' boots clacking down the corridor to his office to hand in transfer requests. Over the years, he fell out with some of the biggest names in football: Terry Venables, George Graham, Barry Bridges, George Best, Denis Law, Willie Morgan, Paddy Crerand, Jim Gregory, Bruce Rioch, Gerry Daly, to name just a few.

Yet rather than destabilising performance on the field, the fact is that the longer Docherty remained at a club – Chelsea and Manchester United being the cases in point – the more successful his teams became. If that was because he managed over time to get shot of those who failed to respond to his methods, then it is hard to hold that against him, on a purely professional basis at least. Of course, the alternative argument is that perhaps he could have won more than one League Cup, two promotions and an FA Cup had his team environments been more harmonious. Even at the two clubs where he achieved most, his reigns eventually came to an end largely because he had run out of allies when he needed them most.

Deteriorating rapport with the board and players at Chelsea meant that when he picked up a one-month ban from all football for abusing an official during a summer tour game in 1967, weeks after leading the club to the FA Cup final, it was made clear to him that his time at Stamford Bridge was at an end. And, most famously of all, he was dismissed by Manchester United within weeks of guiding them to Wembley success in 1977 after revealing that he had been having a relationship with Mary Brown, the wife of the club physiotherapist. Theories abound about why United felt compelled to dismiss Docherty after originally intimating that he could remain in their employ, but the feeling remains that had he not made enemies of influential board members, not strained his relationship with certain players to the limit, and generally been less of a roguish character, his misdemeanour would have been viewed more sympathetically.

Docherty was as unreconstructed as the northern stand-up acts, whom he so admired, that you'd see around that time on shows like ITV's *The Comedians*. Yet time caught up with him. He learned the hard way that the laddish pranks of the dressing-room, the dodgy deals of a typical football club, telling a few porkies in the manner of most football managers and, yes, sleeping with a colleague's wife had a price that had to be paid in the real world.

Former United player Eamon Dunphy, in his masterpiece about the club, *A Strange Kind of Glory*, states that 'the Doc's life at United was lived on a number of levels'. He says, 'He fought with players, behaved as venally as was necessary to survive, socialised with the Busby family one day; dealt with Stan Flashman the next.' Docherty undoubtedly ignored the romantic notion of Old Trafford under Sir Matt Busby in the post-Munich era and scuffled and scrapped, and wheeled and dealed in the same way that he would have done at a hard-up, lower-division club in the provinces. 'Nobody objected,' says Dunphy. 'Until Tommy Docherty fell in love with Mary Brown.'

Yet among the many paradoxes of Docherty's career is the issue of whether the 'Mary Brown Affair' was genuinely a transgression too great for United to ignore or whether it simply gave the club the excuse they'd been seeking to get rid of him. He had, after all, been the subject of investigation by private detectives supposedly working for those with connections to the board. Docherty always insisted that he was 'sacked for falling in love', yet as he looks back on that period now even he admits that he doesn't know what motivated the club's decision.

While Docherty found personal happiness with Mary, to whom he is still contentedly married, he never recovered professionally, bouncing around from club to club, including three managerial stints in Australia. It all ended with an acrimonious departure in 1988 from non-League Altrincham: his 15th managerial appointment. It was an inauspicious, undignified final curtain for a man whose sides are still revered at two of the modern era's mega-clubs and who might, on the evidence of a year or so of high promise, have turned out to be the greatest manager the Scotland team ever had.

Just as Docherty has been a reliable resource for media over the past half-century by virtue of his ready pronouncements on everyone and everything in football, so it is almost impossible to find someone who does not have an opinion about the Doc – although the number of people who declined requests for interviews for this book suggests that many would rather keep them to themselves. The comment from one former player that 'if I haven't got something nice to say about someone I'd rather say nothing' appears to reflect the outlook of many. Even one of Docherty's biggest supporters, former Chelsea man Charlie Cooke, admits, 'I know there are people who would put the boot in on him, but not me.'

Lou Macari, whom Docherty picked for Scotland, signed for United and fell out with on a regular basis, says, 'Along the way he has annoyed a few people, but I don't think that bothers him a great deal. If you are not the forgiving type or can't accept that is what he is like then you can spend the rest of your life holding a grudge against him.'

Similarly, Gordon Hill, the England winger Docherty purchased on three occasions, admits, 'There will be a lot of people who hate the Doc, absolutely despise him. One man's meat is another man's poison, I suppose. At times he would back you up and could help you out in a difficult situation, but would I completely trust the Doc? I wouldn't trust him as far as I could throw him. But I don't think he would ever do anything deliberately harmful to anybody. It was just his nature. His football was the number one consideration.'

Over the years, Docherty has remained mostly unperturbed by adversarial comments, his skin thick enough for them to merely bounce off. As journalist James Lawton once put it, 'Docherty needs our approval about as much as Jesse James needed a credit card.' Besides, Docherty would tell you, football history is punctuated by the unfulfilled promise of men such as legendary former England captain Billy Wright who turned out to be 'too nice' to succeed as managers.

On the one occasion Docherty did take noticeable offence to criticism, when Morgan described him on television as 'the worst manager there has ever been', he launched an ill-advised libel case that led to his own appearance in the dock on perjury charges. He was accused of deliberately lying during a case that collapsed more spectacularly than the poorest team he ever managed. 'It is the biggest regret I have,' he admits. 'I'd never let what anyone said bother me before that.' It was the only time he forgot comments such as, 'If people take the piss out of me I don't mind. If you give it out to them you have to expect to take it back.'

Docherty could dish it out more than anyone, yet there is little evidence of him being the 'foul-mouthed' character one writer described him as a few years ago. In the hours I spent talking to Docherty for this book, not once did the F-word fall from his lips. Even when a 'bastard' slipped out, he quickly added, 'Excuse my language.' It was as endearing as his habit of adding 'God rest their soul' whenever he mentioned someone who had passed from this world.

A man who often failed to walk the fine line between instinct and impulsiveness, Docherty offers a story rife with unfathomable contradictions. At times he could be a fierce disciplinarian, to the point of banishing eight of his Chelsea team from a vital game in the Championship run-in over an after-hours drink in Blackpool. Yet he could be childishly undisciplined himself, as his penchant for starting bread-roll fights in inappropriate situations shows. He loved to be one of the boys away from the field, but was quick to fall out with them in the dressing-room, especially when he attempted to pull them up over behaviour he could easily have been guilty of himself on another occasion.

Players speak of his ability to give a club an immediate lift with the injection of energy he brought to a struggling team, which, in the nature of football management, most were when Docherty arrived. 'He tackled life with an explosive energy that often made him seem like an earthquake waiting to happen,' is the description of Docherty by George Graham, who played for him at Chelsea, United and Scotland.

Yet Docherty's record suggests he was not the man to appoint if you wanted a quick fix. The first five English clubs who appointed him as manager were relegated either that same season or the season after. The two clubs who retained Docherty long term beyond such disappointment, Chelsea and Manchester United, were rewarded, in particular with the style of football and excitement his teams delivered to the fans.

Detractors point to the failure to win more at Stamford Bridge and Old Trafford, yet those who watched their teams under Docherty talk animatedly about the vibrancy that transferred itself from pitch to terrace, the team and players each feeding off the fervour of the other. One example of that is voiced by Brian Mears, a board member at Chelsea during Docherty's reign and son of then chairman Joe Mears. In his 2001 memoir of life at the club, *Chelsea: Football Under the Blue* Flag, Mears junior adopts a tone of disapproval of much of Docherty's behaviour and personality. Yet, like many, he is able to overlook the faults in favour of the thrills. 'His flamboyant ultimate failure was better than the benign success of Vialli,' he states, before addressing the 'dinosaur' comment made about Docherty by celebrity fan David Mellor. 'Whatever history says of Docherty, his contribution to Chelsea was 1,000 times that of Mellor and his ilk.'

Similarly, Richard Kurt and Chris Nickeas, in *The Red Army Years: United in the 1970s*, are aware enough of the manager's flaws to refer to 'Docherty's wankerhood', yet at the same time they acknowledge, 'He played on the fans' erogenous zone – he gave us a young team, predominantly home developed, who truly believed in attacking football, who exhibited a never-say-die attitude and played with the flair, passion and the skill for which United have traditionally stood.'

Brian Clough even said of United at the height of their powers under Docherty, 'They have dragged people from their armchairs who abandoned my game years ago.'

The Doc's preferred method at most clubs was to weed out the ageing and the cynical, offering opportunities to those with young legs and impressionable minds. One such player was the late Peter Osgood, who would describe Docherty as 'one of the few people I can honestly say has really influenced my life'. He added, 'His contribution to the game has not been fully appreciated. Like Clough, he could motivate previously average players to become exceptional ones.'

Docherty's own playing days as a wing-half for Celtic, Preston, Arsenal and Scotland were notable for a combative style that he saw as a necessary platform from which more gifted colleagues, such as the great England winger Tom Finney, could perform. 'The fame and success he went on to enjoy as a manager certainly came as no surprise to me,' noted Finney, adding, 'All his teams put the emphasis on good football – fun was always the name of Doc's game.' But it should not be overlooked that his teams, when required, could complement his love of an attacking game featuring orthodox wingers with the same pragmatism with which he played. There would be times when Docherty abandoned his beliefs for a formation designed to achieve a specific result. He might have been a romantic about the beautiful game, but he wasn't stupid. He regularly voiced his admiration for the achievements of Don Revie at Leeds United. After an FA Cup victory with Aston Villa – against the QPR team he'd recently left – Docherty remarked, 'I would rather be an unpopular winner than a good loser.'

There were periods when Docherty drew criticism for the artisan nature of the football played by his teams, especially in the early days at certain clubs before he had completed the task of installing a young team to reflect his expansive ambition. Certainly, no one who saw Manchester United fighting relegation under Docherty would have predicted what was to come in the following three seasons.

In his early days as a manager, Docherty was considered an innovator. His Chelsea team was acknowledged as one of the first to utilise overlapping full-backs on a regular basis, and he was quick to embrace new training methods, attempt tactical complexities and study the mental approach of teams such as world champions Brazil. Much of that has become buried beneath the public image of a rent-a-mouth. 'My reputation has maybe overshadowed whatever ability I had,' he has said, although adding, without being entirely convincing, 'That doesn't bother me.'

Docherty's long-time colleague Frank Blunstone suggests, 'The trouble is, if you tell too many jokes people treat you as a joke.' But in their study of Scottish bosses, *The Management*, authors Michael Grant and Rob Robertson attempt to redress the balance:

> There was much, much more to Docherty than that. Not for nothing had he managed Manchester United, Chelsea, Aston Villa and Scotland by the time he was 49. He was a focused, hungry, driven manager with a fastidious attention to detail. He was years ahead of his time in embracing sports psychology and media manipulation, in checking the bloodline of players who might be eligible for Scotland caps, in bringing African players to the English league. He was still a serving player when the SFA asked him to compile reports on the opposition at the 1958 World Cup finals. These aren't the acts of someone who was nothing more than a tabloid windbag. Docherty was a manager of substantial talent and vision.

Veteran journalist and author Norman Giller argues, 'I wrote a book with Tommy called *The ABC of Soccer Sense* and people don't quite realise the depth of knowledge of football and tactics that Tommy had. People are quick to pooh-pooh what he achieved and give all the credit to his coaches, but he really did know the game.'

Yet too frequently the accomplishments and ambitions of Docherty's career were undermined by that impetuous Gorbals-formed personality. 'Often the hopes have been mangled by the quirky impulses of his nature,' Lawton wrote during the last days of Docherty's career.

Similarly, his acts of kindness are compromised by tales of ruthlessness, even cruelty. Blunstone relates a tale of Docherty's generosity from an occasion when members of the United coaching staff visited a clothes wholesaler. 'I saw a coat there and thought it was nice, but it was 600 quid so I said, "Bugger that, I expect a suit for that price." Later that afternoon Tommy came to me and said, "Here you are." He had paid for it himself.'

Steve Coppell made sure I knew about Docherty cutting short a holiday in Malta to fly home for his university graduation. 'I remember how impressed and touched my mum and dad were by that,' he says.

But for every tale of sending Coppell and his girlfriend to the Lake District at his own expense; or telling Brian Greenhoff to disappear for a few days during the season with his wife, who was unwell during her first pregnancy; or travelling to Scotland to take George Graham's parents to their son's Scotland Under-23 debut, there is a damning counter-balance. For example, Denis Law's shock at hearing of his free transfer from United after thinking he'd agreed a more graceful exit, or the various players banished to train with the reserves, or the club captains stripped of their role without explanation.

Terry Venables, who went from the status of beloved son to undesirable influence in Docherty's eyes at Chelsea, said, 'One minute you would be a favourite, the next, someone else would be flavour of the month and you were on the outer. He fell out with everybody.'

The words with which the *Daily Mirror*'s Ken Jones reported Docherty's departure from his first managerial post at Chelsea would have been just as appropriate as a summary of his entire career. 'He has always said what he means, often without thought, and rarely with any regard for the outcome,' he wrote. 'He bought, sold, built and destroyed. In five years he came close to greatness but never achieved it. He had teams that were the envy of almost every manager in the country – and then tore them apart.'

Author Sean Egan notes in *The Doc's Devils*, his book about the Docherty era at United, 'Only a psychiatrist would be able to explain why someone who is a warm and generous friend and mentor to people currently in his favour should – as in the Law case – seek to put a distance between himself and people he has decided have outlived their usefulness with a completely unnecessary degree of cruelty.'

Yet Docherty insists that the majority of players who have taken against him over the years have done so simply because that is what happens when players realise they are not the key figure in a manager's plans. He does add, though, 'I was a good judge of a player, but maybe not a good judge of character.' That perhaps contributed to some of the quarrels and is why he confesses, 'One or two weren't good signings, but I got rid of them quickly.'

Whether the public took offence at the infighting within the dressing-room – as long they didn't see it affecting performance on the field – is debatable. Rather, they appeared to lap up the soap opera of his life. As Lawton wrote, 'The great redemption of Docherty, outweighing his cynicism, an unscrupulous streak that he has rarely attempted to conceal, has been his clear love of the interaction between one man, eleven players and a public hungry for colour and incident.'

He certainly provided that. Even if his teams weren't in the points he was usually in the headlines – sometimes unintentionally and not always for the better. Even though the contemporaries he admired most were the likes of Revie and Bill Shankly – for sheer consistency of performance – it was Clough and Malcolm Allison with whom he is more frequently bracketed. The trio occupied the same top table of quotability and rare was the day when one of them wasn't in the news. Docherty himself would concede that his achievements don't measure up to either of those men, Clough having performed miracles over an extended period at Derby and Nottingham Forest, and Allison masterminding Manchester City's domestic and European dominance over a shorter period under Joe Mercer.

It is Allison to whom Docherty's descent from the pinnacle of his profession bears the most striking resemblance. Allison spent the years after his first spell at Manchester City, where he won four trophies in three years, trying to balance his increasingly parodied media image with a quest for glory that took him around various League grounds, foreign fields and non-League arenas. So it was with Docherty, following his departure from Old Trafford. It was little wonder that two kindred spirits should end up working the theatres together for a spell in the 1990s.

While Docherty could match Clough and Allison with his tongue, his greatest feats on the field were creating the promise of what could be – and what might have been. That was particularly so at Old Trafford. When he departed Chelsea in 1967 it felt as though he had taken his team as far as it could go, yet the United team he left behind in 1977 appeared to have the potential to build on its FA Cup triumph. Juventus manager at that time, Giovanni

Trapattoni, was predicting European triumph for them, and even the retired Shankly looked at the imminent challenge to his beloved Liverpool and said, 'There is a team from the East Lancs road that could take the title from us.' Of course, with Docherty in charge, maybe the divisions among the players and his confrontations with those he felt were getting too comfortable after a taste of success would have ensured it all ended in tears anyway. Perhaps ending on a high was the more poetic conclusion.

It is the 'what ifs' of Docherty's career that dominate his story and make him such an intriguing subject. If only he'd not been tempted to Old Trafford – something he now looks back on with some degree of regret – he could perhaps have become the greatest manager his national team ever had. Look at the talent his successors, Willie Ormond and Ally McLeod, had at their disposal in the World Cup finals of 1974 and 1978 and imagine the likes of Bremner, Lorimer, Gemmill, Macari, Dalglish and Souness galvanised by Docherty's dynamism during the white heat of tournament play.

Or suppose he'd been able more often to nurture player relationships for the benefit of a harmonious, united dressing-room. And what if he'd burned fewer bridges, retained more allies for when times got tough? Would Sir Matt have stood behind him when he declared his love for Mary Brown if he'd previously sought compromise rather than confrontation with loyal Busbyites such as Law, Crerand and Morgan?

The stage act Docherty has been performing for three decades might have been unrecognisable from the now-familiar routine. Without the self-deprecation, without the shortcomings, scrapes and sackings, there might have been no act at all. With more trophies, there might have been no need for it in the first place. Undoubtedly, this book would have progressed down an alternate path – one potentially far less interesting. The life behind the one-liners would have been a very different story.

PART ONE

BLUE IS THE COLOUR

'Without ambition one starts nothing. Without work one finishes nothing. The prize will not be sent to you. You have to win it. The man who knows how will always have a job. The man who also knows why will always be his boss.'

Ralph Waldo Emerson (1803–1882)

'Matt Busby said to me, "What are you going to do when you've finished playing?" I said, "I've half a mind to be a manager." He said, "That's all you need."'

Tommy Docherty

1

GLASGOW BOY TO INFANTRY MAN

'Your mother bought all your clothes at the Army and Navy store. It wasn't much fun going to school at the age of seven dressed as a Japanese admiral.'

The Gorbals. The name has a harsh, uncompromising edge that hints at the remorseless austerity of life within its boundaries. Certainly of the existence eked out by its inhabitants in the inter-war years when this district of Glasgow, situated south of the Clyde river, bulged with the overcrowding of its housing and cowered in fear of the 'razor gangs' who ruled its filthy streets.

Home to the Docherty family – who welcomed a son, Thomas Henderson, to the world on 24 April 1928 – was a single room in one of the Victorian-built tenement blocks that symbolised the bleak struggle for survival. These soot-stained 'single-end' dwellings, of which there might be a dozen spread over three or four floors in each building, frequently had seven or eight inhabitants each. Families endured miserable conditions, often frightened of telling the landlord of the latest leak or infestation for fear of being hounded for their rent arrears, or even evicted.

By the time Tommy was delivered into the world to mother Georgina and father Thomas, Glasgow's population, which had barely reached 80,000 at the start of the 1800s, had grown to almost 1,000,000 as the Clyde burped out myriad new industries along its banks. Migrant workers had eagerly taken advantage of employment opportunities, the Gorbals becoming a melting pot of cultures. Irish Catholics, Jews from Eastern Europe and Scots down from the Highlands worked, played, loved and fought in suffocating proximity. The size of the workforce had quickly outgrown the job market, just as surely as the population was bursting at the seams of available properties. Author John Burrowes, taking Florence Street as his example, calculated that seventy-nine children lived in two adjoining buildings – 'closes' – and the most populous close of all housed twenty-six families.

Slowly decaying below clouds of coal smoke, pinned in place for most of the year by the cold air, the tenements had been seen originally as the solution to the urgent need for mass housing. As many as four people might share each of the 'cavity beds' that were squeezed claustrophobically into what were effectively cupboards sunk into the walls, behind doors that remained closed during the day. Docherty recalled being forced to sleep with his father, mother and sister Margaret in a bed that was nothing more than a piece of board inserted into a slot in the wall and topped by a mattress and blankets.

Published in 1935, the novel *No Mean City* offers a vivid depiction of the Gorbals slums, where even darkness brought no relief from the unremitting drudge of tenement existence. Authors Alexander McArthur and H. Kingsley Long wrote:

Night brings no kindly silence to the tenement dwelling of the Empire's second city. The wide streets are deserted; the courtyards are empty; here and there the close-mouths may shelter shadowy figures, but each box dwelling is sealed by its own front door. The tenements themselves are never silent. There are sick children who wail and healthy ones who get restless; half-drunken men who snore and mutter; half-sober ones who quarrel with their wives. In the 'hoose' next door, or in some other 'hoose' on the landing above or below, there may be a party in progress which will last for forty-eight hours. As ever and anon front doors will open to allow some hurrying figure to reach the single landing closet which serves three households.

In common with most Gorbals families, there was no close bond between Docherty and his father, who worked at the Stewarts and Lloyds iron foundry and who his son recalled as constantly fighting against ill-health. 'I never remember my father reading me a story or buying me an apple or taking me for a walk in the park or to a football match,' he says, with no trace of regret. 'That was no different to the norm.' Life for most working fathers consisted of long hours 'at toil' and spending whatever money was not required for rent, fuel or food at the pub. Thomas senior was better than many, however, neither leaving his family short of life's essentials nor coming home drunk to administer the beatings to wife and offspring that were a regular occurrence in many homes.

With little other than the evening radio shows to amuse him indoors, Tommy would be outside until dark playing football with rolled-up newspaper or, if he had been fortunate at Christmas or if a few pals had chipped in the odd penny, a small rubber ball. Or there would be street shows to stage with the neighbourhood children. Showing an early aptitude for comedy by aping the 'wireless' performers to whom he listened, the likes of Sid Field and the Crazy Gang, it was the first manifestation of the repartee that would earn him so many headlines.

When Docherty was only nine – and his mother pregnant with second daughter Mary – his father 'lost the fight to keep himself alive', succumbing to pleurisy. Georgina took a second cleaning job to make ends meet, leaving home at 4.30 a.m. and returning a couple of hours later to wake her children and get the older ones ready for school. At least the leftovers she was given by the middle-class families for whom she worked helped to enliven the staple family diet of 'mince and tatties'.

Even with his mother's income, there was still the occasional need for Tommy to take the family's mantelpiece clock to the pawnbroker, where it would fetch two shillings and sixpence (12.5p) to tide them over until they could afford to redeem it for the original sum plus sixpence interest. His clothes had known previous owners, but were always clean and ironed following Georgina's trips to the communal washhouse. There were even new football boots every couple of years, second-hand of course, but with fresh studs nailed in by the local cobbler. 'They were two sizes too big, massive,' Docherty recalls, 'but they were cheap. She said, "You'll grow into them." She bought them from a place called Barrowland, near Glasgow city centre. There were all these stalls, hundreds of them. You name it, they sold it.'

None of this seemed remotely unusual or unjust. 'You don't know the good times,' Docherty says. 'It's rough all the time and you accept it.' According to McArthur and Long, 'The slums as a whole do not realise they are living in abnormal conditions.'

The extent of the ambition of most young men in the Gorbals was to have a clean home and a pretty wife to look after it. Only those who excelled at football or boxing dared dream of a life beyond the tenements.

The Gorbals' most celebrated sporting figure during Docherty's childhood was boxer Benny Lynch, who in 1935 became world flyweight champion by pounding England's Jackie Brown in Manchester. In *Benny*, his book about Lynch's life, Burrowes has one of his characters summarising the pride felt in the fighter's achievement by saying, 'The only thing they knew about the Gorbals or Florence Street before Benny was that we were the arsehole of the country.'

When Lynch returned to Glasgow as champion, more than 20,000 crammed the concourse at Central Station before he paraded through the banners and bunting of the Gorbals, whose excited inhabitants at last had something of which they could be proud. Even then, a cautionary tale was close at hand. Only 22 when he was crowned champion, Lynch was already a heavy drinker. His career ended three years later: he was knocked out in his final fight while bloated and drunk, and in 1946, aged thirty-three, his booze-worn body succumbed to pneumonia.

Boxing was not for Docherty, who had no love of a fight. Nor at a young age did there appear to be much potential for a career within football, given that he was no better than most boys in the teams for whom he played. Instead, the two men who made the biggest impression on him were from very different professions. He marvelled at the magnetism of the local 'ragman', who handed out toys in exchange for old clothes and ornaments as he drove his horse and cart through the neighbourhood. And then there was Father Joseph Connolly, the Catholic priest who visited the family on most days. 'He never stopped talking football to us,' Docherty said of a man whose support he valued so much that he vowed to reward him with an entire weekly wage packet for use in one of his causes. When he began work he would keep his promise, handing over £1 5s. 9d.

Attending St Mark's School, Docherty was averagely gifted, capable in the basic subjects and reasonably well behaved. 'I was a scallywag,' he admits. 'I would pinch an apple out the shop: mischievous things. As kids we were always pinching something.

The coppers, rather than arrest you, would give you a thick ear. And you were more scared of the priest than the police. The saving grace for me was the Boys' Guild run by Father Connolly. You had to go Mass and Holy Communion or you didn't play football. He reminded me of Bing Crosby in the movies. You used to be able to get in at the pictures by taking a jam jar up to the cashier and that's what we did.* I used to watch people like James Cagney and you copied a lot of the things they did. But then the Catholic priest, Bing Crosby, would put them on the right path. Father Connolly was like that. I used to go to Mass every morning, because if I did that and I was good enough I would be in the Boys' Guild team.'

Unsurprisingly, the football field held greater interest than the classroom for Docherty, and the highlight of the school week was when the games master handed out shirts on Friday afternoon to those selected for the next day's game. Having played in the morning for St Mark's, where future Kilmarnock and Scotland defender Willie Toner was a teammate, Docherty would spend Saturday afternoon turning out for Father Connolly's team, St Paul's Boys' Guild. Those matches offered him his first sight of different areas of Glasgow.

Docherty had almost escaped the Gorbals at the outbreak of the Second World War in an evacuation to Stirling. But when his mother discovered that the family would have to be separated, she announced, 'If we're going to die, we'll die together in our own home.' The family was briefly relocated to the Gallowgate district and finally granted the blessed relief of a council house in Shettleston shortly before the arrival of peacetime. With an inside toilet and three bedrooms it was 'undreamed-of luxury' and made Docherty fully aware of the deprivation of his life thus far. It gave him a vision of future possibilities and he would claim that his background 'was why my ambition in life was to become successful'.

It was Parkhead, home of Celtic, where football dreams were fortified. Now living even closer to the ground, Docherty was a frequent visitor, although he had to content himself with watching only the final 20 minutes after the gates opened to liberate the early leavers. Celtic had broken the grip of dominant rivals Rangers long enough to win the Scottish League Championship in 1936 and

---

* In the days before recycling, stores paid for returned glass jars and bottles.

1938. However, the post-war team, with goal-scoring legend Jimmy McGrory beginning a 20-year spell as manager in 1945, would have to wait until 1954 for its first title as Hibernian and Rangers, built around their 'Iron Curtain' defence, vied for pre-eminence.

Docherty idolised right-back Bobby Hogg, outside-right Jimmy Delaney and inside-forward Gerry McAlton, although it was at centre-half where he played most of his football. His hopes of joining the world of his heroes might have intensified, but first there was real life to contend with. Having left school at 14, he flitted at rapid speed through a variety of jobs – window cleaner, factory worker, bottle worker – that neither suited his temperament nor allowed him sufficient time to play football. But once he had settled into the enjoyable routine of a bread delivery boy, whose work hours were 4 a.m. until noon, his football found a further vehicle for advancement when he was recruited by Shettleston Juniors. The club even offered a £3 signing-on fee, weekly expenses ranging from half-a-crown to £1 and an occasional share of gate money.

Docherty was still employed by the bakery when, at the age of 18, he received his call-up papers several months after the end of the war. Turning down the opportunity to work down the coal mines as a 'Bevin Boy', he was ordered to report for two years of National Service with the Highland Light Infantry (HLI). 'It was the making of me,' he believes. After the somewhat haphazard, hand-to-mouth nature of his early years, he enjoyed the structure, purpose and camaraderie of army life. He learned about teamwork and the importance of relying on one's practised skills at times of pressure – lessons he would carry into his sporting career. 'I learned self-discipline. I was given responsibility and responded well to it.' It was also where he first began to realise that his football ability was something out of the ordinary.

Six weeks of basic training at Whittington Barracks in Lichfield, Staffordshire, took him out of Scotland for the first time, and during three months stationed in Edinburgh he learned about – and took great pride in – the history of his regiment. The daily army rations were a dietary improvement on what he'd been used to, and his level of fitness, always good, was honed to even greater sharpness. 'Willie Waddell, the Rangers outside-right, was there and he was good to me,' Docherty recalls. 'He used to let me miss the passing-out parade so I could get the train to Glasgow to play for Shettleston. Then I woke up one morning and lorries took us to Southampton. We were on a ship for four weeks and ended up at Port Said.'

There was plenty of decent football to be played during that posting to Palestine, the area now recognised as Israel and Jordan. 'When we arrived at camp in Jerusalem, the first thing they asked was whether there were any athletes. That determined which company you went in.' Docherty instantly identified himself to his superior officer as a footballer.

'Who do you play for?' came the demand.

'Shettleston Juniors, sir.'

'Professional?'

'Semi-professional.'

'That'll do. Charlie Company.'

When it came to the business of soldiering, one contemporary of Docherty's explained on the HLI Association's website that his memories of Palestine were of 'extreme boredom and heat, being stuck in the desert for weeks at a time, with only the occasional jaunt into Jerusalem or Cairo to break the monotony'. Yet it was one of those visits to the holy city of Jerusalem, early in his posting, that was to remind Docherty that National Service was no paid vacation, that life in uniform was lived under threat of violence, even death.

Although both sides had fought together against the Nazis, the tension between the British and Palestinians was all-encompassing. Since 1920, the British Mandate for Palestine had placed the region under Britain's administrative control. The Mandate was the League of Nations' recognition of the stated purpose of 'establishing in Palestine a national home for the Jewish people', but in the meantime the British were viewed by both Arabs and Jews as an army of occupation. One local, Elli Baram, told me, 'It was not the easiest of times and there were a lot of underground organisations that were against the British.'

One such group was Irgun, a militant Zionist faction whose leadership included the future Israeli prime minister Menachem Begin. On 22 July 1946, Private Docherty was on guard duty outside the modern, six-storey King David Hotel, in which were housed the headquarters of the British forces and government secretariat. A group of Irgun loyalists, dressed as Arabs, entered the basement kitchens with 350 kg of gelignite and TNT hidden inside seven milk churns. At 12.37 p.m., the explosives were detonated, bringing down much of the building's southern corner, in which the British offices were situated. Amid billowing smoke, the screams of terrified people diving down side streets, police whistles and the wails of bending, crashing girders, Docherty's training – 'all three months of it' – kicked in.

Without conscious thought, he found shelter from the flying debris and established communication with fellow troops. Then, having been stationed on the opposite side of the building to the damage, he was dispatched to the south side. There he was faced with scenes to which no human ever expects to be exposed. 'Carnage, much of it human, of the most unimaginable sort,' was how he described it. One witness recalled, at the moment of detonation, 'bodies falling down off the road and winging through the air'. A YMCA building across the road bore, at third-storey height, a gruesome bloodstain where a man had been blown 150 yards into the side of the building. A young typist had her face ripped off her skull and flung into the road, where it landed, still fully recognisable.

Docherty has always chosen not to describe in detail the bloodbath confronting him, but author Thurston Clarke, who spoke to numerous witnesses for his book *By Blood and Fire*, wrote that 'blocks of stone, tables and desks crushed heads and snapped necks . . . chandeliers and ceiling fans crashed to the floor, impaling and decapitating'. One woman described the dresses of female victims blown up in their offices fluttering through the air like parachutes.

Docherty and his colleagues, their ears assailed by the cries of those trapped amid twisted metal, crackling wires and endless rubble, moved past lifeless bodies to assist those who were staggering and crawling away from the building. Following the momentary surge of elation caused by his escape from serious injury, the realisation hit Docherty that people he knew had been killed. A three-day rescue operation led by the Royal Engineers, booed and stoned as they travelled to the scene, brought out only six survivors from the wreckage. After days spent identifying victims, it emerged that several of Docherty's colleagues were among the 91 people – including 28 British, 17 Jews and 41 Arabs – who had died.

Within his first few days in Palestine, Docherty had borne witness to one of the most infamous terrorist attacks of the twentieth century, an event that would hasten Britain's withdrawal from the area and create a template for future atrocities around the world. The notoriety of the event was multiplied by claims that warning calls were made and that hotel staff either failed to pass on the messages or that the arrogant British leadership simply ignored them. Docherty refused to believe that his commanders could have done nothing had they heard about the threat.

At various moments during the remainder of his tour of duty, Docherty would again come under fire in attacks on his barracks or ambushes during patrols. Describing another upsetting task, he says, 'Some of the soldiers sold their rifles and if they were caught they had to go to Gaza to a prison camp for six weeks. When I was a corporal one of my duties was to take them there. They stripped them off and searched them and you just left them there and went back to Cairo or Jerusalem.'

Nothing, however, would ever match the horror of the Jerusalem bombing. And, like most veterans of conflict, he would carry a new perspective into civilian life. 'When you have witnessed the things I did that day,' he said, 'nothing the game of football will throw at you can ever chasten or unduly upset you.'

In such an environment, moments of beauty, such as seeing Midnight Mass conducted near Bethlehem, and the pursuit of normal activities, such as a game of football, assumed even greater importance. Docherty turned out regularly for the Third Infantry Division alongside various professional players, including Arthur Rowley, scorer of more than 400 League goals. Another teammate was David Beckham's grandfather. Docherty reckoned that his own unit, the first battalion of the HLI, lost only three of the hundred or so matches in which he played.

Shortly before his demob date at the end of July 1948, Docherty was promoted to sergeant and offered the suggestion that he undertake officer training. Although flattered, he declined. With the heightened self-esteem he'd acquired during his two years in uniform he was determined that the next stage of his life would be played out in football kit.

2

NORTH ENDER

'Bill Shankly told me, "Just put on the number four shirt and let it run around, son. It knows where to go."'

Tommy Docherty was experiencing the lightness of step typical of any returning soldier as he turned into his street in Shettleston. The bright sunshine of this July morning, his first back in civilian life, seemed a perfect reflection of his mood. What he saw almost stopped him mid-stride. Rarely would any vehicles other than funeral cars have cause to stop in the street, but here were four outside his house. Puzzled at first, he quickly twigged to their purpose. He barely felt his feet touch the pavement as he made his way excitedly inside and into the arms of his mother.

Knowing he would have officer training to fall back on if things didn't work out, Docherty was determined to devote himself to football. He'd assumed that writing letters seeking trials was the way in, but now representatives of some of the biggest clubs in Britain were outside his front door. Burnley manager Harry Potts sat in one car, Everton's Cliff Britton in another. Manchester United, Football League runners-up in the previous three years and FA Cup winners in 1948, had sent one of their scouts. But it was the sight of Celtic manager Jimmy McGrory on his doorstep that turned his head. 'There was only one team in my eyes,' he states, 'and that was Celtic.'

Reflecting later, he surmised that the fleet of cars were the doing of a division captain in Palestine, former Rangers skipper Adam Little, who had been serving with the Royal Army Medical Corps. How else would the clubs have known of his homecoming? Who else could have alerted them to the talent that had been exiled overseas for two years? He spoke politely to his visitors in turn, while his mother entertained those waiting.

According to another telling of the same story, Docherty recalled as many as ten clubs going to see him. These included Sheffield Wednesday, Newcastle, Middlesbrough and St Mirren, whose representative William Walter told him, 'When I saw McGrory coming into your house and I saw the look on your face, I knew we were wasting our time.' McGrory, too, was expending breath unnecessarily in convincing Docherty to join his club. It was already a foregone conclusion, Docherty's only disappointment being that Celtic wanted him to sign as a part-time professional. He would train on Tuesdays and Thursdays, earn £10 a week – reduced to £8 in the summer – and take a job in O'Connoll's Sports Shop to fill the remainder of his hours and supplement his income. But, he says, 'They gave me £100 to sign and when I gave it to my mother she thought she had won the treble chance on the pools.'

Only weeks after his memorable homecoming, Docherty was given a first-team debut – a home game against a Rangers team on its way to winning the Scottish treble. After a night during which he struggled to sleep, he lined up on the right wing, close enough to the crowd to hear the abuse hurled in his direction from visiting fans. As someone to whom sectarianism was not, and never would be, an issue, the depth of insults took him by surprise. He noted that such issues never permeated the playing field, where the empathy shared by fellow professionals superseded background or religion.

He felt he managed to ride it all well enough to turn in a decent performance in a 1–0 defeat. It was not enough, though, to win him the permanent approval of McGrory, a genial man whose unwillingness to give Docherty more than nine first-team appearances over the next year or so could not dim the young professional's affection for his boss.* Besides, he was getting a thrill from travelling the country and playing for Celtic's reserves, who drew bigger crowds to away games than most clubs' first teams. And he'd come across a man who had already made his mark on world football and was now leaving an imprint on him.

---

* An indication of McGrory's nature was provided later by Archie McPherson describing his successor, Jock Stein, as 'like approaching a shark instead of years feeding your goldfish'.

Lancastrian Jimmy Hogan had been a journeyman inside-forward between the turn of the twentieth century and the outbreak of the First World War, coming closest to glory when he played in an FA Cup semi-final for Fulham. It was as a coach, however, where he found his calling, although not amid the narrow-minded anti-tacticians who dominated the British game. Mainland Europe, where he had spells guiding the fortunes of the Dutch and Swiss national teams and club sides in Austria, Hungary, Switzerland, Germany and France, proved far more open to his ideas. Helmut Schoen, who would lead West Germany to World Cup victory, called him 'a shining example for the coaching profession'.

Most notable were Hogan's periods in Budapest, where he spent the war years coaching the MTK team, having originally been arrested in Austria on the day hostilities began. Sent by the authorities to Hungary to work his war passage, he was considered a 'traitor' by FA secretary Frederick Wall. Hogan, who would return to MTK in 1925 for a further two-year stint, put the emphasis on skill, ball control and on-field strategy – as opposed to the traditional British virtues of strength, power and fitness – and was considered to have laid the foundation for the great Hungarian team that demolished England at Wembley in November 1953. Gusztáv Sebes, coach of the 'Mighty Magyars', whose 6–3 win was the first home defeat suffered by England against a nation from beyond the British Isles, insisted, 'We played football as Jimmy taught us. When our history is told, his name should be written in gold letters.'

British football could barely bring itself to scribble Hogan's name as a footnote, although he did manage to guide Aston Villa to promotion to the First Division after taking over as manager in the wake of leading Austria to the 1936 Olympic final. By the early 1950s he'd pitched up at Celtic Park, where an impressionable Docherty took the opportunity to digest as much of Hogan's knowledge as he could gulp down. 'He used to say [football] was like a Viennese waltz or a rhapsody – one, two, three, one, two, three; pass, move, pass, move. We sat there absolutely glued because we were all so keen to learn.'

On the day Hungary shook English football to its foundations, Hogan would be sat in the Wembley stands with the Aston Villa youth players he was then coaching. Pupils such as Peter McParland and Ron Atkinson would endorse the view of Docherty, who stated,

'The best thing that happened to me at Celtic was the arrival of Jimmy Hogan. This man was a wonder with youngsters.' Yet Docherty witnessed the resistance of the older professionals, who dismissed Hogan as 'theory mad'. It was left to the more junior members of the squad to take advantage. 'I reckon I received my basic coaching from one of the best men at his job in the world,' Docherty said.

It was Hogan who suggested to McGrory that Docherty move from outside-left, where he was spending the majority of his time, to right-half, even though Celtic already possessed Bobby Evans, the national team's incumbent in that position. 'That boy will play for Scotland one day,' Hogan asserted, 'but not as a winger. He's a born wing-half.'

There is no doubt that Docherty looked more like a defender than an attacking player on the football field. He ran with his arms held low, his 5 ft 8 in. frame stooped slightly forward, maintaining a low centre of gravity that allowed him to move more quickly across the ground. It could easily put one in mind of the cartoon character Popeye and was the gait of a man seemingly more intent on disrupting the opposition than attempting creation of his own, which is not to say he was without touch when it came to quick passing and launching an attack. And certainly, as a player and a manager, he always favoured an adventurous approach – even if he understood that his own on-field contribution was more in establishing a platform from which skilful teammates could operate.

As Docherty admitted in *Soccer from the Shoulder*, the autobiography he wrote while still playing, 'I have always had a reputation for being a firm tackler. I have never found that it made me any the worse thought of – not among real footballers anyhow. A wing-half has got to be hard. That's his job.' Hogan could see where those qualities could be most effectively utilised. Yet the fact that only three of Docherty's Celtic appearances were at right-half – he also played on both wings, inside-forward and centre-half – was indicative of the apparent distrust that many at the club held of the coach's opinions.

By the start of 1949–50, with Celtic looking to build on a sixth-place finish the previous season – an improvement of six positions on the year before – Docherty appeared to be no closer to a regular first-team place. His predicament had been brought into sharper focus by the fact that he was about to marry Agnes McKeown, whom he'd met in October 1948 during a club training trip to the holiday town of Girvan on the Firth of Clyde, where Celtic had stayed at the Shelburne Hotel. A friend of the hotelier's daughter, Agnes was, Docherty discovered, 'vibrant' with 'a keen wit', making her a natural companion for a born joker. Their long-distance relationship – consisting of letters, occasional phone calls and visits to Girvan, when money and time permitted – had blossomed to the point of impending marriage.

Docherty had asked Celtic for the use of a club house when he was told that Preston North End were interested in him. He had already been around professional football long enough to know that the very act of informing him of the approach suggested that Celtic were happy to let him go. Preston chairman Jim Taylor and director Bob Smith duly told him that they had been watching him play and that manager Will Scott was keen to take him to Deepdale.

'I never really got the opportunity to make the grade at Celtic,' Docherty says. 'The chairman thought I was too small and at that stage Bobby Evans was a better player. I met Desmond White, the Celtic secretary, in his office in Sauchiehall Street and he told me they were transferring me. I asked, "What is the fee?" He said it was none of my business so I said, "If it's none of my business I am not going." Later, an old player, Chic Geatons, told me, "You want to get a few bob for yourself; ask for a thousand." That got me married.'

Even though he'd spent many hours with army colleagues from England discussing favourite teams and players, Docherty had never seriously contemplated playing there. All he knew of Preston was that they had recently been relegated to Division Two, but still attracted decent crowds and appeared to be ambitious. On offer was a £10-a-week full-time contract, which would leave him worse off because of the loss of his second income, but, crucially, included the use of a house at the rent of 25 shillings (£1.25) per week. 'To a man who went to bed every night with wedding bells ringing in his ears that was the ace of trumps,' he would write.

In November 1949, Docherty became a Preston player for a reported fee of £4,000. 'I had taken a major decision and gone rushing off in a direction I had never thought of,' was how he described the move in *Soccer from the Shoulder*.

He arrived at Preston as the apparent replacement at right-half for Bill Shankly. The Scotland international had left for Carlisle the previous summer after almost 300 games, embarking on a managerial career that would earn him a place in football lore and bring him into opposition with Docherty on many memorable occasions.

In time, Docherty would form a redoubtable combination with Australian centre-half Joe Marston and another Glaswegian, left-half Willie Forbes, signed from Wolves for £18,000. Marston recalls, 'We had a good half-back line. That was the strength in the team. We could read a game and knew where one another were. If you got in trouble there would be somebody to help you out with a shout.'

In his early weeks at Preston, however, Docherty was confined to the familiar environment of reserve-team football – which still seemed like a step up in class and pace from most first-team games in Scotland. As former colleague Eric Jones, a regular second-team player, commented, 'In those days the Central League and first teams were not far apart in ability. You would often find yourself playing against full internationals.' When Docherty finally got his chance in the first team he was picked in the number-seven shirt for a 3–1 Christmas Eve defeat at Leeds.

In the *Lancashire Evening Post*, reporter Walter Pilkington greeted the selection by writing, 'It may be a makeshift move but at least it had the attribute of boldness, influenced by a belief that a good player should be able to play in more than one position . . . [Docherty] was not fast in his position at the outset but was not easily shaken off and showed intelligence and purpose in his methods.'

Docherty, who was married three days after his Preston debut in Girvan's Sacred Heart Church, a few yards from the McKeowns' hotel, felt he had adjusted well to the demands of the English game. He put his easy transformation down to the high level of fitness he'd enjoyed his whole life. When he was restored to the first team in place of the injured Tom Finney for an FA Cup replay at home to Third Division Watford he again felt satisfied with his performance, despite a 1–0 loss. By the end of the season, he'd finally been given the chance to establish himself at right-half, playing 16 more games as Preston finished sixth in the table. The number-four shirt, once the property of Shankly, had found a new permanent home.

Few things in his playing career would give Docherty as much satisfaction as favourable comparison with his predecessor. Shankly had, after all, become a hero after teenaged Tommy had seen him score in a 5–4 Scotland win against England in the first Hampden Park international he attended. 'I idolised Shanks,' admits Docherty, who saw similarities in their preference for attacking football and their quest for peak personal fitness. 'He would chase flies around the field. He was non-stop. Being compared to him was the greatest compliment I had as a player. He used to come a lot when I was at Preston and we got on great.'

In the summer of 1950, as he completed his first pre-season training at his new club, Docherty sensed an atmosphere of optimism. That mood manifested itself in a strong run leading into Christmas, at which time Preston led the division.

Playing in every game of the season, Docherty proved himself an indispensable member of the team. And although his thoughtful distribution alongside tough centre-half Marston proved that there was more to his game than his combative nature, it was that Glasgow tenacity that teammates and opponents would remember most vividly. 'He was a dirty bugger,' is how former Chelsea winger Frank Blunstone puts it. 'I took a few kicks off him. I remember him kicking me at Stamford Bridge one day and he went down making out he was injured. Good thing he did because I think he would have got sent off.'

Arsenal and England inside-forward Jimmy Bloomfield knew that Docherty was the man he'd be facing when Preston were the opponents. 'I wouldn't go as far as to say that I didn't look forward to playing against him, but I knew I was in for a very hard game,' he said. 'At that time he was without doubt the best wing-half in the four home countries.'

According to Frank O'Farrell, who would eventually join Docherty at Deepdale, 'He was a real bundle of energy. He refused to be beaten and was definitely a great player to have on your side. He had great powers of recovery and was very quick.'

Jones recalls, 'Tommy was an excellent player, a hard man when he wanted to be. He could sometimes be a bit naughty. He came from a tough area and needed refining a little bit, but he'd had to look after himself at a very early stage of his life. Players from Glasgow at that time were all self-sufficient. If you weren't, you were knocked about up there.'

England international winger Tom Finney said that Docherty 'tackled as though his life depended on it' and 'didn't know what losing meant'. He recalled in his autobiography, 'Tommy came to Preston a raw prospect, clearly talented and tenacious but with a lot to learn. For all that, he was a kid you couldn't help like. His enthusiasm mirrored that of Bill Shankly . . . He knew how to rough things up and, having faced him in training, I know.'

Marston adds, 'Doc loved to get stuck in; he couldn't help himself. Every training game was competition.'

Jones has painful memories that support his teammates' comments and reveal Docherty's realistic approach to his profession. 'We were great friends and we were against each other one day; first team against reserves. I was playing left-wing and the ball was walloped in my direction. I realised it was not going out of play. I went at maximum speed and the last man at a 45-degree angle was Docherty. I thought, "Doc will not stop; he'll go right through." While I was deciding whether to check inside or push it on and race him, this juggernaut hit me. I went off at an angle and went flying full length. I couldn't breathe and thought he had broken my ribs. He realised he had hurt me and came over to see if I was all right, and I told him in industrial language where to go. I was really angry and upset.

'At full-time he held me back and I thought, "He wants to have a fight!" He said, "I am sorry about that; I don't think I have done any real damage." I said, "It hurts, Tom. I can't breathe. I am not going to fall out with you, but I don't want to talk to you now." He held on to me and let every player get out of earshot and then he said, "Right, Eric. Let me tell you something. You are a ball player. You go past people and you make people look silly. They won't like that and they will do to you what I have just done. If you can't stand that, go and get yourself a job." That is real professionalism, in an unusual sort of way.'

Finney, considered by many the most complete footballer of his generation – winner of 76 England caps and a Footballer of the Year award – has been generous enough to acknowledge Docherty's contribution to his own performance, describing him as a 'very talented and underestimated footballer' and pointing out, 'We had a good understanding of each other's game and Tom was always keen to bring me into play.'

Most of the limited number of games Jones played for the Preston first team were as deputy for Finney on the right flank. 'I owe a lot to Tommy Doc for the way he looked after me,' he says. 'It was general guidance throughout the game. You'd always hear him telling you to hold it or turn or shouting "one-two" or "go". It was controlled communication, which is what makes a team. Many was the time I turned a full-back inside out just through Tommy calling, "Push it. Turn." Before the man is on you, you're past him.'

Docherty, meanwhile, idolised Finney as a player and as a man: modest, kind, correct and the epitome of sportsmanship. He admired the way he executed his brilliant skills without complaint at tough-tackling opponents or exasperation at less-gifted teammates. The more Docherty mixed with Preston fans, on journeys to the ground or around town, the greater evidence he found of the reverence in which Finney was held.

It is Finney who features in one of the most-repeated Docherty anecdotes, a tale that has assumed an air of the apocryphal but which both men insist is true. Docherty, having felt he was making good progress, took advantage of the traditional 'sign here' contract-renewal process to ask for more money. Finney had already been told that he would be on the maximum allowed at the time, £12 a week, with £10 in the off-season. Docherty was informed by manager Scott that he would be on £12 and £8, at which point he insisted on the same money as his teammate.

'But Finney's a far better player than you,' Scott spluttered, to which the quick-thinking Docherty replied, 'Not in the summer he's not!'

According to Marston, 'We looked after Tom Finney because he was our prize. There was a group of us, Willie Cunningham, Doc, Forbes and myself, and if any player took exception to Tom we would look after him. We were good footballers, but we could also sort somebody out.'

As Docherty became more deeply embedded in the club, so his personality would become one of the dominant forces around Deepdale. The ready wit meant that, according to Finney, 'there was never a dull moment', especially when the team travelled. 'We saw a succession of top-line stars down the years but often our best entertainment came via the Doc. He helped to encourage team spirit.'

His manager was happy to acknowledge the importance of Docherty's jokes. 'We are lucky in having two natural comedians and they have helped make this one of the happiest teams I have known,' Scott said. 'Tommy Docherty and Andy Cunningham, our right-back, are great wits. Their cross-talk helps ease the tension before a big match and lifts spirits when we've had an unlucky defeat.'

Marston saw that 'Doc lived for football' and was perfectly suited to an environment where forthright exchanges of opinion were encouraged. 'If players had a grievance or somebody didn't have a good game they would say, "Come on, you can do better than that." We could criticise each other and we had some right arguments if people weren't pulling their weight. Tommy was a 100 per cent player every game and he couldn't stand people who didn't try. If I wasn't having a good game he would say, "Get your finger out." He could stand criticism and you could tell that he could be a manager.'

Finney noted that 'with people like the Doc around you never went into a game anything less than fired up' and added, 'He was always a bit chirpy with the referees and occasionally the mixture of his over-enthusiastic tackling and backchat got him into hot water.'

Jones, meanwhile, remembers a generous nature away from the field. 'I took Tommy for his driving licence and once he had it he bought a brand new Morris Oxford. He said, "Eric, I have got to go on tour with Scotland, I've only had the car two days so would you take it, with your girlfriend, and run it in for me?" He was happy to let me use it. That is the sort of man he was.'

Fans, too, enjoyed Docherty's presence at their club. In a 2011 interview for Football League sponsors npower, North End follower George Gill remembered meeting him at Preston station and being offered a ticket for the upcoming game at Huddersfield. 'I picked the ticket up and watched the match,' he explained. 'Tommy Doc and Willie Cunningham had had a kick or two at a few of the Huddersfield players, which the crowd wasn't very happy about. I went round to the players' entrance again, hopefully to see Tommy, although the Preston players got straight on the bus because the Huddersfield fans were getting a bit intense about it all. Before the bus left they were banging on the side of it and Tommy let the window down and shouted "Bollocks!" to all of them.'

Spring 1951 found Preston taking vital strides towards the finish line in the promotion race, with a run of fifteen straight wins putting them ten points ahead of second-placed Cardiff. Even after failing to win any of the next three games, they clinched the Division Two title with a match to spare by beating Hull in their final home game.

For Scott, it was the first triumph of a managerial career that had taken its initial steps when he arrived at Deepdale in 1923 as trainer under Jimmy Lawrence, his former boss at South Shields, where he had spent most of his playing career. He eventually ascended to the position of club secretary during the Second World War. In 1947, he took up the manager's post at Blackburn, a job that was curtailed by illness.

He had returned to Preston as manager for the 1949–50 season, by which time the team was far from being 'the Invincibles' who had won the inaugural Football League season in 1888–89 without losing a match, winning the FA Cup in the same season and retaining the title the year after. There had been spells in Division Two, the scandal of illegal approaches to players and the triumph of an FA Cup final victory over Huddersfield. The 1948–49 season had seen the club's run of eight seasons in the top flight halted.

Scott had made Docherty one of his earliest signings, continuing the club's long tradition of making excursions beyond the border to acquire talent. The majority of 'the Invincibles' had been Scottish, with Preston among those quickest to identify the need to import the best possible players as professionalism took hold of the game. Docherty felt that Scott and trainer Jimmy Milne, a Dundee-born former North End player, achieved 'a deft blend of English and Scottish styles', with the creative methods associated with the Scots complementing the more direct and robust nature of the Anglos. They maintained such a consistent style of play that Shankly reckoned you could blindfold an ex-Preston player and he'd still be able to describe events on the field.

Scott was no more tactically endowed than the typical manager of the time. 'He would stand on the touchline, immaculately dressed in collar and tie and a trilby,' Docherty recalls. 'I never saw him in a tracksuit in all my time there.'

Nuances such as tactics, preparation and strategy were slow arriving in the English game. Even the post of manager itself had only achieved prominence over the previous two decades. Until the likes of Herbert Chapman, title winner at Huddersfield and Arsenal, who insisted on picking the team and giving the players some semblance of constructive preparation for matches, clubs had been administered by 'secretary-managers', little more than clerks and travel secretaries. The directors, who also acted as selectors, were only too happy to offer up their paid employee when fans and media wanted a sacrifice in times of trouble, so more managers woke up to the fact that taking charge of training was in their interests. The thought of extending that preparation beyond fitness work and occasional kickabouts, however, had still not occurred to many of them.

Therefore the praise that Docherty endowed upon Scott, the first Preston boss to enjoy selectorial privileges, was as effusive as it ever got for most managers of the era. 'He introduced good players and welded them into a formidable, balanced outfit,' was his verdict, reflecting the fact that signing the right players and playing them in the most effective position was considered the extent of managerial expertise. Docherty does concede that he 'encouraged us to play' and that 'every word I received from [him] was constructive'. He also acknowledges that his organisational strength was an undoubted asset, even though Milne was the one out on the training pitch.

The daily routine for Preston's players, many of whom walked or caught the bus to Deepdale from their nearby homes, began at 10 a.m. with approximately eight laps of the pitch, followed by a few further running exercises. Some basic ball work, including shooting and passing, would then be followed by a full-scale practice match in which the first-team defence lined up against the best attackers. With bragging rights on the line, as well as places in the team, the action could be ferocious. After a visit to the gymnasium for some head tennis, the players had the afternoon to play snooker, go to the pictures, do household chores or, in the case of someone like trained plumber Finney, devote time to business interests they hoped would sustain them beyond their playing days. Little attention would be devoted to the specific challenge posed by the next opponent.

Such scenes were played out at just about any of England's 92 professional clubs, the only real differentiation being between those who enjoyed the relative luxury of a separate training ground and those who had to make use of their playing pitch, or sometimes even the club car park. Certainly, Preston were able to approach their first season back in the top flight without worrying that any of their rivals were stealing an advantage with a revolutionary approach to preparation.

With the solidity of half-backs Docherty, Marston and Forbes behind a strike force led by former miner Charlie Wayman – who added to an already impressive résumé from Newcastle and Southampton by contributing 29 goals to the promotion season – North End tackled their task with quiet confidence. Docherty, who felt his own game benefited from playing at an elevated level, was buoyed by an early season victory over Blackpool, one of the First Division's powerhouses. It proved a good yardstick of Preston's potential, and a 4–0 win against Liverpool in the final game cemented them in a very respectable seventh position. Wayman was top scorer again, with 24 goals, and Docherty would describe him as 'the best uncapped and the best footballing centre-forward in the game during my time'.

Despite their promising return, few would have expected Preston to mount a Championship challenge the following season, especially after starting off with a trio of draws and sitting in the lower half of the table in November.

It was around that time that Docherty made known his dissatisfaction on a personal level, telling the club that he would seek a transfer unless they provided him with a better house to rent. The one in which he lived had only an outside lavatory, which Docherty felt was now unacceptable with Agnes pregnant with their first child. When the club declined to move him to a new property or arrange for installation of inside facilities, he told them he wanted to leave. His frustration was increased by a perfectly acceptable club house still being occupied by Eddie Quigley, even though he had been transferred to Blackburn. Issues were eventually resolved and, in truth, Docherty had no great desire to depart. 'I would happily have finished my career there had things worked out,' he says.

As a new year arrived and anticipation mounted around the country over the young Queen Elizabeth's summer coronation, so Preston began buzzing with the excitement of an unexpected run at the League Championship. An eight-game unbeaten spell had been triggered by a November home win against second-placed Sunderland. A further run of only two defeats in ten games found them top of the table by the end of March, leading Wolves on goal average. It was Wolves who'd been overcome 5–2 in the third round of the FA Cup, only for Tottenham to knock Preston out of the competition in a replay. That result at least deepened their determination to see the title challenge through to the bitter end.

In the midst of that effort, they had become involved in one of football's saddest stories. On 14 February, they came up against a Sheffield Wednesday side spearheaded by 23-year-old centre-forward Derek Dooley, who had added 16 Division One goals to the 46 he'd scored to help secure promotion a year earlier. On an icy Deepdale pitch that would have failed to pass a modern-day pitch inspection, he suffered a double fracture of his right leg as he challenged Preston keeper George Thompson. Two days later, nurses at Royal Preston Infirmary discovered that a scratch suffered in the incident had become infected with gangrene and surgeons were forced to amputate his leg. Docherty was among those who visited Dooley's bedside, admitting, 'I struggled to find the right words to say. In such tragic circumstances, everything that came into my head appeared pithy or trite.'

After a loss to Aston Villa and a 2–2 draw at Burnley on Good Friday, Preston remained top of the table, with three teams separated by goal average and only three points spanning the top seven clubs. By the time they took the field at Sunderland the next day, the Preston players had learned that they would be getting a new manager at the end of the season. Scott had announced his intention to retire and a replacement had already been identified in East Fife manager Scot Symon.

Preston missed out on an important victory when a deflected shot gave Sunderland a 2–2 draw, dropping them to second behind Wolves. An Easter Monday win against Burnley brought no change as the other main contenders, Arsenal, Charlton, Wolves and West Brom, were similarly successful. With three games in hand on the leaders, Arsenal appeared to be lurking most dangerously of all in third place.

It was at this moment that Preston stumbled, drawing against Wolves and losing to Charlton in home games, before steadying themselves with a win at Manchester City. Arsenal, whom they trailed by two points after both teams had played forty matches, were up next. Thousands were locked outside Deepdale as Preston produced one of their best performances of the season to win 2–0.

As usual, Docherty updated the table for his teammates in the dressing-room after the game, stressing the value of points in the bank, although they still only had the same number as the Londoners and possessed an inferior goal average. A 1–0 win against Derby in their final match did little to improve that situation – their 1.42 goals scored for every one conceded trailing Arsenal by a tenth of a goal. But at least it meant their rivals had to win at home to Burnley two days later, on the Friday before Blackpool met Bolton in what would turn out to be an historic FA Cup final. 'We had given it our best shot,' Docherty recorded.

As would be the case for at least another couple of decades, there was no shifting around of radio schedules or loosening of rigid Football League broadcast guidelines to accommodate an additional commentary into the schedule. It meant that, once the title decider game had kicked off at 6 p.m., Docherty, having checked all the stations, was reduced to making calls to Walter Pilkington of the *Lancashire Evening Post*. Pilkington was posted in his office and attempting to follow events at Highbury via the wire services, while fielding multiple similar enquiries for the latest score.

In front of a Highbury crowd that included the Bolton Wanderers Cup finalists, Arsenal fell behind after nine minutes, only to march into a 3–1 lead. Just when it seemed Preston's hopes were over, Burnley pulled a goal back with 15 minutes remaining. There was to be no final dramatic twist, however, leaving Docherty and his colleagues to ponder on the implications of having lost the title by such a slender margin. Docherty, like every one of his teammates, questioned whether there was just one thing he could have done differently in a single game that would have produced an additional point. 'I was gripped by a mild form of depression which took a couple of days to lift,' was how he described the experience.

3

PATRIOT GAMES

'The system by which the SFA picked the national team was often as much of a mystery as the function of the human appendix.'

Everything about the experience stuck with him, from the flurry of goals to the taste of the pie he ate on the terraces. But mostly, it was the 91,000-strong crowd, the seething mass of humanity that enabled Hampden Park to breathe and move with a visceral life force of its very own. For Tommy Docherty, watching his nation beat England 5–4 on his first visit to the home of Scottish football a week before his 14th birthday, it was intoxicating.

He would describe being outside the stadium at other internationals and hearing the 'explosion of joy' when Scotland scored, prompting an instinctive need to 'find an air raid shelter'. In *Soccer from the Shoulder*, he said this of the Hampden fans:

They are as much a part of the team as the eleven men in blue down on the field. When the ball goes in the air they will it towards a Scotsman; when a Scot goes into a tackle their bodies tense as they help him fell the enemy. And, when Scotland attack, they are with them, sweeping forward to a man, one gigantic, rampant, clan.

Never would Docherty have dared dream during his afternoon at a wartime international that in future years, as captain and then manager of his country, he would be one of the chosen few who held the fortunes of 'dear patriotic, seething Hampden' in their hands.

Yet on 14 November 1951 he was among those 'eleven men in blue' for a Home International Championship game against Wales in front of 71,272 at the home of Scottish football. The pride he felt for his family on hearing of his call-up was matched only by his surprise. Not only had he not realised he was playing well enough to merit the honour, but he was also well aware of the apparent prejudice that existed within the selection committee against the 'Anglo-Scots', the players who had opted for the more rarefied air of competition south of the border. It was a bias that Docherty himself would go so far towards eradicating when responsible for picking the team himself that the accusations of favouritism ran in the opposite direction. 'The Scottish papers were very unfair,' he says. 'If you were an Anglo-Scot you were a traitor for going to England to earn your living, so you had to be twice as good.'

Ironically, none of his former Celtic teammates were chosen alongside him on the occasion of his debut, but Bobby Evans, the man whose dominance in his position hastened Docherty's departure from Parkhead, sent a good luck telegram. So, to Docherty's delight, did Bill Shankly.

Scotland went into the game as holders of the annual British championship* and having already beaten Northern Ireland 3–0 a month earlier, hence their disappointment in losing to a goal by Ivor Allchurch, the 'Golden Boy' of Welsh football. Docherty's arrival in the team seemed to be well received by reporters – with J.L. McCormack of the Glasgow *Evening Times* predicting 'a solid international career ahead of him' – and his teammates. One of the latter group, legendary Liverpool forward Billy Liddell, travelled home with him, offering encouragement, advice and the assurance that more caps would be forthcoming.

Wales were opponents again a month later when Docherty was selected for the United Kingdom XI team that played in Cardiff to celebrate the Welsh FA's 75th anniversary. According to Docherty, the game 'gave me the feeling that I had arrived in international football'. After the guest team's 3–2 defeat, *Daily Express* reporter Desmond Hackett, one of the sport's most influential writers, described 'wee right-half Tommy Docherty' as a 'great prospect'.

A footnote to the game was Docherty's first-hand experience of

---

* At that time the tournament was spread throughout the season, being consolidated into one week at the end of the campaign from 1968–69 until its demise in 1984.

the parsimonious attitude taken towards the top players by the authorities. Having claimed a meal on the train home, he received a letter from the Welsh FA saying that they would not be reimbursing this 'unnecessary expense': echoes of Stanley Matthews being refused tea and cake by the FA on his way to an international engagement. This was also the era when players would have the choice of a £15 match fee or the jersey in which they had played. Docherty invariably would choose the latter.

Another harsh lesson in the ways of international football was coming his way. He'd felt comfortable in his surroundings and believed that he could thrive with such good players around him. Yet he was left out of Scotland's next game, the Home International climax against England in April, and not even named among the standby players for his country's post-season Scandinavian tour. It was not in the nature of international selectors at that time to offer excluded players any explanation of their decision.

Docherty sensed that the selectors had again been 'preaching insularity' and dressing it up as some kind of patriotism in their preference for the Scottish-based Evans. But there was, he felt, an even more obvious reality to which he was becoming resigned: that international football was a case of 'every man for himself'. It was futile to slog through 90 minutes of hard graft work for the team's cause, executing what he called 'the less obvious virtues', if the selectors, unaware of what really went on and swayed by the occasional piece of skill, weren't going to notice. 'In international football, I found out, it is fatal to play for your side,' he confessed. 'Play for yourself all the time. That's the only way you can stay in the team.'

Inevitably, that culture led to disjointed team performances and he adds, 'I looked forward to getting back to my club because you knew you were playing with a team that had a bit of understanding.'

Proof that he had not been forgotten completely came via a pair of Scotland B games in the autumn of 1952, draws in France and against England. And with Preston's push for the Championship keeping him at the forefront of bulletins from south of the border, Docherty was picked at right-half to play against England at Wembley: his second cap and first taste of the oldest football rivalry of them all. The game ended in a 2–2 draw, and Docherty played again – this time at left-half – in a home defeat against Sweden a month later. 'I had a taste once more for international football,' he noted. 'I didn't want it to be my last.'

For a while, it looked like it might be.

Having come so close to winning the League Championship in the 1952–53 season, it was the FA Cup that kept Preston in the chase for honours one year later. But even as he was helping his team beat a path to Wembley, Docherty discovered that the Scotland selectors appeared to have forgotten the way to his part of Lancashire. Ignored for the three games during the season against Scotland's British rivals, he was eventually back in the national team four days after the disappointment of Cup final defeat to West Bromwich Albion. As captain, no less.

Docherty admitted he was 'flabbergasted' when asked by manager Andy Beattie to lead the team against Norway at Hampden Park in one of Scotland's warm-up games for the forthcoming World Cup finals in Switzerland. Scotland had earned their place, along with England, via their performance in the Home International Championship, which had also doubled as a World Cup qualifying group, although the three games in the 1953–54 season had brought them only one win – in Belfast – a draw in Glasgow against Wales and a home defeat against England. The selectors, of course, were never slow to react to defeat with wholesale changes and on this occasion introduced five new caps, including Preston teammate Willie Cunningham. Docherty was given his favoured number-four shirt, with old rival Evans playing at left-half.

Even though only 25,000 were interested enough to attend the match, Docherty would say that his 'badge was bulging with pride' as he marched out at the head of his team. He had the further satisfaction of walking off with a victory, albeit after an unimpressive team performance, and setting up the only goal for Aberdeen's George Hamilton.

Four changes were made for the return game in Oslo two weeks later, a 1–1 draw, and four more new caps were awarded in a 2–1 defeat against Finland. Docherty, rested for that final game in Helsinki, remained uncertain of his status as team captain and bemused by the fact that the selectors had apparently got this close to the tournament without a clear idea of their strongest team. The decision to take only 13 players to Switzerland suggested they had finally hit upon their preferred line-up – not that they were in any hurry to share that information with the manager.

Docherty discovered his own fate as captain via Cunningham on the day before Scotland's opening game of the tournament, against Austria, in Zurich. His clubmate, who had assumed that his leadership role against Finland had been temporary, had been called into the selectors' meeting and emerged with the news: 'They've replaced you as captain.'

'I was dumbfounded,' was Docherty's response, although he was quick to offer his support to Cunningham. His opinion of the selectors' understanding of the game sank even lower, if that were possible. They were sending Scotland into a World Cup – beginning with a match against one of the top teams in the world – with an inexperienced team containing only one man who had won more than six caps. Yet things were about to get even more chaotic.

Austria were considered one of the tournament favourites: they were a fluent, technically adept team whose feature was the way in which skipper Ernst Ocwirk would move forward into attack from his centre-half position, in the style with which Franz Beckenbauer would later dominate the West German team. Scotland offered hard work as a counter and played well to keep their defeat down to the first-half goal scored by Erich Probst. Blackpool's Allan Brown, a brave but unlucky character who had missed two FA Cup finals through injury, sacrificed his attacking game to drop deep from his inside-left position and neutralise Ocwirk. It was rare for British football's adherence to the rigidity of the WM formation to allow for such strategic thinking and the selectors were, predictably, unimpressed enough to complain that Brown had not attempted enough shots.

The following day, four months into his job and two days before the second game of the tournament, against Uruguay, Beattie announced his resignation as Scotland manager. According to Docherty, 'He told me he was totally fed up with the way the Scottish FA ran the show.' To have taken such a course of action after an encouraging performance in difficult circumstances demonstrated the extent of his frustration. What irked him in particular was that the SFA travelling party appeared to include more officials than players.

The haphazard nature of the venture led Alec Young to write in the *Daily Mail*, 'As for the way the Scottish Football Association conducted affairs for the World Cup, it would make a good Whitehall farce.'

If Hungary's recent 6–3 and 7–1 victories over England at Wembley and in Budapest respectively had revealed British football as lagging behind the rest of the world at international level, the events of the World Cup were further exposing both its tactical deficiencies and its outdated ambivalence towards the sport's premier event. England, upset by the United States in their belated first World Cup finals in Brazil four years earlier, made it out of their group this time by virtue of a 4–4 draw against Belgium and victory over Switzerland, but were no match for the technical excellence of Uruguay in the quarter-finals, being beaten 4–2.

Uruguay had already shown their liking for British defences when handing out a 7–0 thrashing to Scotland in Basle. 'They tore us apart,' Docherty admits. 'I remember saying we were lucky to get nil. There had been no preparation at all. We looked at Uruguay and they had these light cotton shirts with V-necks, short pants and little stockings with no shin guards, and boots like slippers. We had these Mansfield Hotspur boots with toecaps, big woollen stockings, long pants and thick shirts. We were knackered by the end of the national anthems.' From their kit to their swift passing, the South Americans were playing a different game, building on a two-goal half-time lead as the Scots slipped further into demoralisation.

Not even Uruguay could match Hungary in the semi-final, losing 4–2 after extra time to the Olympic champions, who were then upset by West Germany in the final, blowing a 2–0 lead against a team they'd already thrashed 8–3 in an earlier contest.

British, and particularly English, club football might have been admired for the week-in, week-out relentlessness of the title race, the human drama and glamour of the FA Cup and the rollicking goal-fests that each competition produced, but it was becoming clear to those, like Docherty, with a mind capable of thinking a little deeper that changes in methods were required.

The advanced play of Ocwirk, the non-conformist roving of Hungarian centre-forward Nándor Hidegkuti, the swift interchanging of the South American teams – all showed what possibilities existed if one looked beyond the boundaries of a British approach that had altered little since the new offside law of the 1920s saw the centre-half adopt a more defensive role. 'Many in the game were convinced that change was inevitable,' Docherty would recall. 'I decided I wanted to be at the forefront of such changes.'

4

FINAL HURDLES

'Jimmy Milne told us, "Get out there and play them off the park." Well, we got out there at least.'

His fate at the World Cup finals in Switzerland – losing the captaincy of his country and experiencing a pair of humbling losses – completed a miserable few weeks for Tommy Docherty. The tournament had proved to be anything but the antidote he'd sought to an FA Cup final defeat that was both disappointing and, in his view, perfectly avoidable.

Preston had begun the 1953–54 season with high hopes, having lost the Division One title to Arsenal by, literally, a fraction. They also kicked off with a new man at the helm. Continuing their tradition of Scottish links, the club had given Will Scott's old job to Scot Symon, a former Dundee, Portsmouth and Rangers wing-half who had represented his country at football and cricket. During six years as manager of East Fife he had achieved the considerable feat of leading the cash-strapped coastal club to a pair of League Cup victories, a Scottish Cup final appearance and third place in Scotland's top flight.

Possessing a grasp of tactics greater than the typical manager of the era, Symon was also known for seeking perfection, criticising his players for their performance in the League Cup final of 1947 before he let them crack open the champagne.

Even though it was generally anticipated that Symon would be at Deepdale only until the managerial seat at Rangers became vacant, Docherty took to him, finding him to be a fair and honest man who 'showed respect for every player [and] proved himself good at man management'.

It wasn't enough, however, to mount another Championship challenge. Preston won only seven of their first seventeen League games, although when they clicked they won handsomely, putting six past Sunderland and Sheffield Wednesday and posting other scores of four and five. If that suggested a team that could turn it on sufficiently on their day to challenge for the FA Cup, then that was borne out by comfortable 2–0 victories at Derby and Lincoln and a 6–1 home thrashing of Third Division Ipswich to reach the quarter-finals.

Leicester City, top of Division Two, gave Preston what Docherty described as 'one hell of a battle'. After a 1–1 draw at Filbert Street, the underdogs led 2–0 in the replay before Charlie Wayman pulled one back and a late equaliser arrived via Morrison's volley. The woodwork denied both teams in extra time, giving the opportunity for a crowd of almost 45,000 to enjoy a second replay at Hillsborough, where Jimmy Baxter, Bobby Foster and Tom Finney secured a 3–1 Preston victory.

Docherty made his mark on a tense semi-final against Sheffield Wednesday with a bulldozing tackle that saw inside-left Jackie Sewell carried off on a stretcher. No one suggested he had deliberately set out to injure his opponent, but he had given notice of a certain intent when he'd told reporters that he would 'concentrate on holding Jackie Sewell wherever he may wander'. Already behind to a Wayman goal, Wednesday bandaged up their wounded man and sent him back on, but were effectively a player short for the remainder of the contest. Preston made sure of a place at Wembley via a second goal, by Baxter.

West Bromwich Albion were to be Preston's opponents in the final, having ended the romantic run of Port Vale with a 2–1 semi-final victory, assisted by Ronnie Allen's debated penalty and the Third Division side's disallowed equaliser.

By the time the final came around several weeks later, Preston were favourites with the recent formbook as well as the public. Their League performances after reaching Wembley were impressive, a six-game unbeaten run within their final eight matches ensuring a finish in the top half of the table. 'Nobody in the country at that time was playing football of the quality of Preston,' wrote Docherty.

Joe Marston suggests, 'I think it came from the footballers they picked. We were noted for our short game, although we could handle ourselves if it got rough. We weren't a big, tall side who could play kick and rush. We could all play football and sometimes we got bollocked because we did too much with the ball.'

West Brom, meanwhile, had fallen disappointingly short in challenging Wolves for the title after losing five of their seven League games following the semi-final. The view of Bob Pennington of the *Daily Express* was typical, predicting, 'It is still Preston, the perfect blend of Anglo-Scottish artistry, to win.'

The public's desire to see the popular Finney picking up a winner's medal might not have reached the clamorous levels of the previous year's campaign on behalf of Blackpool's Stanley Matthews, but it still made Preston the neutrals' choice. Assisted by the increased sales of television sets before the coronation, more than 10 million viewers had watched Matthews and his Blackpool team win the dramatic 1953 final. That statistic had finally scared the football authorities into scheduling the English game's showpiece match on its own weekend, after the conclusion of the League season.

Yet the exclusive attention on Wembley might have played a part in shaping Preston's fate. Symon chose not to treat the occasion like 'any other game'. While every available building and lamppost in their hometown was being decked out in white and blue, the players were spirited away to Weybridge, on the outskirts of London, on the Wednesday before the final.

Docherty maintains that Symon made a mistake in changing a familiar routine – even though he would do likewise during his own managerial career. Not only did the squad travel two days earlier than was usual for a London game, but they did no meaningful training once they arrived. Instead, they 'stewed' – Docherty's description – forced to settle for light workouts in between waiting for the next meal. There was not even a television in the hotel to alleviate boredom, and players quickly tired of reading books or newspapers. When they made a Thursday-night visit to the cinema, Docherty thought it entirely appropriate that they saw the prisoner-of-war movie *Stalag 17*.

'A change of programme may be all right for a side that has had too much football or one that is having an indifferent spell and needs pepping up,' he argued, but that wasn't the case for Preston. Of course, hindsight makes it easy for Docherty to take a dim view of Symon's planning, but he insists that it was apparent even as the game approached that all was not right: 'As the monotony increased, the tension built up in every one of us. I think we all knew the atmosphere was wrong.' While Preston's men became 'bored and irritated', West Brom trained at home and arrived in London on Friday afternoon.

Docherty feels that the approach to the game itself was flawed. He accuses Symon, who would go on to win six Scottish League titles and five Scottish Cups in thirteen years as Rangers boss, of being 'unhelpfully laconic'. He merely told his players to let West Brom do the worrying. As a manager, Docherty would also prefer to focus on his own team's performance, but rarely to the extent of being oblivious to or blasé about the opposition's capabilities. He felt that lethargic preparation and the manager's lack of urgency led to a poor mental state among the Preston players.

After Finney recovered from a thigh injury, Preston were able to take to the field with a full-strength team: Thompson, Cunningham, Walton, Docherty, Marston, Forbes, Finney, Foster, Wayman, Baxter and Morrison. But 'proud Preston were putrid' wrote Docherty in his first autobiography, concluding that an early realisation that things were not clicking made them try too hard.

The morning rain, London's first for three weeks, had cleared away by kick-off, but the clouds that persisted reflected the gloominess of much of the play. Docherty settled with a couple of first-time passes and a crisp tackle, but rarely ventured much beyond halfway in the early stages.

West Brom, matching Newcastle's record of nine final appearances, took the lead after twenty-one minutes after Cunningham mis-hit a clearance and winger George Lee's scuffed left-foot shot ran to the far post for centre-forward Allen to finish. Docherty led an immediate Preston response, firing in a diagonal cross from the right for an unchallenged Morrison to head past the keeper.

Docherty quickly recovered his wind after taking the ball in the midriff and, as he resumed his role, attracted what he would have considered a highly complimentary remark from BBC commentator Kenneth Wolstenholme, who ventured that he was 'looking uncommonly like Bill Shankly'. Thoughtful, if not always successful, in his attempted use of the ball, Docherty had his first shot after 42 minutes, firing wide from the edge of the box. It was no great surprise. After four full seasons in the team, he was still waiting to find the net. 'Shooting was not one of my strong points,' he would confess.*

That opening had been created by Finney's run and cross, but the impact of Preston's talisman was fleeting. On one occasion his left-foot shot ended up closer to the corner flag than the goal, on another he ran almost the length of the field with the ball, only to slip as he tried to deliver a cross.

The half-time message from Symon and Jimmy Milne was simply to 'keep playing your own football', and Docherty and Finney combined to help create a second goal in the 52nd minute, their exchange leading to an opportunity for Wayman to round the keeper. Referee Arthur Luty stood firm when surrounded by Albion players convinced that Wayman had been offside.

Docherty was down again after 61 minutes, having taken the ball in the head. 'Still as tough as ever,' noted Wolstenholme as he marched back into the action, looking like the soldier he once was. A couple of minutes later, Docherty was once more in the thick of things, with an unfortunate outcome. Bobby Foster was unable to control a loose ball just outside his own area and Albion left-half Ray Barlow pounced, striding into the box where Docherty was stationed. The ball bounced past Docherty and, as Barlow attempted to go inside him as well, the two players collided. Docherty felt Barlow had run into him; the referee agreed with the Albion man that he had been body-checked. 'The worst that should have been given against me was an indirect free kick,' Docherty wrote. In another account, he explained, 'Ray had actually overrun the ball when I executed the challenge but he regained control just as I slid under him. Ray went over my right shoulder; his knee caught me on the way.' Allen struck the penalty beyond Thompson's right hand.

Docherty made an important tackle as Irish international Reg Ryan drove towards the Preston area a few minutes later, but neither side were going to be proud of their attacking efforts by the end of the 90 minutes. It was Albion, though, who produced just enough to win the game, outside-right Frank Griffin running on to a lofted through ball to slide a shot past Thompson with only two minutes remaining.

---

* Docherty's first Preston goal was at Huddersfield five years after signing, sparking a run of four goals in successive games.

'We knew we were in for a hard game, but they just got breakaways,' Marston remembers. 'On the winning goal, our full-back got caught up the field and left the right-winger. I cut across and just missed him. The bottom fell out of the bloody world because time was just about up. The ball was hit from nowhere in defence and he was there on his own. I was just about a yard short.'

Preston never threatened an equaliser. 'I sat in the dressing-room feeling utterly devastated ... this was disappointment as never before,' recorded Docherty, whose sympathy extended easily to teammate Finney, whose disappointing contribution would be highlighted, somewhat unfairly, as the main reason for Preston's downfall.

The club's post-game dinner at the Savoy, where singer Petula Clark and comedians Norman Wisdom and Al Read provided the entertainment, did little to brighten the mood, although the subsequent reception given to the team by almost 40,000 outside Preston Town Hall was uplifting.

After returning home from the disappointing World Cup campaign, Docherty teamed up with half-back Joe Dunn to open a café in Cannon Street, close to Deepdale. Docherty had mentioned the idea to Dunn in casual conversation and his teammate persuaded him to put his money where his mouth was. The Olympic Café was a successful venture, with Docherty and Dunn happy to help out after training, cutting sandwiches and doing some simple baking. The reputation of the food, and the welcome, grew to the point where teams such as Tottenham and Chelsea would often stop there on Fridays upon arrival for the following day's game.

Such activities were more than a mere alternative to spending their spare time at the snooker hall or in betting shops. This was the age of the maximum wage, where all most players could hope for was to finish their careers with enough money to set them up in their own house. Most professionals in the game, approximately 70 per cent, earned less than the 1954 maximum of £14 per week. Even Preston's achievement in reaching the FA Cup final had only brought sufficient commercial spin-offs to allow the players to share £550.

Money had been pouring into football and its related industries since the resumption of competitive play after the Second World

War. The 1948–89 season had seen a record total Football League attendance of 41.3 million, while the football pools companies had an estimated 10 million people filling in their coupons every week by the start of the '50s – all of which had little impact on the men around whom the sport revolved. Young professionals were encouraged to take up an apprenticeship, both to safeguard them against an early end to their sporting ambitions and to give them a trade for later life. Others, including some of the biggest names in the sport – Matthews, Mortensen, Finney – invested in business ventures in the hope of avoiding the post-football search for the next pay packet. As Docherty explained, 'I had the initial idea for the business with one eye on my future. At the time I didn't know what I wanted to do in my life once my playing days were over.'

Back in his day job, Docherty was not surprised to find that Symon had returned to Scotland to succeed Bill Struth at Rangers, meaning Frank Hill became Preston's third manager in little more than a year. Hill, another former Scotland international half-back who had won League Championships under Herbert Chapman at Arsenal, was coming off an unremarkable six-year stint as Burnley manager. Under his leadership, Preston finished in the lower half of the table, a worrying five points away from relegation. In a highly competitive season, however, they were also only 12 points behind champions Chelsea, whose attempts to recapture such glory in future years would soon be down to Docherty.

Eric Jones recalls that Hill did little to earn the players' support. 'Tommy was a very strong-willed person, not afraid to nominate himself, and he hated Frank Hill – as I did,' he states. 'So you can work out for yourself that he wasn't the nicest. We would play in all weather on a practice pitch outside the ground and at half-time one day Frank came along with his fancy white shorts and said he was having a game. Tommy said, "What a bloody opportunity. See what I'll do to this fella." Well, he dumped him in the mud and Hill said, "There's no need for that." Doc just replied, "If you come on here you'll play as hard as we do."'

Jones perhaps overstates his colleague's antipathy towards the manager because Docherty himself would call Hill a 'colourful character with a tremendous sense of humour', although he was no great admirer of his tactical awareness. While admiring Hill's desire to play attacking football, he felt he lacked the pragmatism required to ensure that his team didn't leak goals. FA Cup defeat by 5–2 against West Ham, a modest Division Two side, was typical of a 1955–56 campaign that saw Preston avoid relegation by only one point. Indicative of their continued attacking ability, enhanced by the £27,000 signing of Aston Villa centre-forward Tommy Thompson, they ended up scoring more goals than they conceded, despite winning only 14 matches. Towards the end of the campaign, Docherty made another of his transfer demands, although once again he would still be at Deepdale when the following season arrived.

Like an increasing number of younger players around that time, Docherty – inspired by the likes of Hungary and Austria – was keen to dig deeper into the strategic and technical side of his sport. While he might not have been able to glean much from Hill, at least his continued presence in the Scotland side was broadening his horizons.

Picked for the single-goal victory in Cardiff in October 1954, and pleased with his performance, Docherty was dropped for the next game against Northern Ireland. Eight changes later, he was back for the December contest against Hungary. In front of more than 113,000 on a frosty day at Hampden Park, he faced his greatest test as an international footballer: nullifying the threat of Ferenc Puskás. It was a role he happily took on without any great idea of how to accomplish it. In the end, he settled for the same energetic tackling and chasing that saw the Scotland team as a whole perform above themselves. As he said in *Soccer from the Shoulder*, 'All I could do was constantly reposition myself, harass and hustle the man until he inadvertently offered me a glimpse of the ball, whereupon I'd attempt to get a toe on it.'

Unable to match Hungary technically, Scotland worked themselves into the ground, even after the visitors took a 2–0 lead. Two minutes before half-time Docherty's pass allowed Bobby Johnstone to set up a goal for Tommy Ring, although Hungary quickly added a third before the interval. Johnstone headed home ten minutes into the second half and Docherty even had a shot turned over the bar by the keeper before a late breakaway sealed the Magyars' 4–2 victory.

Any Scottish smugness at having put up a considerably better fight against Hungary than England had managed was wiped away later in the season. For Docherty, it was another miserable Wembley experience, a thrashing during which Manchester United's Duncan Edwards made his international debut and Wolves forward Dennis Wilshaw scored four goals. On their way to what was then their biggest defeat in the Home International Championship, Scotland conceded four times inside half an hour. Docherty would have been more thrilled with the way he drilled an 84th-minute free kick beyond Bert Williams from outside the box for the final goal of the game had his team not been 7–1 down at the time.

Frank Blunstone, who played on the left wing for England that day and would later coach under Docherty, recalls how the result enabled him to needle his boss. 'If he had a go at me I'd just say, "You remember that game at Wembley? 7–2." He'd just reply, "Fuck off," which I suppose still gave him the last word!'

Docherty was discarded for a 3–0 win against Portugal, but was named for the end-of-season trip to Europe. Having sat out a draw in Yugoslavia, he was surprised to be told as the team coach departed the game that he would be included against Austria. His selection was one of five changes, which produced both an impressive 4–1 victory in Vienna and Docherty's assertion that it was 'the best Scottish team I have ever played in'.

The final game of the tour brought Puskás into Docherty's sights once more. Hungary were 3–1 winners, but only after Scotland led at half-time through a goal set up by Docherty for Gordon Smith. The home team turned the game around after switching Nándor Hidegkuti to create havoc from the right. Puskás was to place his admiration for Docherty on record in his autobiography, writing, 'I was confronted with a man who played very well. He was dogged in his pursuit of me. I found it difficult to settle into my normal rhythm and play the ball as I pleased.'

Docherty must have wished that the Scottish FA had found a place for the Hungarian maestro on its selection panel. Although picked for a Great Britain team that lost 4–1 against the Rest of Europe in Belfast for the Irish FA's jubilee during the following season, it was not until the 1956–57 campaign that Scotland looked in Docherty's direction again.

That season had begun with Preston's players getting used to yet another manager, Hill having been replaced by former England half-back and Burnley and Everton boss Cliff Britton. Having led Burnley to the FA Cup final and Everton to promotion in 1954,

Britton had departed Goodison Park after a series of confrontations with the directors over the availability of transfer funds and perceived interference in the running of the team.

Docherty would say that 'he never got on with him' and that there was universal dislike for Britton among the players. That may be an overstatement, as Frank O'Farrell, for example, found him sympathetic to his need to make return trips to London after his transfer from West Ham while his daughter was receiving treatment at Great Ormond Street Hospital. Yet even he admits, 'He was not liked by everyone.'

A strict Methodist, Britton frowned upon the consumption of alcohol, and Docherty joked to O'Farrell that he 'would ban us from eating wine gums'. Britton's habit of checking up on what time players got home in the evening and questioning their commitment to the club was never going to make him popular, and trainer Jimmy Milne often found himself playing peacemaker. 'He was as hard as a fireside poker, without its occasional warmth,' wrote Docherty, who was also unable to ever rid himself of the image of Britton standing picking his nose while Milne led training. A comment Britton passed about Finney did not endear him to Docherty either. 'He said to me, "If Tom Finney trained harder he would be a better player." I said, "But he is a genius to start with!" What a load of rubbish.'

According to Docherty, Britton 'appeared to believe you could never relax without becoming casual' – a belief that Docherty himself would constantly challenge throughout his managerial career, often to the opposite extreme. Constantly on edge and lacking in interpersonal skills, Britton did manage to translate his strong disciplinarian methods into a more solid unit on the field. In time Docherty conceded that he 'got the first team playing wonderful football'. And his army experience made him able to appreciate the manager's assertion that good habits acquired via practice would be performed more naturally in matches. As an example, he would have his wing-halves spend an hour shadowing an inside-forward during training.

As someone who was becoming increasingly fascinated by football strategy and formulating stronger views on the game, Docherty was relieved to have a manager of whom he could say, 'From the tactical footballing side, he was a lap or two ahead of the rest.' His growing respect was such that in his first autobiography, published in 1960, he urged the FA to make Britton the England manager and predicted that, if they did, they would be beating the world within two years.

According to O'Farrell, '[Britton] could talk about the game, the tactics and so on and we'd put his ideas into practice during training.' He even staged tactical team talks on Friday afternoons, leaving O'Farrell far more impressed then he had been with his former West Ham manager Ted Fenton, who'd left such things to senior players like Malcolm Allison and Noel Cantwell.

Yet Britton's start at Preston was anything but auspicious, losing the first four games of the season before breaking out of the slump by thrashing Cardiff 6–0. With Finney scoring prolifically from a central position, Preston progressed to a third-place finish in the table. They missed out on second place to Tottenham only on goal average, although were a distant eight points behind Manchester United's ill-fated champions – the final title for the 'Busby Babes' before tragedy struck on a Munich runway in February 1958.* North End teased their fans with thoughts of another long FA Cup run, reaching the fifth round before losing in a replay at Arsenal.

Preston's improved form encouraged the Scotland selectors to give Docherty another chance, naming him against Yugoslavia in their third game of the season. His presence in the team was welcomed for unusual reasons by Charlton defender John Hewie, who had spent his first 21 years living in South Africa with his expat Scottish parents. 'The Doc met me at the station,' he recalls. 'What I remember most about him was explaining to me what all our teammates were saying. My Dad had lived in South Africa for 30 years by that time so I couldn't understand their Scots accent.'

After a 2–0 victory, the Scottish *Daily Mail* concluded that Docherty's 'ball-winning skills and intelligent use of the ball fortified Scotland'. The paper's prediction of a 'regular place' was always risky in light of the selectors' track record, but Docherty was in again for the late-season game against England, a match that was to provide

---

* Docherty, like so many within the football world, would be cut deeply by the news of the tragedy that befell United. His wife, Agnes, recalled him weeping as he listened to the news reports of the plane crash that would leave 23 dead.

him with another lesson he would take into management.

Leading 1–0 at half-time, Scotland were instructed by captain George Young, the Rangers defender, to sit back when play resumed. Docherty voiced his disagreement with the orders for him to adopt a deeper position and left the dressing-room knowing 'we had made a big mistake'. Sure enough, Scotland surrendered control of the game, allowing Edwards to dominate the midfield and score a winning goal five minutes from time.

Docherty had provided the Wembley crowd with their pantomime villain when he was ruled to have up-ended Preston colleague Finney – causing him to be carried from the field – and then shaken his fist in protest at the Dutch referee, an act of some rebellion in a more genteel age. *Daily Express* reporter Bob Pennington said that Docherty still looked 'tense and drawn' after the game when he attempted to defend his actions. 'I knew Tom was going to move to the left at that moment and as I plunged forward and got the ball he tripped over my foot and knocked himself out as he fell on George Young's boot,' Docherty claimed. 'To be penalised and then booed when I was quite innocent was a bit much. When Tom recovered and came back ... I knew he did not hold it against me. But I never felt or played the same after that.'

Scotland's bid to qualify for the 1958 World Cup began with a 4–2 home win against Spain, Blackpool's Jackie Mudie scoring three goals, and continued with a 2–1 victory in Switzerland. The team moved on to Stuttgart for a friendly against West Germany and, with Young unfit to play, Docherty was asked once more to captain his country. He 'fancied our chances' against the reigning world champions in front of an 80,000 home crowd and such optimism proved well founded as Bobby Collins scored twice in a 3–1 victory that gave Docherty 'tremendous satisfaction and pride'.

Resentment was not far away, however, with Young apparently upset that Docherty had begun discussing tactics with players as soon as he was named captain instead of waiting until closer to the game. Impatient by nature, Docherty was also far enough advanced in his football education to believe that tactics were too important to be reduced to last-minute instructions blurted out in the dressing-room.

Four days after beating Germany, Scotland faced Spain again in Madrid. Young, hoping to be recalled, learned during a protracted team announcement by Sir George Graham at a team dinner that he wouldn't be. Docherty saw this as a positive, forward-looking move, with no sentiment attached. Meanwhile, Young, who still had supporters within the squad, moodily refused Docherty's request to pose for a squad picture as they left for the Bernabéu Stadium. Scotland lost 4–1, with Hearts' Dave Mackay suffering an ankle injury during a disappointing international debut. Docherty showed his human touch, recognising the distress Mackay was feeling and assuring him, 'Don't worry, Dave. You'll have another chance. The best is yet to come.'

For Mackay, and for Scotland, the prospect of a second World Cup finals still loomed large.

5

TO HIGHBURY AND BEYOND

'The ideal set-up at a football club is to have three on the board – two dead and one dying.'

Harold Macmillan, elected as the new Conservative prime minister earlier in the year, might have had Tommy Docherty in mind in July 1957 when he announced that 'most of our people have never had it so good'. While the country had finally shaken off its shroud of post-war austerity in favour of the gleaming cloak of economic boom, production growth and full employment, Docherty himself felt dressed for success both on and off the field. Despite the setback in Madrid, Scotland were poised to clinch a place in the World Cup finals; Preston had returned to the upper echelons of English football; his café business was thriving; and he was now the father of three children. But if a week was a long time in politics – as one of Macmillan's rivals, future Labour prime minister Harold Wilson, would say – then Docherty was about to discover that a year in football could make a whole world of difference.

On the domestic front, the 1957–58 season was another of which Preston could be proud. Runners-up behind Wolves, although this time by a convincing five-point margin, they won eighteen of twenty-one home games and scored one hundred League goals, thirty-four of them via Tommy Thompson. Had they not lost four of their first six games they could have run the champions even closer.

Continued involvement with the Scotland team offered Docherty an opportunity to discuss training at other clubs. He filed away physical exercises aimed at different parts of the body and started to build a dossier on teams, tactics and formations. Playing against some of the best European national sides had exposed him to the way players' movement off the ball and freedom to roam from assigned positions could add flexibility and fluency.

As captain he had the opportunity to put some of his ideas into action. In Scotland's first game of the season, in Belfast, he neutralised Northern Ireland's twin strikers by playing deep alongside his centre-half in order to pick up the extra forward, Billy Simpson. After a 1–1 draw, Irish skipper Danny Blanchflower praised Docherty for his tactical thinking, while the Scotland selectors complained that he had not been more attacking.

One month later, Scotland won the game that enabled Docherty to start imagining pitting his wits against the best teams on the planet. A 3–2 victory against Switzerland secured a place in the 1958 World Cup finals in Sweden, where the Scots would be joined by all three other home nations. A home draw against Wales and a 4–0 defeat against England at Hampden Park managed to dampen enthusiasm and saw Docherty omitted for the Scots' final home warm-up game against Hungary. At least he had his letter from the Scottish FA confirming selection for the World Cup. Yet all that brought was a rift with Preston that would end his nine-year spell at the club.

Scotland were scheduled to finish preparation for the World Cup with a friendly against Poland in Warsaw, before kicking off their programme in Sweden against Yugoslavia in Västerås a week later. Yet in the meantime Cliff Britton had informed Docherty that his first responsibility was to Preston's five-week tour of South Africa, departing 7 May and returning 11 June, which would cause him to miss the biggest tournament in the world. Docherty's attempts to reason with the club directors met with a sympathetic response, but they told him it was down to the manager. Docherty suggested a compromise that would see him join Preston for the first part of the South African trip before he flew to Sweden, an arrangement he had enjoyed with previous managers in other summers when required by Scotland. He informed Sir George Graham of the Scottish FA that he would be unavailable for Scotland's preparation, but would be there for the tournament itself.

Britton, however, told him that early departure from South Africa would mean the club going to the expense of taking an additional player. It was all or nothing. Docherty was angry at the club's attempts to keep him out of the World Cup, and also felt that going along for part of the South Africa tour was a well-deserved perk. Yet when the party flew off, accompanied by speculation that Britton was wanted by Italian club Juventus, Docherty was not on the plane. Instead he trained with the Scotland squad in Girvan.

'I'd had all the injections for South Africa,' he explains, 'but Britton never took me. I had always gone on tour and then gone with Scotland or vice versa. Britton was an awkward customer and I learned a lot from him on how not to manage.' Even Tom Finney, who rarely had a bad word to say about anyone, agreed that Britton's man-management skills left something to be desired.

Docherty believed he was still a candidate to captain Scotland in the World Cup. But he was never to set foot on the field in Sweden. Eddie Turnbull of Hibernian was given the right-half berth against Yugoslavia, with Liverpool goalkeeper Thomas Younger continuing his recent captaincy role.

The plan had been for Scotland to be managed by Manchester United's Matt Busby, but as he continued his convalescence after coming close to death in Munich, the responsibility fell to trainer Dawson Walker. Interviewed by Gary Imlach for *My Father and Other Working-Class Football Heroes*, Turnbull was dismissive of Walker. 'He'd never played the game, certainly not as a professional,' he said. 'We were possibly the only nation there without a manager or a coach, the only country that didn't have a figurehead.'

Wing-half Dave Mackay, fulfilling Docherty's prophecy with his recall to the squad, described the team's preparation as 'shambolic'. Unable to believe Busby was not properly replaced, he was full of praise for Docherty's attempts to instil some order. 'Tommy filled the vacuum as best he could. He was merely a player, with no official sanction. He was not even the captain and was not selected to play in any of the games, but in times of crisis, leaders emerge.'

Even had Busby been in Sweden, the selectors would have been in charge of picking the team. Turnbull described them as 'potato merchants and what have you', while the *Weekly News* weighed in with, 'I can't see a soul on the selection committee with either the time or the qualifications to take our World Cup hopes and fashion them into a well-disciplined outfit with a proper plan of campaign.'

The players more or less set their own training routines, while Docherty was given the task of watching Scotland's other group opponents, Paraguay and France, compiling scouting reports based on the 7–3 victory by the French. He was never asked to present his findings and doubted that his work was even looked at, saying, 'I think they just wanted me out of the road.' He watched from the sidelines as 17 players were used by the selectors during the tournament, which continued with a 3–2 loss against Paraguay in Norrköping and a 2–1 defeat to France in Örebro.

Docherty sought solace in the opportunity to absorb as much as he could from the terraces. The players were given a pass to all the games – standing enclosures only, of course – but as the tournament progressed, fewer seemed interested in taking advantage. For his part, Docherty was seeking out 'techniques I had never come across before' and made sure to see the final three games played by eventual winners Brazil. He spoke to as many people as possible, including the professor who worked with the Brazilians on mental preparation, who stimulated him to 'find out as much as I could about sports psychology'.

Back home after Brazil, inspired by the 17-year-old Pelé, had beaten the host nation in the final, Docherty confirmed his intention to leave Preston. Whereas his previous noises to that effect had been idle threats, this was serious. His relationship with Britton had gone past the point of repair.

He recalls, 'I wanted to buy a little newsagent and tobacconist across from Deepdale. That was my ambition after I finished playing. The shop was available for 500 quid. I was at Preston nine years and nine months and I was nearly due a testimonial worth £1,000. I was a bit short of what I needed for the shop so I asked the club if I could borrow it in lieu of my benefit to secure my future. Britton said, "No, they won't do it." If they thought that highly of me after so long then I might as well move.'

Docherty even wondered whether Britton's insecurity with his vocal presence at the club was responsible for the recent 'vindictiveness' of his manager. 'Maybe he just thought I was a cocky little so and so who needed taking down a peg or two,' he wrote in his autobiography. If that was the case, it was a feeling with which Docherty would later be able to empathise, most notably when he had Terry Venables as captain at Chelsea.

Docherty felt it was significant that he was never asked to change his mind about leaving and, in the meantime, was ordered to train alone. As the new season approached, he was told by Britton that Arsenal manager George Swindin had arrived to see him. Swindin had publicly told Britton he would pay the fee Preston wanted for their wing-half.

Embarking on his first season as Arsenal manager, Swindin explained why he was prepared to spend money on a player who, at 30 years old, hardly fitted into his stated recruitment policy. 'We need youth,' he said. 'Docherty is the one exception. We need his experience and personality as a short-term investment until our own young men mature.'

While Preston and Arsenal eventually settled on a fee reported at close to £28,000, Docherty considered Swindin's approach for a couple of days, watching Arsenal lose 2–1 at Preston in the first game of the season, before deciding to undertake what he would call the 'great adventure' of moving south. 'I suppose everybody who has ever kicked a ball wants some day to play for Arsenal, and I was no exception,' he said. He had no idea that Manchester United had also enquired about making him part of their post-Munich rebuilding, although Britton had given Arsenal first option. Docherty admitted later that his admiration for Busby was such that he 'might not have been able to refuse' a United offer.

Saying his farewells and packing up his home and family, Docherty was straight into the Arsenal team for a 3–0 victory over Burnley, in which he scored his only goal for the club. But it was the atmosphere around Highbury that impressed him more than the team's performance. Entering the famous marble halls as a home player, enjoying the luxury of heated changing-rooms, the issuing of a club blazer and tie: these were the things that persuaded him he had arrived at a 'football college'.

Docherty sensed it wasn't love at first sight for the home crowd. Previously an abrasive opponent, he now felt that his constant shouting at teammates during matches was not going down well with his new supporters. Not until Arsenal beat local rivals Tottenham 3–1 in mid-September – part of a sequence that saw them score twenty-five goals in winning their first six home games – did he sense acknowledgement of his wholehearted approach to his game.

Acceptance within the dressing-room was achieved more quickly and would remain throughout his Arsenal career. John Barnwell, a young inside-forward when Docherty arrived, recalls, 'He came in full of enthusiasm and desire. Tommy was very vocal and technically he was a much better player than he was given credit for. He gave the impression of being an exceptionally strong player – which he was – and vicious in his tackling. But I always thought he was a fair tackler.'

Docherty would say towards the end of his career, 'I have gone home looking like an advertisement for blue-black ink. I have also handed out my share of punishment. It's not a pastime for namby-pambies who want to perform or watch delicate tricks of footwork or ball control executed while the opposition stand off and wait.'

Barnwell supports Docherty's self-assessment. 'He never moaned about things; he just got on and played. I remember a terrible tackle on him and at half-time you could see the gash right down his leg. He just strapped it up and went back out. You wouldn't have known he was injured. He was a hard man and a great motivator. He lifted the team to higher levels when he was playing. Off the pitch, he was always the joker and had a one-liner for everything. He would make comments on most things – whether you agreed with them or not was something else – and he was a livewire. If you had a party he was the first one you would invite.

'He was a big influence. You learned a lot playing in front of Tommy. I would be on the same part of the pitch and he liked a lot of conversation, always for the betterment and encouragement of teammates. He was a good leader.'

Docherty's competitive instincts were to get him into trouble over the season of goodwill. Having been booked during a 6–3 defeat at Luton, the Gunners' third consecutive loss, he made his displeasure at certain decisions known to referee Ken Stokes as they left the field. The official informed Docherty that he would be reported to the FA, and a charge of using foul and abusive language was duly laid against him. In one retelling of the story, Docherty admitted calling Stokes a 'homer', but denied that he had used obscene language.

His version of events at the time was, 'Mr Stokes pulled me up for an alleged foul. I did not dispute the matter, but later he called over to me, "I shall be reporting you, Docherty." I stake my life on it that I only turned round and said, on the spur of the moment, "It is you who should be reported."'

One month later an FA disciplinary committee made Docherty the first Arsenal player for four years to receive a suspension[*] when they banned him for fourteen days and fined him £50, almost three weeks' wages, plus the costs of his personal hearing. 'I will just have to abide by the FA decision,' he commented. 'But it is never too late to learn a lesson and it is this: I shall not even say "hello" or "good afternoon" to a referee in future in case my intentions are mistaken.'

Docherty, who feared a reputation as a troublemaker would harm his future prospects in the game, spoke diplomatically of the damage to his club's reputation: 'The last thing in the world I would ever want to do is anything that could be regarded as a slur. I am proud of being an Arsenal player and have always tried to set an example.' The club's response, meanwhile, was typically proper. Secretary Bob Wall announced, 'The FA have dealt with the matter and we would not presume to criticise their decision. I am sure Tommy would not either.'

Privately, Docherty felt the punishment was 'grossly excessive' and he was not alone in that view. Journalists brought to light the potential conflict of interest in having club officials sitting in judgement on rival players. The three-man panel adjudicating on this case had included the secretary of Nottingham Forest and Chelsea chairman Joe Mears, who would soon become the closest boardroom ally of Docherty's career. One columnist urged, 'I demand Arsenal must make an appeal against this verdict, and the players' union should use this as a test case against a system that has no place in British football.'

Backing from Arsenal fans came in a more tangible form. 'I've received over £50 from supporters,' said Docherty during his ban. 'Of course I can't keep it. I shall give the lot to a church charity. And if I don't get round to answering every letter I want them to know how much I appreciate a wonderful gesture.'

Before starting his suspension, Docherty volunteered to test a new kind of boot with a 'ridged crêpe sole', according to descriptions, in an FA Cup replay against Colchester, keeping his feet securely on the slippery surface in a 4–0 win.

With or without Docherty in the line-up, it was the team's ability in front of goal that helped them to third place in the table in his

---

[*] Ironically, the previous suspension had been given to Doug Lishman after being sent off for a tackle on Docherty in a match against Preston.

first season, albeit a distant 11 points behind champions Wolves. Jimmy Bloomfield argued several years later, 'Tommy came to Arsenal when we were having a struggle. In his first full season we finished third, our best for a long time, and it was largely due to him. My overriding impression of the Doc was his tremendous dedication and his will to win. I never knew anyone who had more of these things. He had the sort of enthusiasm that rubbed off on everyone around him. He is the quickest-witted person I have ever known in the game. His tongue could sometimes be biting if you were on the receiving end.'

Full-back Billy McCullough adds, 'I thought Tommy was a good player to have in your team, but I wasn't very fond of him, to be honest. He was a funny person and sometimes he could be very cutting to people.'

Arsenal had gone to the top of the table in February by beating Leeds and had then overcome Manchester United 3–2 at Highbury in what Swindin called the 'best performance of the season'. Docherty was described as 'dazzling' by one reporter, while Barnwell scored twice as Arsenal went 3–0 up inside half an hour. A week later, however, they were being labelled 'washed-out quitters' by Desmond Hackett as they crashed 6–1 at Wolves. Their challenge derailed and confidence undermined, they failed to win any of their next six matches.

Even so, their final placing was to be the club's best performance during a barren spell that began after their 1953 Championship triumph over Docherty's Preston and would not end until success in the European Fairs Cup 17 years later. Following the death of manager Tom Whittaker in 1956, former Gunners and England wing-half Jack Crayston had taken charge, resigning after a 1957–58 campaign that saw the team finish in the bottom half of the table and lose in the FA Cup to Third Division Northampton.

Another old boy, former goalkeeper Swindin, had been given the manager's post in recognition of his success at Peterborough United, whom he had led to three consecutive Midland League titles and an appearance in the fourth round of FA Cup. 'A good guy but by now out of step with the revolution that was taking place in English football,' was Docherty's damning assessment. He was, therefore, encouraged to find that the club had also appointed a forward-thinking coach in future West Ham and England manager Ron

Greenwood. The former Championship-winning centre-half at Chelsea had been serving as manager of Eastbourne United.

Greenwood was among the new breed of tactical innovators – schooled at the FA's training centre at Lilleshall in Shropshire – who were finding their way into the country's dressing-rooms. An advocate of playing thoughtfully out of defence, he was given responsibility for training and tactics, an advance not universally welcomed by the Arsenal players. 'Ron was one of the first FA coaches,' Barnwell recalls, 'and the senior professionals of the time had a great wariness of them. But he impressed his thoughts onto the squad and the team started to flourish. There were four or five of the old era who were very against change. But times were changing and Doc was very open-minded about it.'

In fact, Docherty positively welcomed the presence of Greenwood. 'It was Ron who got me really involved in coaching and showed me more about tactics and preparation,' he explains. 'I used to go to Baker Street on Tuesdays and Thursdays with people like Malcolm Allison, Jimmy Hill and Bill McGarry – a smashing group of people. We were learning how to improve on individual skills, exercises and drills to improve players' technique and knowledge of the game.'

Having enrolled on a course at Lilleshall, he was guided by Walter Winterbottom and rubbed shoulders with future managers such as Dave Sexton and Don Howe. By now he was recognising the opportunities ahead and saw coaching qualifications as a necessary tool to 'open doors' in the game. 'I went to get a preliminary coaching certificate and ended up getting a full badge,' he recalls proudly.

At Highbury, Greenwood saw Docherty's role on the field as a defensive one, a similar move to that which the club had made with Joe Mercer in the final years of his career. The two men spent a lot of time in conversation and, according to Docherty, 'The more I learned the more I realised how much there was to learn.' Greenwood's training routines were organised, purposeful and dynamic, a stark contrast to the sessions at Preston. Docherty even found himself working with weights for the first time.

Swindin was given the freedom to spend on transfers that had largely been denied his predecessor, and Docherty travelled to Wales to help him persuade Mel Charles, the brother of Welsh legend John, to move to Highbury. Another Scotland international, Jackie Henderson, was signed from Wolverhampton, with McCullough recalling, 'Jackie was a big buddy with the Doc, but he was never allowed to go out with him. If I was there it was all right, but his wife wouldn't let him go out with the Doc on his own in case he got him into trouble.'

Meanwhile, a total of 17 professionals had left Highbury by the end of Docherty's first season, including Welsh wing-half Dave Bowen, who was succeeded as captain by Vic Groves. 'There was a lot of turmoil on the playing side,' Docherty recalled. 'Players wanted to leave and had become unsettled and we never really took off.'

There was further disorder in store when Arsenal concluded the season with a trip to Italy. Docherty was spoken to on several occasions by the local referee during a 3–1 defeat to Juventus, a game that left him limping on bloodied and bruised legs and displaying stud marks on his thigh. One Juventus player, Enrico Paul Sivori, claimed, 'It was all Docherty's fault. He kicked my ankle and was always trying to trip me. He should have been sent off, but when he stayed on I retaliated. I pulled his hair and when he tried it again I kicked him.' Swindin described the events as 'disgraceful' and pulled out of negotiations to play a further game against Bologna after fulfilling their fixture against Fiorentina. 'We just dare not risk any more injuries,' he said.

On the Scotland front, evidence of the difference to Docherty that Busby might have made had he been able to influence World Cup selection was provided when he recalled him to the team against Wales five months later – Busby's belated first game at the helm. Chosen at left-half alongside his old school pal Willie Toner, Docherty helped his team to a 3–0 win, in which Huddersfield's Denis Law scored on his debut. Three weeks later Docherty played in a 2–2 draw against Northern Ireland. With Andy Beattie replacing Busby and beginning his second spell in charge of the national team, Docherty played in his 25th and final international at Wembley in April 1959. Summing up his Scotland career, he said, 'During the time I played for Scotland they had a lot of good players but never a team consistent enough to achieve things.' He bowed out on the wrong side of a 1–0 scoreline, but the Scottish side had not yet seen the last of him.

Busby had recognised enough potential in Docherty as a manager and coach to ask him to scout England in a Villa Park international against Wales late in 1958. 'I felt I had a foot on the management ladder,' Docherty said. Having failed to win selection for Scotland's summer programme, he moved himself up another couple of rungs by enrolling for further instruction and testing at Lilleshall. The events of the 1959–60 season were about to hoist him inexorably towards a coaching career.

He had already begun to realise that he'd rather make an early entry into the profession than eke out a prolonged playing existence in the lower divisions. 'Not for me the Saturday afternoons before a few handfuls of spectators, labouring through the game an ageing and forgotten star,' he wrote in his first autobiography. Then, with Arsenal having won only five of twelve games, Preston visited Highbury. With 20 minutes played, Docherty attempted to intercept a cross and collided with centre-half Bill Dodgin. Pain shot up from his ankle, and his own fears were reflected in the worried look on the face of Tom Finney, the first man to come to his aid. The ankle was broken.

Having sold his interest in his café following the move to London, all that was left for Docherty during his lay-off was 'reflection and introspection'. He began approaching clubs about the possibility of employment once he had completed his coaching qualifications. He also began refining what could have stood as his coaching manifesto: his file of preferred training methods and tactics. He studied team formations, ranging from the defensive approach of Italian sides to the localised versions of the sweeper system, such as that employed by Mercer's Sheffield United. Not only did he study ways of implementing similar strategies, he formulated plans to combat them.

An insight into the all-consuming nature of Docherty's passion for football – not to mention his ability for great acts of generosity alongside the vindictiveness – comes from Dave Mackay's recollection of his transfer around that time to Tottenham from Hearts. Docherty insisted that Mackay and his wife, Isobel, stayed with him and Agnes in Cockfosters while he looked for a house. 'They were very kind to a new boy in town and looked after me well,' Mackay recalled. 'Tommy was obsessed with football, even more than me, and little else was discussed in that household. I can see him now at the dinner table getting agitated about some player, manager or official, only stopping his stream of invective when Agnes quietly put his dinner down in front of him. He'd be silent as he ate and then seconds after the final mouthful had slipped down his gullet, he'd start back up where he had left off.'

Mackay could tell that Docherty was destined for management, adding, 'Tommy was not a rebel or a troublemaker, as he has sometimes been portrayed. He was merely passionate and knowledgeable, and they were two qualities that the men who ran the game lacked the most.'

Even though he was filling his time productively, the competitive spirit within Docherty pushed him towards a quick return to the playing field. When he announced his intention to walk 16 miles a day to build up his leg, Swindin told him, 'Forget that crazy idea. You are only going to do what the doctor orders, and no more.'

But by the time he returned to the first team against Fulham in April, with Arsenal on their way to finishing 13th in the table, he recognised that his love of playing was now secondary to his desire to coach. The Highbury crowd, to whom Docherty had 'quickly become a folk hero' according to the *Daily Sketch*, would have been dismayed to learn of such developments, yet his teammates were unsurprised. 'I always thought Tommy was cut out to be a manager,' says Barnwell. 'That was his style and probably by the time he was at Arsenal the best of his playing days had been used up. He was already thinking about it.'

Docherty's off-season began with an eye-opening visit to Hampden Park to see the great Real Madrid side of Puskás, Di Stefano and Gento annihilate Eintracht Frankfurt 7–3 in the European Cup final. It continued, as usual, at Lilleshall, swapping ideas and methods with the likes of Allison, Sexton, Frank O'Farrell, Bob Paisley, Billy Bingham, Peter Taylor, Phil Woosnam and Malcolm Musgrove.

By now, word of Docherty's interest in coaching was circulating, resulting in an approach by Barnet, then in the Athenian League, to see if he would work with them two evenings per week. It was unpaid, but was both close to his home and an opportunity to put his ideas into practice. Whatever the impact of Docherty's input, Barnet did not exactly set their league alight and the only consistent mention of his contribution in copies of the *Barnet Press* during that time was when he arranged for injured players to receive treatment at Highbury.

Yet such was Docherty's desire to move into coaching full-time that he told Swindin that he had no interest in a transfer to Blackpool, a move that might have allowed him to extend his playing career for a few more years. The Seasiders had offered £10,000 and, according to Docherty, he was 'flabbergasted that Arsenal were thinking of selling me'. Having spoken twice to Blackpool manager Ron Suart, he informed Swindin and Greenwood that his coaching interests, and the notion of a possible café partnership with Henderson, made him want to remain in London. 'I will never play for any other club,' he said a few days later, even though he had been left out of the team.

To those unaware how completely the coaching bug had bitten him, there was no evident waning in Docherty's appetite for an on-field scrap. Such was his ongoing reputation that one reporter commented tongue-in-cheek after a game against Burnley, 'What's up with tough-guy Tommy Docherty? I actually saw him return to the scene of a heavy tackle and carefully replace a divot!' He also ended up with seven stitches in a leg wound against Chelsea, after which the club ordered him to start wearing shin pads.

It was hardly the happiest of times to be an Arsenal player, however. In September, director Jimmy Joyce resigned, claiming that chairman Sir Bracewell Smith and the board were holding back the team. The following month, protesting fans made Swindin aware of their dissatisfaction with results and the way in which players such as Docherty, Herd and Henderson were being offered for sale as part of an apparently haphazard attempt at rebuilding. England midfielder Bloomfield, meanwhile, was stating that he was 'finished with Arsenal'. The players were driven to releasing a statement through skipper Groves supporting their manager and directors and claiming that 'team spirit has never been higher'.

A route away from Highbury presented itself to Docherty in January 1961 when he read a report stating that he had asked for permission to apply for the vacant coach's position at Chelsea. At that stage he'd known nothing about the job, but when England manager Walter Winterbottom said that he'd suggested him or Burnley's Jimmy Adamson for the role, he pursued the opportunity. 'I want to do the right thing by Arsenal,' he said after being given the club's blessing to speak to Chelsea. While Docherty waited for his interview, Adamson was ruled out of contention by League champions Burnley's involvement in the European Cup. Vic

Buckingham, who managed West Brom to FA Cup triumph at Docherty's expense in 1954 and was now in charge of Ajax Amsterdam, emerged as a rival, along with ex-Chelsea centre-half Roy Bentley and Reading coach Bobby Campbell.

Chelsea manager Ted Drake, the former Arsenal centre-forward, had been working without a chief coach for two years since Albert Tennant, with whom he had won the Division One title in 1955, had become manager at Southern League Guildford. But with the club flirting with relegation after straddling the New Year with a run of nine matches without victory, the board had told him to bring in outside help. It was significant that it was they, rather than Drake, who interviewed Docherty. He gave a confident, even cocky, performance, encouraged by chairman Joe Mears informing him, 'There are three other directors here and we know nothing about football.' Docherty recalls thinking, 'I am in with a chance here!'

Asked what he thought of Chelsea's defence, Docherty responded, 'A jellyfish has more shape.' When vice-chairman Charles Pratt sought out his motives for wanting to be a manager, he shot back, 'If you ask, you'll never know. If you know, you need never ask.'

While Docherty and Campbell were being interviewed, Buckingham was reportedly laid up in Amsterdam with flu. The press speculated on whether Buckingham would get the chance to stake his claim, but Mears, whose last intervention in Docherty's career had been to help get him banned, was impressed enough by the Arsenal man to call and offer him the job. Five days after meeting the Chelsea board, Docherty's appointment was announced. Of his employers' willingness to release him from his contract, he said, 'I'm grateful to them. It is a typical Arsenal gesture. I always wanted to retire as a first-team player.'

Meanwhile, the *Daily Express* delighted in outlining the task ahead. 'Docherty ends his playing career at 32 to shoulder the big job of ending the jeers at Stamford Bridge and drilling Chelsea's youngsters into a First Division power.' He couldn't wait to get started.

6

COMMANDING THE BRIDGE

'I took the players to see the Wailing Wall, but we couldn't get near it for Sunderland supporters.'

Ted Drake had been lying through his teeth. 'We wanted a man with real zest and experience, yet young enough to be out with the players in any weather,' he'd told reporters when Tommy Docherty was introduced as his chief coach. 'Tommy has an absolutely free hand to get on with the job. Everybody here will be backing him a million per cent.' But when Docherty turned up for work he found the manager in his office and was met with, 'I didn't want you here. I wanted Vic Buckingham.' Welcome to Chelsea.

Drake, the former Arsenal and England centre-forward, would at least remain true to his comment that the training ground would be the coach's domain as 'my office is 200 yards from the pitch and it's tough tying in the desk work with everything else'.

Having watched his new team draw 2–2 at home to Blackpool, Docherty quickly observed that practice sessions lacked pattern or purpose. On the personnel front, the team contained some promising young players, with even more waiting to step up from a successful youth team, and a motley group of senior professionals, who, ironically, included Bobby Evans, the right-half who had barred Docherty's path into the Celtic team.

'We obviously only knew Tommy as a player,' says winger Frank Blunstone. 'Ted Drake was a pure manager. We didn't have a coach; we just had a trainer, Albert Tennant, who only did fitness. Ted never came out in a tracksuit and we never saw him during the week. We were struggling a bit. The team that won the Championship [in 1955] was a good one, but it was getting on.'

Docherty adds, 'I was lucky in that we were winning the FA Youth Cup twice and we had some fantastic young players. Dick Foss did a great job with that team and I inherited eight or nine of the best under-18s in the country. But Ted never saw the young players because he only ever saw anyone on match days. He never came to training.'

The early games made evident Docherty's biggest problems. While the team, spearheaded by young genius Jimmy Greaves, was capable of scoring six against Newcastle and Cardiff, they had shipped the same amount against Wolves and Manchester United before Docherty's arrival and would concede four at Burnley* and Tottenham. A tighter defence, shielded by a more solid midfield, were the priorities, but to say Docherty achieved immediate success would be an overstatement.

A 4–3 win on the final day against Nottingham Forest – with Greaves scoring all the goals to take his tally to forty-one for the season – saw Chelsea finish 12th, an improvement of three places on the time of Docherty's arrival. But now the source of all those goals was leaving for AC Milan.

While the Professional Footballers' Association had spent the first half of the season fighting for the abolition of the £20-per-week maximum wage, going to the brink of strike action, Greaves was looking at the banker option of unrestricted riches abroad. Even with the PFA having won the pay battle – although their fight for greater freedom to move at the end of a contract would go on a little longer – Greaves cited the opportunity to advance his career, as well as the financial opportunities, in Italy when announcing his decision. Denis Law, bound for Torino from Manchester City, and England strikers Gerry Hitchens (Aston Villa to Inter Milan) and Joe Baker (Hibernian to Torino) had made the same judgement.

According to Docherty, Greaves was having second thoughts as his departure date loomed, but his earlier promise and Chelsea's need for the £80,000 transfer fee meant that matters were beyond the point of no return. 'One of the biggest disappointments of my

---

* The Burnley game ended in a 4–4 draw but the League champions were fined by the Football League for fielding a weakened team, having rested 10 first-teamers prior to their European Cup quarter-final and FA Cup semi-final engagements.

career was when they sold Greavsie,' Docherty says. 'I think if we had kept him we could have won the League four or five times. He is the best goalscorer I have seen.'

When, several months later, Greaves decided he'd had enough of Italy, Chelsea sent secretary John Battersby to discuss a possible return. Docherty is convinced that had he been given the chance to outline his plans to the England forward, he could have convinced him to rejoin Chelsea instead of Tottenham. 'I was told by one or two younger directors that John Battersby was told to go out to Milan but "don't bring Greavsie back". In other words, make him an offer that he won't accept because Chelsea needed the money they'd got for him.'

Docherty feared the worst as the 1961–62 season kicked off. Drake, he believed, was becoming more distant and barely tolerant of his presence at the club. It rankled when the manager, writing in the club's handbook, welcomed new trainer Harry Medhurst and spoke about the reserve and youth-team managers, but made no mention of Docherty. Meanwhile, the squad had lost its best player and contained some who 'if it had been up to me, wouldn't have been allowed within a mile of Stamford Bridge'. Docherty recalls, 'I noticed very quickly that Ted kept playing a lot of his old pals, like the Sillett brothers, goalkeeper Reg Matthews and Sylvan Anderton. Some people weren't interested in how they played, just how long they played. The youngsters were champing at the bit.'

After Chelsea won only one of their first six games, Drake suggested Docherty return to action, even though he'd not played for nine months. Having warmed up in a London Challenge Cup game against Wimbledon, he lined up at left-half against Sheffield United, the team whose sweeper system he had studied so closely. Included at the expense of unhappy 18-year-old Terry Venables, Docherty felt that well-timed diagonal balls, behind the full-backs and intended for the speedy Bobby Tambling, would break down the Sheffield defence. Held 1–1 at half-time, Chelsea romped to a 6–1 victory with Tambling grabbing a hat-trick. 'Tom Docherty could have planned this comeback as a training exercise,' said one report, noting Chelsea's 'spells of absolute fluency and intelligence'.

But this was no new beginning. Docherty played a couple more games and Chelsea failed to win any of the next three. The board had run out of patience. As Docherty stood waiting for his manager so that they could take a flight to Scotland for a scouting trip, he was approached by Battersby and told, 'Ted Drake has gone.' Docherty thought he meant that Drake had departed for the airport. He was corrected. Drake had been removed with six years of a ten-year contract remaining and given a reported £9,000 pay-off. Asked to take temporary charge, Docherty called Drake to wish him luck, goodwill that he said was not returned, and set about what he knew would be a long process of rebuilding.

Chairman Joe Mears stopped short of publicly describing Docherty as a caretaker manager, saying, 'Tommy Docherty's title is still chief coach.' But he did emphasise that he had 'a completely free hand' and seemed to be using him as his model when he painted a portrait of a prospective manager. 'We are moving in the same direction as West Ham: that is towards the idea of the manager in a tracksuit who is really a coach. The directors are in favour.' Mears suggested that money would be available for new signings, although he warned, 'We would not spend as much as £100,000.'

Blunstone remembers, 'We expected Tommy to get the job. He hadn't really had the chance to bring in his own ideas; we were still working on Ted Drake's.' Certainly, Docherty felt there was much he could do without an old-school manager reining him in – and if he could rid himself of a group of grumpy, uninterested senior players.

A stark outline of life at Chelsea was offered by left-half Frank Upton, who had been the final player signed during Drake's reign but had rarely featured in the first team. 'I am disappointed,' he said. 'The spirit is not the same as at Derby. The difference in atmosphere is remarkable. There are too many cliques in the Chelsea dressing-room and I've found it a little hard to mix with them. Some of the players have been at Chelsea for years and look on me as an outsider who might push one of their mates out of the team.'

Docherty would have agreed with that assessment, but as caretaker – even if that was not his official title – he still felt unable to change things as quickly as he would have liked. His first four games in charge were lost while conceding 15 goals and, with the team bottom of the table in December, he identified to the board the players he felt he could sell to raise funds for new signings.

Blunstone, who along with full-backs Peter and John Sillett was a survivor of the title season, was relieved to find he was not considered surplus to requirements. 'Ted Drake was a great friend of the Sillett brothers and their father, Charlie, but Tommy didn't have a good relationship with them. He clashed with a lot of the old players, but for some reason he got on all right with me. I didn't go out of my way to make that happen. I was on 25 quid a week and he called me in and I thought, "What have I done? I am in trouble." He said, "I have been thinking. I am going to give you a fiver rise." I told him I didn't know why because I'd signed a contract and was happy but he said, "You are giving a lot more effort than half of these, so you are getting an extra fiver."'

All some others got was an opportunity to put themselves in the shop window in a series of specially arranged friendlies. 'The youngsters wanted to listen and wanted to get on,' Docherty explains. 'They would put a lot of time into what you were trying to teach them. The other lads, the 30-year-olds, you couldn't tell them anything. They said, "Mr Drake said we should do this," and I had to reply, "Well, he is not here any more." I sensed friction with a lot of the older players and the only thing to do was to get them away.' Meanwhile, Mears's stated willingness to pay £90,000 to bring an unhappy Greaves back to London was trumped by Tottenham's £99,999, while Celtic rebuffed Docherty's attempt to court half-back Paddy Crerand by calling it a 'typically English stunt'.

Docherty's slow start prompted continued speculation about the long-term inhabitant of the Chelsea manager's office. Youth-team coach Foss was said to have his supporters in the boardroom, while the availability of Archie Macauley following his resignation from Norwich set further tongues wagging.

Chelsea's first win under Docherty came at his old Highbury home, a 3–0 win against Arsenal being the first of four games without defeat. The Chelsea board responded by showing enough confidence in Docherty to break the club record by spending £38,000 on 20-year-old Cardiff forward Graham Moore. Cardiff manager Bill Jones revealed the characteristic impulsiveness with which Docherty had conducted business, admitting, 'I was astonished. Chelsea phoned me yesterday morning from London and four hours later Tommy Docherty was on the line from a Cardiff hotel. Moore was seen at 10.30 this morning and four hours later it was all completed.'

As New Year approached, Desmond Hackett was telling *Daily Express* readers that 'Chelsea's form since [Docherty] took over is certain to make him the Chelsea chief in time for a Hogmanay celebration'. Hackett was wrong by only a couple of days. On 2 January, Docherty offered the board the reality that it would be hard to avoid relegation but that the development of the squad would mean a probable immediate return to the First Division. The response came from vice-chairman Charles Pratt. 'We think you have done a very fine job in very difficult circumstances,' he said, offering him £60 per week to take the job permanently. Docherty skipped out of the meeting and gave his team the news as they prepared to travel to Blackpool for a few days before facing Liverpool in the FA Cup.

Having lost that game 4–3, Docherty – despite his warning to the boardroom – was not about to concede the inevitability of relegation in public. 'I honestly don't think we'll go down,' he told reporters. 'There are 15 games to play and we need 20 points.' They got nine, winning only twice during the run-in and finishing three points adrift at the foot of the table. Docherty reiterated to the board his belief that imminent changes would ensure a swift promotion.

Helping him to deliver on that promise was a new assistant coach, Dave Sexton, a former inside-forward with the likes of West Ham, Leyton Orient, Brighton and Crystal Palace who would establish himself as one of the country's sharpest football minds. A member of the famous think tank at West Ham – where players spent afternoons discussing tactics at Cassetari's cafe on the Barking Road – and a regular attendee at FA coaching courses, Sexton was quickly identified by Docherty as his right-hand man and appointed within weeks of his confirmation as manager. 'I liked him and his ideas,' Docherty explains. 'I valued his expertise as a coach and we worked well together. I was responsible for tactics and Dave did the coaching and training.'

The careers of the two men were to remain closely linked, with Sexton called upon to succeed Docherty after his two most successful managerial stints. Docherty would never be entirely convinced of his colleague's credentials as a manager, believing him to lack the necessary force of personality, but in the meantime he knew he had a valuable aide.

Blunstone illustrates the difference in the personalities of Docherty and his assistant. 'Dave was a funny bugger, very quiet,' he states. 'I remember when he was Chelsea manager going with him to Cambridge City to watch a centre-forward, Ian Hutchinson. I drove and he never bloody spoke to me. Not a word. It wasn't because he was rude; he just wasn't a great communicator.'

Frank O'Farrell, a teammate of both Docherty and Sexton, describes the latter as 'a bit of an intellectual'. Recalling his West Ham colleague, he says, 'Some players, all they knew about was horses. But during pre-season training we would have a break at lunchtime and have a quiz. Dave would buy *The Times* and he would set the questions.'

Ken Shellito recognised that Docherty was by now more inspired by strategic thinking and the challenge of man-management than training-ground routines. 'Tom didn't enjoy coaching. Dave did. Tom did the management and organisation and Dave did the day-to-day work. They worked terrifically as a team and were opposites.'

Blunstone continues, 'Tommy had trained us up and down the terraces: all the old type of training. Tommy was not a great coach and didn't read the game that well. But he got the best out of people and was clever to let Dave get on with it. Tommy did the motivating in the dressing-room. If players weren't doing it then Tommy could give them a bollocking and get them going.'

John Hollins, an FA Youth Cup winner waiting for his first-team break, recalls, 'Dave Sexton was the best coach I ever worked under. He always had a thought, an idea, was trying to make you better and make you think. We'd all be guinea pigs. "Just try this" or "just do that". He kept changing the game.'

Ron Harris, another youth-teamer who would progress to the status of club captain, adds, 'When Tom first came to the club nobody knew what coaching was about. You used to do two warm-up laps and had a kick-about. Dave brought a new dimension and took coaching to a different level.'

Docherty quickly saw the players' respect for Sexton. His total trust in him was probably helped by his notion that Sexton was not cut out to be a manager, nor appeared to want to be one. It made for an easy relationship. Docherty was later to prove that such amicability was elusive with anyone he perceived as a potential threat to his authority. As Shellito adds, 'I ended up going to several clubs with Tom as his number two. It worked because he knew I didn't want his job. People like Dave are worth their weight in gold. They don't want your job; they just want to work with you.'

The final weeks of Chelsea's relegation campaign had helped Docherty complete his diagnosis of the team's health. According to Hollins, 'There was going to be a change, a revolution, and I don't think Tommy could change the way the older players felt. It was ingrained in them to think, "We'll just stay steady; we won't try things." But Tommy was going to bring all the young kids through, the team that won the FA Youth Cup. That was Ted Drake's legacy to Tommy.'

Shellito adds, 'We'd had a lot of us young players pushing through and a lot of senior players struggling along. Tom cleared away a lot of the older ones. The club had a magnificent player-development system and Tom wanted to get us in there to prove ourselves.'

Ron Harris believes Docherty saw greater dependability among the younger players. 'His philosophy was that youngsters never cheat you,' he explains. 'When you are young and the ball looks like it is going out, you still run after it. When you get a little bit older you don't bother. Providing you played ball with Tom and were honest, he would go with you and he would motivate you to play for him.'

With 94 goals conceded on the way to relegation, it was not hard to see where immediate surgery was required. Docherty had already shown faith in young full-backs Shellito and Allan Harris, who says, 'Tommy wasn't worried about what people thought. He would put young players in if they deserved it. He had a big reputation as a player and he got a lot of respect from us that way.'

But further reconstruction was clearly required. Docherty ventured to East Stirling and had his eye captured by left-back Eddie McCreadie – not the intended subject of his attention – and eagerly signed him for a bargain £5,000. Ideas on how best to utilise such talent sprang from a summer trip to the World Cup finals in Chile. Docherty returned further enamoured with champions Brazil, in particular the way they used full-backs to broaden their attacking options.

Shellito says, 'I remember Tom and Dave saying to me and Eddie, "We are going to completely change the way we play," and that was the instigation of attacking full-backs. It was so enjoyable. Before that you wouldn't be allowed to cross the halfway line. They completely changed that so we could get forward and play, while someone else would get back for us. So many clubs followed it, and I am a firm believer that Tom and Dave were the two who brought that to England. It was completely new. We played 4–2–4 and we wanted to play football. We wanted to pass the ball, not just kick it up there. That was the point when Chelsea changed from being an Accrington Stanley to playing very European-style football."

Blunstone confirms, 'We started getting full-backs to overlap and I had to drop back, like a rotation thing. Me and Chopper [Ron Harris] had to fill in if Eddie came forward. We worked hard at it and then the press accused us of being a team of bloody runners. They said it was all movement and no skill. Well, there was a lot of bloody skill in what we were doing.

'I remember a friendly against a Continental team who played with a sweeper. Dave said, "When we start attacking I want you to run inside off the touchline every time and take the full-back in with you. That will leave room for Eddie." I kept running the full-back in and hardly got a kick and Eddie got all the credit. But when I came in, the first one Dave and Tommy came to was me and said I did a fantastic job. Reporters were thinking I had a stinker, but I was doing my job. Dave was clever like that.'

Speed throughout the team was an important component of a proposed pattern of play that would feature swift passing, movement off the ball and quickness of mind in covering for teammates. One of Chelsea's early season wins would be described in the press as a 'victory of perpetual motion'. Later in the season, Docherty would explain, 'We learned to do simple things at speed. We rehearsed new moves, free kicks and corners, and when we had mastered these plans we introduced them into match football.'

Hollins adds, 'We got at people. As soon as they got the ball back we got at them. If we could get the ball back in their half it was a much shorter journey to goal than dropping back and letting them attack us. We were an energetic team.'

Renowned weight trainer Bill Watson, who had worked successfully with recent champions Tottenham and Burnley, was brought in to increase players' agility. Bobby Tambling and Barry

---

*   England manager Alf Ramsey appeared to endorse that view later in the season when he asked Chelsea to play a training game against his team to help them prepare for a match against France.

Bridges would provide the pace up front, while Bert Murray and Blunstone occupied the wide midfield positions and Venables would orchestrate from the centre. Having shipped out well over a team's worth of players and seen the potential of the youngsters in his midst, Docherty felt there was no need at this stage for further transfers.

And he was not bothered about pandering to the sensitivities of players of whom he disapproved. One group 'whose efforts had not impressed me' were ordered in for extra training. They were joined by former England winger Peter Brabrook, who had refused the offer of a new contract and was sold to West Ham for £35,000. In offloading others who had held out for more money – including former captain Andy Malcolm, who went to Queens Park Rangers, centre-half Mel Scott and winger Mike Harrison – Docherty felt he was sending a warning to the rest of the squad, many of whom were young and impressionable.

Malcolm's transfer came only days after Docherty had described him as one of the six best players in the division. When it became clear that Scott was in the group who wanted to look elsewhere he quickly joined them on the sidelines. 'What is the point of playing them?' Docherty said. 'They might leave us at any time, so I am making my plans without them. I am annoyed they should want to leave Chelsea.'

Brabrook's departure meant that the last survivor of the 1954–55 team was Blunstone, of whom Docherty said, 'I could have asked no more of him in attitude and application. He set a fine example to the younger players.'

Docherty struck an untypically cautious note on the eve of the new season, saying he would rather spend an extra year in Division Two if it meant getting his team better prepared for future success. Instant promotion with a team ill-equipped for the highest level didn't interest him. 'I want us to be on a playing par with the best clubs in the top division,' he told reporters.

Armed with a £5 pay rise, Chelsea's players attacked the new campaign with no such reservations. A line-up featuring seven teenagers won the opening game at Rotherham through a goal by twenty-one-year-old captain Tambling, and then beat Scunthorpe and Charlton at home by three and five goals respectively. A 6–0 thrashing of Cardiff in October had reporters marvelling at the free-kick move that had broken the deadlock, Upton providing the finish after a McCreadie dummy, a Blunstone pass and a set-up by Moore. According to one report Docherty 'summoned up all his modesty' to say, 'Don't make too much fuss; we don't want other teams to know too much about it.'

A 4–2 home win against Newcastle prompted Desmond Hackett to come up with this glowing account in the *Daily Express*:

> For years Chelsea has been an arid area starved of real team football. Solitary gems have gleamed at Stamford Bridge where some of the greatest players of all time have paraded their skills. Alas, the setting was drab and even the finest of footballers must have a strong supporting cast. But these Chelsea young men of 1962 are a team. A team of rich promise, flowing with good football, high confidence and ablaze with the rare quality of team spirit. The man who has inspired this 'All for Chelsea' spirit is manager Tommy Docherty, the fittest team chief in Britain.

By the time Luton were beaten on Boxing Day, giving Chelsea eleven wins and a draw in twelve games, Docherty's side sat six points clear of Sunderland at the top of the table. Led by the prolific Tambling and Bridges they were the division's top scorers and, significantly, boasted the best defensive record.

It appeared that only a freak of nature could derail their march to the title. It did. The worst British winter on record took hold and six snowy, freezing weeks passed before Chelsea played another League game. During December, as thick fog and smog over London had hinted at the disruption to come, Docherty – always with an eye on a photo op – had his players train in protective, surgical-style masks. He created more headlines by flying his players to Malta during the worst of the winter. It was hardly the most successful of trips: the weather was bad and a game against Valletta was marred by crowd trouble and ended with a dispute over Chelsea's share of gate receipts.

When they returned, defeat at Swansea was the first of five consecutive League losses. A couple of FA Cup wins – a run ended at Manchester United in the fifth round – were their only successes until they beat Derby 3–1 at Stamford Bridge to record their first points for three months. 'Pathetic,' was how Docherty described a home performance against Huddersfield. 'It's worrying.'

A response to the bad run was the £45,000 signing of West Bromwich Albion's Derek Kevan, an experienced and uncomplicated forward not at all in the mould of Docherty's preference for quick-footed poachers. Kevan had been allowed to leave Albion to avoid 'dressing-room disruption'. His acquisition showed that Docherty could sometimes douse his idealism with a splash of pragmatism, although it was not to be the greatest advertisement for his foresight. He'd persuaded chairman Joe Mears that without Kevan they would not win promotion and, even though that goal was to be achieved, Docherty was disappointed to find he'd signed a player who appeared overweight and unsupportive of his methods. 'He mistook discipline for dictatorship and we were forever at odds,' he recalled.

A maddeningly inconsistent Chelsea were contending with Stoke and Sunderland for the two promotion places. After defeat at Norwich, Docherty claimed that 'the players seem to be losing their enthusiasm'. A 66,199 crowd at Stamford Bridge was not enough to rekindle sufficient fire to overcome Stoke, whose 1–0 win gave them a firm grasp on promotion with two games left. Docherty had ordered 18-year-old Ron Harris to stick close to Stanley Matthews, 30 years his senior and on his way to winning a second Footballer of the Year trophy. Docherty glows as he recalls, 'Chopper was great: a born leader and great captain. He used to say, "I might not be able to play but I can stop people playing."' Such was the gusto with which Harris approached his task that even his own fans protested at the rough treatment he meted out to the nation's favourite player.

This was no time for niceties, however, a fact Docherty reflected in his team selection for the penultimate game at Sunderland, where a draw for the home side would ensure their promotion. Chelsea needed a win to stay alive. Selecting a team that would 'shut them out but also snatch a precious goal', he omitted Bridges, Murray and Moore in favour of a pair of battering-ram strikers in Kevan and defender Upton. 'Frank was useless,' Docherty laughs. 'He trapped the ball further than I could kick it. But he was a smashing lad and did a job for me.'

Blunstone adds, 'Frank had no skill, but was hard; a 100 per center. It surprised us all. We had not practised with Frank up front or talked about it. We didn't even know until we got up there. If it had been Dave Sexton who'd thought it up he would have tried it in training.'

Also selected – for only his fourth Chelsea match – was Tommy Harmer, the 35-year-old former Tottenham forward picked up the previous September from Watford. Even Harmer admitted, 'My job was to play alongside the youngsters in the reserve side,' but Docherty had been impressed by his uncomplaining, unselfish attitude. In return, Harmer said that his new boss 'restored my faith in myself'.

Brian Mears, the son of the Chelsea chairman, had accompanied Docherty and Venables to watch Sunderland play against Luton a few days earlier, and the manager admitted to him that his selection was not the best Chelsea team, merely the best for the job. In front of a Roker Park crowd that had begun queuing the previous night, Moore and Upton were instructed to unsettle Sunderland centre-back Charlie Hurley, who liked to play out of defence. That combative approach permeated the entire Chelsea line-up, with seven of the first eight free kicks and three of the game's five bookings chalked up against them. Tambling recalled, 'We went up there with a side packed with defenders and people who could look after themselves.'

Chelsea were a goal up at half-time after a Tambling corner deflected into the net off Harmer's thigh. Pinned back by the wind and by their opponents in the second half, they held on for a crucial win that meant victory in their final match would see them accompany Stoke into the First Division.

Chelsea's tactics brought a wave of criticism, forcing Docherty to respond, 'This is still supposed to be a man's sport. We've dropped too many points already through trying to play too much football in a division in which some opponents play it too near the marrow. This had to be a tough, raw match. A whole season's work was at stake.'

Tension before the decisive game at home to Portsmouth was so high that centre-half John Mortimore suffered a nosebleed in the dressing-room, but the maligned Kevan eased nerves by converting a Tambling cross after two minutes. From then on it was a romp, Tambling scoring four goals in a 7–0 victory to take his season's total to thirty-seven and Ken Jones describing events in the *Daily Mirror* as 'a night of football fantasy that could only happen at Stamford Bridge'. The celebrations began long before the final goal went in and Docherty responded after the game by sending his players into the stand as the fans gathered below. With no microphone to hand, Docherty cupped his hands and bellowed, 'I promise that we'll give you a team to be proud of.' On such a joyous night it hardly mattered that barely anyone heard him.

7

BLACKPOOL OR BUST

'Football is a rat race, and the rats are winning.'

If one season encapsulated the Tommy Docherty era at Stamford Bridge it was 1964–65. Chelsea rolled out the kind of exciting football that reflected both the personality of their manager and the colourful scene that was establishing itself on the streets near Stamford Bridge. Visually, it was the season when Docherty ditched Chelsea's white shorts and introduced what would become the iconic Chelsea kit: royal blue shirts; royal blue shorts with a broad white stripe and white numbers; white socks.

'I felt we were living in a new, modern age and wanted Chelsea to reflect this,' said Docherty, whose instincts as a showman led him to throwing open a pre-season training session to which 3,000 fans flocked, along with the national media. It took six hours for the players to sign all the required autographs and pose for pictures. On display were the team's new training outfits, different colours for reserves and first team, whose uniform included eye-popping candy-striped shorts. Peter Osgood noted, '[Tommy] was an expert at keeping on the right side of the media, plying them with champagne and nibbles.'

Ultimately, despite winning their only trophy under Docherty, the season would end in a failure that was both glorious and futile, partly the consequence of a managerial decision that was both brave and impulsive and would have consequences beyond just that season. It would ultimately help to rip Docherty's team apart.

Before that, Chelsea had given a strong hint of the challenge they would mount to the established order in their first campaign back in the First Division. Having spent the post-promotion summer of 1963 on a team holiday in Cannes, followed by a playing tour of Israel, Docherty prepared for Chelsea's top-flight return with typical lack of sentimentality. He shopped around some of the men who'd helped make it possible, selling Derek Kevan to Manchester City for £38,000 and Graham Moore to Manchester United for £35,000. 'Neither fitted into my style of play,' he confessed, although Kevan would later contend, 'I could never have settled with Chelsea. Docherty was too dogmatic. I think he only took me to Chelsea to frighten the others into playing better.'

For a time, Moore was used as bait in an attempt to land Charlton Athletic defender Marvin Hinton. Citing the 23-year-old's 'uncanny knack of reading the game,' Docherty spent much of the pre-season trying to sign him – at one point offering Barry Bridges in part-exchange – before eventually completing a £35,000 deal one game into the season.

After Chelsea opened with a pair of 0–0 draws, some critics took issue with the focus they believed Docherty was placing on defence. They had perhaps expected more after he'd spoken of the potential £100 per week his players could earn if they went top of the table. 'We're already the third-best paid team on basic wages; only Everton and Spurs are better,' he claimed. 'And I'm not going back into the First Division just to establish myself and my team. We want to get right up there.'

Yet after hearing the Turf Moor fans booing in the second of those goalless contests, outspoken Burnley chairman Bob Lord accused Chelsea of footballing 'murder'. In mitigation, Chelsea had been hampered by an injury to Bobby Tambling and, with substitutions still two seasons away, Docherty argued, 'Our handicap made it imperative that we should adjust ourselves and rely on saving a point.'

That cut no ice with Lord, who ranted, 'There's nothing wrong with all-out defence for the last three or four minutes if you're winning by a goal, but to play it for forty out of forty-five minutes like Chelsea is a negation of all we have looked for in football. Fans pay their three shillings for entertainment. They want to see an attacking game. Tommy Docherty may feel the technique is fine from his point of view, but not one spectator in a thousand will be concerned with technique.'

Although not one to be swayed by critics, Docherty would ensure that there was little opportunity for anyone to gripe about Chelsea's entertainment value over the next few years. The team's swagger and flair blended perfectly with the explosion of show business and youth culture that led to this patch of south-west London, with the King's Road at its heart, symbolising Britain's 'Swinging '60s'. While musicians, film stars and fashionistas – from Marc Bolan to Mary Quant – frequented the shops and eateries close to Stamford Bridge, celebrities such as Richard Attenborough, Tom Courtenay, Alan Price and Tommy Steele were often to be found inside the ground. *Likely Lads* star Rodney Bewes recalled a whole group of northern actors following Chelsea around the country.

By mid-season their team was tucked in behind eventual champions Liverpool in fifth position, which they held to the end of the campaign. Along the way they scored four or more goals in seven of their twenty victories, although the manager's pragmatic side still announced itself with four consecutive 1–0 wins to finish the campaign. There had been a splash of glamour with an FA Cup third-round replay defeat of Tottenham in front of 70,123 – the biggest attendance of the season – and Docherty's assessment was, 'We were all quite happy after having just come up.'

Midway through the season, Docherty made a show of publicly thanking his 31 professionals – 19 of whom had come through the club's youth system – for their efforts. After his 30-minute talk he announced, 'I know they're all getting paid well, but I thought it would be nice to thank them too.' It was typical of Docherty to create headlines out of what might have been considered a routine internal meeting.

While Frank Blunstone and John Mortimore brought experience to the team, there was further advancement for the club's young talent. Midfielder John Hollins and wide man Peter Houseman made the most of their opportunities, with Docherty describing the former as one of the club's most intelligent players. Hollins feels that the 'energy and enthusiasm' with which Docherty attacked his job was reflected in his team selections. 'He would say, "He is not bad, let's put him in and have a look." Others would think a player was too young, so credit to Tommy for that. He got me in the team when I was 17 at Swindon. They were flying and it was a 30,000 crowd, but he was fearless. He said, "You're playing." Simple.'

So impressed was Docherty with his protégés that he told reporters that he was done with the transfer market. 'I don't think we will ever have to buy a player again, certainly not a big-fee player,' he stated. 'I want to get my players when they're about 15 or 16. I can then mould them the way I want them.'

Docherty felt able to relieve 15 club scouts of their duties, retaining only Jimmy Thompson, the man who unearthed Jimmy Greaves, Bobby Tambling and Hollins. He explained, 'We are not buying players, we are looking for youngsters. Jimmy was the only scout we had in the past when we found so many great boys. All we want now is a steady influx of two or three good youngsters a year.'

At one stage, Docherty attracted the disapproval of the Football League for the number of inexperienced players he fielded in a League Cup tie. The competition would not fully achieve major status until it was afforded the glamour of a Wembley final in 1967, and while some leading teams opted out altogether, Chelsea sent three teenaged debutants into action in their 3–0 defeat at Swindon, with Hollins joined by nineteen-year-old forwards Dennis Brown and John O'Rourke. 'We are not going to allow the Cup to be turned into a second-team tournament,' was the grumble emanating from League headquarters.

Docherty also came under physical attack during a game at Goodison Park, where a stone thrown from the crowd struck him in the face, although he insisted that no action be taken against Everton. He was in a less forgiving mood when Tambling, by now replaced as team captain by Venables, turned up late for treatment on his calf injury and was fined £5.

Having signed a three-year contract in the summer of 1964, Docherty continued his evolution of the Chelsea team into the new season. Tambling was switched to a wider forward position to accommodate George Graham, a young recruit from Aston Villa. Spotted during a reserve game, the aerial threat Graham could offer and the modest £5,000 fee prompted Docherty to move quickly for the 19-year-old Scot, although only just quickly enough.

'I went to spend some time with my brother in Poole and I looked around Southampton,' Graham explains. 'The manager, Ted Bates, wanted me. If my brother hadn't lived in Poole I would probably have signed there and then, but because I was staying overnight, I said, "Let me have another day to think." When I got to my brother's there was a message from Chelsea. They got in touch and I told them Southampton had offered £25 a week. Tommy said he'd give me £30, so not only was it more money, it was Chelsea, who were a fantastic team.'

Having explained that he would make his decision during a holiday in Majorca, Graham was shocked to find Docherty at the airport in the early hours of the morning with his contract. 'Luckily for me, Bobby Tambling got injured in preseason and Tommy put me straight into the team. I couldn't stop scoring, so when Bobby came back, I played up the middle with Bobby left and Barry Bridges right. We were an exciting team, youngsters at the top of their game. It was a joy playing between Tambling and Bridges. Someone would knock it to me and I'd hold it up or flick it on to one of them coming through.'

Chelsea prepared for the new season with a six-game European tour, Docherty explaining his desire to 'play ourselves into fitness through matches'. He also pointed out that 'I want to be known as the best manager in Europe with the finest team in Europe' and added, 'My players have three-year contracts; I have a three-year contract. I'll be very disappointed if we haven't won the Cup or the League by the time those contracts run out.' He was confident enough in his players' ability to compete on all fronts to ensure that their contracts included a contingency for winning trophies, along with the usual weekly bonuses for League position, wins and attendance. It looked like they would be cashing in as they began the season by winning seven and drawing three of their first ten games.

For the first time, television viewers were sharing in events at Stamford Bridge following the launch of BBC2's new Saturday evening programme *Match of the Day*, which featured an hour of highlights from one of the day's leading games. Chelsea featured in the programme's second week, beating Sunderland 3–1 at home. Such was the attraction of Docherty's team that they were shown three times within the first seven weeks. By February, however, club chairman Joe Mears had banned the cameras from his ground for the remainder of the season. 'Football must stand by its own performances to attract live audiences,' he said. 'I can't see why in these days when we are still seeking ways of winning back the public we should instead encourage them to stay away to watch sport on TV screens.' It was a view typical of those within football who failed to acknowledge the possible benefits of showcasing their 'product' to a wider audience, especially with the BBC giving no advance warning of which game was being shown.

In the midst of Chelsea's early run Dave Sexton was formally named as first-team coach rather than merely assistant. In January, however, he would become manager of Orient, leaving with the assurance that 'working under Tommy Docherty has been wonderful'. The disappointment felt by the Chelsea players would be mirrored nearly four years later by the Arsenal squad's regret when Sexton – who had joined them as coach a season earlier – took over from Docherty at Stamford Bridge. Graham, a future Gunners player who would therefore suffer Sexton's departure twice, says, 'Dave was a big influence on me and a lot of other people at Chelsea. He was the studious coach while Tommy was the motivator. Their different styles worked. When a partnership works well the manager tells the number two how they want to play and he carries it out, doing the majority of the coaching work. They were a good combination.'

Docherty, meanwhile, was the subject of an ambitious attempt by Sunderland to persuade him to succeed Alan Brown, who had moved to Sheffield Wednesday. He was 'flattered', but the offer was dismissed, as was his team's unbeaten run when they lost 2–0 at home to a George Best-inspired Manchester United. The setback was a springboard to another impressive sequence, only three losses in the next twenty-one League games. That left Chelsea top of the table, three points clear of division newcomers Leeds, who held a game in hand. Docherty's team were also through to the quarter-finals of the FA Cup and awaiting the two-legged final of the League Cup. The whole of English football, it appeared, lay at their feet. 'I could see no one stopping us in our quest for glory,' Docherty said. Perhaps he should have looked in the mirror.

Docherty offered *The Times* an insight into his methods and philosophy. His love affair with attacking full-backs had intensified following visits to watch Real Madrid in training and he described his desire to use them, as well as half-backs, to add an extra man to the attack. 'It is a concertina movement; we demand mobility,' he said. At this stage of his career, Docherty, skilled in giving the reporters a disposable quote, appeared to be less adept at articulating his strategic thoughts. Contradicting himself somewhat, he explained that Venables was the only player 'given free rein to improvise', yet in the same breath said that the others were 'encouraged to play by ear, not sticking to rigid positions'.

In training, he said, 'The accent is on accuracy, high speed and endurance, a mixture of strength and finesse, with no players in practice games allowed more than two consecutive touches. Running off the ball and playing the ball quickly are the basic things for us.'

According to Venables, this was all a world away from the 'laid-back approach' of Ted Drake, who often seemed interested only in practising his golf swing. But while younger players thrived under Docherty's instructions to play with ambition and innovation, Venables felt 'the older players resented Docherty and his new ideas'. The mood of the veterans was exacerbated by the manager's obvious preference for young legs over experienced heads, and an abrasive communication style that worked more effectively on wide-eyed youngsters.

Hollins explains, 'As we had grown up all together as players, you thought, "Well, he has given us the chance to play so let's give him the chance to have a go at us. Take it on the chin and get on with it." We were all learning the game.'

It is why young players such as Allan Harris recall, 'I enjoyed his company and he was well liked,' while Peter Brabrook had a totally different view. 'We didn't see eye to eye, but, then again, no one liked him,' he said. 'He just wasn't anyone's cup of tea.'

Docherty had proved – notably in the vital promotion game at Sunderland – that he was flexible enough to tailor his team's approach to the opposition and the need for a specific result. Yet in general, and increasingly as his confidence in his charges grew, he was happy to shape his teams and tactics according to the players' strengths and his ingrained desire for carefree football. 'He let the opposition worry about us,' says Ken Shellito. 'Tom thought that once you started telling players that the opposition can do this and that, it makes them feel inferior. His policy was, "We are the best; go and show them." He wouldn't put dread into you. Even if you got beaten he would say, "What are you worried about? You played well, but you lost." Managers have not got that luxury now.'

The strength of Docherty's teams at their best – at Chelsea in the mid-'60s and at Manchester United a decade later – was their attacking capability. 'We played the same way, home or away,' says Ron Harris. 'We weren't told to hang back or anything like that. You were encouraged to get forward.'

Blunstone explains, 'I remember the press getting on to Tommy after we won a game 4–3 because we'd let in some goals and he said, "I don't care if they score four as long as we score five." That was his attitude.'

Hollins continues, 'He would pick a team and go for it: attack, attack, attack. Sometimes you would win by four or five goals and you'd think, "This is really easy."'

Allan Harris adds, 'Tommy used to talk a little bit about the opposition, so that we had a good picture, but he would let us get on with our own job and concentrated on motivating his own players.'

It was something, according to many, at which Docherty was expert and which he describes as 'a gift'. Shellito says, 'He could talk to players and get them ready to go out there and play. He realised what players wanted to do. Tommy Harmer couldn't go out without a smoke, so he let him go into the toilet for a cigarette. Later, at QPR, Tony Currie had to have a quick glass of whisky and Stan Bowles his last bet. Tom let them do it because if you restrict them you're not going to get the same player. They loved him for it. When players came off the field, Tom wouldn't praise or criticise them, he'd just ask, "Did you enjoy that?"'

Blunstone, who played under Docherty at Chelsea and coached for him at three clubs, explains, 'He understood how to treat people. For example, at Chelsea the one he used to swear and kick up the arse all the time was Peter Osgood. That was the only way Ossie responded, so Tommy would go for him. Others you just gave a pat on the back and said, "Come on, you are not doing it." The players loved it. There were odd occasions at Manchester United when Tommy would come in at half-time and would go in the loo and let lads sort it out among themselves, which they loved. Arnie Sidebottom wanted to come off every time he had a knock, but Tommy would shout, "Get back on and don't you dare come here." Tommy knew who to pick on.'

But it would be stretching the truth to say he got it right every time. Board member Brian Mears recalled Docherty's attacks on Bridges, who would leave the club an unhappy man in 1966. 'Docherty made his life a misery sometimes over missed chances,' he noted.

Speaking to *Kings of the King's Road* author Clive Batty, Tambling called Docherty 'the greatest motivator of players I have ever known', recalling the same method of confidence bolstering employed by the likes of Shankly, Allison and Clough. 'He used to build us up so that we felt ten feet tall. He would pick his moment to boost the confidence of an individual and we all got the treatment at some time.' Docherty frequently used the media to deliver that message. 'When you read the things that were written about you, you started to believe you could play a bit,' Tambling said.

Charlie Cooke, who would join Chelsea from Dundee the following season, suggests, 'Initially, Tommy was fantastic at getting people up, winding them up and getting them buzzing. People wanted to play and would lay their bodies down for him and the team. He had that initial effect. When he had been around a bit maybe keeping everything buzzing was not so easy because people get used to each other.'

The confidence Docherty showed in young players was a trait he would continue at other clubs. They would, naturally, respond in return. According to John Boyle, 'If he said, "There's a wall, I want you to go through it," you only say, "How?" not "Why?"'

Venables believes, however, that Docherty encouraged paranoia among some players, citing the example of winger Mike Harrison, who had been at the club since the mid-'50s. Harrison was convinced that Docherty used to eavesdrop on dressing-room conversations to find out who was on his side. Venables recalls an occasion when Docherty fell into the room when the door was opened quickly and another when he was found hiding in a cupboard.

If it was a deliberate plan to keep the players off guard, then it went along with another tactic Bridges would describe in an interview a few years later. 'I had my troubles with him as everyone knows,' he admitted. 'He could really get us going. Sometimes he would say things at half-time that would make us annoyed. Then we would go out and play our legs off just to prove him wrong. I suppose he used to say things to make us angry or frightened. But it used to work. Players' reputations don't worry him.'

Docherty, though, rarely gave his players the kind of full-on rant that one of his successors, Alex Ferguson, would make a feature of the Old Trafford dressing-room. While Docherty could be quick with a cutting comment, bawling at players was not his style. 'He was quite calm,' Shellito remembers, 'even if things were going badly.

I remember we played at Birmingham once and I made a stupid mistake and we lost a goal. He came to me at half-time and said, "Ken, are you a good player or a bad player?" I said I was a good player. He said, "Well, go out and prove it because in the first half you proved the opposite." He did that instead of giving me a rollicking. It was not very often you got blasted. He thought, "What is the point? It's not going to change the result." He would rather wait and talk to people sensibly.'

Docherty admits that this approach creates another contradiction. 'It was unlike me because I am a fiery person and a quick decision maker. But I would leave it. You think, "Well, they'll still be here Monday so I'll have a go at them then."'

Ron Harris recalls, 'You knew when he was upset even if he didn't throw tea cups. If you weren't doing well, he would tell you why he thought you weren't and what he expected of you.' And Hollins adds, 'He thought about it. If someone made a stupid mistake he would say, "Learn from that. I don't want to see it again."'

According to Cooke, 'When we played poorly he never ranted and raved, although you could see his disappointment. He was a banterer, never a blusterer. He was not one to push people around and in training he was not one for the old English FA thing of shouting, "Stop. Listen to me," when half the team are down the field and can't hear him anyway. He would talk to you in the dressing-room or on the way to the field.'

However, Docherty's detractors – of whom there are many – argue that while he might not have been a shouter, he could instead be too quick with a put-down, too willing to make a player the butt of one of his wisecracks. Sometimes he did it in order to deliver a serious underlying message; at other times he simply couldn't resist the opportunity for a gag and was insensitive to any upset it might cause.

Graham looks back with an acceptance of Docherty's contradictory nature and an understanding of its foundation. 'Some managers are thoughtful and quiet, and others, like Tommy, are brash and up front. He was great fun but he was very black and white. He would either bawl you out or you were the best player in Europe. And what a sense of humour. You could never take him on with one-liners. He could be cutting, but a lot of Scottish people are like that, very blunt in their opinion, and sometimes people take it as hurtful. It is the Scottish trait. They don't bullshit.'

Graham, along with many others throughout the years, experienced the great kindness of which Docherty was just as capable as he was of being mean and petty. Picked for his first Scotland Under-23 international against Wales at Kilmarnock, Graham was astonished when Docherty flew to Glasgow, rented a car and drove to Bargeddie, taking Graham's mother out for tea and driving the family to the match. 'He could be enormously generous one moment, almost vindictive the next. Just as you felt like getting your hands round his throat he would reduce you to helpless laughter.'

His young captain, Venables, had the most complex relationship with Docherty of any of the Chelsea players, describing it as 'certainly pretty fiery' and echoing Graham's comments about anger one minute, humour the next.

Docherty saw his comedy act as just another way of creating a relaxed atmosphere in his squad. Early in the 1964–65 season, he instigated the practice of having his players spend the night before games, even those played in London, in a hotel. This, he hoped, would make his team more focused and enhance team morale.

Yet there is plenty of evidence of Docherty's insistence on fun overriding his sense of order and decorum. Venables said the manager could be 'more of a kid than the young players'. He recalled stern words if results were going against the team, with Docherty warning the players against 'fooling around' and to 'get serious'. But, Venables added, 'Straight after the game he would start pulling stunts and making us laugh.'

Says Ron Harris, 'Tom would joke as much as any of the players. Sometimes you used to think, "Christ Almighty, he is the manager and he is doing things that the players do." On one occasion Docherty grabbed Hinton in the post-game team bath and gave him a love bite on the neck, breaking away to declare, 'Explain that one to the missus.' There are tales of the Doc's penchant for beginning food fights by hurling bread rolls around in hotels and aeroplanes.

Reflecting on Docherty's love of a laugh, Harris argues, 'He got away with it,' but such incidents were bound to create uncertainty among the players as to the manager's attitude to club rules and discipline.

As manager at Arsenal, Graham's strictness would earn him the nickname 'Gaddafi', an approach he admits came partly from seeing

Docherty in action. 'He liked to stand on the bridge and walk the deck at the same time, a mistake for any manager to make,' he once wrote. Docherty, however, contends, 'I would not socialise too much with the players. I would go out for a drink with them, buy my round and then leave them to it. I wouldn't go out all night with them.'

Graham continues, 'I was never friendly with the players when I went into management, because it is very difficult to be pally and socialise with them and the next day discipline them or tell them they are out of the team.' Docherty might disagree, but one has to question whether that played a role in what would transpire at the end of the season to undermine Chelsea's title challenge.

It was Championship contenders Manchester United, the first team to beat Chelsea earlier in the season, who again pricked their bubble as the business end of the campaign approached, administering a 4–0 beating at Old Trafford.

Two days later, Docherty had to lift his men for a major trophy challenge, the first leg of the League Cup final against Leicester. He had once again used the early stages of the competition to test emerging players, including forward Jim McCalliog, Joe Fascione and Windsor-born Peter Osgood. Chelsea's initial successes were low profile, although Docherty attempted to elevate the significance of a weakened team's second-round victory over Birmingham by calling it 'the greatest exhibition I have ever seen from a Chelsea side'.

Hyperbole aside, wins against Notts County, Swansea and Workington, after a replay, did not exactly fire west London with cup fever ahead of a semi-final against Aston Villa, the inaugural tournament winners four years earlier. Eighteen-year-old John Boyle, a versatile Scot, marked his first-team debut with a long-range 83rd-minute winner in a 3–2 victory at Villa Park, before a 1–1 home draw in the second leg set up a final against the trophy holders.

The crowd of only 20,690 at Stamford Bridge for the game against Leicester said much about the competition's status, as did the fact that both stages of the final were played on Mondays – an unfashionable night for football before the advent of Sky Sports. To Docherty, however, the importance was evident. He sensed that a first trophy could advance his team's development, giving them a taste of the addictive nature of winning and the confidence that comes from a medal on the mantelpiece.

Not for the first time, he chose an important game to spring a selection surprise. With Bridges injured, his choice at centre-forward was not the precocious Osgood but left-back Eddie McCreadie. After Leicester twice came back to equalise after a goal by Tambling and a Venables penalty, McCreadie proved – just like Tommy Harmer at Sunderland two years earlier – that Docherty possessed a lucky touch in these matters by driving home the winning goal. It meant that the manager could justifiably argue that he had switched McCreadie 'not as a publicity stunt as some of the press believed, but because he had pace and was very direct'.

Twelve days later, Chelsea faced Liverpool in the FA Cup semi-final at Villa Park, having earned that right by beating Northampton, West Ham, Tottenham and Peterborough. The 1–0 win against Spurs had been preceded by scenes of fans queuing for two miles to buy advance tickets, while Third Division Peterborough – spearheaded by Derek Dougan – never threatened to repeat their earlier upset of Arsenal as Chelsea eased home 5–1.

The build-up to the Liverpool game featured another television-related row, with the Professional Footballers' Association threatening to prevent its members playing if cameras were seen rolling at the stadium. Viewers missed a convincing 2–0 win for Liverpool, although John Mortimore appeared to have headed Chelsea into the lead until offside was awarded. Docherty claimed his players had suffered from nerves and 'didn't have enough experience', while Liverpool manager Bill Shankly reportedly pulled one of his motivational masterstrokes by pinning what he claimed was a prematurely prepared Chelsea FA Cup final brochure on the dressing-room wall.

The nine days between FA Cup defeat and the opportunity to secure the League Cup proved eventful for Venables. After a 1–1 draw at Everton, Docherty decided that his team was getting a 'Venables complex' and left his skipper out against Birmingham. 'I want to get the team straightened out before it is too late,' Docherty claimed. 'Terry has been playing badly. He has been holding the ball, getting caught in possession.'

Venables attempted to remain diplomatic, saying, 'I am not complaining, but I just cannot understand it.' Despite Chelsea's 3–1 win, he would be back for the League Cup, but the rift between skipper and manager would soon become much wider.

Chelsea had frequently sought out overseas opposition for friendlies and such an approach found its reward at Filbert Street. They had even recently won 1–0 in Duisburg against the West German national team, whose manager Helmut Schoen said, 'It is only a question of time before Chelsea becomes a soccer power in Europe.' Much to the disgust of the Leicester fans, who vented their anger with booing, Chelsea approached the game like an away leg in European competition.

Docherty proved again he could be a pragmatist, and according to Boyle, preferred to the more positive option of Graham, Chelsea 'played for the 0–0 from the kick-off'. The newspapers were kinder than the home fans, with one report saying that the tie was 'won by courageous defence'. It might not have been the most prestigious of the three trophies Chelsea had been chasing, but victory was celebrated fully. 'I was especially pleased for the board, particularly Joe Mears, who had given me the opportunity to manage and backed me all the way,' Docherty remembered.

Chelsea won only one of their next four games, concluding that run with an Easter Monday defeat at Liverpool, whom they'd beaten 4–0 on Good Friday. They needed to win their final two matches to remain in the title hunt and, with those games being at Burnley and Blackpool, Docherty chose not to take the team back to London. Instead, he set up camp at the Cliff Hotel in Blackpool. It was to prove the most momentous excursion of his career.

The exact detail of what happened on the evening of Wednesday, 21 April 1965 was somewhat confused at the time and is still not totally clear several decades later. What is undisputed is that Docherty's Chelsea were never the same again.

Two days after losing at Liverpool, Chelsea's players were out in Blackpool. According to the subsequent newspaper accounts of nineteen-year-old Pauline Monk and eighteen-year-old Shirley Clarkson, the players were joined by the two girls in the Queen's Bar. They had a 'few lagers' and left in time to make Docherty's 11 p.m. curfew. The exact role of the girls would be the subject of contention in the ensuing days, with Venables telling the press that they were merely drinking close by. The captain's girlfriend even announced her confidence that nothing untoward had occurred. In another comment,

Venables used the phrase 'picked up' about the girls they had been talking to, which left Docherty having to apologise to an irate father. The truth, however, was that the presence – or otherwise – of any girls was irrelevant to the main thrust of the story and merely provided the newspapers with an extra layer of titillation.

Having returned to the hotel to meet their manager's deadline, Venables, Hollins, Bridges, Graham, Hinton, McCreadie, Fascione and Bert Murray slipped out again, via a fire escape. Reports said that the players visited a Greek restaurant and a bowling alley. 'We just talked about the game,' Hollins insists. 'What had gone wrong at Liverpool and how we could beat Burnley.'

Graham says, 'We were a team full of characters, lots of young Cockney boys, always up to tricks. It was really funny some of the things we got up to and Terry Venables was always at the head of everything. On this occasion we were up in Blackpool for nearly a week and we thought the midweek curfew was a bit early. We were young boys being a bit silly. We broke the curfew and paid the consequences.' Even Venables would admit that the players' actions were responsible for 'making a confrontation inevitable'.

Docherty recalled sitting with other members of his staff when a hotel porter, ex-professional footballer George Honeyman, informed him that a fire escape had been opened and that there were reports of disturbances. The porter assured Docherty that it was his players, not a resident rugby team, who were responsible and accompanied him to check on the rooms. Docherty sat up and awaited the players' return.

According to Honeyman, the players arrived with a couple of girls, who were turned away, and Docherty immediately addressed the players in the lounge. This version doesn't have much support elsewhere. Docherty's own story is that the porter informed him after 3 a.m. that the players were back at the hotel. Meanwhile, one hotel guest was quoted as having been woken at 2.50 a.m. when 'doors started banging, people shouted along the corridor and the noise was terrible'. Maximising his own moment in the spotlight, he concluded, 'I thought we were being invaded.'

Taking a hotel pass key, Docherty began opening doors again. Entering the room shared by Hollins and Bridges, he asked if the players were sleeping, pulling back the bed covers to find them still wearing their suits. 'I could have laughed if I hadn't been so fuming mad,' he admitted. It might sound like a comedy scene that has progressed from embellishment to established fact over the years, but Hollins confirms, 'That did actually happen. We came back and got into the hotel and Tommy had been checking the rooms while we were out.'

Docherty was angry enough to put all eight players on the first train to London on Thursday morning, sending word to the club to dispatch reinforcements. 'I think it was over the top,' Hollins argues. 'We probably weren't going to win the League anyway so maybe it was a way of saying, "Look what they have done to me," rather than having to say, "We didn't win it." We weren't going around Blackpool shouting and hollering. We had two lagers and then came back.'

Ken Shellito, a long-time Docherty ally, understood at the time why such drastic action was taken, even though he now accepts it was probably handled with unfortunate indelicacy. 'We had plenty of free time. We had a curfew and it was broken and Tom was devastated. We'd had some great nights and he just said to be back in at a certain time. That was not asking much. A lot of them disagreed with me, but it was the right thing to do. We did have a bit of leeway and Tommy was let down.'

To make Docherty's anger and embarrassment more acute, it had been only eight months since he had stated publicly that his players could be trusted in such situations. 'Our treatment of each other is based on respect,' he'd said proudly. 'If I say they can have a night off then they'll probably have a few beers and a sing-song. If I say bed by ten, then they'll be in bed by ten.'

In the time it took for the players' train to arrive at Euston, the world knew that the miscreants were on board, punished for breaking a curfew. Hollins recalls, 'On the way back we talked about what we were going to do. We said, "Why don't we go home, change suits and go back and watch the game?" We got to Euston and were walking down the platform with blazers on, and there were press people running around with cameras and everything. We thought, "Crumbs, the Beatles must be on the train." We turned round and there was no one else there. They were there for us. They were saying, "You have been doing this. You have been doing that." We said, "No, we haven't."'

Such was the clamour that police had to clear a path for the players to squeeze into a mini-bus to be driven to Stamford Bridge. 'It was worse than being a criminal,' Bridges commented. The mention of the possible involvement of girls and a lack of specific detail encouraged the public's imagination to run wild. 'It makes me feel as if everyone is looking at me and wondering what I was up to,' said Venables.

One unnamed player told a reporter, 'People must be thinking there was a right old orgy. But nothing. No booze. No birds. Just a couple of drinks while we were talking about football and then a meal . . . We wouldn't have complained at a fine and a telling-off. But this is awful.'

The players initially wondered who had been unable to resist passing on such a juicy story to the press. Docherty suggested that the hotel was responsible for the leak. But *Daily Express* reporter Norman Giller explains, 'It wasn't hard to find out about it because Tommy released it himself. He was determined to show who was boss and used the situation to strengthen himself. It was appalling at the time because he put his own needs before the team. There is no way he should have reacted the way he did. It just needed internal discipline, not to hang the players out to dry. He put a lot of marriages in trouble with that one.'

Docherty responded to questioning from reporters with this statement:

The incident which led up to the disciplinary action was reported to me and I went round town last night to investigate. I am no angel myself. I was disciplined in my playing days. I happened to believe the old saying about all work making Jack a dull boy. But what happened this week was the limit. These boys have not only let down me and their club but all the Chelsea supporters. They have been completely disloyal. While the lads are in training they are under very severe discipline. They are more or less told where they may go and what they can do and how much they can drink etc. I expect them to be in by 11 p.m.

The eight players disappeared into a café close to Chelsea's ground. 'We all collected together and decided we had to get the story done properly,' says Hollins. 'So we went into Denmark Street, where we knew some people in the offices, and we called up [football journalist]

Peter Lorenzo, who we thought would help put it straight. We met him and chatted and said, "This is way over the top."'

The players emerged with a statement of their own, which made the front pages of many of the next day's newspapers:

> We have done nothing to be ashamed of. We have not been the subject of any complaint from a member of the public or any member of the staff at our hotel. We have done nothing about which we could not talk freely. We admit to a breach of club discipline in that we were late back to our hotel. If necessary we can obtain proof of the way we spent every minute of the evening.
>
> We are shocked by the punishment, which we believe is out of all proportion. We are also distressed at the way it was announced by Chelsea FC because of the reaction [*sic*] it must have had on our families and the general public. We have worked tremendously hard this season and are sorry it has ended like this. It has not been in our nature to misbehave. Anyone who has seen us play should know that we could not play as hard as that unless we were dedicated to fitness and to the game.

They concluded, 'We are too professional to do anything to harm our careers or risk our reputations,' and stated an intention to take their case to the Chelsea board. Yet in the meantime, chairman Joe Mears had cut short his holiday in France and was saying, 'I am sure Tommy Docherty has done the right thing.' Having contacted his fellow directors from his home in Richmond, he added, 'We are behind Tommy, even if it costs us the Championship.'

The following day, Friday, the banished players announced that they would make the 200-mile drive to watch their colleagues at Burnley, although it was later suggested that this was at the urging of a television company. Saying they would have no contact with Docherty during their trip, they issued another statement, in which they admitted having gone out after curfew and returning to the hotel at 2 a.m. 'None of us was drunk, nor was there any disturbance,' they said. 'There were no girls in our company.'

Inevitably, Chelsea lost at Burnley, by an overwhelming 6–2 scoreline. 'I fell out with Tommy over that,' says Blunstone. 'He did it all too publicly. I said, "They went out so you have got to punish them, but you punished the rest of us." Those of us who behaved ourselves got hammered. Those other buggers could say, "Look what happened without us." They were young players and Tommy was upset at what they had done, but he made a quick decision.'

By the time the Monday newspapers landed, everyone had – on the surface at least – kissed and made up, although the picture of Docherty and the banned players training together was obviously and unconvincingly staged. Six of them were back in the team for that night's game against Blackpool after Docherty painted a not entirely convincing picture of a house united. 'They asked to see me. They admitted they had done wrong. We both gave our points of view, and there was some give and take until the whole thing was cleared up and, I hope, forgotten.' That wish would be a forlorn one.

In the end, even victory in the final two games would have given Chelsea only sixty points, one behind champions Manchester United and runners-up Leeds, but obviously Docherty could not have known that when he exercised his sanctions against his players. He would never get as close to the Championship again. Ron Harris argues, 'I think Tom would tell you it was the worst thing he did, sending home eight players when we still had chance of winning the League. He acted on impulse. If he had fined them a week's wages there wouldn't have been the same fuss. Things started to go wrong after that.'

Shellito counters, 'Even though the team could have achieved a hell of a lot more, I still felt that the punishment fitted the crime. If Tom hadn't done it maybe he wouldn't have achieved anything anyway. You've got to have a certain amount of discipline. If you say, "We might lose this game so I won't do it," that is wrong. If you don't go by your own beliefs you have got no chance.'

Graham would admit in his autobiography, 'We were in the wrong no doubt about that, but the Doc used the silly incident to score points against us, when a verbal rocket and heavy fine would have done the trick.' He says now, 'Tommy probably was impulsive in his decision. It was sad because we had the makings of an outstanding team. It was a shame the way it fell apart after that.'

Leading football figures were invited to comment on Docherty's action, with few offering much backing. Danny Blanchflower argued, 'It was not a public crime and Tommy was impulsive to make it public. There's no one more sincere about the game and the club.

But I feel he's been a bit rash.' PFA secretary Cliff Lloyd described himself as 'shocked' and called it a 'very sad thing for football', although a more supportive Bill Shankly felt he knew Docherty well enough to state that 'he must have had ample justification'.

At the time, Docherty pondered, 'How can you win the Championship with disloyal players?' But what he does not appear to have considered was the hurt caused to Chelsea supporters by what amounted to a virtual throwing-in of the towel, and to those blameless players whose ambition of winning the biggest prize in their profession was undermined by his stance. A fine would have maintained those players' hopes of achieving what Docherty had been driving them towards for the previous 40 matches.

His actions meant he ran the risk of pitting himself against the whole squad. As Blanchflower warned, 'Young men have a way of remembering hard punches; they continue to think they were not fair.' And veteran QPR manager Alec Stock added, 'It has become fashionable for the younger managers to air all their troubles and beat their players about in public.'

Admitting that he gave up any hope of the title 'on a matter of principle', Docherty would say he 'did not regret my action in the least'. Yet he was clearly wrestling with his decision when he told reporters a few days later, 'If I had known what the effect would have been, I would rather have cut off my right hand. I still think I was right, but it has been a lesson to me. Maybe I shall have to deal again with players who step out of line and I shall know what I must do.' According to Murray, Docherty apologised and 'told us he would never do anything like that again'.

So why did he feel he had to do it this time?

'I was stupid and impetuous,' he admits. 'I was a young manager inexperienced in that kind of situation. I could have had the same result by fining them a couple of weeks later.'

As an example of how he matured over time he tells the story of meeting a pair of his Manchester United players in a pub on a night when socialising was supposed to be off-limits. Accepting their offer of a drink, he downed a gin and tonic and left. 'When they came in the next day, I gave them a letter saying they were fined a week's wages. There was no shouting and bawling. When I was younger I might have gone in and dragged them out.'

Given the deteriorating state of their relationship one has to ask whether it was the participation of Venables in the Blackpool incident that informed Docherty's response. Did he jeopardise the season just to re-exert authority over someone with whom he felt his previous influence was dissipating? Ron Harris suggests, 'Terry had a big sway with some of the players and his relationship with Tom was coming to an end. I think his being involved in this was the last straw.'

Docherty argues, 'Terry was the ringleader. He was the king of the kids. There were some you knew would have gone out anyway, but others, like John Hollins, just followed whatever Terry did.'

Venables felt that Docherty's stance on the Blackpool incident was the culmination of a growing number of smaller disagreements with his players, and with him in particular. He had broken a previous curfew on one of the team's London-based sleepovers, singing with the band in the ballroom of their Kensington hotel rather than being in his room by 9 p.m. 'Perhaps that was why Docherty was so eager to believe that I must have been the ringleader,' he said.

Docherty viewed Venables as the strongest personality in the dressing-room. It was why he was club captain. Yet he believed that he was becoming a 'disruptive influence', recalling him challenging the manager in front of the players and apologising in private later. 'We would be working on a free kick on the training ground and I would outline a move,' Docherty explains, 'Terry would say, "It won't work." He was pessimistic; sometimes they worked, sometimes they didn't. But he should have a word in private, not in front of the team. I didn't mind if it was his way or my way as long as it was best for the team, but that is trying to take away some of your authority. Someone like Ron Harris would do anything you asked, but Terry would question everything.'

While Docherty ended up concluding that 'Terry was trying to run the show', Graham recalls, 'Both were very opinionated and very talented in their own way. Terry was an outstanding young player who already had his own views on the game and was a strong character.'

Brian Mears enjoyed a close-up, yet detached, view of the Docherty–Venables double act, noting that the player was 'always watching and learning, soaking up the knowledge of every talented person who crossed his path'. Yet as Venables became more self-assured he became 'too much for the Doc to handle'. Mears recalled, 'Sometimes I would drop in on the Doc's surgery as he gave his team talks. [He] would turn to Venables and ask him for his comments. Venables would infuriate Docherty with a shrug of his shoulders or a look of total bewilderment at the Doc's tactics.' To Mears, the response to events in Blackpool was no great surprise. 'The volatile Docherty was always a short trip away from the self-destruct button. I saw the power struggle between Venables and Docherty reaching crisis point.'

Giller observes, 'Tommy and Terry were always at loggerheads and they just didn't respect each other. But Terry was such an important cog in that Chelsea team, Tommy shot himself in the foot.'

Venables felt misunderstood. He saw the questioning of his manager, initially welcomed by Docherty, as merely the action of a young player seeking self-improvement. 'I had such a thirst for knowledge about the game,' he argued, believing Docherty 'began regretting his encouragement, because my constant questions became a bit of a bugbear for him'.

The quick-witted Venables also thought that Docherty, like a comedian who resents his straight-man partner getting the limelight, would become 'furious' if he made the players laugh with a joke of his own. With the benefit of hindsight and years of managerial experience, Venables accepts that responsibility for the rift was mostly his and is able to identify the inexperience of both men in their respective roles as the root of the problem, even suggesting that Docherty should have 'taken me to one side and straightened me out or given me a dressing-down in front of the group'. In later years, they have got along without any problem.

Blunstone puts it plainly. 'Tommy didn't like Venners,' he states. 'Terry wanted to be top dog and so did Tommy, so they clashed. It wouldn't surprise me if his decision in Blackpool was partly because Venners was involved. Tommy would go to extreme lengths to get rid of someone if he didn't like them.'

The Stamford Bridge career of Venables, and several others, was indeed coming to an end. 'I realised that if I could not trust players then it was time to move them on,' Docherty explains. It is one of the defining statements of his managerial career.

8

DIVIDED WE STAND

'Charles Pratt certainly lived up to his name. I said to him at our first meeting, "Mr Chairman, when I want your advice I'll give it to you."'

The biggest day in Tommy Docherty's managerial career at Stamford Bridge still lay ahead when Chelsea convened for their Australian tour in the summer of 1965, but even he acknowledges the unavoidable truth: 'Things were never the same after Blackpool.' He could no longer completely trust certain of his players, while some of those disciplined publicly by their manager felt their own sense of betrayal. The extent of the rift was such that only three of the 'Blackpool Eight' would represent the club when Chelsea played in the 1967 FA Cup final. According to George Graham, 'We lost confidence in the Doc because he had overreacted.'

As Docherty and 19 players headed off for several weeks in the southern hemisphere, the assumption among the media was that the time away would 'forge again the old spirit of friendship and trust'. At the airport, Docherty announced that 'Chelsea's spirit is as good as ever'. The truth was somewhat different, Bobby Tambling telling author Clive Batty that the atmosphere 'was like a morgue'.

Peter Osgood, who had not wanted to go in the first place because his wife, Rose, was close to delivering their first child, argued that Blackpool 'had polarised the two main men at the club – Docherty and Venables' and concluded that 'the club was not big enough for both of them'.

The first half of the 1965–66 season would be punctuated by regular reports of fall-outs between Docherty and the players, some of them terminal. In October, Jim McCalliog decided he could wait no longer for regular first-team football and was eventually sold to

Sheffield Wednesday for £40,000. Then Barry Bridges told Docherty he wanted to leave after hearing that Osgood had been promised a run of ten games. Docherty resisted, insisting that he had told Osgood he would get a chance to prove himself, but had not mentioned the specific number of games. In later years, Docherty would proudly recall making the ten-game promise, which suggests, of course, he'd been less than truthful with the unhappy Bridges, who was anxious to remain in contention for a place in England's World Cup squad.

The prospect of selling Bridges did not sit well with some Chelsea fans, one of whom, Mike Greenaway, organised a petition to protest. 'We appreciate that Tommy Docherty is a brilliant manager and that he has a difficult and lonely job,' he said. 'But we object to him criticising the supporters so strongly and to the fact that Bridges may be sold.'

That criticism had come when a home defeat to Leicester prompted Docherty to say of the Chelsea crowd, 'They are useless, a waste of space. I wish we could play all our games away. They are either silent or critical.' His comments provoked a pile of letters to national newspapers, many of them reminding Docherty that it was the fans who effectively paid his wages. Bridges would stay for now, but there was to be no happily ever after for him at Chelsea.

Eddie McCreadie was the next to request a transfer, making no attempt to hide his motives. 'There is a rift between Tommy Docherty and myself that is beyond repair,' he said, calling it 'a matter that can never be solved'.

Docherty announced, 'I know the reasons for all these requests, but I am not worried. Anyone asking for a move is wasting his time.'

With Christmas looming, it was Venables who lost the spirit of goodwill after being dropped for what he believed were reasons unrelated to his form. 'I have been left out because of something personal between the manager and me,' he claimed, although he added, 'I am not jumping on the transfer bandwagon.' However, that issue would soon be taken out of his hands.

Early in 1966, Docherty handed the captaincy to Ron Harris and six weeks later announced that Venables was available at £70,000, leaving the player 'completely stunned'. Docherty stated, 'It's in the best interests of the club that we part company. I do not wish to elaborate' – although he had complained after a loss to Everton a couple of days earlier that there were 'too many big-heads in the team'. Venables conceded, 'I suppose this has obviously been building up for some time. It seems the manager and I do not quite see eye to eye.'

At least one player's Chelsea career had ended amicably. Frank Blunstone had remained at the club after retiring following the 1964–65 season because of injury, beginning a long off-field partnership with Docherty. 'Tommy gave me a job as youth-team manager, which was fantastic as I had done no coaching,' he explains. 'I was only 29, so I took it on and got my coaching badges.'

But the fact that so many players were open in acknowledging that they did not get on with Docherty demonstrates not only a different age, before players had media advisers sanitising their comments, but also the depth of feeling that clearly existed.

Norman Giller, who spent a lot of time around Stamford Bridge in his role with the *Daily Express*, says, 'Tommy would put himself first, the club second and the player third. He wouldn't give a monkey's about players complaining. Loyalty to Tommy was a two-way street, and if a player was loyal to him, for example Chopper Harris, he would go to the front line for him. But if he felt there was somebody, such as Terry Venables, who was doing things to undermine him, he would be a very bad enemy.

'Things used to become public knowledge very quickly because there were a lot of leaks at Chelsea. I was friendly with a lot of the staff and hardly anything could happen without it becoming public. The players were close to people like Ken Jones and Nigel Clarke of the *Mirror*, and I'd put myself in that category.'

In his autobiography, future chairman Brian Mears said, 'The Docherty–Venables team was to implode under the weight of their own expectations, relationships going sour, becoming hopelessly routine, dazed, confused, blurred, almost bankrupt of ideas.' The remarkable thing, therefore, was that in the midst of such discontent and disruption Chelsea produced another good season.

It was conflict of a physical nature that provided the biggest story of Chelsea's first foray into Europe. After winning the title in 1955, the club had infamously been persuaded by the Football League not to participate in the first-ever European Cup. Their first-round tie against Roma in the Inter-Cities Fairs Cup,[*] courtesy of winning the League Cup, must have made them wonder whether they'd have been better off staying at home again.

What would unfold in Chelsea's contest against Roma was typical of the culture clash in early European games between English and Italian clubs, with their differing philosophies about how their sport should be conducted. A year later, Burnley players would be set upon by their opponents at the final whistle in Napoli before their dressing-room was invaded by armed police. At the same stadium in May 1970, Swindon, leading 3–0, were declared winners of the inaugural Anglo-Italian Cup when violence broke out on and off the field, forcing the final to be abandoned.

Later that year, Arsenal's team were attacked by Lazio players in a Rome backstreet after a post-match banquet following a Fairs Cup tie. Gunners skipper Frank McLintock explains, 'In those days, the difference between Italian football and English football was remarkable. In our opinion they would be sly. They would fall over looking for free kicks and spit on you – all that stuff. We would tackle from behind and go in with big crunching tackles that they thought were unfair, so the ideologies of the two camps were poles apart.'

Docherty had already articulated a similar view when writing, 'When these foreign sides come over here they are greeted with the tackle. And that frightens them to death. When they get back home they howl about the rough handling they have had in England. You would think we had been chopping their legs off with meat axes.'

Having flown to Italy to watch Roma play, Docherty was convinced he had seen a weakness in their *catenaccio*, the version of the sweeper system employed by many Italian teams. He had another concern, however, which he addressed by taking his squad to Roma's training session in Mitcham for what the newspapers described as a 'spot-the-signor session'. Docherty explained, 'All the Italians look alike when you first see them. I want our men to get a good look at them.' Putting aside the *Carry On* film phraseology, Docherty's worry highlights the journey into the unknown that European

---

[*] The forerunner of the UEFA Cup, the tournament was so named because it was originally conceived only for cities that hosted trade fairs.

football represented for English clubs in the days before widespread television coverage of overseas teams.

Chelsea won the first leg at Stamford Bridge 4–1, with Venables grabbing a hat-trick. The incident with the deepest repercussions, however, occurred after McCreadie had received a shin-gashing kick from Leonardi, who later grabbed the Chelsea full-back by the throat in a separate incident. McCreadie hit out and was sent off, prompting a campaign in the Italian press warning about the physical English opponents coming to town.

Docherty saw trouble looming when there was no Roma representative to meet his team at the airport, a common courtesy in European games. Having only heard through a journalist that the game had been moved from Olympic Stadium to the smaller Flaminio Stadium, he then discovered that the kick-off had been moved from afternoon to evening and that Chelsea had been refused permission to train at the stadium. He warned, 'They will obviously try to provoke us.'

Those attempts began before kick-off. Having watched Roma fans directing insults and phlegm at the team coach, Chelsea's party made their way to the pitch, where chairman Joe Mears was struck by a tomato thrown from the crowd. There was a more sinister edge during the game, with a ceaseless barrage of coins, stones, cans and bottles of urine aimed at the players. Roma, meanwhile, went through their repertoire of dark arts: elbows off the ball, stamping on toes, pulling hair and pinching skin. 'I don't think I ever saw players face such provocation and hostility,' Docherty recalled.

Coming out for the second half, Chelsea players attempted to protect themselves by remaining close to their opponents, who tried to evade their markers and run for cover as a new wave of missiles fell upon them. As the visitors maintained the goalless scoreline, Boyle was felled by a bottle and McCreadie had a lucky escape when another hit him on the shoulder. The most alarming near miss came when a piece of iron railing, apparently aimed at Graham, landed without finding its target. Docherty claimed, 'Even when the bottles and the heavier objects were coming down, all the police seemed to stay in the dressing-rooms.'

When the final whistle sounded, with Chelsea's aggregate lead undisturbed, the players huddled together and raised their arms for protection while leaving the field. Windows were shattered as the coach drove away from the stadium and for a while there were fears that the vehicle would be overturned. Docherty told reporters, 'My players acted even better than I thought possible. Not once did any of them give a hint of retaliation. I am proud of them.'

Labour sports minister Denis Howell sent a message to chairman Mears congratulating the team on their 'wonderful conduct and composure', while Roma would be banned from European competition for three years.

One might have expected such a victory in the midst of adversity to have fostered greater harmony and brotherhood. Yet even this triumph was set against a backdrop of unrest. According to Venables, there had been a 'fundamental difference' between Docherty and the players in how to approach the second leg. Marvin Hinton had been playing as a sweeper in recent games, but Docherty felt they 'could get done' if they adopted that method in Rome. Venables ignored the manager's instructions and ordered Hinton to continue to take up a sweeping position if he felt there was a threat, saying he was reflecting the desires of the players.

Victory over Austria's Wiener Sportklub in the second round, in which Chelsea overcame a first-leg deficit, was relatively serene, even though Hinton was sent off in the first game for a head-butt and Wiener's Adolf Knoll was dismissed in the return for a kick at Boyle. That produced the spectre of a return to Italy to face AC Milan, who won the first leg 2–1 but were beaten by the same score in London, with Graham, scorer in both games, and Osgood getting Chelsea's goals. In the days before the away goals rule, Chelsea lost the toss for home advantage in the play-off, which was drawn 1–1 after Milan cancelled out a Bridges goal in the closing moments. After 120 minutes the tie was decided on another toss of a coin, which came down in Ron Harris's favour.

TSV 1860 Munich, beaten by West Ham at Wembley in the previous season's Cup Winners' Cup final, were overcome in the quarter-finals, Osgood heading the only goal after 78 minutes of the second leg after a 2–2 draw in the German snow. Barcelona would be the semi-final opponents.

Meanwhile, having chosen not to defend the League Cup because of their increased commitments, Chelsea's domestic exploits were carrying them towards a fifth-place finish in the table and had earned them a second successive FA Cup semi-final appearance. As

Frank Bough said when introducing one of the club's regular appearances on *Match of the Day*, 'Chelsea have been the rave of Division One ever since they left Division Two.'

Their Cup progress began in the most emphatic fashion, beating both the previous season's finalists, Liverpool and Leeds. The 2–1 victory at Anfield gave the manager particular satisfaction. According to Brian Mears, 'Docherty was desperate for revenge. I never saw him take a game so seriously. He saw Liverpool as the yardstick by which we measured our success.' Chelsea hit back from an early deficit to win through headers by Osgood and Tambling. Departing Anfield with the cup, so that he could return it to FA headquarters, Docherty described the game as 'the most satisfying performance' since becoming manager.

It was before the Leeds game in the fourth round that the nation heard the team nickname that is commonly attached to the era, 'Docherty's Diamonds'. In the build-up to the tie a TV crew followed Docherty and captured him yelling at his charges, 'Come on, my little diamonds.' By now, Osgood was the one sparkling most brightly, converting his trial run into a permanent place. He had been described by *The Times* as a 'west London Hidegkuti' and was considered an outside bet for Alf Ramsey's World Cup squad, eventually making the provisional 40-man roster, along with Bonetti, Bridges, Hinton, Hollins and Venables. Chelsea's attempts to pair him with Arsenal's England forward Joe Baker came to nothing when Joe Mears announced the club's refusal to pay the player a signing-on fee.

Docherty did bring in a new face, however, when he paid West Ham £35,000 for full-back Joe Kirkup, whom he saw as finally replacing the injured Ken Shellito. Having completed the deal just in time to arrive at Luton Airport for a flight to Munich, Docherty displayed his publicity flair when he realised that Manchester United had just landed back from their historic 5–1 hammering of Benfica in a European Cup quarter-final tie. It was the game that truly marked the beginning of the George Best phenomenon, with the Portuguese media describing him as 'El Beatle' and his performance propelling him towards the kind of public profile enjoyed by the Fab Four themselves. Seizing an opportunity, Docherty ensured that his flight was held while he manoeuvred himself into the next day's press photographs with Best, who was sporting an oversized sombrero.

After Tambling scored the only goal against Leeds, less glamorous opponents were waiting in the fifth and sixth rounds. Shrewsbury were beaten 3–2 at Stamford Bridge, and Chelsea then overcame Hull City 3–1 in a replay, having been held 2–2 at home.

Docherty's achievement of guiding Chelsea into the last four of two tournaments was gaining him widespread attention. In Europe, he had proved adaptable enough to tone down the attacking bias of his team's style of play in the League, where he felt his players' skill, pace and commitment was enough to sweep aside weaker opposition. He understood that against technically proficient, defensively minded overseas teams a more patient method was required – even if his players were apparently not always totally in accord with the specifics of those tactics.

As the semi-finals loomed, Spain's Atlético Madrid made known their desire to offer Docherty a two-year contract totalling £30,000. With just over a year left on a Chelsea deal worth only a third of Madrid's annual offer, he was also reported to be a target of FC Cologne. A regular visitor to Germany, he was even said to have been learning the language. 'I am flattered by the suggestions,' he commented.

The next few days did little to raise Docherty's stock. He'd hoped that the change of routine in staying in the Leamington countryside rather than in Birmingham city centre would reverse the fortunes of the previous season's semi-final at Villa Park. He also thought that wearing the black and blue stripes of Inter Milan as a change strip would provide inspiration. Yet with inches of clinging mud turning one of the season's most important games into a lottery, it was former Chelsea player McCalliog who inspired Sheffield Wednesday to a 2–0 victory, scoring the second goal himself.

Hollins recalls, 'We had got to two semi-finals and lost both in very, very heavy conditions. We tried to outrun and outpace them, but we lost goals and were always chasing the game.'

Desmond Hackett, in typically acerbic mood in the *Daily Express*, was in no mood to impart sympathy. 'Chelsea did everything wrong and in my opinion the major blunder was that Docherty sat on the touchline,' he wrote. 'It appears to be a shade late in the day to start coaching a team from the touchline. Docherty's place was up in the stand where he could read the true pattern of the game.' He continued, 'Docherty should have told the players of the futility of trying a short-passing game on a pitch that ended up like a well-rutted pig farm.'

It was another pivotal moment in Docherty's Chelsea reign. Barely had the players knocked the mud off their boots before he was announcing plans for an immediate reshaping of the team. Graham recalled that he stated in the dressing-room that 'we still had a great future ahead of us; then told the press he was breaking up the team'. Graham argues, 'London in the '60s was a great period, full of buzz, and at Chelsea we had an outstanding young team that reflected that. I still wonder what would have happened if it hadn't all broken up so quickly. We could have been one of the greatest teams of that era.'

With the first leg at Barcelona being played four days after the FA Cup tie – following a League game against West Brom, squeezed in on Monday night – Docherty declared, 'The players to be sold may not even make the journey to Barcelona. One or two might be missing from the team. We have been a little weak in a couple of positions and we have been looking for players to do something about it.'

Typically, Docherty wasted no time in making his first move, flying to Scotland to sign Dundee midfielder Charlie Cooke for £72,500. It was the final straw for Bridges, who was left out of the West Brom game and was therefore already in a bad mood at the airport the following day when his new teammate arrived. 'The Doc was the easiest guy to speak to of all the managers I had,' says Cooke of the man who pitched him into the middle of a civil war. 'He could think on his feet and is quick with his tongue. I travelled down to Heathrow from Edinburgh with him and the whole party was waiting to board the plane for Barcelona. Tommy made a few introductions. I was trying to talk to some of the Scottish guys when Barry Bridges stormed out. I had no idea what was going on. I didn't realise it was a big do. I thought he was just going home. So my arrival there was clouded by that.'

Bridges explained to journalists, 'It's my decision not to go out to Barcelona. It was a waste of time going after being left out against West Bromwich. I didn't have an opportunity to tell Mr Docherty on Monday because he rushed off to Scotland to sign Cooke. I told him I didn't want to go when I saw him at the airport. We exchanged a few words and then he agreed that I could go home. I don't see how it can lead to anything else but my asking for a transfer again.'

Venables, meanwhile, was determined to speak to Docherty about his future during the trip and accepted that he would soon be sold. It was hardly the most conducive atmosphere in which to play an important game, and Chelsea were probably relieved to come away only 2–0 down.

Cooke played in the second leg, which was delayed by a postponement due to a waterlogged pitch – worsened, according to some, by Docherty getting the fire brigade to turn their hoses on it in order to gain more preparation time.* It was the new signing's shot that deflected in off Gallego for Chelsea's first goal. An effort by Harris was disallowed after Tambling fouled goalkeeper Miguel Reina, the father of future Liverpool number one Pepe. The plan all night had been to test Reina physically and it paid off after 80 minutes when he turned the ball into his own net under a challenge from Graham. With the scores level on aggregate, Chelsea again lost the toss for play-off site, going down 5–0 at the Camp Nou.

The season, and this particular team, had reached the end of the line. The trophy that might have exorcised the ghost of Blackpool had not arrived. Venables had been sold to Tottenham for £80,000 even before the resolution of the Barcelona tie; Bridges and Murray left for Birmingham City. Early in the next season, Graham, top scorer over the past two years, went to Arsenal in exchange for striker Tommy Baldwin and £50,000. Venables would write ruefully, 'Docherty lost patience with us. He simply gave up too soon.'

Graham says, 'I had been very happy as part of what had become a very good Chelsea team. But it looked as though the team was going to break up. Terry had moved to Spurs and there were other players ready to get away. The writing was on the wall and I thought it was the right time [to leave].' His Highbury move was, however, 'a culture shock'. He explains, 'I had been 19 when I joined Chelsea. It was an exciting time. We had very funny, comical players. When I joined Arsenal everything was so professional and I thought, "What have I done?" You noticed it in the training and the way you did things at Arsenal.'

---

* Asked by reporters about the state of the Stamford Bridge pitch, Docherty replied with the classic line, 'Conditions were so bad this morning that the chairman's wife couldn't shave.'

Graham's future achievements at Highbury as a player and manager prove how successfully he eventually became assimilated into the Arsenal way, although he would cross paths again with Docherty, who claimed he had got the better end of the Graham–Baldwin deal.

It was the sale of Venables that caused Docherty the greatest soul-searching, knowing the adverse reaction it would provoke from fans and the accusations that he'd done it purely out of spite for events in Blackpool. It was why it took him a year beyond that incident to bite the bullet. But he insists that Venables had become a 'luxury', that his interest in coaching was becoming a distraction, that his apparent desire to undermine him in front of teammates had gone far enough, and that he now had a better player in Cooke. 'I should have sold him earlier,' he concludes.

McCreadie recalled Docherty telling him, 'You lot broke it up, not me. If everyone had played the game it could have been different.' But not everyone could play the Docherty way.

Bonetti and Tambling had ended the 1965–66 season by asking for transfers after refusing new contracts. Chairman Joe Mears agreed to pay them the additional money they wanted without consulting Docherty, who pointed out the potential damage of such action. Such was the relationship between manager and chairman that Mears apologised and rescinded the offer. Yet on 1 July, with England preparing itself for the start of the World Cup, Docherty lost his closest ally when Mears, who was also Football Association chairman, collapsed and died suddenly in Oslo.

'His death affected me a lot,' admits Docherty, who describes his boss as a 'caring and understanding' man. 'He was the best chairman I worked for by miles. He was always straight with you and gave you an answer where others would just hum and haw. It was either, "We can't afford him," or "Go and get him." He would never offer an opinion on who should play. I was spoilt.'

Docherty remembers only once asking for Mears's advice on the playing side, during a coach journey to Grimsby just after he had signed Graham Moore.

'Are you all right, Tom?' asked Mears. 'You look a bit uneasy.'

Docherty replied, 'I have just got a little problem. We are going well and on a good run and we have signed Moore. I am wondering whether to keep things as they are or bring him in.'

'Are you asking me?'

'Well, I am fishing.'

Far from being proud to have his opinion sought, Mears barely paused before telling his manager, 'That is what I pay you for – to make those decisions.'

According to Brian Mears 'they had mutual respect for each other and Docherty knew exactly how far he could push things', but his relationship with new chairman Charles Pratt was to be strained and unproductive. 'Docherty could barely conceal his contempt for him,' said Mears.

English football returned to work in the summer of '66 with a spring in its step and a smile on its face after the triumph of Alf Ramsey's team, but clouds still managed to find their way over Stamford Bridge as Docherty refused Bonetti permission to report late for pre-season training after his stint with the England squad. Bonetti took the time off anyway, even though Docherty – 'out of spite' according to Bonetti – had signed Millwall's Alex Stepney. Bonetti was fined and responded with another transfer request. Docherty told the two goalkeepers they would play in alternate games, a situation that suited neither of them. Both men informed Docherty they would prefer that selection was made strictly on merit. After playing only one game, Stepney – whom Docherty said he had signed because he had feared Bonetti would be leaving – was sold to Manchester United, with Bonetti quietly wishing it was he who was moving north. Stepney would depart with memories of Docherty's 'juvenile behaviour and the ludicrous idea that he could play me and Peter in alternate matches'.

Come November, Hollins became the ninth player in little over a year to ask for a transfer, saying he was 'fed up'. Docherty responded angrily, threatening an inquiry into the action of other clubs. 'How can he be fed up when he is earning £100 in a team top of the First Division, is a member of the England Under-23 side and is on the brink of full international honours?' he asked. 'I put it down to England's training sessions and being tapped up by another club.'

As 1966 drew to a close, Docherty announced that he would be at the club until 1972. In fact, he wouldn't make it out of 1967. 'I have signed the next five years of my life over to Chelsea,' he declared, calling his employers 'the greatest club I have ever known'. Aware that it might have been hard for some people to take that at face value, he continued, 'Despite the rows, the storms, mounting transfer requests and apparent non-stop bickering between players and myself over the last three seasons, I'll stick with Stamford Bridge and so will all the players if they have any sense.'

He continued, 'Some people may laugh, but Chelsea are essentially a happy club. Most of the trouble has arisen because, unlike most clubs, I have always given my players complete freedom to air their complaints in public. I've always been outspoken, but I've never regretted a word I've said. The players have had the same right, but not any more. In future they will have to get permission to speak from me. The squabbling is over.'

That might have made it more difficult for internal rows to find their way into the public domain and perhaps the face of the club would improve cosmetically, but it would not prevent the blemishes turning septic under the surface.

Again, results – for a while, at least – managed to speak louder than all the background bickering. Chelsea rained on West Ham's opening-day parade, spoiling Upton Park's celebrations for its World Cup winners, Bobby Moore, Geoff Hurst and Martin Peters. Cooke capped his League debut with a goal and Chelsea achieved a victory that launched a ten-game unbeaten run, the club's best-ever start. The sequence included a 6–2 win at Aston Villa – where Tambling scored five – and four appearances on *Match of the Day* in the space of nine weeks. They'd also been chosen that season, along with Fulham, to stage the close-up action sequences that the show used in its opening credits.

New arrivals Cooke and Baldwin loved what they discovered at the club. 'I got exactly what I wanted,' says Cooke. 'I wanted to go to England, but I didn't want to play for Manchester United or anybody like that. Chelsea were the team at the time. I knew the reputation they had as a young, up-and-coming side – a busy team with young, quick boys, a team for the future. They had a lot of energy and were a good skilful side.'

Baldwin had come from an Arsenal regime under Billy Wright and then Bertie Mee where he was expected to undertake his share of hard graft and defending. The Docherty approach, by contrast, was 'a real breath of fresh air'.

The turning point of this season, however, arrived when Chelsea – top of the table – visited Blackpool in the League Cup and lost

Osgood with a broken leg in a tackle with Emlyn Hughes, the future Liverpool and England captain. From there they slipped to ninth in the League, clearly missing their precocious young striker, who, although he would return to play for England and become one of game's most iconic characters, was probably never quite the player he'd promised to be. 'The loss of Osgood was a big blow,' Docherty admitted, describing him as 'a player with an abundance of skill, a good football brain, terrific vision and an eye for goal'.

Tony Hateley, a centre-forward in the old Tommy Lawton mould, was bought from Aston Villa for £100,000 as a replacement. Docherty believed that his aerial ability would give his team an extra dimension, yet he would end up describing him as 'probably my worst' signing. Hateley was unable to blend with the swift, fluent nature of Chelsea's football, while the team struggled to accommodate the different approach required to utilise his strengths.

'We won the League Cup with an attacking style,' says Hollins. 'When it came to 1967 we changed the way we played. Instead of having very fast forwards like Barry Bridges, we changed to Tony Hateley, and Charlie Cooke had come in. I think the side we had earlier was a much better footballing side, but Tommy had decided that it was time for another revolution.'

It was Hateley who modelled a new training device that Docherty had discovered in Germany, a special jacket with pockets in which sand and stone could be placed. 'It's like hitting yourself over the head with a hammer; it's great when you stop,' said Hateley, while Docherty explained, 'After training with that extra load, the boys are like two year olds when they return to normal kit.' Hateley did score one of the goals as Chelsea beat Real Madrid 2–0 at Stamford Bridge to win the somewhat spurious International Charity Cup, but those Chelsea fans who would soon take to booing their new signing probably thought there were occasions when he'd gone out to play wearing his weighted outfit.

Another new face appeared on the scene at Tottenham in March when Docherty made 16-year-old forward Ian 'Chico' Hamilton the youngest-ever Chelsea player. 'The Doc started me off,' he says. 'I enjoyed playing for him. We used to train with Chelsea on Tuesdays and Thursdays at Brent Cross and the Doc kept in touch with certain players he had taken a little shine to. I was taken on from school when I was 15 and then he put me in at Tottenham.

He obviously had confidence in me and geed me up.' Hamilton made his mark by heading Chelsea's goal in a 1–1 draw. 'There were 50-odd thousand there, and I was taking corners and everything, and then I got that header past Pat Jennings. I am not saying I had a great game, but I did score. Then me and my mum had to get the train home.'

Hamilton, who would play only four Chelsea games before a transfer to Southend, recounts his other overriding memory of his brief time as one of 'Docherty's Diamonds'. 'I didn't really drink – I wasn't allowed – and we went to play in San Sebastian in northern Spain,' he begins. 'Doc said to me, "Would you like to try a little bit of champagne?" I was only used to light and bitter so I had a couple, and a few jars. Next day I wasn't too good, but we had to travel and Doc was being poorly in the back of the bus. The coach had to keep stopping and would open the back door for the Doc to be sick.'

Back on the field, Chelsea's performances were up and down enough to induce nausea in the hardiest managerial stomach. Having ended 1966 with eight winless games that effectively ended any Championship aspirations, Chelsea continued inconsistently, saving their best for the FA Cup. Once more, this being the Docherty era, nothing ever ran smoothly. Not even on the path to Wembley.

Tambling's winner at Huddersfield set up a fourth-round match at Third Division Brighton, where the players' ticket allocation became the dominant issue. With men such as Bonetti and Hinton living in the Brighton area, Docherty appealed to the board for a greater allocation of free tickets. Policy dictated that they received two free and a further ten for purchase and, having asked the directors to explain to the players why the allocation could not be flexible on this occasion, he voiced his concerns in the press, saying, 'I thought it was an unfair offer and told the directors.' The board had told him that they did not need to defend themselves, while the players resented the apparent implication they might want additional tickets merely to sell them.

Docherty felt the situation created a barrier between him and the board, who were already upset that their manager had attracted a £100 fine and an FA warning before Christmas for 'ungentlemanly remarks' to a referee after an FA Youth Cup match at QPR. Things, he felt, would have been much different had Joe Mears been around.

In the meantime, he tried to show his players a good time by the seaside. Undeterred by the memory of Blackpool – or confident that those responsible for events there were no longer at the club – he based his squad in Brighton for a full week, allowing them to visit a club on Tuesday, dog racing on Wednesday and a casino on Thursday. His own week was interrupted by a summons from the board to explain his public comments on the tickets, after which his team drew 1–1, with Boyle sent off.

The club chose the day of the replay to announce a public reprimand and to warn Docherty about his future behaviour. Docherty felt 'humiliated and not a little miffed' by Chelsea's decision to go public with their actions, although maybe it gave him a little more empathy with the feelings of the 'Blackpool Eight'. Having been ordered not to voice personal views on club matters in public, he found it odd that club secretary John Battersby immediately went out and spoke to reporters. At least an easy 4–0 win, with Tambling scoring twice and Hateley and Cooke left out of the side, gave them a smooth passage into the fifth round.

Chelsea returned to Brighton before their next two Cup games, the superstitious Docherty ensuring they stayed in the same hotel and replicated their training routine in Worthing. One difference was that five days before Hateley and Tambling found the net in the 2–0 win against Sheffield United, Docherty fielded his entire first team in a reserve fixture against Gillingham, claiming they had requested it in order to 'try out one or two moves'.

Sheffield Wednesday, Chelsea's conquerors in the semi-final a year earlier, now stood between them and a return to the last four. A game described by Desmond Hackett as 'an affront to a noble competition' was decided when Baldwin forced home the only goal in injury time.

For the third year running, Chelsea faced a semi-final at Villa Park, with Leeds their opponents this time. Despite the continued excellence of Manchester United and Liverpool throughout the '60s – champions twice each, FA Cup winners and, in United's case, European Cup winners – it was Chelsea and Leeds who best reflected the two extremes of football philosophy in England. That conflict would reach its climax in the dramatic, brutal FA Cup final matches of 1970, but even three years earlier the personalities of Leeds and Chelsea were well enough defined under the leadership of the pragmatic Don Revie and the more idealistic Docherty to offer a fascinating contest.

In climbing out of the Second Division and towards the upper reaches of the First, Leeds had become known for a brand of football out of keeping with the skilful, thoughtful style for which Revie had been known as a player. Their rise was associated with a disproportionate number of controversial incidents and ugly games, their football based on the philosophy of not losing. In this regard, Revie was merely one of the first managers to acknowledge the harsh realities and higher stakes of the modern game, although many believe he allowed his team to overstep acceptable boundaries. Frank McLintock's view that 'they were a great side, but they just got too dirty, too cynical' is hardly untypical among their rivals.

Yet Docherty had a grudging admiration for teams like Leeds and Liverpool, saying, 'They may not be attractive to watch, but they have an efficiency.' In trying to match their success, he had sometimes resorted to big-game team selection that went against his basic philosophy and had even spoken in support of playing defensively away from home. Yet he was still considered a flag-bearer for adventurous football, his colourful, lively personality helping the attacking label to remain attached to his team at most times.

Hackett, though, had apparently fallen out of love with the Doc. His reports in the *Daily Express* increasingly criticised Chelsea's 'drab' approach, and even after seeing them score four against Brighton he'd promised to 'walk home from Wembley bare-footed' if Chelsea won the FA Cup with such unattractive football.

Before the semi-final Docherty said that 'we are hoping Tony [Hateley] can disturb Leeds in the air' and he did just that five minutes before half-time. Cooke squirted free of two Leeds players, set off down the left and curled a right-footed cross towards the penalty spot for the centre-forward to head inside the near post. It seemed symbolic that two of Docherty's most recent signings had combined for the goal that looked like finally breaking the club's semi-final jinx. Having denied Leeds space and possession in the second half, Chelsea conceded a late free kick for Hollins's foul on Norman Hunter. Giles played the ball square for substitute Peter Lorimer, who enhanced his reputation for the fiercest shot in football with a screaming effort into the top corner. Yet as Leeds celebrated, referee Ken Burns, who had earlier denied Leeds a goal for offside, indicated he had not given permission for the kick to be taken. When Burns blew his whistle for the final time a few minutes later, Docherty hugged Osgood on the bench and then raced to the field to embrace his Wembley-bound players.

Osgood had been at the centre of yet another club controversy in the build-up to the game. Docherty demanded that his player be allowed to go on the club's summer tour of the USA and Bermuda as a reward and as an opportunity to continue his rehabilitation in different surroundings. Club doctor Paul Bayne advised against it, and the board sided with him rather than the manager. A furious Osgood immediately demanded a transfer, claiming, 'I shall never kick another ball for Chelsea. What are the board trying to do? Destroy me?'

Once Wembley was secure, it was time for player bonuses and tickets, again, to become issues of contention. Rumour reached the Chelsea players that their opponents, Tottenham, were receiving anything up to ten times the two free and ten purchased tickets allowed by FA regulations. This was considered the unwritten norm. Standard practice was that less than half of those would be needed to fulfil needs of friends and family, leaving plenty to be sold at a profit to the touts: a nice 'earner' as a reward for reaching the final. Profits for this game, the first all-London final of the century, would be healthy, with a 10-shilling (50p) ticket fetching as much as £10 and a 70-shillings seat changing hands for £30.

Docherty warned his players of 'serious trouble' if they looked to profit in such a manner, saying it robbed real fans of the chance to acquire tickets. Yet he attracted suspicion for being seen with a large amount of cash himself. 'As manager I received 100 tickets from the club for the Cup final and I had to pay for them myself,' he responded. 'It's ridiculous to say I sold them to touts.'

Years removed from the issue, Docherty happily concedes, 'The players were selling tickets – but that was because the wages then weren't what they are like now. It was a chance to pick up an extra bonus. The players did it and I did it.'

The players ended up receiving up to 20 tickets, but it was still being argued about on the day of the final – as were the bonuses. Again, the players heard stories that the Spurs men had been promised £2,000 each for winning and £1,000 if they lost: many times the amounts written into the Chelsea contracts. Word was that Tottenham's board had agreed to increase the amounts to be paid once a place in the final had been secured, although Docherty, aware that FA regulations forbade the rewording of contracts in mid-season, doubted the veracity of the story.

Several players warned Docherty at the Hendon Hotel that they would refuse to play, forcing a late deal to be struck. The squad would reportedly share between £12,000 and £19,000 if they won, but would have to be content with £50 appearance money if beaten.

'Pratt was furious,' Brian Mears recalled. 'The players were upset; the problems were further compounded by disputes over ticket allocations. Mighty fine preparation for the biggest day in the club's history.' Describing the players as being in a 'puerile mood', he added, 'It was beyond silliness.'

Docherty's insistence that 'we must be the happiest team ever to go to Wembley' was pure fiction, as he would admit in later years when he described the mood as one of 'mean-mindedness and bickering'. It was becoming the familiar off-key song of Stamford Bridge.

Having stated, 'We are not going to Wembley to entertain; we are going there to win,' Docherty sent out this team for his first return to the FA Cup final since losing as a player 13 years previously: Bonetti, A. Harris, McCreadie, Hollins, Hinton, R. Harris, Cooke, Baldwin, Hateley, Tambling, Boyle. Sub: Kirkup.

The player whose name stood out most when Docherty perused the Tottenham line-up was that of Venables in the number 10 shirt. 'I don't think he's as good a player now as he was when he was playing for Chelsea,' he said. 'I don't anticipate too much trouble from [him]; my men know his game too well.'

Docherty had used the forum of the final to announce that he would be toning down his public pronouncements. In a statement that, paradoxically, earned him more headlines than ever, he said, 'I'm through shooting my mouth off. I've blabbed too much in the past when the best policy would have been to keep my mouth shut.' Docherty's resolution barely lasted the duration of the post-final dinner.

If he'd hoped that his team would do his talking on the Wembley pitch, it soon became clear that they'd become tongue-tied. 'I would love to have won the Cup for Joe Mears, God rest his soul,' he says. 'But we just didn't play.'

Docherty looked nervous as he walked out at the head of his team, glancing behind a couple times as if to check that skipper Ron Harris had remembered to follow him, before taking his seat on the bench alongside his son Tom. BBC television's Kenneth Wolstenholme warned viewers not to be fooled by the 4–3–3 formation that appeared on screen. 'Don't kid yourself they stick to any rigid plans,' he said, while co-commentator Walter Winterbottom, the former England manager, politely refused to predict a result, even though Tottenham's 23-game unbeaten run made them most people's favourites.

Cooke spent the early part of the game running from deep positions, although his distribution let him down too frequently. The wing play of Jimmy Robertson and the central threat of Alan Gilzean comprised a more likely threat, and Spurs made the first chance when Frank Saul's half-volley was blocked by Allan Harris. Jimmy Greaves and Robertson had further efforts saved by Bonetti. Chelsea's aimless passing meant that they had to rely on efforts individually created, Hollins forcing a save from Jennings from 20 yards and Cooke's brilliant run ending with a right-foot shot that was tipped over.

Tottenham took the lead in the final minute before half-time after Mullery was given room to break from midfield. His low shot hit a defender and fell to Robertson, who fired past Bonetti. Midway through the second half, Spurs scored a second, Robertson heading on for Saul to shoot past the keeper's left hand.

With Cooke well marshalled by Dave Mackay, Chelsea's chances of getting back into the game were becoming more remote. Hateley headed over after good play by Baldwin, but with five minutes left there was suddenly a glimmer of hope when Boyle curled the ball in from the left and Tambling headed home while the Spurs defence waited for Jennings to claim the ball. Yet Chelsea's belated urgency failed to create a further opening and Tottenham had little problem in holding out for victory.

'We learned a hard lesson and got a bit of a chasing,' says Hollins, while Cooke's summary is, 'The final was shit. I can't tell you how bad we were. I felt physically sick. I was so disappointed for the team. We played crap, abjectly, terrible.'

Some of the repercussions were aimed at Docherty, with Hinton believing he was wrong to make him play as a man-marker against

Gilzean instead of his usual roving, sweeping role. 'Players are always great tacticians after the game,' Docherty recalled dismissively. But even Spurs manager Bill Nicholson said the decision 'made our task easier', noting, 'In previous matches he used Hinton as a sweeper and took three out of four points off us. Alan Gilzean did not like playing against a sweeper.'

Ron Harris dismisses the notion that Chelsea's players were affected by the off-field shenanigans. 'I don't think it was a distraction,' he says. 'I don't think it made any difference to the way we played. We didn't perform at all against Spurs and I don't think it had anything to do with us demanding more tickets or whatever. That was all pushed to one side.'

Docherty arrived at Chelsea's post-game banquet in a dark mood. He had not been due to speak at the dinner, but when chairman Charles Pratt used his own time on the microphone to praise the Chelsea teams of the past, he felt compelled to step forward. It had only been at his urging that the players, still angry over the bonus issue, had agreed to attend the event and Docherty was not going to sit back while their efforts were ignored. 'I was beginning to think that the people responsible for this club getting to Wembley – the players – were not going to get any mention at all,' he announced. 'So a big thank you, lads. You've been terrific.' Pratt might have been fuming, but, as Docherty explained, 'By this stage I couldn't care less what the board thought of me.'

Cooke recalls, 'If we had won it could have been different. Five months later Tommy was gone and I think losing at Wembley was a contributing factor. It was the beginning of the end for Tommy Doc at Chelsea.'

9

THE ROAD TO ROTHERHAM

'I told the chairman, "I'll take the club out of Division Two." I did – into Division Three.'

Tommy Docherty's famous quote about taking Rotherham United out of their division in the wrong direction sums up the haphazard path his career took after Chelsea's Wembley defeat. In the space of 18 months he went from the FA Cup final to Division Three, back to the First Division for barely a month and finally into his fourth managerial job in English football. All three of the teams he managed immediately after Chelsea would suffer relegation not long after Docherty's arrival at their training ground. Suddenly, having been among the hottest managerial properties in the country, it appeared there was nowhere meaningful in England for him to go.

The end at Chelsea was not long in coming after the disappointment of the FA Cup. Again, the party that set off on their summer trip – to the USA and Bermuda – could hardly be described as happy travellers after the recent bonus dispute. The players issued a statement saying they had 'been treated shabbily' by a 'stingy' board.

When the tour reached Bermuda the final downward spiral of Docherty's Chelsea career gained full speed. First, he was angered by the 'dirty tactics' of a local side after a 2–0 win in which reserve-teamer Barry Lloyd was sent off for a comment to the referee. The next day, the same thing happened to Tony Hateley in a 4–3 victory over the Bermuda national team. At the end of the match, Docherty was reported to have said, 'That referee should never be let loose on the field. He should be locked in a cage.' In response Bermuda FA secretary Joe Ferreira shouted back, 'Docherty! You may do this in England, but you don't in Bermuda.' The two men continued to argue as rain soaked them.

Docherty recalls that when he went to the field to remonstrate, the referee had barked at him, 'Get off the field, white man.' At the time he denied insulting the match official, but in his most recent autobiography he describes his response as 'the first thing that came into my head, which was derogatory and politically incorrect'. He'd previously told author Brian Clarke that he'd said, 'You should be swinging from a tree, not refereeing.' Docherty remains adamant that he made no reference to skin colour, nor did he swear – although in another account he tells author Clive Batty he told the referee to 'fuck off'. The exact wording is largely irrelevant, however. It was Docherty's general tone and demeanour that led to the incident being reported to the Football Association.

Board member Brian Mears was not exactly surprised at how events transpired. 'I had seen his behaviour on previous trips when moderation, like mediocrity, had no place on the agenda,' he recalled. 'Docherty was out of control. There is a fine line between cocking a snook at the establishment and simply being a clown.'

While Docherty waited to hear what the FA made of it all, Chelsea plummeted. The sale of Tony Hateley and Allan Harris to Liverpool and QPR respectively could hardly be said to have destabilised the side, yet after ten League games Chelsea were 19th and already out of the League Cup.

Peter Osgood recalled sensing that results and the looming FA hearing were wearing heavily on Docherty. Describing a defeat at Southampton, he said, 'I noticed him under pressure for the first time. The press wanted to know what was wrong and Tommy tried to laugh it off by saying it was just one of those things ... He didn't seem to give a shit what they thought.'

The media would soon have their big story. On the first Friday of October, with Docherty never having been invited to any hearing, he arrived at Stamford Bridge to be informed that the FA had suspended him from all football for a month. He would not even be allowed to pay to watch a game. Taken into consideration, the FA said, were reports of other run-ins with officials during the summer tour and his previous punishment resulting from the FA Youth Cup game. Yet even Bermuda FA secretary Ferreira was 'surprised at the severity of the punishment'.

Docherty was stunned. He believed he had gained an unwarranted reputation as a troublemaker, something he knew sat uneasily with chairman Charles Pratt. He knew his deteriorating relationship with the Chelsea board couldn't take another blow like this. 'I always said back then that if anything happened to the chairman [Joe Mears] I would leave before long,' he says. 'I knew things would never be the same.'

As well as the rows about tickets and bonuses, he'd been forced to release his number two, Jimmy Andrews, and coach Tommy Harmer as cost-cutting measures and had spoken up for John Hollins against the directors when he asked for a pay rise. He resented things like Pratt's insistence that he be told team selection for events as insignificant as the London Five-a-sides.

When Docherty was ordered to attend that afternoon's emergency board meeting he recognised that 'the writing was on the wall'. Mears admitted later that 'top of the agenda was Tommy receiving his P45', calling his position 'untenable' and describing the club as 'a Casablanca of gossip and unrest'. Docherty wasn't going to give the chairman his moment. 'We can't go on like this, Tom,' said Pratt wearily, but before he had the chance to dump his manager, Docherty asked to be excused and brought in a crate of champagne. Popping a cork, he announced, 'I knew what was going to happen. Say no more, Mr Pratt. Have a drink instead. I resign.'

As Mears put it, 'The most exciting episode in the history of the club had ended as it started, with the style and class of Tommy Docherty.'

While reporters and players waited around the ground, Docherty eventually emerged. 'It's over. I have not been pressurised,' he declared, before being driven away by Agnes in their Jaguar. Pratt proved just as adept at putting a friendly face on events. 'The board have unanimously accepted Mr Docherty's resignation. No pressure was put on him. We part on good terms.' He did, however, acknowledge that the club were 'not pleased at the FA suspension'.

Skipper Ron Harris described himself as 'shocked', although his comment that 'the boss had as many good points as bad' was hardly a ringing endorsement. Years later, he contends, 'There were a couple of people on the board who Tom didn't get on with, so this was an excuse to get rid of him.'

Osgood, who told reporters that 'this is a bad blow for Chelsea; we'll be in trouble without him', recalled later, 'Us players didn't know what to think. Most of us had fallen out with him at one time or another, but we liked and admired him. He'd been good to me, signed me, gave me my break, stuck with me now when I was clearly not the same player as before my leg snapped, helped me buy a house, bought me drinks, told me jokes. The fact that we weren't turning it on was down to us, not Tommy.'

Those in whom Docherty had shown faith all had reasons for being sorry to see him go. Tommy Baldwin, who said he 'wasn't the tough regimental man that people make out', regretted the departure of a manager who was not afraid to have a beer with the boys. John Boyle mourned the loss of someone who 'encouraged us youngsters to play'.

Charlie Cooke voices disappointment at the speed of Docherty's departure. Only a few players had the chance to say goodbye, although Osgood and Hinton went to visit him in the days that followed. 'On the day he left I never saw him,' Cooke explains. 'He drove out and a couple of guys, including Chopper, said goodbye, but I never had the chance. And I never thought it was right to pick up the phone to my ex-manager. You just didn't do that, so I never talked to Tommy Doc for years.'

Having settled as a coach in Cincinnati, Ohio, Cooke adds, 'About five or six years ago I still had never really talked to him. I called him and said, "Tommy, I am here in Manchester with my wife and we have just flown in on our way to Greenock. I would love to come and say hello." I felt I owed him a conversation and to say thanks for the opportunity he'd given me. I wanted to let my wife see somebody from my past. He drove into Manchester and we had lunch. He was fantastic, just the same guy I remembered.'

Docherty's profile meant that events at Stamford Bridge made the front-page lead in several newspapers, with reports saying he had been granted an £8,000 pay-off. Speculation centred on possible job offers from Europe.

Soon, Docherty was taking the opportunity to look at himself, saying, 'Possibly I'm too impulsive; possibly I could be more understanding. Those are things I am going to try to change,' he said, sounding like the habitual smoker who says he is really going to quit this time. But he also added, 'I do worry what people think about me and I want to be liked. But if a decision makes me disliked I can't afford to worry about it.'

Meanwhile, as assistant manager Ron Suart – the former Chelsea player and Blackpool boss – took temporary charge, Stamford Bridge faced up to its loss. A 7–0 defeat to Leeds 24 hours after Docherty's departure brought it sharply into focus. Chelsea fans on the same train back to London as the team made their unhappiness known, prompting a reply from Pratt, who reasserted his claim that the board had placed no pressure on Docherty, but admitted 'things had been boiling up'.

Regret over the implosion of Docherty's Chelsea reign continues in some quarters even to this day, as does the debate about the success of that period. Detractors point to the failure to win more than a promotion and one cup competition, the same argument made by those who denigrate similar achievements in a comparable time frame at Manchester United. Yet fans who watched their teams under Docherty talk animatedly about the vibrancy he restored to the clubs, the excitement he generated on the terraces. Average attendance at Chelsea increased 30 per cent to 35,000 during the Docherty years.

Chelsea historian Clive Batty reminds readers in *Kings of the King's Road* that Chelsea had won only one trophy in their fifty-five-year history before Docherty's arrival. The near misses, he argues, 'showed the football world that Chelsea were a force to be reckoned with, raised the collective pulse of the fans and, crucially, provided the players with all-important big-match experience'. It was Dave Sexton who would be the beneficiary of that, returning to lead Chelsea to FA Cup and European success. But Batty asserts, 'Doc will be remembered as one of the club's finest and most influential managers.'

Brian Mears's memoir about the club is revealing. Even though he adopts a consistent tone of disapproval and disappointment with Docherty, in the final analysis he comes down absolutely in support of him, able to overlook the faults in favour of the excitement and achievements. 'In my view Docherty should have his own statue in the Village complex,' he wrote in *Chelsea: Football Under the Blue Flag* in 2001, comparing his impact to that of Ruud Gullit in the '90s. 'The parallels are obvious. Both joined Chelsea at a time when the club was becalmed. Both managers triggered huge changes in the team . . . neither suffered fools gladly and both were to fall foul of the structure that their cocksure proclamations had outgrown and eventually alienated.'

It has become another of Docherty's famous one-liners. Probably even he doesn't remember if he ever really said it. While discussing the problems and pressure of his latter days at Chelsea with wife Agnes, he sighed and commented, 'Things could be worse. I could be manager of Rotherham.' Within a few weeks, he was.

'I enjoyed my time at Rotherham, but I took the job too quick,' he says. 'That has always been my weakness. It wasn't that I had the feeling that I might never work again, but I wanted to work again as soon as I possibly could.'

Docherty's German connections had prompted talk of a move to that country, but it was Greek side Panathinaikos who were first to offer him a job. They promised £10,000 a year, plus a home, a car and a sizeable operating budget, and flew him and Agnes out to take a look. They were an attractive proposition, especially when weighed against enquiries from Sydney-based team Hakoah and Peterborough United.

While he considered his options, Docherty's first activity after his suspension was to go with 17-year-old son Michael when he signed professional forms for Burnley. He had originally been an apprentice at Chelsea, but youth-team manager Frank Blunstone explains, 'I said to Tommy, "He is your son, but he has to go. It isn't fair. I give him twice as much work as any other bugger because I don't want people to think he is getting away with anything." Also, he'd sometimes be sitting in the dressing-room when one of the senior players was moaning about Tommy. That wasn't fair on him or the players. So we sent him to be an apprentice at Burnley, where they had a good reputation with young players.'

Looking back at that time, Michael explains, 'I grew up knowing I had a famous dad who was playing football and was in the spotlight and all I wanted to do was emulate or better what he achieved. Mum wanted me to go into architecture or maths, but I just wanted to be a footballer. At Chelsea, I had to prove that I warranted the right to be there. It was a big ask to leave home at 15 and a half and go to Burnley. I got homesick and the only time I saw Dad cry was when he dropped me off.'

Michael, born in 1950, was the oldest of four Docherty children.

After Agnes lost another baby in a miscarriage following a fall at home, he was followed into the world by Catherine, in 1954, Tom, two years later, and Peter, in 1964. If Docherty was a frequently absent figure from the family home, then he was hardly unique among those in his profession.

'It is all-consuming if you do the job correctly,' says Michael. 'And he is as good as it gets. I had the same problem latterly when I went into coaching and in retrospect it probably cost me my marriage after 25 years. I was constantly travelling. Building a foundation for your family is difficult.'

As proud as Docherty was of Michael for following in his professional footsteps, Blunstone recalls having to give a brutal assessment in later years about his youngest son, Peter: 'Agnes said to me, "Have a look at Peter and let me know what you think." After the game I said to Agnes, "Tell him to concentrate on his schoolwork. I'll say no more." Tommy thought he would make it, but Agnes knew I would give her an honest answer.'

Looking at his own career options after his departure from Chelsea, Docherty found his interest piqued by an approach from Coventry City. Chief executive and former manager Jimmy Hill arranged a meeting with chairman Derrick Robbins, but when Docherty returned from Greece, having decided against a move there, he heard on television that former Manchester United captain Noel Cantwell had been chosen to lead the newly promoted First Division side. Hill was soon on the phone again, apologising for the mix-up and informing him that Rotherham United wanted to ask him about replacing recently fired Jack Mansell.

What was that Docherty had said a few weeks earlier about curbing his impulsive tendencies? After one meeting with chairman Eric Purshouse and his son, Lewis, the local butcher, he was ready to tether himself to a club struggling in Division Two rather than wait for a bigger offer. 'Everyone was friendly, honest and easy to deal with,' he explained. Purshouse's confidence in his new manager was such that he announced, 'If he decides to sell the ground, providing he can provide good reasons, he can do it.' As if to prove his commitment, Docherty bought a house in nearby Whiston, from where he could also go to see Michael at Burnley more easily.

The Rotherham players were as surprised as anyone to discover the identity of their new boss. 'Tommy was a real big name, a real superstar,' says Roy Tunks, then a teenaged goalkeeper. 'We thought, "What the hell is he doing coming to Rotherham?" I remember this big Jaguar pulling up in the car park and in those days you were the bee's knees if you had one of them.'

First-team keeper Alan Hill recalls, 'I was shocked when I saw the news on television. We arrived at ten as normal the next morning and were told to report back at 3 p.m. Four of us went down to the barber for a haircut because we'd heard the Doc could be tough on that. Tommy came bouncing into the dressing-room and asked, "What is wrong with this club?" He said he would change things and was full of enthusiasm. We went into the indoor area and he put on this training session that nearly killed all of us.'

Fitness was once again going to be a key characteristic of Docherty's team, as defender Colin Clish remembers. 'I was out with hepatitis when he arrived. When I came back I was sick at my first training because I went straight back into a tough session.' Midfielder Les Chappell adds, 'Tommy was one for really hard training. He used to say to us, "Train like this during the week and on Saturday it will be like a holiday."'

Promoted to the Second Division in 1951, Rotherham had missed out on further elevation four years later on goal average, but since then survival had become their biggest concern. 'I took this job with a long-term object in mind,' Docherty stated. 'I shall be doing all the coaching myself and my immediate aim is to pull them up the table.'

Along with making his players fitter, he set about improving their self-esteem, as Hill recounts. 'We were playing Millwall in his first game and he told us, "When you report for training tomorrow bring an overnight bag." We had never done that. He took us to be measured for two suits: a club suit and any other one we needed. We travelled to the Green Park Hotel in London and after dinner we walked to the London Palladium. Taxis were stopping and waving at him and then, during the show, Bruce Forsyth, who was compère, announced, "I'd like to welcome Tommy Docherty and his new team, Rotherham United."' It filled you with confidence and made you feel important.'

Docherty would continue to build up his players, whether by taking them to train in Blackpool or Scarborough before FA Cup ties or delivering well-chosen words. Chappell adds, 'All the lads held Tommy in awe because of what he had done. He was a superb motivator. He'd go round the dressing-room geeing you up, telling you that you were better than the other team.'

Camera crews crowded in front of the dugout at The Den as Docherty's new team fought out a 0–0 draw, after which he spent half an hour talking to reporters. 'Tommy was looked upon as glamorous,' says Tunks. 'He had that hint of showbiz about him and he lifted the profile of the club.'

Docherty quickly shed nine squad members, and by the season's end seventeen of his twenty-two players were products of the club's own youth system. Tunks continues, 'Tommy was bright enough to work out that he had to compromise, that he wasn't dealing with Peter Osgood and Bobby Tambling. But we had a good group of youngsters. He gave me my debut when I was 16. I turned up in the morning to go and play in the Northern Intermediate League for the Under-18s and he said, "Come back this afternoon, you are playing against Birmingham." Tommy was a great motivator more than a tactical coach and he put a lot of the young lads in.'

Hill says, 'Tommy would change players very quickly. You always wondered if it was your turn.' Believing their workloads failed to match their salaries, Docherty also got rid of the club physiotherapist and groundsman, with trainer Albert Wilson taking on their duties.

On his way to Millmoor was a future stalwart of England's defence, centre-back Dave Watson, whom Docherty had seen playing for Notts County's reserves. Guaranteeing first-team football to the 21-year-old who both looked and was built like a light-heavyweight boxer, he agreed a player-exchange deal valued at £5,000, which included Welsh winger Keith Pring. 'I didn't actually meet the Doc before I signed,' Watson recalls, 'but he had briefed his assistant. Obviously I knew the Doc's reputation and the manager at Notts, Billy Gray, said I should go. I got on great with him from the start. I was young and hungry for success and the Doc liked young players.'

Watson made his Rotherham debut on the left of midfield in a 6–0 hammering by QPR, with Chappell recalling, 'He was marking Rodney Marsh and we thought, "Bloody hell, he won't play again for about a year." To Tommy's credit, he saw something in him.'

When Docherty prepared for an FA Cup third-round game against Wolves he earmarked his new signing for right-back. Watson recalls, 'We had quite a few central defenders, but I believe that some of the senior players had a chat with him and I ended up playing centre-half.' He proceeded to mark Derek Dougan out of the game as the Millers pulled off a 1–0 upset. 'Dougan was a big figure at that time and I was lucky enough to have a good game, and we won,' Watson adds.

'You could see he was quality,' says Hill of a man who would remain at centre-back, apart from a brief, successful spell as centre-forward shortly after being transferred to Sunderland for £100,000 in January 1970.

After winning by a single goal at Aston Villa in the fourth round, Rotherham's Cup adventure ended with a 2–0 replay defeat against Leicester, a match Hill remembers for a pre-match incident as Docherty introduced players to a group of friends in the dressing-room. When the chairman entered, he asked what was going on.

'I'm getting the lads used to shaking hands with the King for when we get to Wembley.'

'It's the Queen, Tommy.'

'It'll be the King by the time this bloody lot get there.'

The money from the Cup, plus an increase of 3,000 per game in attendance and the proceeds from transfers, temporarily offset some of the club's financial problems. But after a flurry of victories took them out of the relegation places, failure to win more than two of their final eight matches condemned them to the drop. This was becoming the pattern of Docherty's managerial career: take over a team, fail to prevent relegation, earn the chance to bring them back up. In the modern era he might not have had as many second chances. At Rotherham, the board accepted that he had faced a tough task and sent him and the squad on holiday to Spain.

He might now have had only a Third Division club in his charge, but Docherty was still a capable salesman, persuading goalkeeper Jim Furnell to exchange the marble halls of Highbury for the wooden tea huts of Millmoor. Having lost his place to Bob Wilson shortly after playing in Arsenal's League Cup final defeat against Leeds, Furnell was looking for a fresh start, but admits, 'You don't go from Arsenal to Rotherham without a good reason and I went there on Tommy's reputation alone. He was a charmer. I was a little bit fed up at Arsenal and he told me what Rotherham were going to do and it sounded good. It was a big drop for him, but he was going to run it like a First Division club. He'd had a gymnasium built with all the mod cons and we got club suits. For all intents and purposes we were a First Division club in the Third Division.'

According to an interview he gave on the eve of the season to *Goal* magazine, the environment suited Docherty. 'I'm glad to be rid of the glamour,' he said, failing to sound convincing. 'We are not far short of being a very good side. Our Cup run made the boys believe in themselves.'

Docherty had been persuasive in the boardroom, getting Purshouse to agree to increased salaries and a points-based bonus scheme. Hill explains, 'I remember him saying, "Big Man, I want to see you after training." I thought I was on my way but instead he offered me an increase in wages, from £25 to £35, and said he was putting us all on another £17.50 per point. That was First Division wages.'

Furnell adds, 'Tommy was trying to get us back up and was prepared to pay for it. But the club was nearly bankrupt, and we didn't have a sheikh, we had a butcher. He didn't want to pay the bonus. If we won he wouldn't come into the changing-room. If we lost he would come in and say, "Well played, lads."'

Docherty adds, 'There were times when we crossed the halfway line and the chairman would be screaming, "Offside!" To be honest I think it's a bit of a fallacy that the win bonus makes much difference. Appearance money made players play when they were not quite fit, but money can't make them play any better.'

Whether or not the cash made a difference, it proved a costly start to the season for Purshouse. When Rotherham beat Southport 3–1 at home they had lost only one of their first ten games and sat third in the table. Watson remembers, 'I was confident that relegation was a blip and that the next season we would be flying. Being so new to professional football, I never thought about the club losing the Doc. It came as a big shock to me when he left us all behind.'

As happy as he was with his team's performance, Docherty's initial surge of enthusiasm had been waning. He was looking longingly at the First Division, the place to be if he wanted to reach his full potential. As only one of the next seven games was won, that feeling intensified. Newspaper reports that Docherty had been approached after Wolves sacked Ronnie Allen were untrue, but while Rotherham were losing at Stockport on the first Monday of November, events unfolded that would take him back to west London.

Queens Park Rangers' 4–3 defeat at West Ham had left them bottom of Division One with only two wins from seventeen games. Alec Stock, the loveable manager who had led them to the League Cup as a Third Division team in 1967 and won two successive promotions, was fired. The next day, Rangers chairman Jim Gregory was on the phone to Millmoor, requesting permission to speak to Docherty.

Once again, impulse took over. A chairman who could so quickly and casually fire the manager responsible for a Wembley triumph and promotion from Third to First Division in little more than a year was one to be wary of. 'I should have given considered thought to it,' Docherty admitted. Yet he 'couldn't resist the challenge of a move back to a struggling First Division club to try and resurrect it'. He accepted Gregory's job offer the first time he spoke to him, despite the warnings in the headlines about Stock's departure.

Meanwhile, Hill – unable to reclaim his place from Furnell after a broken hand – recalls, 'We were sorry he was going, but it was only a matter of time before he went to a bigger job. To me, he was one of the best managers. I worked with Brian Clough and he was similar, filling you full of confidence and making sure training was always different. If you put your lot in, Tommy liked you. He could tell if players were cheating.'

The son of a fish-stall holder, Jim Gregory had invested millions from his successful second-hand car dealerships into QPR, the club he'd supported all his life and of which he had been chairman since 1965. He had managed to persuade Purshouse to release Docherty 'without any strings attached' and with no compensation payment. 'Where Jim was great,' says Docherty, 'was that if he wanted a player or he wanted you as a manager then no one would beat him. He always got who he wanted. But he was a crook, a gangster. Horrible.'

Gregory explained that he'd pursued Docherty because 'his drive, enthusiasm and experience were what were needed for us to keep our heads above water in the First Division'. Meanwhile, Docherty had been impressed with Rangers in Division Two and had, mistakenly, predicted that they would not look out of place in the First Division.

Rangers winger Roger Morgan recalls, 'There was a different

quality in the First Division. You might get two chances in the top flight and you must take the opportunity and score, whereas in the lower leagues we might have been having twenty shots a game.'

The newspapers took considerable delight in pointing out the task Docherty faced in return for his £6,000-a-year salary, with assistant manager Bill Dodgin Jr on the verge of departure and five players having submitted transfer requests. 'Every job has its problems,' he responded. 'I would not have accepted the position if I did not believe I could make a success of it.'

Dodgin would leave for Fulham within a couple of weeks. Having originally commented, 'Tommy Doc and I used to be teammates at Arsenal and I think it is fair to say we are contrasting characters,' he'd then said that he 'could foresee no problems working together' before finally moving to Craven Cottage to work under new manager Johnny Haynes.*

On the playing side, right winger Ian Morgan announced his withdrawal from the transfer list. 'I was impressed with Mr Docherty's attitude to the players when we met him,' he said. 'He asked us to give him 100 per cent cooperation and he has put all the transfer-listed players back on full first-team money.'

Twin brother Roger adds, 'I remember Doc putting his arms around me and Ian and saying, "I want to build a side around you two and some of the younger players. Are you with me?" He wanted you on his side. If you have got five or six young players in the first team you can build around them, like Manchester United did with Scholes, Giggs, Beckham and those players. But he didn't have the quality of players at Rangers.'

Among those at Docherty's disposal were a couple of familiar faces. Allan Harris, who had been sold twice and re-signed once by him at Chelsea, was able to give his new teammates an endorsement of the incoming manager. 'Alec Stock being fired was right out of the blue and then, even more surprising, Tommy Doc turned up,' he says. 'He was a likeable guy, a character, and he knew his football.' In another corner of the dressing-room, Barry Bridges, signed from Birmingham that summer, probably offered a less charitable assessment.

A 2–0 home defeat against Burnley in his first game in charge

---

* Dodgin took charge of the team within a matter of days when Haynes decided that management wasn't for him and stepped down.

– with a team selected by Dodgin – was the first time Docherty had seen Rangers play since catching their opening game on *Match of the Day*. Burnley's team included six players aged twenty-one or under and, not for the first or last time, Docherty diagnosed QPR's problem as too many older players, stating his intent to 'give the kids a chance'.

Ian Gillard, a future England left-back, was one of the teenagers who would earn a first-team opportunity. 'There were a lot of mixed feelings,' he explains. 'Tommy was a very forceful man who knew what he wanted and the senior pros weren't too happy about it. Obviously the young lads were going to take their places and there was a lot of excitement among them. He was great with them, gave them a lot of belief and encouragement.'

Roger Morgan continues, 'It was a new regime, a new way of doing things, and some of the senior players resented him. Some of those he wasn't going to get on with, he made them train at the ground on their own. He was very strong-willed and established his authority straight away.'

He did so by making former England goalkeeper Ron Springett and centre-back Bobby Keetch train at Loftus Road while their teammates were at the club's training ground in Chiswick, and by fining defender Tony Hazell and forward Dave Metchick for a fight during a practice match.

For the trip to Everton, Docherty appointed twenty-year-old Frank Sibley as captain and was able to call upon Rodney Marsh, the star of Rangers' rise through the ranks, who had missed all but one game during the season after breaking a bone in his left foot. The result was a 4–0 defeat, but Marsh then scored the first goal in a 2–1 victory over Nottingham Forest.

And that was it. On 5 December, Docherty, who had again promised on his arrival at Loftus Road that people would find him 'less impetuous', resigned after 28 days in charge.

Having initially warmed to Gregory, Docherty would recall, 'I found Jim arrogant to the point that he appeared to have no interest in any ideas about the team and club but his own.' According to Morgan, Gregory was typical of many chairmen of newly successful clubs. 'After I went to Tottenham, I never even saw the chairman,' he explains. 'But at a smaller club, the chairman feels part of everything. He wanted to be in the dressing-room to talk to players, which never happened at Spurs. That was the domain of the players and coaches.'

Having identified his former Rotherham captain, Brian Tiler, as someone who could strengthen the team, Docherty was frustrated by his chairman's unwillingness to discuss the matter. After various unreturned calls, he tracked Gregory down at a health farm and was promptly refused permission to spend the £35,000 Rotherham demanded. Docherty's response was emphatic: 'It isn't going to work between us. I'm leaving.'

His public explanation was terse. 'It's a matter of principle,' he said. Gregory, meanwhile, was more expansive. 'Tommy telephoned me with an ultimatum,' he said. 'He told me that unless I gave him the money to buy a player he would accept an offer to join a Spanish club. I was on a diet of water at this health farm. At that moment I felt like reaching for something stronger.'

The Spanish club in question were revealed as Atletico Bilbao,* who were said to be offering £7,000 per year and who stated that 'his appointment is provisional'. Docherty was reported to be flying to Bilbao to finalise his contract, but *Daily Express* reporter Norman Giller warned presciently, 'The Doc is notorious for changing his mind and I believe there is still a chance that this character will decide on English football.'

While Docherty considered his next move, Gregory installed veteran winger Les Allen as manager. The former Spurs Double-winner's first action was to drop teenagers Gillard, Mick McGovern and Alan Glover, all promoted by Docherty, explaining, 'I feel it's time for experienced players to take over.'

Gillard recalls, 'The club was all over the place. From my point of view, I'd made my League debut and things started to look up in my career and then all of a sudden Tommy is out and you don't know what is around the corner. Les left us all out and brought the senior players back again.' Yet Allen's approach would work no better, with Rangers eventually relegated with what was then a record-low 18 points.

Docherty was not done with Queens Park Rangers, however. He'd be back as manager a decade or so later. The double act with Jim Gregory was good for a bit more entertainment yet.

---

* The club had been ordered to change its name from Athletic Bilbao during the rule of General Franco because of a ban on the use of English-language names.

10

VILLAIN OF THE PIECE

'Doug Ellis said to me, "Tommy, I'm right behind you." I said, "I'd rather have you in front of me where I can see what you're doing."'

Tommy Docherty's new managerial position was, he recalls, determined by a car crash. He'd sat in a London hotel and agreed to manage Atletico Bilbao and was excited at the prospect of re-energising his career overseas. Then came news from Spain that club president Julio Egusquiza had been killed in a road accident. 'The new man came in and had his own ideas about who he wanted to appoint,' Docherty explained. But there would soon be a new name running one of England's most famous clubs, Aston Villa, and he wanted Docherty as manager.

Having been relegated in 1967, Villa had fired manager Dick Taylor and then struggled in the lower half of Division Two under Tommy Cummings. Things were even worse in 1968–69 and Cummings was sacked early in November with the club bottom of the table. The backdrop to this slide down the League had been a long-running ownership battle, with chairman Norman Smith and the board under pressure to sell the club.

Docherty heard through a friend of the Mears family that a banker called Pat Matthews wanted to meet him to discuss the Villa job. Matthews had helped to construct the Birmingham Industrial Trust, which had 44-year-old travel agent and Birmingham City director Doug Ellis as its figurehead. Docherty was quizzed on the Villa playing staff and, having recently been in Division Two and plotted the club's FA Cup downfall, breezed through his exam. He was then introduced to Ellis, scoring an early point by reminding him that he was premature in asking to be called 'Mr Chairman' before the projected £750,000 purchase of Villa had gone through. Another of Docherty's classic lines emanated from the meeting: 'Doug smiled and there was warmth in his smile. About half a firefly's worth.'

Docherty chuckles at mention of Ellis. 'He was OK,' he says. 'He was harmless. He just wanted to be involved. He wanted to be in the dugout with you and he used to come out to watch training wearing a tracksuit.'

There was no doubt who the Villa fans wanted to inherit the team from caretaker-manager Arthur Cox. Docherty's name was chanted throughout the home game against Charlton, a day after his exit from Queens Park Rangers, although the Birmingham *Evening Mail* was championing Matt Gillies or Johnny Carey, recently departed from Leicester and Nottingham Forest respectively. Eleven days later, with the Bilbao opportunity having disappeared and Ellis and Matthews installed in the boardroom, the supporters got their wish. At £9,000 per year, half as much again as Bilbao were reported to have been offering, Docherty was quids in.

He spoke publicly of his plans to keep the club in Division Two and stressed the importance of developing young players. His squad, meanwhile, received a taste of his often-abrasive style of management at their first meeting.

'What am I like if you cross me?' he asked goalkeeper John Dunn, who'd been with him at Chelsea.

'You'll chop our legs off, boss,' was the reply.

'Right, gentlemen, see you at training.'

The arrival of Docherty, one of a new generation of Scottish managers inspired by the likes of Busby and Shankly, was entirely appropriate to Villa's rich history. It had been a Scot, George Ramsay, who established them among the elite of English football by winning six League titles and six FA Cups between 1894 and 1920. So revered was he that Villa placed a Lion Rampant on the club badge.

Docherty was being looked to for rather more modest achievements, and fans were happy enough when his first game, against Norwich, was won 2–1. Two days later, Docherty returned to Millmoor to buy his former Rotherham captain Brian Tiler after Ellis made available the £35,000 that QPR's Jim Gregory had withheld, although the largesse stopped short of funds to buy Dave Watson.

A 41,250-strong Villa Park crowd saw Tiler score the only goal of his Boxing Day debut against Cardiff, and another single-goal victory followed at Carlisle. The comments of home manager Bob Stokoe illustrated what was becoming the familiar Docherty pattern of putting pragmatism before poetry in the early stages at any new club. 'I'd rather sweep the streets than play like Villa,' Stokoe scoffed. Docherty had warned on his first day in the job that his initial approach would be 'ultra cautious', but there would be more criticism a few weeks later after a 1–1 draw against Charlton failed to light up *Match of the Day*. Geoffrey Beane noted in the *Evening Mail*, 'Unhappily there is growing evidence that Villa, in their determination to climb the table, are prepared to resort to strong-arm tactics.'

Bookings accrued at a rate considered unusual for the time – twelve in as many games – and it is perhaps significant that one of Docherty's transfer targets was noted midfield hard-man Brian O'Neill, who eventually left Burnley for Southampton after Villa's reported £50,000 bid failed.

Defender Charlie Aitken explains, 'Tommy wanted us to be physical all right. He was aggressive and the training was geared in that direction.' Even Docherty confesses, 'The only important thing was getting safe. Playing well and losing was no good; we needed to get results.'

As fate would have it, Villa began 1969 with a home tie in the third round of the FA Cup against QPR. For Docherty, it was an immediate chance at some form of redemption, an opportunity to ram Gregory's stubbornness back down his throat. 'I didn't think I had a point to prove,' he said later, but someone as emotionally charged as Docherty would have relished the draw. So, too, did the Rangers fans, who marched through Birmingham with 'We Hate Docherty' banners.

Villa's faithful, on the other hands, were smitten. As Docherty, dressed for the cold in a leather coat with sheepskin collar, made his way round the pitch to the benches on the halfway line, youngsters shoved magazines under his nose to sign. Even a goal-bound shot by Ian Morgan after 39 minutes couldn't lower the energy level around the stadium. An equaliser just before half-time by Brian Godfrey was celebrated with the fervour of a trophy-winner, and after 69 minutes, several fans raced onto the pitch after the ball fell at the feet of inside-forward Barrie Hole, who swept in the second goal. At the final whistle, they poured on in their hundreds, Docherty racing against them to reach the players with his own congratulations.

One report described the game as 'a victory for team and crowd', although not before Villa had come in for some criticism for slowing the game down in the closing minutes. 'I saw no fault in our tactics,' said a glowering Docherty. 'Leeds have played like this for years and pray God I should be as successful as Don Revie.'

Confident enough to place his free £50 bet at the opening of a bookmaker's shop on Villa to win promotion in 1969–70 at odds of 12–1, Docherty's popularity with the Villa fans grew further after winning a fourth-round FA Cup tie against Southampton. Having squandered an early 2–0 lead at The Dell four days earlier, they came from behind in the replay when Peter Broadbent netted a header and Martin converted a Dave Rudge cross, prompting the appearance of 'Docherty for Lord Mayor' stickers around town. Within a matter of weeks, Docherty's presence had more than doubled attendance to almost 40,000. The effect on the players had been no less galvanising.

'A breath of fresh air swept through the club,' was full-back Mick Wright's description. 'We thought, "Hallelujah, salvation is at hand." It was as though we had stepped out of the darkness into the modern era. The arrival of Tommy Docherty was the best thing that happened to me in my career.'

The media continued to recognise Docherty's news value. Family entertainment magazine *Reveille* featured an interview and *Goal*, the weekly football publication launched at the start of the season, began its four-part 'X-ray on the Doc'. Over the course of the series, reporter Chris Coles interviewed former players, ex-teammates, rival managers, his bosses at Villa and his current players. The uncontroversial nature of the magazine meant it was a mostly favourable portrait. Manchester City and former Villa manager Joe Mercer called him 'a man of decision' and someone who 'makes his mind up quickly', although that had not always been an asset. 'I have always admired his professional qualities of drive and dedication,' Mercer added. 'But there are no shades of grey with Tommy. It is either black or white. You like him or you don't.'

Doug Ellis offered a view that jars, with the benefit of hindsight. '[He is] an intensely devoted family man who hates being away from his wife and children. To my knowledge he rings his wife twice a day to keep in touch, whatever else may be going on.' Ellis continued, 'He is a God-fearing man without being deeply religious. He will not hesitate to pop off to church from time to time. This is the private side of Docherty.'

If Docherty offered up a prayer for a headline-catching draw in the fifth round of the FA Cup, he was rewarded with a game that thrust his past in front of him again. Villa were sent to Tottenham – although the home team mistakenly printed some tickets with Southampton as the opponents. Asked for a status report on his relationship with his former manager, Terry Venables commented, 'Everybody says he has changed, but I can't believe it. I don't harbour any grudge against him. Any feeling there was between us is now in the past.' A 3–2 defeat saw Docherty declaring his pride in his team and sent them full of confidence back to Division Two duties. When they beat Sheffield United it meant they had won eight of ten League games under their new boss. Victories were harder to come by towards the end of the season – only two in the final ten matches – but Villa showed their resilience in a series of draws and ended up 18th, having lost only four times in the League since Docherty's arrival.

Peter Broadbent, the former Wolves and England man whose intelligence in midfield played an important role in Docherty's early games but would soon be sold to Stockport, said, 'He makes players feel as though they're the best in the world. He will go up to a lad who only a few weeks ago was struggling and say, "You are the best in the League." The player believes it because he wants to. He goes and plays as if he is indeed the best.'

A summer trip to the United States to play games against the Atlanta Chiefs saw Docherty sign Zambian players Emment Kapengwe and Freddie Mwila from the host team, a forward-thinking move at a time when black faces and overseas imports were a novelty in the Football League. But, as throughout his career, overseas jaunts were also an excuse for japes and jokes. Aitken recalls a mid-season trip to Majorca where Docherty began one of his infamous food fights by throwing bread rolls at a group of Germans at a barbecue and also explained, 'He would burst into your room, throw a bucket of water over you, then run out again.' Another time he connected the door handles of two rooms by rope and kicked the doors so that the players within tried, unsuccessfully of course, to open them.

'When I was manager we knew when to have a laugh and a bit of fun, and we knew when to be serious,' Docherty insisted, even after the warning signs at Chelsea about blurring the lines. Broadbent's wife, Shirley, would comment, 'They were a big club and a good crowd of players, but I think they were too fond of a good time. When Docherty came in he wanted to be one of the boys, and you can't be like that if you want to be a manager.'

Reading the newspapers during the summer of 1969, it appeared that it was not only the Apollo 11 astronauts who were shooting for the moon. Docherty was supposedly trying to sign Charlie Cooke, Jim McCalliog, Jimmy Greenhoff and Rodney Marsh. Any of them would have represented a giant leap for a team that had recently been fighting the drop to Division Three, but such was the Doc's PR skill that the stories were afforded some credibility.

The players who did arrive were less eye-catching. Chico Hamilton, Docherty's former Chelsea charge, was signed for £40,000 from Southend, and Celtic midfielder Pat McMahon joined on a free transfer. The latter had been another of Docherty's impulse acquisitions, as commercial director Eric Woodward recalled: 'He was reading the Glasgow Saturday evening sports paper when he saw that Pat was available, and he got straight on the phone and did the deal. That was how Tommy was: he gambled on his instinct.'

The capture of Luton's 21-year-old Bruce Rioch caused a little more excitement, arriving with his younger brother Neil, a defender, for a combined £100,000, nine-tenths of which was attributed to the former. Midfielder Bruce had once scored four goals in a trial game for Docherty at Chelsea before going into hospital. 'When I came out, they already had their quota of 15 apprentice professionals,' he explained.

For Neil, it was an ambition fulfilled. 'I played for England Under-18s with Michael Docherty,' he remembers. 'We beat Belgium 2–0 and Michael, who was very much like his dad, said, "You'll do for my team." I said to him, "Ask your dad if I'll do for his."' Meanwhile, former club captain Vic Crowe returned from Atlanta to take charge of the reserve team.

Once again, Docherty focused on style as well as substance, overseeing the introduction of a new kit that did away with the club's traditional claret shirts with light blue sleeves. Instead, the jerseys were now completely claret, save for the light blue collars and cuffs. With them were worn sky blue shorts. When the kit was premiered against a young Italy team, fans initially booed, believing it was the opposition running out.

Some of Docherty's pre-season comments had more than a touch of cosmetics about them: Dick Edwards touted as an outsider for the England World Cup squad, Barry Lynch compared to a young Bobby Moore, and winger Mike Ferguson credited with the potential to be another George Best. All nonsense, of course, but the cumulative effect of the summer's activities was that a team that had spent the previous season staving off relegation was now considered a promotion favourite. 'It didn't go that way, did it?' laughs Hamilton. 'Expectations were very high. We had what looked a good blend of players, but things didn't seem to work out.'

Neil Rioch adds, 'There was a lot of positivity surrounding the club. The fans had taken to the Doc in a big way and everybody expected good things. He made you believe in yourself. He was very positive as a person and you followed that. We started staying away the night before matches, even before home games. You knew you were at a big club.'

Brother Bruce adds, 'There was immense enthusiasm and excitement around the club. I remember driving to the stadium the first time, seeing the size of it, and they were putting in private boxes. There were enormous events taking place on and off the field.'

Yet Docherty admitted years later, 'I never felt we were good enough to win promotion. I thought it was going to be another tough season, only I didn't realise how much.' If anything, the heightened anticipation ended up weighing down, rather than inspiring, his players. Tiler was not being complimentary when he said that the opening game of the season, at home to Norwich, felt like a Cup final. After it was lost 1–0, Docherty – pictured on the programme cover in full American Indian headdress – claimed, 'I don't want to be top until April.' But nor did he want to be bottom, which is where Villa found themselves after gaining only two draws in nine games. Even radical team changes were having no impact. When, finally, Rudge grabbed a 77th-minute winner against Hull, it was the first time all season Villa had been in the lead.

Docherty was aware of the feelings of *Schadenfreude* Villa's plight inspired. To many, he was a show-off who deserved nothing less. 'I'm having quite a chuckle at the fact they are chuckling at my present position,' he said. 'Some of them must be pretty small people if this is the best thing they have to do.' Support was forthcoming from Derby manager Brian Clough, who announced, 'People should stop knocking Docherty. Everybody seems to be laughing at him, but I think this is wrong. Tommy is good for the game.'

Yet there was also criticism from within, with some players blaming Villa's struggles on Docherty's approach to training. In anticipation of the energetic style he'd employed at Chelsea, Docherty had instructed coach Arthur Cox to work harder than ever on fitness during pre-season. 'It was the hardest training I have ever encountered,' says Bruce Rioch. 'I remember my first session. I thought we'd finished, but then I realised it was only the warm-up.'

Players were instructed not to drink from Wednesday until Saturday evening, while even the morning of a match would often feature a tough fitness session followed by a competitive six-a-side game.

At the time, Aitken had described Docherty as 'easily the hardest of the four managers I have played under', adding, 'The training is sharp but only comes in sharp concentrated sessions. We enjoy it because it is never boring.' But in later years, without the need to toe any party line, some Villa players gave author Richard Whitehead a more honest perspective. 'We trained like maniacs,' said Edwards, 'but we were over-trained.' Jimmy Brown, a young Scottish midfielder, felt that it had a detrimental effect. 'You couldn't train like that and play,' he argued. 'We would be fine for the first half-hour of games; then we'd all be struggling for breath.'

Yet Hamilton feels that element is overstated, arguing that training always seems harder when a team is not winning. 'There was some moaning and nagging, but you know you will have hard days and you have to do it. If you are having a great streak then everything is hunky-dory and it's far easier.'

Even so, where team spirit, enforced by the power of the manager's personality, had seen them through the honeymoon period of Docherty's first few months, now it needed more. According to Aitken, it wasn't forthcoming. 'It all just fizzled out with Tommy because tactically it went to pieces.'

If he wasn't gaining points, he could still capture headlines. His decision to force Hamilton, Ferguson and Wright to get their long hair cut or be left out of a League Cup tie against West Brom created a front-page story alongside the death of Ho Chi Minh, the communist leader of North Vietnam. Then Docherty gave Brown his Villa debut in a defeat at Bolton when still 16 days short of his 16th birthday, the club's youngest first-teamer.

The Hull victory began a sequence of twelve games in which only two were lost, but by now problems were escalating. 'There was a split in the dressing-room,' Hamilton explains. 'With Tommy, you either liked him or you didn't. It cut the players down the middle and got worse as the season went on. I thought I had made a great move, but we made a bad start and never got over it. A lot of disruptive things went on, with people talking behind his back. It just got worse and he never got on top of it.'

Neil Rioch contends, 'It would have been amazing if we had achieved success that season, given what was going on in the dressing-room. There were three separate camps. There were the new boys like me and Bruce, Chico and Pat McMahon; the existing players that Doc got on well with; and then there were those who the Doc was leaving out or didn't get on with. He had a problem with them and they had a problem with him. You could see how he treated the ones who weren't in his favour. It wasn't great.'

By way of example, he continues, 'We didn't have a training ground so we would use various different locations and get a coach there and back from Villa Park. On the way back one day there was a stand-up argument. A senior player who knew he and some others weren't playing the next day had been told by the Doc they still had to come to the game. He asked, "Will we be able to bring our cars on to the car park?" and was told, "No, you have got to park on the street." These were senior players who had to be at the game or be fined, but were prevented from using the car park. I thought that was shocking, but this was the sort of thing that was going on.

'Once you have cracks in the dressing-room, it follows that you have them on the pitch. There was no togetherness; you had players pitted against each other. The atmosphere was awful and Doc was certainly aware of it. But rather than try to change it, he did things to make it worse.'

Bruce Rioch saw what he felt was the error of Docherty's ways when he began his own managerial career. 'When you are trying to move players out but they are on contract and you just push them to one side, you don't get the response from everyone. If you can transfer the lot, then fine. But he knew the players he didn't want involved long-term and they were basically outcasts. If you push half a dozen to one side, it does create disharmony. Sometimes you have to keep them involved.'

Mick Wright's summary to Whitehead in *Children of the Revolution*, his study of the club in the 1970s, was that 'the dressing-room was split down the middle between people who stayed loyal to Tommy and wanted to play for him and people who disliked him intensely'. Edwards, Hole and Ferguson fell into the second camp after Docherty fined them £100 each for breaking club rules by drinking on a Thursday night, another story that made the front pages and in which could be heard echoes of Blackpool. Two weeks later Edwards and Ferguson were banned from the ground 'pending investigation into alleged disciplinary irregularities', while Hole was transfer-listed and fined again after refusing to join a training session at Lilleshall. 'There were internal disputes and a lot of infighting,' said Rudge. 'It drove a wedge between the players.'

Wright continued, 'The Doc's character was that if you were for him and gave 100 per cent, he would support you. If he felt for whatever reason that you were not giving your best then he could turn against you.'

Villa ended 1969 at the foot of Division Two. Local businessman Brian Evans issued a statement from shareholders that suggested, 'The feeling is that we may need new management.' A seven-hour board meeting the following day offered Docherty a vote of confidence, even after he fell out with director Jim Hartley when asked about the team. Docherty told Hartley that he didn't ask him how to make nuts and bolts so he should not ask about players. As has become football tradition with such statements of support, the board's confidence quickly ran out. 'I knew it was no such vote at all,' Docherty would find himself saying three weeks later.

The new decade began with an FA Cup exit to Charlton in a replay and a 5–3 home defeat against Portsmouth, after which, on 19 January, another board meeting was held. Docherty was ordered to arrive at 4 p.m., but was still waiting to be summoned several hours later. When the call came he was informed that he and Cox had been fired.

Bruce Rioch had already suspected that all was not well. 'We were away in the hotel ready for a game and I could hear a conversation Doc was having in the hall. I can only assume it was with a board member. What we were hearing wasn't pleasant and you felt that something was going to happen. Not long after that it did.' Despite feeling he had been played out of position as an orthodox forward in his early games, Rioch was sorry to see Docherty's departure. 'I was one of Tommy's boys and you want to do well for the manager who buys you. And he had been great at helping me and my wife settle in.'

Docherty was disappointed and surprised at his dismissal, believing that Ellis wanted him to stay and could have done more to pressure the directors into supporting him. Ellis admitted, 'I was in favour of giving him more time, but it was a board decision. It was hardly Tommy's fault, looking back.'

'I didn't get long enough there,' Docherty states simply, before contradicting Ellis's comments at the time. 'Doug wanted success last night, not tomorrow. There was great potential there, but I had only about 15 months. Some people expect it to happen overnight.'

Chelsea had been, and Manchester United would be, rewarded by giving him the time that Villa couldn't spare. But Docherty felt the club 'panicked' and were influenced by directors such as former player Harry Parkes, who was no fan of his. 'This is the worst setback of my career,' Docherty said on the day of his departure. Wright, who recalled finding his manager in tears in his home in Sutton Coldfield, said, 'He loved Aston Villa and he desperately wanted to stay.'

Whitehead suggests that Docherty believed factions on the playing side were unsupportive, specifically Vic Crowe and recent signings Tiler and Bruce Rioch. This was denied by Crowe and Rioch, although when reports emerged that the players had opposed Docherty's removal, a statement was issued to the contrary by Tiler, Godfrey, Edwards, Dunn, Anderson, Lew Chatterly and George Curtis, an early season £25,000 signing from Coventry. The players pledged support for Crowe, who had been placed in charge.

According to Hamilton, most players were disinclined to take sides. 'I think we were surprised when he went,' he says. 'But players will just get on with it. If managers leave, they leave. It's a shame, but we have a game to play.'

Graham Leggat, a former Scotland teammate who had moved from Rotherham to Villa to coach the third team for Docherty, handed in his resignation, while many fans sent letters and a signed petition to the Birmingham *Evening Mail*. That show of support for Docherty was enough to prompt a further response from the directors, who announced, 'There has been much talk of magic, but the job of the board is not to deal in magic but in facts.'

The harshest fact against Docherty's impact at Villa Park was the relegation that duly arrived at the end of the season. 'When I took over, Villa were in a shambles,' said Crowe. Yet the following season they reached the final of the League Cup, going on to win promotions in 1972 and 1975 and the League Cup in 1975 and 1977. Neil Rioch says, 'There was a massive change when Vic took over and players who had been frozen out were suddenly part of the squad again. Brian Godfrey, for example, was made captain and led us to the League Cup final and promotion.'

But Hamilton suggests, 'The Doc built the club up. He was the start of it. He bought players like Bruce Rioch and me and others. It was making them gel that he didn't quite get right, but we did turn it around.'

When it came to the direction Docherty's career would now take, *Daily Express* writer Norman Giller accurately predicted, 'My guess is that he will pick up the managerial reins with a Continental club,' arguing that 'the Doc has become too hot to handle for English League clubs'. More to the point, his on-field record since Chelsea – his teams had between them won 28 of 98 League games – made it easy to question whether the aggro that seemed to come with Docherty was worth putting up with. Giller predicted, 'I expect this granite-hard Scot to be back in League business before two seasons are through.'

In fact, it would be three inevitably unpredictable years before Docherty managed again in the Football League. But when he did, it would the biggest job of all.

PART TWO

RED DEVIL

'If we do not know ourselves to be full of pride, ambition, lust, weakness, misery and injustice, we are indeed blind. And if, knowing this, if we do not desire deliverance, what can we say of man?'

Blaise Pascal (1623–1662)

'I must be the only football manager to be sacked for falling in love.'

Tommy Docherty

11

TO HULL AND BACK

'There is a place in football for the media. They just haven't dug it yet.'

Everything about 16 December 1972 was miserable, unless you were a Crystal Palace fan. The weather over Selhurst Park was dark and gloomy, the pitch wet and heavy in appearance, as though it had been sweating under the oppression of the day. The afternoon's contest between two struggling teams was anticipated keenly only by the home fans, for whom First Division life was still enough of a novelty for visits of a club like United to be among the highlights of the season. A month after the government's introduction of pay and price freezes in a bid to halt inflation, those who had travelled from Manchester to be among the 39,484 crowd might have been wondering if their day, and money, could have been better spent in pursuit of Christmas bargains. ITV commentator Brian Moore would shortly be announcing for viewers to digest in the following day's highlights that 'Manchester United simply don't know what day it is'. For Tommy Docherty, it would be one of those days that changes life for ever.

He had travelled to the ground on the suggestion of Bert Head. Knowing Docherty's proclivity for selecting English-based players during his 14 months as Scotland boss, the Palace manager had urged him to look at Glaswegian left-back Tony Taylor. Not far from where Docherty sat awaiting kick-off, United manager Frank O'Farrell, overcoat buttoned against the chill, plonked himself down alongside Sir Matt Busby and club chairman Louis Edwards. O'Farrell, who had guided Leicester to the FA Cup final in 1969 and back to the First Division after losing their top-flight status in their Wembley season, knew he was reaching crisis point in his

18-month endeavour to steer United back onto the glorious path followed by Busby's teams.

Where Wilf McGuinness, a former 'Busby Babe' had failed after being given the job on Busby's recommendation in the summer of 1969, so O'Farrell had appeared he might succeed two years later. In the first half of 1971–72, United played the kind of football they'd not achieved since their night of European Cup glory in May 1968. Inspired by the genius of George Best, they led the First Division by five points in December, only to go into meltdown after Christmas and finish eighth. They now found themselves 20th in the table, with only O'Farrell's former club and today's opponents below them.

While Palace paraded £100,000 signing Alan Whittle, the little blond forward whose flurry of late-season goals helped Everton to the title in 1970, United began the game without their defining figures. Bobby Charlton was missing with flu, Denis Law was tucked up under a blanket on the substitute's bench, and George Best was believed to be on a Spanish beach after walking out on the club. In their places were Welshman Wyn Davies, on the downside of a fine career; Ted MacDougall, signed for £200,000 after scoring copious goals for Bournemouth, including nine in an FA Cup-tie against Margate; and former Nottingham Forest winger Ian Storey-Moore, who had the skill and dark-haired charisma to compensate partially for Best's disappearance but not the durability. Docherty would recall that the trio were 'virtually anonymous'.

The afternoon highlighted United's shortcomings. Pulled apart by Palace, they looked disorganised and uninterested, gave the ball away with alarming regularity and were two-down at half-time after full-back Paddy Mulligan was twice set up by Don Rogers. The winger with the Zapata moustache added a third himself after the break.

Storey-Moore,[*] who allied a powerful, gliding running style to deft close control, made some flashy runs into the heart of the opposition defence, but when Palace sprang back into attack Rogers

---

[*] Having had one of the most distinctive names in football, Storey-Moore tended to be called only 'Moore' after his £200,000 transfer to United earlier in the year – although you can bet that in the days of names on replica jerseys the most would have been made of the revenue potential in his double-barrel.

curled a shot just over. Moments later, Whittle saw a similar effort drop in for 4–0. 'If you love the game of football you don't know whether to be glad for Palace or sad for United,' said Brian Moore dolefully. 'It's a long, long time since they've known such bitter times.' When Law gave up the ball and Rogers went away to round Alex Stepney for the fifth, capping Palace's greatest day since promotion in 1969, Moore described United's state as 'total and utter confusion'.

By now, there was no such uncertainty in the minds of Edwards and Busby, who still wielded considerable power in his role as director and club figurehead. But when Docherty found them locked in discussion after the game, the last thing he was expecting was for Busby to say, 'There's a lot of trouble in the camp. Fancy the job?'

'You've got a manager,' Docherty replied.

'We won't have by Wednesday.'

As a shocked Docherty suppressed a nervous laugh, Busby added, 'Think about it,' and told him how highly Scotland players Law and Willie Morgan rated him. Busby had been seeking references. Law had returned from a summer trip to Brazil raving about Docherty's 'abilities and adaptability' and, in the wake of O'Farrell's departure, would confirm, 'The Doc is as good as anybody I know. He can get United out of the hole we're in.'

Docherty's unease was compounded by the fact that O'Farrell was a former teammate and a good friend, godfather to one of his children. When he ran into him a few minutes later he felt duty bound to confide.

'Between you and me, I have just been offered your job. You're getting the sack this week.'

'I am not surprised,' was O'Farrell's resigned reply.

'What should I do, Frank?'

'Take it. If you don't, someone else will.'

Docherty, his head in a spin, barely noticed the taxi ride and flight home. The most famous team of all wanted him as their manager. A couple of years earlier he couldn't have bought himself a job with a top English club.

It had been inevitable that Docherty would be forced to leave British shores if he was to get a half-decent job after Aston Villa. 'There was some interest from other parts of the country, but I didn't fancy them,' he says. The only acceptable offer of work from

England early in 1970 had been as a columnist for the *Daily Mail*.

'I am ready to come abroad to work,' he said while in Spain shortly after his exit from Villa Park. He was enjoying the hospitality of Malaga club president Antonio Rodriguez, who'd offered him a family holiday while making up his mind about taking over the team. Meanwhile, Celta Vigo and Real Betis were also said to be interested in having him take a similar path to English managers Ronnie Allen and Vic Buckingham, who were at Atletico Bilbao and Barcelona respectively.

In the end, Docherty was out of football for less than three weeks, announcing that he was heading to the Portuguese city of Oporto to become manager of FC Porto on a contract that would run until June 1971. 'I thought this would add to my education and my knowledge of the game,' he explains. Exact details of his deal were withheld, but it was reported as the most lucrative of his career so far. It was agreed that his children would remain in England, with Michael at Burnley and the others attending boarding school in Staffordshire.

Porto's first game after Docherty's arrival was a 1–0 home defeat to leaders Sporting Lisbon and he quickly realised that there would be 'no time for sightseeing'. Club president Afonso Pinto de Magalhães explained that he would take charge of all financial issues while Docherty had responsibility for everything football-related, a task he undertook with vigour, watching as many Portuguese League games as possible.

'It was good out there and I enjoyed it,' he says. 'You are only the coach. You weren't involved in any administration work. You had a press officer who gave all the bulletins to the journalists and you didn't sign the players. They would say, "There are 20 players. Get on with it." One day they might tell you, "Here's a new centre-half," even if you didn't think you needed one. And if Portugal were playing, the season would close down and they might suddenly tell you that you were going off to Brazil for ten days.'

In training, Docherty worked with an interpreter and spent the evenings having lessons in the local language, although he fell back on his native tongue in moments of high tension: 'I could say what I wanted if I lost it. I couldn't get into trouble because they didn't know what I was saying.'

The club was plodding along in mid-table, drawing crowds of

around 20,000 in the 80,000-capacity Estádio do Dragão, and Docherty recalls identifying players from Académica Coimbra and Vitória Setúbal who could improve the team. Given his previous experiences with directors and his new boss's outlining of duties, he was thrilled when de Magalhães went ahead and acquired them. The opportunity to concentrate purely on football matters did lead him, he believes, into training his players too hard in his early weeks at Porto. But he quickly realised his mistake of approaching things as he would in England, making no allowance for the slower game and hotter weather in Portugal. Training sessions were changed to an earlier start time and more emphasis was given to ball skills over physical fitness.

Docherty's impact was not quite as he recalls in his 2007 autobiography, where he talks about taking over the team in 14th place out of 18 and raising them to sixth. In fact, Porto finished ninth of 14 teams before Docherty headed to Mexico in the company of men such as Arsenal coach Don Howe, Stoke manager Tony Waddington and Ipswich boss Bobby Robson to watch the brilliant Brazilians win the World Cup.

The greater impact of Docherty's tenure at Porto was felt during his full season with the club, 1970–71. His team began modestly, winning only one of their first five games. But after suffering only a single defeat in the final fifteen games of the twenty-six-match season – including a streak of eight victories – they rose to third place in the table, four points adrift of champions Benfica and one behind Sporting. They completed the season unbeaten in thirteen home games, but it was the failure to gain more than one point away from home against any of the top five teams that undermined ambitions of a serious title challenge. They did at least qualify for the UEFA Cup (as it would be called after changing its title from the cumbersome Inter-Cities Fairs Cup). In the Taça de Portugal (Portuguese Cup), Porto's hopes were ended by Vitória Setúbal 2–1 on aggregate in the quarter-finals.

'It was a very enjoyable experience, and what was especially gratifying for me, having run the gauntlet between the board and the fans at Villa Park, was to see how the Portuguese fans warmed to me,' Docherty remembered.

Rumours of a return to England had surfaced midway through the season when Blackpool were seeking to replace Les Shannon.

Before they settled on Bob Stokoe, the comments of a club director had suggested interest in Docherty, who warned, 'Any approach would have to be made through the proper channels. I am under contract and have no complaints about life out here. I miss the day-to-day involvement of English football but am still very happy here.'

Nottingham Forest fans had chanted Docherty's name when poor results piled pressure upon Matt Gillies and, more significantly, Sir Matt Busby announced that he was returning, albeit temporarily, to the Manchester United managerial chair in place of McGuinness, who was found to be out of his depth. Docherty was mentioned as a possible long-term replacement, along with O'Farrell, and a poll of Northern-based readers of the *Daily Express* identified him as the fans' favourite for the job.

Yet that still lay some way in the future. When his contract with Porto expired, the club made it clear that their intention was to appoint a new manager. Docherty's dented pride was balanced by his desire to return home. His hope was that his time in Portugal, where he'd done a solid enough job without the British tabloids dogging his steps, had gone some way towards re-establishing his credentials.

Author Tony Pawson's comment that Docherty 'was as likely to kill off his patients as to cure them' was the kind of view he feared was prevalent in boardrooms. 'Will they look at my record,' Docherty pondered, 'and say I did a great job at Chelsea and a sound one at Rotherham? Or will they harp on the QPR incidents and say I failed at Villa Park in a job I never had time to complete?'

At least the football public appeared to have no qualms. In another newspaper vote, Scottish fans named Docherty as their choice to replace Bobby Brown, whose tenure as national manager had begun with the famous 3–2 victory over the world champions at Wembley in 1967 and was about to end following a 3–1 loss in the same setting and subsequent defeats in a pair of summer friendlies. Docherty, whose 30 per cent of the vote beat Jock Stein into second place, responded, 'It's very nice to see that the fans still have faith in me, but it doesn't mean very much.'

Meanwhile, the club appointments with which Docherty was linked were hardly of the profile to which he was accustomed. Grimsby were said to be interested until they named Lawrie McMenemy, leaving Hamilton Academical as the front-runners after three directors met Docherty in London. 'I was very impressed with the people I met,' he said, 'and with the ambitious plans.' When he eventually informed them that he was declining their offer, Orient were the next club to be mentioned.

When Docherty finally announced he was back in employment, it was not so much the club that was the surprise, Second Division Hull City, but the fact that he was employed as assistant manager to former Arsenal teammate Terry Neill. The Northern Irishman, who had made his Highbury debut in the latter stages of Docherty's period at the club and captained them at the age of 19, had been player-manager of Hull for a season, a dual role he would take for his country as well.

Given his continued playing commitments, Neill had identified the need for some experienced help. Docherty says, 'I had not been back long and Terry called to say he was looking for a first-team coach if I was interested. He was player-manager, and you can't do both jobs properly.'

Neill followed a 'hunch' after chatting to Docherty at a dinner, explaining, 'I remembered how kind Tommy had been to me when I first arrived at Highbury, and was only too pleased to do him a favour by giving him a year's contract at Hull and a reintroduction to English football after his spell at Porto. He was happy to be back.'

Accepting that, for Docherty, Hull was obviously a stepping stone to another job, Neill had felt confident that the potential at Boothferry Park would prove attractive, having just finished fifth in the table and reached the FA Cup quarter-finals. Docherty acknowledged the promise at Hull and the local support, but admitted that his chief motivation was 'because I wanted to be involved in British football again'. He was even unconcerned by the presence of general manager Cliff Britton, who had been a hindrance to Docherty's involvement in the World Cup while his manager at Preston and with whom Neill admitted to having an uneasy relationship.

While Docherty told reporters, 'I do not consider my job to be a back seat,' Neill commented, 'Tommy's help and advice are going to be a tremendous help, although decisions still rest with me.' Hull chairman Harold Needler played down the potential for conflict with Docherty in a subordinate role, saying, 'We are thrilled to have

Mr Docherty here. I'm sure he will work well with Terry.' So well did the two men get on that Docherty, with his own family still living in the south, would babysit for his manager and take Neill's daughter, Tara, for long walks in her pram.

Docherty's first words of advice were his familiar refrain about the virtues of young players. Hull were represented around that time by fine players such as record scorer Chris Chilton, who was bound for Coventry, forward Ken Wagstaff, midfielder Ken Knighton and goalkeeper Ian McKechnie, but after a defeat and a win in the first two games of the season Docherty urged Neill to give reserve striker Stuart Pearson, a former trainee post office engineer, his first-team debut. The forward who would play a key part in Docherty's career over the next few years justified his future boss's faith by scoring in a 1–1 draw at Cardiff, before getting the only goals in wins over Birmingham and Blackpool.

'We are not going to miss Chilton, even though he's a great player,' Docherty enthused. 'We expect Pearson to be even better. I have had a lot of great players under my wing, including Peter Osgood, and this Pearson lad will stand alongside them all one day. He goes out and runs like he never wants to stop. He will be the answer to our goal-scoring worries.' He would indeed solve a problem for Docherty, but that was three years away.

Between propelling Pearson into the Hull team and signing him for Manchester United, Docherty had an important passage of his career to fulfil. It began when journalist Ken Gallacher asked if he could give his phone number to Hugh Nelson, chairman of the Scottish FA. Brown had departed as Scotland manager in July, and Gallacher hinted to Docherty that Nelson would not be calling to talk about Arbroath, where he was also club chairman. After a heavy defeat to Liverpool in the League Cup, Hull travelled to lose another one-sided game against Bristol City, and while there Docherty met with SFA representatives. The opportunity offered to him was to take charge of European Championship qualifiers against Portugal and Belgium and a friendly against Holland, with the prospect of a full-time £8,000-per-year contract if results were satisfactory.

Needler, whom Docherty describes as a 'lovely fellow', gave his blessing and agreed to keep him on the payroll in case things did not work out. In a second meeting in Glasgow, it took only 15 minutes for Docherty to formally accept the SFA's offer, although he was taken aback when secretary Willie Allen warned him not to talk to the press and said he'd prefer if they never found out. Docherty, who'd seen enough SFA committee men over the years to be underwhelmed by them, shot back, 'They'd see me sitting on the bench at Scotland matches and work it out. They're very good like that.'

Assessing his time at Hull, Docherty says, 'I was happy there and gave them my all.' He would continue to look out for them, often fulfilling unofficial scouting missions while on Scotland duty and inviting Needler to be his guest at an Under-23 international in Aberdeen. 'Tom had a side of beef waiting for him,' Neill recalled. 'He is a very generous man at times. Tom can be all things to all people, but I can only speak as I have found him. He has been a good friend to me over the years.'

Docherty believed this new role gave him a chance to prove wrong those who said his career was floundering. He recognised that such negativity had adversely affected him and sensed that his usual exuberance was missing on occasions, even though he'd worked effectively with Neill. Proud to have captained his country, the opportunity to manage them at this critical junction of his career was 'an enormous boost to my morale'.

He made a point of seeking out those journalists who had been supportive. Not only did he want to thank them for helping him get the job but he felt that a good working relationship with the media was even more important in international management than in club football. 'I was appalled by England's breakdown in public relations in Mexico,' he said of the previous year's World Cup. 'There was an atmosphere of hate and hostility towards [the media] that could have been avoided by the right approach.'

Docherty's tactic with the media throughout his career was, wherever possible, to give them what they wanted. He understood the conduit they provided between team and fans and was smart enough to know the importance of creating allies, recognising the role journalists could play in projecting him and delivering stories in the way he desired. 'I always knew that in the journalism world you have got a job to do as well as I have,' he explains. 'So the better the relationship we have, the better for both of us. I appreciate the fact that the editor will tell a reporter to go and check out a story and if the reporter doesn't have a good relationship with the manager then he gets agitated.'

Norman Giller of the *Daily Express* was one of those closest to Docherty, operating on a 'friendship basis'. He adds, 'We would socialise. I don't think reporters do that with players and managers these days. I would call him one of the most entertaining people ever to cross my path – a gag a minute. He was an old-school Glasgow comedian with a punchline in every conversation. No matter what he was saying it would lead to a joke, even at the most serious of times.

'Tommy made our lives much easier and he had a set line when you phoned him: "I've got nothing to say. What do you want to know?" He was the king of using the media. When Tommy had something he wanted to get out, he knew which papers to go to. He would even know the edition times. He had an open line to Vic Railton, who was like a sounding board. Nine times out of ten, the first stories would appear in the *Evening News*. He was a fantastic self-publicist and fantastic at deflecting things away from the news that we wanted to be writing about. If there was something that he wanted to hide he would come up with something better.'

Docherty continues, 'With the media who played the game with me, I would tell them if I had a good story, but sometimes I would say to them, "Don't use it until Thursday." I felt, right or wrongly, that some let me down. Usually that was when they printed something about me without speaking to me about it.'

John Rafferty of *The Scotsman* recalled Docherty being popular with Scottish journalists because he gave them good quotes, recognised the pressures and problems of their profession, and 'tried seriously to cooperate with them'. According to Rafferty he was 'shrewd in his assessments and showed a tremendous memory for detail'.

As Docherty began his new role, it was his relationship with the Scottish players that would prove even more important. As usual, he wasted little time in getting started.

12

DOC'S TARTAN ARMY

'I had so much time to spare as Scotland manager I used to sit watching the pigeons in the park. Even they were walking in a 4–2–4 formation.'

Don Revie picked up the ringing phone in his office. 'Can I come and see you?' asked the familiar voice of Tommy Docherty. 'I have been appointed manager of Scotland.' Having admired his Leeds United adversary during his Chelsea days, Docherty had wasted no time in approaching him as a way of establishing rapport with an important core of his new squad. 'I want to talk about Peter Lorimer, Billy Bremner, Eddie Gray and David Harvey. I want Billy to captain the side, so can I speak to him?'

Docherty continues, 'Don said to come up the next day. When I saw Billy, I told him, "I want you to captain Scotland all the way to the World Cup." He was over the moon and Don thanked me for the way I had gone about it.'

Asked if he saw something of himself in the notoriously fiery Bremner, Docherty replies, 'Not really. He was a better player than me. But he was a good leader, and I think that came from Revie and the camaraderie they had there. I said to Billy, "When I give you a night out, you are in charge. Anything goes wrong, it is down to you and I will cut your legs off."'

Docherty's opening message when he assembled his first squad a month later was to remind them of the burden of responsibility they bore, that they represented a nation and their behaviour should reflect that. Victory over Portugal and Belgium was vital, he believed, even though they were effectively eliminated from reaching the European Championship quarter-finals after losing three qualifiers in a row. Seeing the games as valuable preparation for future World

Cup contests, as well as being decisive for his own future, he stressed the importance of making sure everyone understood the aims of the squad, the problems they faced and the role each man would play. Seeing the players only intermittently made it imperative that clear and concise communication was achieved.

Hibernian's Pat Stanton recalls, 'You saw all the bits and pieces about Tommy long before his appointment and knew he was a larger-than-life character and had been very successful. But you didn't know quite what to expect. He was easy to get along with. He was bubbly and enthusiastic and always cracking jokes, but he liked to win as much as anybody and had good knowledge as well.'

Given his recent spell at Porto, Docherty was well acquainted with his first opposition. The majority of the Portuguese team came from Benfica, while three of the squad were his former players, including Jose Rolando, who made the starting line-up in midfield. 'He knew Portugal very well,' says Aberdeen goalkeeper Bobby Clark. 'He was well versed and sounded very authoritative. He gave a good team talk because he knew them inside-out and I remember he used black grapes and green grapes as the players.'

The identity of his own squad had been eagerly anticipated. Having suffered what he felt was the prejudice directed at English-based players during his own career, Docherty was determined that a player's location would be no barrier to selection – so much so that he would end up with a reputation for favouring 'Anglos' over those in the Scottish League. While it is true that he certainly increased that quota, it should be noted that they accounted for only fifteen of the starting positions in his first three games.

As Lorimer pointed out, however, 'At that time the Anglos were hated. Scotland had this view that every time the country was beaten in an international fixture it was because the Anglos did not have the right attitude.'

One of the new selections caused a particular stir when named in goal for Docherty's debut at Hampden Park. Bob Wilson's very English tones were already becoming a familiar feature of the BBC's football coverage so it came as a surprise to many to learn that his parents were both proud Scots. Docherty took advantage of a change in regulations, allowing parentage to determine football nationality, and selected Arsenal's Double-winning goalkeeper even though he was a former England schoolboy international. It had been when appearing for that team in West Germany before the host nation's full international against Scotland that Wilson first encountered Docherty, asking for his autograph. 'Tommy Docherty never dreamt he would eventually be manager of Scotland,' he said years later. 'Less possible still was the thought I would be his first selection as goalkeeper.'

Docherty insisted, 'He has every right to be in the Scottish team, both on account of ancestry and ability. To hell with his accent, he's as good as Gordon Banks. He should give us a strength and confidence at the back we have been lacking.'

Even Clark, who had grown up in the Shettleston area of Glasgow, with Docherty as one of his heroes, accepted this new threat to his ambitions. 'Picking players because of their ancestry was fairly new,' he explains. 'But Bob was a really good goalkeeper and I was prepared to compete with him. It was a chance for me to work with an experienced goalkeeper and somebody who had a similar background, having a physical education background and a teaching degree like I had.'

Wilson's Highbury teammate George Graham, who had wanted to quit Docherty's Chelsea, also earned a first cap. So did centre-half Eddie Colquhoun, rewarded for Sheffield United's impressive return to the First Division, and Hibernian's English-born winger Alex Cropley, who recalled, 'I was playing well, but I didn't think I was playing that well. I think it was a kind of publicity stunt to get the punters in.'

A fifth debutant, the smooth Aberdeen defender Martin Buchan, would appear as a late substitute, while there was a recall for mercurial Celtic winger Jimmy Johnstone, of whom Docherty said, 'I felt I could handle him. He needed coaxing; emotionally he was often up and down.'

He continues, 'I had no problem with wee Jinky. I caught him a couple of times on tour with birds in the room. I knocked on the door and said, "Wee man, you had a couple of birds in here an hour ago. Don't do it again." He said, "OK, gaffer," but when I shut the door I listened. He turned to his roommate and said, "Some man, isn't he? He doesn't give a toss."'

This, then, was Docherty's first Scotland line-up: Wilson; Jardine, Colquhoun, Stanton, Hay; Gemmill, Bremner, Graham; Johnstone, O'Hare, Cropley. Stanton was the only player remaining from defeat to the USSR in Scotland's previous match, in which he had also been captain. New skipper Bremner responded to his appointment by saying, 'Tommy has lifted us into a winning mood already. I have never known spirits so high.'

Interviewed for the match programme, Docherty outlined his intention of elevating the mood of the nation. 'I get a thrill out of watching Scots like [boxer] Ken Buchanan or [driver] Jackie Stewart on TV. There's no reason why the Scottish team shouldn't give Scots everywhere the same thrill.'

The prevailing mood of excitement manifested itself on the pitch, with Docherty more confident of victory as the game wore on, especially after Bremner fed Derby's John O'Hare to fire Scotland into a first-half lead. Rui Rodrigues equalised after 57 minutes, but the ever-threatening Johnstone found an advancing Archie Gemmill to shoot Scotland back into the lead and the home team controlled the rest of the game. 'I felt I was now back in the big time,' was how Docherty greeted the final whistle. Eusébio, Portugal's most revered player, noted, 'Mr Docherty has done wonders with the Scottish team. They were unrecognisable from the side we beat in Lisbon last season.'

Talk before the game against Belgium at Aberdeen's Pittodrie ground four weeks later was that Docherty had already done enough to convince the Scottish FA that his post should be made permanent, a position strengthened by a 1–0 victory against a team who had won their previous six matches. O'Hare scored a well-taken early goal, while young Celtic striker Kenny Dalglish earned his first cap.

Few international matches were considered meaningless in this era; certainly not a December meeting with the Netherlands in Amsterdam. The country that had supplied the two previous European Cup winners, Feyenoord and Ajax, would provide the toughest test so far of Docherty's revitalised outfit. That Scotland finished the game disappointed not to have earned a draw was indicative both of their performance and the heightened expectations under their new manager. Predictably, Johan Cruyff, who would inspire Ajax to two more European Cups before taking the 1974 World Cup finals by storm, was the home side's most effective player, his performance nothing short of a masterclass. He scored the first goal after five minutes when he took a pass from Piet Keizer, beat two men and shot past Wilson.

Scotland responded by carrying the game to Holland in the second half, and Gemmill hit the post before the outstanding Graham netted an equaliser. O'Hare headed against the bar as Scotland broke out after Dutch pressure, but Ari Hulshoff scored a scruffy winner inside the final two minutes. Despite the defeat, the SFA had seen enough, offering Docherty a four-year contract worth a reported £8,000 per year before they left Amsterdam. Docherty's response, typically, was to raise the hopes of fans even further by announcing, 'Scotland must succeed. No country in the world possesses as much natural talent as we do. Possibly Brazil, but that's all.'

In international football terms, it had been a relatively busy period, with three games in seven weeks. But now the reality of the job was about to kick in: five months without a match. There were only so many hours one could fill watching club games or talking to reporters. Docherty spent too many hours in his office at Scottish FA headquarters, sometimes amusing himself by feeding the pigeons perched outside his window.

'That's what I didn't like about international management: the gaps between games,' he explains. 'If you didn't do something very well then you had to wait until the next training session in a few weeks to put it right. At a club you could put it right on Monday.'

At least he didn't have a board of directors to answer to. 'Working with the SFA was a lot different to a club. No one wields the power like the chairman of a football club. You have carte blanche to go wherever you want and you are not accountable to anyone. I had to recommend my 22 squad players for internationals to the committee so, out of consideration, I used to get a folder for them with the players all written down. I remember them thinking, "This is very organised. We're going places here." And then someone said, "And what is your team?" I said, "The players will know that before you, gentlemen."'

Docherty did have to establish some important points of principle. 'I remember someone bringing in my post and it was all open. I was told Willie Allen, the SFA secretary, had done it so I went to see him. He told me, "Under the minutes of the association, the secretary can open all mail for the manager." I said, "Not any more. It could be personal stuff. I could have a boyfriend or a girlfriend or it could be a personal contract. You can open my mail when I can open yours."

'Ken Gallacher used to pay me £100 a week for a column in the *Daily Record*, which was almost as much as I was getting for managing my country. Willie Allen tried to stop me but I said, "There is nothing my contract to say I can't." They didn't like anyone answering them back, but I let them know from day one it was my way or not at all.'

Clubs were not always so compliant, however, and plans to work more closely with his players and their teams were frequently frustrated. Docherty had wanted to stage regular squad training sessions and also planned a series of lunches and meetings with Scottish club managers, explaining, 'I know their problems when it comes to letting players go for international duty. I want to sort things out so they are inconvenienced as little as possible.' Yet those lunches were poorly attended and discussions over the release of players were mostly fruitless.

There was at least a chance to look at some younger players when he selected a Scottish League team to face the Football League at Middlesbrough in March. A 3–2 defeat was encouraging, given that the opposition included the likes of Bobby Moore, Geoff Hurst and many of the players expected to represent England at the 1974 World Cup.

It was an older, more familiar name who caught the headlines, though, when Docherty selected a provisional pool of 30 from which he would pick teams for upcoming internationals at home and a trip to Brazil to participate in the summer's Independence Cup tournament. Denis Law was back, three years after his last Scotland appearance. Docherty had always had an apparent soft spot for the striker, having been a teammate on Law's debut. He had offered friendship and advice and had shown Law around Highbury when he was considering a transfer to Arsenal from Huddersfield.[*]

In naming his squad, Docherty felt compelled to cite Hibernian and Aberdeen as the Scottish clubs in whom he was disappointed after their reluctance to make available defender John Brownlie and

---

[*] They had fallen out, however, after Docherty criticised Law's decision to sign for Manchester City over Arsenal. 'He may regret it,' Docherty said. 'He wants to stay in First Division football, but if he stays at City I doubt he'll do that.' Law refused to shake Docherty's hand when they next faced each other on the field.

keeper Clark respectively for all the games. 'It actually helped me when Martin Buchan transferred to Manchester United because the club immediately said I could have Martin, plus Willie Morgan and Denis Law,' he said. 'That was first-class cooperation. I am looking for help with the bosses and in turn I will help them. I've made it clear that if they are cooperative when I want their players, I'll forget about their men when the clubs are heavily involved in their own commitments.'

Scotland were finally back in action against Peru, quarter-finalists at the 1970 World Cup and destined to wreck the Scots' hopes in Argentina in 1978. Law was named captain and, with Wilson having torn up his knee in an FA Cup semi-final, Kilmarnock goalkeeper Ally Hunter was given his first cap, another selection that proved Docherty's open-mindedness. 'He wasn't frightened of the old firm,' says Buchan. 'With all the home games in Glasgow, if you were playing for Scotland, whether you were from Partick, Kilmarnock or Manchester United, you were keeping a Rangers or Celtic player out of the team. People weren't very fond of that.'

Scottish *Daily Mail* writer Brian Scott recalled, 'He did something which I found quite remarkable at the time. He looked beyond Celtic, Rangers, Hibs and Hearts, looked beyond that pool of teams for players. He was prepared to give anybody a chance regardless of which club they played for as long as they had ability.' Another who fell into that category was West Bromwich Albion midfielder Asa Hartford, chosen only months after a proposed £170,000 transfer to Leeds fell through when he was discovered to be suffering from a hole-in-the-heart condition.

O'Hare and Law were the second-half scorers as Scotland gave a thoroughly professional performance to beat Peru 2–0. 'Denis's influence on the other players is remarkable,' said Docherty. 'They all have great respect for him. He sets a great example by training hard and building up team spirit.' Yet, in just over a year, Docherty's relationship with Law would come to an ugly end.

Scotland were considered favourites for the Home International Championship, largely on the basis that escalating violence in Belfast meant that no teams were travelling there for football matches, giving Docherty's men the comfort of three home games. The Irish were beaten by late goals by Law and Peter Lorimer, before another Lorimer strike did for Wales four days later. It was hardly a classic match, and only 21,000 turned up, but Docherty was pleased with a third successive clean sheet and a fifth win in six games. Victory over England, surprisingly beaten at home by Northern Ireland, would secure the British title, although Docherty – enough of a patriot to be photographed in full kilted glory before the Welsh game – had done his best to put games against the old enemy into context. 'Beating England is not the be-all and end-all for me. But any match against English opposition means my players will be given the sort of test that will prepare them for the World Cup.'

This was the infamous occasion when Sir Alf Ramsey arrived in Scotland with his England team and was greeted by a journalist shouting, 'Welcome to Scotland, Sir Alf,' to which he replied, 'You must be fucking joking.' There was little bonhomie on the field, either. One report said that that it was 'not a match for faint hearts or weaklings', while *Goal* magazine's headline announced, 'Britain's prestige hits rock bottom in Hampden's SOCCER SAVAGERY.' Editor Alan Hughes wrote of the 'disgraceful actions of a dozen or so thugs in football shirts', while SFA chairman Nelson stated, 'If that was international football, it is a shame. The public have a right to be entertained.' By the end of a match in which 46 fouls were committed and the captains were ordered to cool down their players as early as the 18th minute, England emerged as winners via a goal by Alan Ball, who further angered the 119,000 crowd by giving them a V-sign.

Docherty took heart from Ramsey telling him that he could see an improvement in his team. Besides, he was excited about what lay ahead in Brazil, where Scotland would take the berth originally offered to England in what had been conceived as a tournament for previous World Cup winners. The fact that Italy and West Germany had also declined did little to dampen Docherty's enthusiasm, although the June/July date for the event meant that some clubs insisted on keeping players at home for pre-season training.

Jock Stein had declared Celtic trio Johnstone, Hay and Dalglish unavailable. 'But he said, "You can take that little sod Macari,"' Docherty chuckles. 'He wanted him out of his hair.' In general, Docherty remembered Stein as being supportive but described Rangers manager Willie Waddell as 'belligerent, obstinate and most unwilling to help'.

Law was again included in Docherty's plans. 'I said to him, "I'm not being disrespectful, but I don't think you can do 90 minutes any longer. I want you to give me your lot for 30 minutes." He came out and he was great.'

Scotland's 18-man squad arrived in Rio de Janeiro five days before their opening game in Belo Horizonte – scene of England's historic defeat to the USA in 1950. Swimming in the morning and training after lunch was Docherty's chosen approach, although Buchan recalls an incident that might have put the Copacabana out of bounds. 'Walking along the beach, there was a very steep drop into the water,' he says. 'I was swimming and this extra large wave slammed me into the sand and hurt my back. I didn't tell anybody because I didn't want the lads being banned from the beach.'

The performance against a good Yugoslavia team seemed to support Docherty's methods, Macari scoring both goals in a 2–2 draw and Morgan missing a late penalty. Czechoslovakia, who would be in Scotland's World Cup qualifying group, were the opponents in Port Alegre, where a small crowd watched a dull 0–0 affair.

Victory over Brazil in front of 130,000 at the Maracanã Stadium would mean a place in the final, and Docherty called it a 'real test of our international credentials, our character and resolve'. It was without doubt his biggest game as an international manager – 'the game I had been longing for' – and he focused his preparation on convincing the Scotland players they could match the world champions for skill.

'He gave you a lot of confidence,' says Clark. 'We had good games against Yugoslavia and Czechoslovakia and we were disappointed only to draw. We felt we were as good as any opponent, even Brazil. You know in a game like that you are going to have to pick their pocket, but we didn't give them a lot of opportunities. We worked very hard.'

Having delayed kick-off by claiming to have been held up on the way to the stadium, Brazil fielded eight of the starting line-up who had overwhelmed Italy in the World Cup final, an injured Pelé being the most notable absentee. Docherty countered with: Clark; Forsyth, Colquhoun, Buchan, Donachie; Bremner, Graham, Hartford, Morgan; Macari, Law.

Brazil would not display the level of petty fouling and spoiling that marked their mean-spirited performance in the 1974 World Cup, but nor were they the artists of two years earlier. They had not even touched the ball before committing the first foul of the match on Graham after seven seconds.

Scotland enjoyed the pedestrian pace of the game made necessary by the heat, 'Stroller' Graham in his element and the impressive Morgan injecting occasional bursts of urgency. Graham tested Leão with a long-range shot before Forsyth, shirt torn and hair wild, surged into the box with more Highland belligerence than Brazilian grace and saw his shot parried. When Morgan switched to the left he was hacked down almost at the waist by Clodoaldo but got up to skip past two defenders, forcing a frantic clearance. After another foul, Macari helped on a Hartford free kick and Graham's diving header was tipped over. So comfortable did Scotland look that Graham even had time to try some ball juggling just before half-time. 'I grew more confident of us achieving a sensational result,' said Docherty.

Brazil increased the tempo after the interval, and where the Scots had previously appeared composed and untroubled in defence they now began to look over-elaborate and precarious. Clark turned a header by Dario over the bar and Gerson headed wide of an open goal. It was no great surprise when Scotland's rearguard was finally breached with ten minutes remaining. Rivelino hit a low diagonal cross from the left and Jairzinho scored with a diving header before setting off on the kind of celebration that had become familiar in Mexico. 'It was a shell of a cross from Rivelino, tremendous speed,' says Buchan. 'If you got on the end of it you were as liable to score an own goal as clear it.'

Brazilian manager Mário Zagallo was forced to concede, 'I was very nervous during the game. It could very easily have been the other way round.'

In the aftermath of a successful South American campaign, noted Scottish journalist Jack Harkness wrote, 'Scotland has found a new hope under Tommy Docherty,' and remarked on the 'bouyant mood of optmism' surrounding the team. Docherty himself enthused, 'The World Cup is coming up and we could not be better prepared.'

Clark states, 'That was a great trip. It was fun, a lot of good football and a good chance to build a team for the '74 World Cup. If the Doc had stayed that trip would have been instrumental in forming the basis of the squad for West Germany.'

Approaching the first game of the new season, a World Cup

qualifier in Denmark, one report stated, 'Docherty has kicked away the blinkers and widened the horizons.' Certainly, in a three-team group that also included Czechoslovakia, nothing less than qualification for the finals was expected.

Docherty's choice of ten English-based players in a squad of eighteen to travel to Copenhagen once again attracted criticism from some Scottish managers, the very group he felt were hindering his team selection. Stanton argues, 'He obviously knew the English-based players and the type of competition they were in, but if there was someone within the Scottish game that was deserving of consideration, he did that as well.' Docherty, whose habit of taking notes during scouting trips on a small tape recorder was considered a revolutionary technological advance, responded, 'I am prepared to travel anywhere anytime to watch any player who can help Scotland.'

The performance he witnessed in Denmark was, he reckoned, the best of his reign. Macari and Norwich's Jim Bone scored before half-time, and Aberdeen's Joe Harper, on his debut, and Morgan netted in the second half as Scotland breezed to a 4–1 win.

Citing the example of Scotland's poor preparation at the 1958 World Cup, Docherty approached the return game four weeks later adamant that nothing would be taken for granted. 'Nowadays that's not on,' he said. 'We will approach the match as though the first had never taken place.' While David Harvey kept a clean sheet in his first international, Dalglish capped a fine display with a goal, and Lorimer got the second, triggering a happy night of celebration – full of patriotic songs – for Docherty, his team and the reporters. 'It had been my great ambition to lead Scotland into the World Cup finals,' he wrote. 'But fate was to intervene.'

When his telephone rang a couple of days after his trip to Crystal Palace, Docherty was prepared for it to be Matt Busby and knew exactly what he would tell him: 'I'll take the job.' The following day, he was informed by Willie Allen that Manchester United chairman Louis Edwards had requested permission to speak to him about the Old Trafford position. Docherty suspected that SFA chairman Hugh Nelson knew he had already been approached, but as a club man himself he turned a blind eye to what was common practice within the game. Before long Docherty was listening on his car radio to the story of Frank O'Farrell's departure, which ended up sharing the headlines with news that

United had eventually run out of patience with George Best and 'sacked' him as well, stating that the transfer-listed star 'will not be again selected for United'.

By the end of the week, during which Docherty was widely and accurately touted as successor to his old Preston teammate, he had shaken hands in the back of a car with chairman Louis Edwards on a £15,000-per-year contract and been introduced formally as the new manager of Manchester United. 'I wouldn't have left my role as manager of Scotland for any other job,' he said.

When Docherty packed up his SFA office and bade farewell to the pigeons, he did so as the most successful manager, in terms of results, his country had ever had. In twelve games, his only three defeats had been to the major powers of Holland, England and Brazil. All four qualifying games in major tournaments had been won and his overall percentage of success was 66.7 (seven wins, two draws, three defeats). Only Alex McLeish, who recorded a 70 per cent record in his ten games in charge in the next century, has bettered Docherty's mark at the time of writing.

As with Chelsea, previously, and Manchester United, later on, the impact would not simply be measurable in results. Docherty instilled a passion and confidence in his players that would continue beyond his own tenure as manager. An example is the dressing-room speech before his first game against Portugal, as recounted by George Graham in his autobiography: 'Right lads, ye're wearing the greatest shirt ye'll ever wear. Just pride alone will make ye six inches taller when ye run out on tae the pitch.'

Graham adds, 'Tommy was very similar to how he had been at Chelsea. It was always fun in his company. He was first and foremost a lover of football, but obviously a very, very proud Scot. He used that patriotism – as most Scottish managers do.'

Docherty had originally voiced the hope that 'something can be worked out' to allow him to continue to guide Scotland's World Cup efforts while at Old Trafford. But the SFA understandably insisted on a full-time managerial appointment. Qualification was duly clinched with a home victory over Czechoslovakia, and Scotland would fly home from West Germany in 1974 as the only unbeaten team in the tournament after beating Zaire 2–0 and drawing with Brazil and Yugoslavia.

It was the 0–0 contest against Brazil that was the defining game of Scotland's tournament, with Willie Ormond's team once more proving the equal of the champions. Rarely, though, can a team's personality have changed so much between tournaments as Brazil's from 1970 to '74. In place of visionary defenders like Carlos Alberto they had hatchet man Luís Pereira, while Rivelino had mutated into a snarling sneak, constantly trying to get Hay sent off and settling for whacking Bremner in the face. The neutrals who fell in love with this team four years earlier were all rooting for Scotland, and the image of Bremner holding his head in anguish after coming within inches of a dramatic late winner is one that all Scotland fans of a certain age will carry to the grave.

In the final reckoning, it was the Scots' failure to fill their boots against Zaire that saw them eliminated on goal difference. Observing the finals, Docherty reckoned that 'having got there, there was something missing'. Perhaps it was that spark, that additional dose of self-belief – which those close to Docherty often discuss – that was the absent ingredient. It is intriguing to contemplate how things would have turned out for Scotland's 1974 squad, which had its share of world-class talent, had Docherty taken them to the finals rather than the genial Ormond, a former Hibernian legend who had been promoted from his job at St Johnstone.

'I had a great squad of players. I am not saying we would have won it, but we would have done well,' is Docherty's verdict. 'The players were there and I picked them. They all knew the system and they would have had a year's more experience. There weren't a lot of quality players that you could have brought into the squad, but Willie took over from me and he scrapped a lot of the players. He should have had a longer look and then decided who he liked.'

Buchan suggests, 'I think it could well have been different [under Docherty]. I think we might have scored more goals against Zaire. They played out of their skins, but we should have been pressing for more goals, and perhaps if we had approached the game a bit differently we might have scored more.'

There is a case that Docherty's powerful personality might have made his players more focused. It is questionable whether a skilled media manipulator would have allowed his men to boycott reporters, knowing the distraction such an issue would become. And, given his relationship with the two men, it seems unlikely that Bremner and Johnstone would have attempted – or certainly not got away with – their drunken night in Oslo before a pre-tournament friendly. 'One of the Doc's great strengths was his discipline. He was a tough man,' was the opinion of Lorimer, who noted, 'He knew what unchecked players were capable of getting up to.'

Bremner and Johnstone had been seen by Ormond in full, embarrassing flow in a student tavern – breaking a team curfew in the process. But the manager retreated from the scene and got a member of his support staff to remove them, taking no further action. Did the indulgence of Ormond set the wrong tone prior to a major competition? As BBC broadcaster and journalist Archie McPherson noted, 'You must have a leader who is prepared to dirty his hands.' For better or worse, Docherty had proved at Chelsea that he was prepared to do that. 'This was an occasion where [the manager] had to stamp his authority on players who were misbehaving,' McPherson told a documentary crew in 2011. '[Ormond] didn't have that control. They didn't fear him.'

Having been the man who brought Johnstone back from international exile, it's unlikely Docherty would have been afraid to play him in West Germany, where the Celtic winger failed to get on the field. McPherson contends that Ormond chose to 'play safe' by sticking throughout with Morgan, rather than risk the maverick Johnstone – even when games such as those against Zaire and Yugoslavia were crying out for a touch of the unorthodox.

Stanton recalls being impressed with the way Docherty approached working with the likes of Bremner and Johnstone. 'There were two or three strong characters in the group and I think he handled them the right way. They were terrific players and had their opinions. Instead of going up against them and having confrontation, he let the lads have their say. He knew what kind of people they were and they responded well. Had he approached it like, "I am Tommy Docherty and I am telling you," it might not have worked. He allowed you your place, but he had that ruthless streak if you stepped out of line or let him down. He went out of his way to welcome you and look after you, but you would be mistaken if you took the kindness as a weakness.'

Docherty had quickly established with his squad that, whatever they had been used to, excessive socialising would now wait until after games. Lorimer observed that 'attitudes would have to change', something that young Arsenal midfielder Eddie Kelly, who had made his Under-23 debut under Brown, discovered to his cost. Docherty recalled that he 'told [Celtic's] George Connelly and Eddie Kelly when I caught them with a bird that they'll never play for me again', although Kelly explains, 'I was in the Under-23 squad and after one of the games we had a bit of a party in one of the hotel rooms. Tommy Docherty came up and came into the room. It was nothing different to what I had done at Arsenal after games. It was me and two other players. A little while later Bertie Mee told me that Tommy had told him on the phone that I would not be picked for Scotland. I couldn't believe it.' Kelly's unofficial 'ban' was not made public until many years later, but he never did play a full international for his country.

Buchan states, 'Doc wasn't intimidated by anyone. He'd had big names at Chelsea so he was used to it. He had been a Scottish international so there was no feeling of inferiority. He jollied them along when he had to and handled the egos very well.'

Clark adds, 'What I liked was that Tommy was always completely in control and he had a nice way about him. I liked his jokes. He loved it if somebody asked if he slept well. "I slept like a log," he'd say. "I woke up in the fireplace." I remember George Graham not laughing and saying, "Remember, I had him at Chelsea so I've heard them all before." Tommy could be the captain of the pirate ship. He handled the whole group well, so if there were any pirates in the squad he could put his arm round them and be the man in charge. He could bring the whole group together in a way where nobody really noticed what was actually happening. I liked little things like, after a midweek game in the Home Internationals, opening the bar in the hotel. It was a free bar, but everybody would be in that room together, so it was controlled. He wanted people to have a few beers and they didn't have to sneak off to do it. He was able to make a working unit and he did it in a fun way.'

Docherty would ponder, 'Perhaps having got the momentum going, if that United offer hadn't materialised and I'd stayed on with Scotland, we might have climbed tall mountains together.' As inevitable as it is that he should imply that his country could have achieved more with him at the helm, it is also not unreasonable to consider whether, in fact, he had found his true managerial calling in international football. Even he wonders whether he should have sought to return to it later in his career, although the long tenure of Jock Stein between 1978 and 1985 might have denied him that opportunity with his own country.

Study the long-term timelines of his periods as a club manager – as we have at Chelsea and Aston Villa and will do shortly at Manchester United – and one thing is apparent: familiarity bred contempt. Docherty's players talk of the galvanising effect of his personality and passion over a short period. Yet dressing-room rancour could become more prevalent the longer he stayed in one place. His put-downs, his clowning around, his financial wheeling and dealing became wearisome for some players over time.

Docherty might not have maintained the patience and tolerance towards those 'strong characters' of whom Stanton speaks if forced to work with them on a permanent basis. The intermittent nature of international management made it easier.

The problem, however, was that 'there simply wasn't enough work to keep me occupied and energised'. Manchester *Evening News* man David Meek was told exactly that when he asked Docherty about rumours linking him to Old Trafford. 'I interviewed him on the Hampden Park steps and he said he'd love the United job,' he remembers. 'As prestigious as it was being manager of Scotland, he missed the day-to-day action of club management.'

But had he found a way to conquer the frustration of long periods without matches, international football might have offered him the environment where his relationships with players remained fresh and productive, one where the squad reported for Scotland duty looking forward to an outlook and approach different to their day-to-day clubs' management. If there were players he failed to get along with he could have simply omitted them from his squad, rather than allow a feeling of mutual contempt to fester in the dressing-room.

It is exciting to think what Docherty's galvanising energy could have done to a team during the whirlwind of major tournament football. It could have been his perfect platform.

Even at the time of his appointment, journalist Norman Giller, who had followed his Chelsea career close up, suggested, 'He will benefit from not having daily contact with his players.' He said it would 'lessen the risk of his becoming involved' and would not give him time to 'poison the atmosphere around him'. As Docherty himself puts it, 'In international football there was no chance for players to stir up any trouble in the dressing-room. The players looked up to you.'

Bob Wilson's verdict is, 'I think he was perfect for international management. The Doc's enthusiasm was infectious, making his international players feel ten feet tall.' And, without referring specifically to Docherty, Graham states, 'Some managers are better having players for three days at a time, whereas when you are a club manager you have them for seven days every week, every month, every year. On the international scene you can be very pally with them and motivate them, whatever style you choose, because you know afterwards you might not see them for several weeks. Certain managers suit being an international manager.'

Jim Reynolds, writing in the Glasgow *Herald* in 1987, argued, 'It was the enthusiasm and ambition of Docherty which sparked off Scotland's impressive World Cup qualifying record. It was Docherty who left the foundation and injected the pride which has seen the Scots in the World Cup finals on the last four occasions.' And, according to Brian Scott, 'Tommy Docherty was bold and brash, but he knew his football and he got the fans talking. He clearly had the respect of the players. [We were] intensely disappointed when he left to go to Manchester United.'

Kenny Dalglish has remained a big fan of the man who gave him the first of his 102 international caps, saying, 'The Doc was great for the game in Scotland. He got everybody involved, got everybody behind the national team. He gave the whole place a lift.' He concluded, 'When Manchester United offered him the manager's job at Old Trafford it was brilliant for him but a great pity for Scotland.'

13

UNITED WE FALL

'I remember a young lady approaching our chairman, Louis Edwards, and asking if he was really a millionaire. He told her that he was before he met me.'

Much is made of size of character in football. The likes of 'Big Mal' Allison and 'Big Ron' Atkinson earned their nicknames for reasons beyond mere results; Brian Clough was doomed at Leeds from the moment he tried to prove he was 'bigger' than dressing-room forces such as Billy Bremner and Johnny Giles; various Manchester United players of the modern era discovered the folly of challenging the enormity of Sir Alex Ferguson.

Old Trafford in the final days of 1972 was not over-blessed with football talent. Martin Buchan, who arrived earlier in the year, states, 'I got a shock when I joined how many poor players there were in the first team. The squad was a curious mixture of superstars and lads who would not have got a game in Aberdeen reserves. There was a lot of rebuilding to do.'

What it was crying out for was someone who, by sheer magnitude of personality, could haul the club out of its quagmire of mediocrity, an individual undaunted by the ghosts of past glories and the continued physical manifestation of those triumphs in Sir Matt Busby and many of his beloved players.

Theories about the failure of Wilf McGuinness and Frank O'Farrell to build on the club's success of the 1960s typically centre on the fact that both were somewhat diffident in their approach, overshadowed by the presence of Busby in the Old Trafford corridors or burdened by the weight of Stretford End opinion. Whatever kind of fist Tommy Docherty made of his new role, no one would ever accuse him of not having the ego, brashness and, at times, brutality to tackle the task.

David Meek, who was covering United for the Manchester *Evening News*, suggests, 'Wilf had been feeling his way into his first job and had problems managing people his own age. Frank was an accomplished manager but lost the players and felt he'd never be successful until he had his own team rather than Busby's team. It needed someone to create a bit of mayhem – a bit of fire and brimstone – and no one was better at doing that than Tommy, although he would say later that he couldn't have been as successful at United without the spade work of McGuinness and O'Farrell. He had to clear out the dead wood, even though it is disrespectful to talk that way about players who had performed heroics. They were too old.'

One of Docherty's protégés, Brian Greenhoff, adds, 'It needed someone to come in and do a dirty job, someone who wasn't frightened of the consequences. Doc wasn't.'

For better or worse, Docherty would have the club riding on the tail of his double-vented, wide-lapelled jacket into the new decade. As Richard Kurt and Chris Nickeas put it so neatly in *The Red Army Years*, 'A Seventies Old Trafford was surely no place for an O'Farrell – but it was made for the Doc, Seventies Man incarnate. Put him in a kipper tie, in *Man About the House*, next to a Party Seven or behind the wheel of a Capri – does he not fit perfectly within your mental image?'

Almost the first public words that Docherty spoke as United manager addressed the issues of the past. 'It has been suggested that Sir Matt's influence has been too strong. What rubbish. I will not hesitate to seek his advice.' He does confirm, however, the power Busby wielded, saying, 'Matt ran the show. If I wanted a player and Matt didn't like him then he could influence the other board members. They didn't know a centre-half from a mince pie.'

But having chosen to bring Busby along with him into the club's new era, many of those held dear by Sir Matt would be consigned to history, bundled up and thrown out like old clothes going to the jumble sale. After all, Docherty had been warned by O'Farrell, 'Watch out for the old pros. They are not doing it for me.'

Docherty might have been comfortable with Busby at his shoulder in the latter days of 1972, yet four years and a half years later his relationship with the club and its figurehead would reach the point where he saw conspirators lurking in every Old Trafford shadow. How much Busby himself might have been behind the private investigators who ended up tracking Docherty's movements, or the huddled groups of directors and hangers-on whispering disapprovingly in the boardroom and in nightclubs, remains a matter of conjecture. What is certain is that Docherty alienated enough influential people to ensure that the greatest triumph of his football career would be insufficient to protect him from the consequences of the biggest personal turmoil of his life. But what an incredible journey it was in the meantime. As author Eamon Dunphy states, 'Under Tommy Docherty the next five years would read like a cheap novel.'

It began with the right words and good behaviour. Introduced as manager on 22 December, an excited Docherty declared, 'It is a privilege to be asked to join a club like Manchester United. My aim has always been to be the best manager in football. And I know that at Old Trafford I will get the best possible chance of proving that I have what it takes.' There was the usual 'changed man' stuff as well. 'I've learned from my mistakes,' he said. 'I used to talk first and think later. Now it's the other way round.'

Yet Frank Blunstone, who would soon join Docherty's staff, recalls only a minor change from the man he'd known at Chelsea. 'He was older, a bit wiser. But you still had to watch him; he was a crafty bugger.'

Docherty met his players at the Mottram Hall hotel in Cheshire and the following day was presented to the Old Trafford crowd before the game against Leeds. He then watched a team selected by coaches Paddy Crerand and Bill Foulkes – European Cup winners both – lose a first-half lead given to them by Ted MacDougall when Allan Clarke grabbed a disputed 88th-minute equaliser. Boxing Day brought a 3–1 defeat at Derby, leaving United bottom of the table. For all the talk of scaling the pinnacle of his managerial ambition, Docherty had seen enough to know he'd never get there with the current group of players.

It was towards his former Scotland squad that Docherty looked for reinforcements. First, he and Busby travelled to London to sign midfielder George Graham for £125,000. Arsenal manager Bertie Mee had thoughtfully set Graham up in a hotel meeting room to meet all the clubs interested in his transfer-listed player and

Docherty emerged to describe his new recruit as 'Britain's Günter Netzer'. Graham found his old Chelsea boss more enthusiastic and energetic than ever, noting, 'I had never known the Doc so bubbling and buoyant, even though United had a relegation battle on its hands.'

One day later, Docherty paid £100,000 for twenty-year-old Alex Forsyth, the direct, powerful Partick Thistle full-back he'd picked four times for Scotland. The new signings wore the red shirt for the first time in a home friendly against Hull, in which Docherty signalled future intentions by leaving out MacDougall and Wyn Davies. Ironically for Graham, his competitive United debut was at Highbury, where his old team won 3–1.

By now, Docherty was beginning to lose the players he did rate. Ian Storey-Moore, constantly troubled by ankle ligament injuries, would miss more games than he played as his career limped towards its inevitable premature ending. Sammy McIlroy was out for the rest of the season after he and his wife were involved in a car crash in which he suffered a punctured lung and four broken ribs. Any hopes that the FA Cup might give the club a lift lasted the two minutes it took for Wolves captain Mike Bailey to score the only goal in United's third-round tie at Molineux.

Two more Scots were summoned. Discovered by Crerand during a scouting trip to watch a different player, Jim Holton, a hulking brute of a centre-half, cost £80,000 from Shrewsbury and would prove to be one of Docherty's most effective, and most controversial, signings until he too was struck down by injury. As United scrapped for First Division survival, the Stretford End accepted him as a hero, the kind of committed individual they could imagine taking into battle in the escalating war on the terraces. To others, the crude effectiveness of the 21-year-old made him an unworthy heir to the Busby Babes' bloodline.

Forward Lou Macari, born in Edinburgh with Italian ancestry, invoked no such ambivalence, becoming an Old Trafford hero over the course of a decade at the club. Desperate to leave Celtic, for whom he'd signed at aged 14 and scored 57 goals since his debut in 1970, he had all but agreed to join Liverpool when Docherty hijacked his move.

'Jock Stein said I had done well, but when he offered me a contract it was only a fiver rise, to £55 a week,' Macari recalls. 'I was raging. Having spent time with the "Anglos" in the Scotland team you knew that in England you could earn up to £200. I had a child on the way and my father had just died so I was looking after my mother, and I was determined I was not going to take a £5 pay rise.

'A couple of weeks later I got a call from Jock saying that a car would pick me up in the morning and that I was going to England, not knowing where. We stopped in Southport for a sandwich and a short while later I was driving into Anfield to meet Bill Shankly. There was no negotiating: he offered me £180 a week and said they'd agreed a fee of £180,000. Jock and Shanks were best of pals and I was more or less smuggled into Anfield to sign.'

Macari took his seat in the Anfield stands to watch his prospective teammates take on Burnley in an FA Cup replay. As fate would have it, Liverpool's directors' box had not enough space for the full contingent of visitors from United, so Crerand scuttled away to find that his seat was next to Macari and Celtic assistant manager Sean Fallon. Shocked to find that Macari was there to join Liverpool, Crerand conferred with Docherty at half-time and told the player, 'Don't sign anything. We'll sign you.'

'As soon as I knew United were interested, I was heading for Old Trafford,' Macari says. 'As a Celtic supporter and player you had a natural affection for United, and they had Best, Law and Charlton – massive names.' Also seeing greater opportunity for immediate first-team football at United than at Liverpool, whose settled side was on the way to winning the League title, Macari was committed even before discovering that he'd be on £200 per week.

With a £200,000 transfer agreed, Macari was to find that he had entered a very different world. 'The Doc and Jock were chalk and cheese. Jock was a real disciplinarian with a very serious approach, would never let you out of his sight. He wanted you away to bed at 10.30 and you got up, ate breakfast and dinner when he told you. Doc was the opposite. He'd said, "We'll give you a shout in the morning and head to Manchester." I thought it would be about 6 a.m. to get back for training. But I was sitting in my room and it was 11 a.m. when I went and knocked on his door and he was still in his bed. He said, "You don't need to train, it's only West Ham."'

That life with Docherty rarely travelled along a smooth road was proved during the drive south when his brand new Mercedes was struck from behind by a lorry. Macari, in the rear seat, was fortunate to escape injury. Docherty recalled, 'We were very lucky. It could have been a really nasty one. There was fog about and this lorry following us had evidently been hit from behind.'

A less heralded signing was that of the versatile Mick Martin, whose £25,000 transfer from Bohemians initially appeared to be at the expense of midfield colleague Gerry Daly, who was left to sweat over the possibility of United returning for him at a later date.

Docherty had now spent £525,000 on five players in the space of a couple of weeks. An influx of new blood was nothing new whenever he took over as manager. After all, his appointments were all at struggling teams. This was a change of direction, however, in that he was writing big cheques rather than dipping into the pool of younger players as he had done at Chelsea. It was not just that he'd found himself at a club with money – in fact, United had gained a reputation for parsimony by making only one major signing, Burnley winger Willie Morgan, in the three years after their European Cup triumph. It was more that he couldn't find the required talent within the club. Star players were losing their power and ill-equipped replacements were coming off the once-prodigious production line.

Blunstone's initial sight of United's set-up after becoming youth-team coach later that year illustrates the depth of the problem. 'The first time I went there [former assistant manager] Jimmy Murphy said to me, "Look at the youth team and see what you think." I watched a game and Bill Foulkes was coaching. He said, "What do you think?" and I said, "Bloody hell. Awful." They couldn't put two passes together because Bill was of the old school, who liked to just bang it. I called them all in and said, "From now on we are going to do things different." I wasn't knocking Bill, but we had to learn to play football and build from the back. We did a lot of shadow football, playing without opposition. I said to the right-back, "Pull out wide here and the keeper will give you the ball." He said, "I wouldn't want it here on Saturday. What if I lose it?" I said we would concentrate on making sure he didn't lose it. You had to teach them how to position themselves to receive the ball so they could see the whole field of play. A couple of months later he said,

"I am enjoying my football now because I am getting touches on the ball.'"

Macari and Holton made their debuts at home to West Ham, at the expense of Davies and European Cup-winner David Sadler. Tartan scarves and Scottish headwear were in evidence among the 50,878 crowd as fans embraced what had quickly become dubbed 'Mac United'. When Macari converted a cross from fellow Scot Morgan after eighty minutes to complete a comeback from two goals down you could almost hear bagpipes emanating from the terraces.

But not every Scot at Old Trafford was getting carried away on a wave of Rob Roy-ism. It soon became evident that Inverness-born MacDougall would never form the partnership with Macari of which Docherty had spoken. Substituted after 56 minutes in a 0–0 home draw against Everton – which lifted United from the bottom of the table – MacDougall's early exit with the non-playing Denis Law was perceived as him leaving in a strop, rather than, as he describes, a simple attempt to beat the traffic. MacDougall believes that the support offered to him by the Stretford End angered Docherty.

A goal poacher who relied on the kind of service he'd had at Bournemouth and would enjoy at future clubs such as Norwich and Southampton, MacDougall sensed that no one at United was interested in making life easier for a First Division newcomer. He'd feared the worst on hearing of Docherty's appointment via a car-park conversation with Morgan. 'That's me gone by deadline,' he'd predicted. The source of his concern was being the only player substituted in an International XI managed by Docherty for Geoff Hurst's testimonial a few months earlier. Although Docherty would claim that MacDougall wanted to move back to the south – he would sign for West Ham for a reported £160,000 in March – the player argued, 'I never wanted to leave the club I'd idolised as a kid.' His suggestion that 'it was a hopeless cause' was supported by the story of a picture taken of United's Scottish contingent, with Docherty instructing MacDougall to stand on the end of a row so that 'when you leave it will be easier to clip you off'.

Davies would soon be heading to Blackpool for £14,000 as Docherty settled on Macari and Kidd as his preferred strike force. A scorer on his 19th birthday at Wembley in 1968, Kidd could 'do a fine job', according to his new manager, who said, 'It was a disgrace the way Brian Kidd had been buried at Old Trafford.' Kidd, whose appearance at Crystal Palace was only his fourth start of the season, claimed that O'Farrell had made him play in a withdrawn role, but spoke in glowing terms of the impact of Docherty, who'd told him, 'You've got the ability. Don't worry, you'll get your chance.' Kidd claimed, 'Tommy Docherty brought me back from the dead. He has given me my appetite for the game back.'

With so many new players to bed into the team and the debilitating weight of a relegation fight upon them, it was never likely to be a period of carefree football. After six weeks without a win under Docherty, captain Bobby Charlton said, 'We are trying to cram what should take a few seasons to discover into a few weeks. We are having to return to basics.' It was Charlton's two goals, one a penalty, that finally brought the new boss his first win, 2–1 at home to Wolves.

Thereafter, six wins and only two losses in the next ten games momentarily lifted United as high as twelfth and allowed them a more relaxed final two weeks of the season before finishing seven points clear of relegation, in 18th position. Yet some observers struggled to comprehend the football to which they felt a club with United's rich reputation and history were stooping in their days of need.

It was not long into Docherty's reign that Meek was warning his *Evening News* readers, 'Manchester United's fight for their First Division lives is going to be a rugged one. It's going to upset the purists.' After the Wolves result, the *Daily Express* noted that the manager was applying 'fierce commitment and a belief that, in football, ideals are something you reserve for tomorrow'.

Holton, the personification of that commitment, was sent off in a friendly at Porto and returned from suspension to earn another early finish after scoring in an important 2–1 home win against Newcastle. The apparent head-butt that he landed on the back of Malcolm Macdonald's skull was merely the most obvious of United's indiscretions, according to the visiting centre-forward. 'United were crude, not only in their tactics but the way they played. It is a terrible shame that a great club like this should have to resort to such methods,' Macdonald said, before adding, provocatively, 'Holton was sent off because he was obeying instructions from the bench.

I heard somebody shout, "You've done one; now do the other."'

Docherty, who threatened to report Macdonald to the Football League for the last comment, responded, 'People seem to have made up their minds that United are going down and perhaps they don't like it when we show them that it is not going to happen. I resent these accusations that we are a dirty team.'

But eminent journalist Brian Glanville was forced to note that United had become 'a very difficult team to love these days' and ventured, 'Unable to play their way out of trouble there is an evident temptation to try to kick their way out.' Docherty's players all insist that they were never sent out with instructions to play unfairly, although Graham would admit, 'There was no doubt that we were using the physical route to survival. It was all desperate stuff and not pretty to watch.'

Buchan argues, 'The Doc did the best with what he had. I never played for a manager who said, "Don't try to score." Defensively we weren't one of the worst and you worked on things during the week with the intention of scoring more goals than the opposition, but we didn't do it often enough.'

United, of course, were hardly alone in placing the emphasis on getting results. Despite the dazzling sambas of Brazil's 1970 World Cup winners and the interchangeable, technical mastery of 'Total Football' practitioners such as Holland and West Germany, the English game in the early '70s was a frequently bleak landscape. For all the raw excitement of life on the terraces – even in an age of dwindling attendance – and the increasingly glossy and colourful way in which the media presented the game, it was functional, organised teams such as Leeds and Arsenal who typified what was happening on the field. Players such as Rodney Marsh, Alan Hudson, Frank Worthington, Charlie George, Stan Bowles and, when he could be bothered, George Best, are remembered and revered from this time because they stood out from so much around them, not because they truly represented what was going on in the game. It appears that United, because of the romantic blanket in which the club had been swathed since the 1950s, were held to higher values than other clubs.

Writing in *Goal* during the summer, Ken Jones would lament the lost lustre of Manchester as a footballing city – Malcolm Allison having recently headed south to Crystal Palace from Maine Road

– and, in particular, United's unattractive image. He claimed that two testimonial committees had recently chosen not to have United as opponents for their players and voiced his fears, unfounded as it turned out, for United's pulling power at the turnstile. 'What we are forced to accept is a different Manchester United,' he concluded.

The fact that he was still able to write about United as a First Division team was due to late-season results such as an impressive 1–0 win at title-chasing Leeds, where a goal by Trevor Anderson, bought by O'Farrell from Portadown for £12,500, virtually condemned Don Revie's team to finishing second.

Such success, however, could not disguise that there was much reconstruction still to be done. One of the pillars upon which previous glory had been built, Best, was apparently already gone, and a second, Charlton, spared Docherty a difficult decision by announcing his retirement once the threat of relegation abated. 'If United had gone down I would most certainly have carried on,' he announced at his farewell press conference, despite admitting that the thrill of playing had disappeared.

Docherty accepted Charlton's decision without any attempt to dissuade him from his course. There was 'no point of friction', according to Charlton, who had appreciated his manager's willingness to allow him to set his own fitness agenda and the empathy he'd demonstrated towards the difficult issue of knowing when to bow out.

There was no fairytale sign-off in his last League game – a defeat at Chelsea – although he did score twice in his last outing for United, a 4–1 win at Verona in the Anglo-Italian Cup. United's participation in a second-tier tournament remembered more for numerous ugly scenes on the pitch and in the stands than the success of English teams such as Swindon, Stoke and Blackpool, says much about United's status. The Verona game did, however, give Docherty the chance to introduce Graham as his new club captain, even though Buchan had been led to believe by O'Farrell that he would inherit Charlton's mantle.

'I captained the side in my second game for United when Bobby was injured,' Buchan recalls. 'It was expected that I would eventually follow Bobby, but there were one or two twists or turns. It was a great honour, but I think I was a leader without being captain.'

Graham admits, 'I was surprised, but the problem was that there were not many senior players there so Tommy selected me. Unfortunately it came when my playing career was fading away.'

The third member of the 'holy trinity' – Denis Law – would not be around to experience his countryman's captaincy. And therein lies a tale that would come back to haunt Docherty.

Despite starting only nine games all season, and only three under his former Scotland boss, Law felt secure in his future. After all, hadn't Docherty promised the man known as 'The King' a job for life at the club – in front of witnesses? Yet on the day before the season finale at Stamford Bridge, Law was summoned by Docherty and told he was being released on a free transfer. With a new house recently purchased in the Manchester area and a wife in mid-pregnancy with their fifth child, Law was disinclined to move anywhere and felt he could still contribute. He had also lined up a testimonial game against reigning European champions Ajax at the start of the following season. After 11 years at Old Trafford he decided he'd rather leave the game than find a new club and reached apparent agreement with Docherty that he would announce his retirement after his benefit game. Unfit for the next day's match, he drove up to his birthplace of Aberdeen to pick up his children after an Easter break.

The next day, Docherty offered the *Evening News* the list of players who were being released. Alongside the name of European Cup-winning full-back Tony Dunne was that of Law. Once the story had been reported in print, it was quickly picked up by broadcasters, and Law was astonished when he heard of his free transfer while watching *Grandstand* in a pub with friends and family.

The sequence of events is unflattering to Docherty yet, almost as an automatic response it seems, he disputes it. 'Denis said that, but it wasn't true,' he claims. 'It wasn't a problem with Denis.' Docherty appears to have forgotten, however, that it was this episode that landed him in trouble when he took Willie Morgan and Granada TV to court for libel several years later. It was when he was forced to admit that the version he'd given under oath was untrue that his action collapsed and he found himself facing charges of perjury.

'I felt Denis's best days were gone, so in recognition of what he had done for the club I decided to give him a free transfer,' Docherty continues. 'I told him first rather than just put out a list. Matt was against it. He wouldn't say you couldn't do it but would say, "I think you are making a mistake." I think it was out of sentimentality rather than ability. Someone had to do it. I got the reports from [physiotherapist] Laurie Brown that he would play on Saturday and be having treatment all week.'

Law chose not to reveal his story to the media at the time. It was only after Morgan described Docherty as 'the worst manager there has ever been' that Law's version of events in support of his former teammate received an airing in court. For now, he kept quiet. Instead, he signed for Manchester City, scored a goal that has gone down in legend with his last touch in League football, and went to the 1974 World Cup finals.

It was a confusing turn of events to those, like Graham, who had witnessed Law and Docherty get on 'like old friends' after the player's recall to the Scotland team but now witnessed 'a coldness and distance' that 'could be measured in fathoms'.

Macari admits, 'As a young player, when you see Denis Law playing for Manchester City, you are scratching your head and thinking, "How can this happen?"' Stepney, meanwhile, called it 'a great injustice and an insult'.

Docherty made a summer addition to his backroom staff when he signed disillusioned Brentford manager Blunstone as youth-team coach, although his arrival at Old Trafford was delayed. 'I drove up to Manchester and I saw Tommy and agreed fees and everything,' Blunstone explains. 'On the M6 on the way back this big lorry suddenly came in front of me across the central reservation. I saw another car swerve and then "Bang!" Next thing I was in Walsall hospital for two or three months. The lorry driver had got me out just before the car went up in smoke. I had broken my jaw, femur, ankle and five ribs. Tommy came to see me and I said, "Whatever you do, don't make me laugh." The bastard, he never stopped. He said the job was still mine when I was ready, and my wife was able to stay at a hotel in Walsall – all paid for by United before I had even done a day's work for them. That was Tommy.'

Meek was another who was grateful for Docherty's thoughtfulness after articles criticising United's turnover of managers prompted the board to tell him he was unwelcome in official club circles. 'It was a black mark against me, and lesser men than Tommy would have said I was *persona non grata*,' he explains. 'He ignored that. I made my own travel arrangements and I was always on the same train or at the same hotel, but eating on my own. He would shout across the restaurant, "I see you are eating with all your friends." He never let the directors having me in bad odour affect our relationship.

'I enjoyed him because you could talk to him man to man. After O'Farrell not wanting to upset anyone, it was quite refreshing to meet the Doc and for him to say things like, "We were crap today." It was like a breath of fresh air. I had a lot of freedom. He used to allow me to go down to training sessions and talk to the players. I think he was pretty fair with the journalists. He didn't have favourites that I was aware of and he treated everybody at face value.'

If any single season in English football managed to obliterate once and for all the spirit of the '60s, it was 1973–74. The two defining moments of that decade had been England's triumph in 1966 and the fulfilment of Busby's European Cup dream on the same Wembley turf two years later. Now, in 1973–74, England would fail to qualify for the World Cup finals, precipitating the sacking of Sir Alf Ramsey, and United would be relegated from Division One.

The nation as a whole was under no illusions that the swinging times had long gone. As Prime Minister Ted Heath took on the unions, industrial action by the mineworkers meant Britain would soon be bracing itself for the loss of street lighting, early closedown of television stations and power cuts. Evening football matches would be cancelled, and from the first day of 1974 the nation's factories and offices were reduced to a three-day working week to preserve fuel. Even the usual cheer of the Christmas post would be rendered sinister by IRA bombs arriving in mailbags on mainland Britain. The festive season would find United searching for their first League win for more than two months and sitting in 20th position, which the new three-up, three-down regulations meant was no longer a safe one. United fans, in particular, felt their emotional health mocked by Slade's feel-good anthem 'Merry Christmas Everybody', which entered the charts at number one. They could connect far more easily with the state of emergency that Heath's Conservative government were forced to declare for the fifth time during their term of office.

Docherty could have announced a similar condition of panic

after just one game of the season, a shambolic 3–0 defeat at Arsenal. Even after beating Stoke and Queens Park Rangers in their first two home games, United were described by one reporter as 'pink-cheeked second-formers lost in the desert'. QPR's Stan Bowles went as far as claiming, 'They're the worst team we've ever met.' To many it had seemed inconceivable that United could spend another season batting against relegation. Typical was the view of the ever-loyal Norman Giller, who'd assured *Daily Express* readers that they would be 'in touch with the leaders before the race is over'. Docherty himself stated, 'I want us to be in things right to the finish.' Yet the only thing they were in was deep trouble.

The extent of United's disarray was evidenced in a mid-September game at Leicester. Having seen Stepney score during a penalty shoot-out in a pre-season tournament game in Spain, Docherty gave him the responsibility for real. Stepney duly scored and would net the only goal against Birmingham five weeks later. As late as the final game of 1973, he was still the club's joint top scorer. It was hardly one of Docherty's finer strategies: a piece of 'look at me' management that threatened to provoke ridicule and undermine his other players. Even Stepney claimed that it was a poor reflection on Docherty.

The more prosaic attempt to rectify United's problems was a return to the safety-first approach that had upset so many. In becoming the first team to take a point off eventual champions Leeds, Docherty's players were accused by *The Sun*'s John Sadler of resorting to 'the behaviour of the hooligan'. Criticism even came from Docherty's old Hull colleague Terry Neill, who called United's tactics 'brutal'. Docherty responded with, 'What's the point in coming here and having a good open game and losing 6–2? We get relegated and I get the sack.' The tactics were not exactly successful, however, with the Leeds game marking the first in a 14-match sequence in which United won only once.

In the midst of that run came one of those incidents that seemed designed deliberately to destabilise Docherty's players. Having failed to score in eight games, Macari was ordered to play for a combined United reserve and youth team in a testimonial at Mossley. He refused, at which point Docherty told him he would be fined two weeks' wages and placed on the transfer list. Macari spoke to Professional Footballers' Association secretary Cliff Lloyd and was advised to turn up for the match, where he ran the gauntlet of reporters who had clearly been tipped off about the story in their midst. Docherty declared his surprise at seeing the player and told him he could go home, before telling the pressmen, 'Everyone not with us is against us. Every player's attitude must be right.'

After an absence of only one match, Macari was back in favour and no serious transfer discussions took place. He never did figure out what had prompted the episode, saying, 'I couldn't get my head around what was happening there.' Docherty's later explanation was that he felt Macari was lacking commitment because he was unhappy at playing in attack rather than midfield. 'Having established my authority as manager and made my point, I was more inclined to discuss his role in his team,' he added. The episode hints at the same insecurities evident in Docherty's big-name player relationships at Chelsea, the same need to suppress any personality he perceived as a potential threat.

Graham had witnessed similar episodes at Stamford Bridge and would again lose his manager's favour in mid-season when the captaincy was taken from him, reportedly via Docherty snatching the match ball in the dressing-room and giving it to Morgan. The new skipper claimed he was told by Docherty that Graham had asked to relinquish the responsibility because it was affecting his form. Wondering why his friend was still not speaking to him several days later, Morgan approached Graham, who said he'd been led to believe by Docherty that Morgan had been manoeuvring for the role.

Divide and rule, but to what purpose? It was all very well for Docherty to comment after his eventual departure on the political atmosphere within the club, but he was responsible for an element of that himself. Graham would write, 'There was so much backstage acrimony in those early months at United that even Captain Bligh would have thought twice about skippering a team that was in a painful transition period.' And, having lost that captaincy, he appeared to be a victim of more Docherty-manufactured acrimony, saying that 'our love–hate relationship touched rock bottom as he gave me the "leper" treatment'. Graham was dropped and told to train with the youth team, but stubbornly refused to ask for a transfer that would have cost him money.

Four decades on from his United days – which he describes as 'the biggest challenge of my playing career' and 'my biggest disappointment'– Graham is forgiving of a man he now happily gets along with. 'One of Tommy's biggest assets was that he wasn't afraid to make decisions. The only problem was sometimes he got it the wrong way round: he could be 70 per cent wrong and 30 per cent right. People don't realise that when you are in football management you have got to make decisions, and most of the time you have to make unpopular decisions. Tommy would never brush that aside.'

According to Graham, 'Some of the old guard were said to be plotting against the Doc because they resented the way he was ruthlessly reorganising things.' One of those stalwarts, reserve-team coach Foulkes, was sent home after a falling-out with Docherty early in 1974 and told to stay away from the ground. Yet a couple of weeks later, in which time Busby had returned from holiday, Foulkes was back in his role, with Docherty saying, 'I am pleased that this problem has been solved in the best interests of the club.'

Recovered from his injuries, the more avuncular Blunstone arrived at a struggling club in the autumn of 1973 and, despite the potential for unrest, remembers being pleasantly surprised by the mood he discovered. 'It was a good atmosphere. Tommy could make a good atmosphere – although he could make a bad one as well.' According to Blunstone, the relationship at that time between Docherty and Busby contributed to the kind of positive environment that helped override individual squabbles. 'Matt would come out of his office and have a coffee and a chat. But he never interfered, and Tommy loved Matt. I remember being in the boardroom after we'd played badly and everyone was feeling down and Matt said, "Listen, we played at Burnley one day at Christmas and lost 6–1 and then we beat them 6–0 on Boxing Day. So smile when you lose and laugh like hell when you win."'

Docherty and Busby worked together on what had previously seemed an unlikely solution to United's difficulties – the extension of an olive branch to George Best – although both claimed the other had been the driving force behind the return of the wayward superstar. Busby had been to see Best in hospital during the summer, while he was suffering with a thrombosis in his leg, and suggested it was time to return to football.

Docherty would tell BBC's *Match of the Seventies* years later, 'We weren't blessed with too many good players, so Matt and I had a chat one day, and it was on his suggestion: he thought it would be a good idea to bring George back. I was trying anything because

Tommy Docherty with first wife Agnes on their wedding day at Sacred Heart Church in Girvan on 27 December 1949. (Press Association)

Preston North End's 1954 FA Cup finalists: (back row) Harold Mattinson, Bill Cunningham, Joe Walton, George Thompson, Tommy Docherty, Joe Marston, Bill Forbes; (front row) Jimmy Milne (trainer), Tom Finney, Robert Foster, Charlie Wayman, Scot Symon (manager), Jim Baxter, Angus Morrison. (Press Association)

Dressed for success. Chelsea coach Tommy Docherty arrives at Stamford Bridge for the first day of preparation for the 1961–62 season, by the end of which he would be the club's manager. (Press Association)

Docherty uses a Subbuteo table to give a tactical briefing to his Chelsea players at their training ground in Ewell. Ever the public-relations expert, he had allowed some local youngsters to listen in. (Press Association)

FA Cup final managers Tommy Docherty and Bill Nicholson lead out their Chelsea and Tottenham teams at Wembley in 1967, with captains Ron Harris and Dave Mackay behind. (Press Association)

Docherty meets up with his former Chelsea players Allan Harris and Barry Bridges during his 28-day spell as Queens Park Rangers manager in 1968. (Press Association)

Another year, another club. Tommy Docherty raised fans' hopes of an Aston Villa revival during the summer of 1969 but was dismissed with the team battling against relegation. (Press Association)

Docherty spent too long for his liking in his office at SFA headquarters while boss of Scotland, yet international management could have been the ideal long-term career for him. (Press Association)

Manchester United chairman Louis Edwards introduces Tommy Docherty as the club's new manager in December 1973. The pair would form a close bond. (Press Association)

Tommy Docherty was merely the latest manager to believe he could 'handle' the wayward George Best. The two are pictured at Heathrow Airport, bound for Lisbon, after Docherty had welcomed Best back into the United fold – although not for long. (Press Association)

Wembley defeat in 1976 was the fourth FA Cup final loss of Docherty's career. All he could do was attempt to console the likes of Brian Greenhoff and Gerry Daly after United were upset by Second Division Southampton. (Press Association)

A major trophy at last as United beat Liverpool in the 1977 FA Cup final. Docherty is at the centre of celebrations, along with (left to right) Stuart Pearson, Tommy Cavanagh, Lou Macari, Gordon Hill and Frank Blunstone. (Press Association)

A few weeks after victory smiles at Wembley, Docherty was left to present a brave face to the media after his sacking as United manager following the revelation of his relationship with Mary Brown, wife of club physio Laurie Brown. (Press Association)

Docherty's post-United career became a series of mostly unsuccessful engagements, including a return to Loftus Road in May 1979 for a second spell as manager of Queens Park Rangers. (Press Association)

Tommy Docherty leaves court with Mary during his trial for perjury, which had resulted from a disastrous libel case against Willie Morgan and Granada Television. (Press Association)

Docherty acknowledges the Chelsea crowd during a game in 2010. While his relationship with Manchester United has been a remote one during the latter years of his life, he enjoys a warm welcome when he returns to Stamford Bridge. (David Shopland)

we were a bit desperate.' According to David Meek, however, Busby left the decision entirely up to Docherty. Busby had already been stung by accusations of interfering in the reigns of O'Farrell and McGuinness and was clearly sensitive on this topic. When his book *Soccer at the Top* was serialised and published that autumn, a sentence appeared in capital letters to stress that he'd not interfered in Best's relationship with O'Farrell.

Best, who during his United absence had been linked with clubs as diverse as Swansea, New York Cosmos and Durban City, and an indoor tournament in Toronto, met Docherty early in September. Together they mapped out a pathway back to the first team, one that called on him to lose 10 lb and regain match fitness over several weeks. 'He is in marvellous condition considering the length of time he has been out of the game,' Docherty announced. 'No one can say when he will be fit to play again. That is up to him. I think he will train religiously.' Best had always had a reputation as a good trainer – when he wasn't absent – and Docherty expressed confidence that United's players were 'looking forward' to his return. With more optimism than foresight, he concluded, 'His problems outside soccer are behind him.'

Six weeks later, Docherty picked Best for the victory over Birmingham, saying, 'I don't expect him to be the George Best of two years ago, but in half a dozen or eight games I think he will be.' Yet by the time he'd played that number of games the comeback was almost over. Bearded and bloated, Best experienced only two victories during his twelve-game revival. He scored goals in defeats by Tottenham and Coventry and performed capably for the most part, but glimpses of his old outrageous talent were rare.

His final game in a United shirt was a 3–0 defeat at QPR on New Year's Day, after which he failed to turn up for training on the Thursday before an FA Cup tie against Plymouth. In his numerous retellings of the story, Best maintained that his deal with Docherty was that such absences would be tolerated and hushed up as long as he put in the additional work later. When he turned up at Old Trafford on Saturday to find he had been left out, he felt his manager had reneged.

Docherty insists that Best arrived at the ground – smelling of alcohol – at 2.35 p.m., after the official team sheet had to be submitted. Best went to his grave disputing that. He claimed that he attended the pre-match meal and was taken aside by Docherty and Paddy Crerand more than an hour before kick-off and told he was not playing because he had missed training. Crerand contends that the team sheet had been prepared in advance without Best's name. 'Paddy knows the truth and has always supported my story,' Best wrote, before delivering his verdict on Docherty. 'I think he is a funny man. But he can also be a bullshitter.'

Whatever the facts of that day, the greater truth appears to be that Docherty had simply had enough of the late arrivals, non-appearances and indications of drinking. If that constituted a breach of the promise he had made to Best on his return, then so be it. Surely there was a limit to how much he was expected to tolerate?

Graham, who became a noted disciplinarian as a manager, contends, 'I think Tommy handled the George Best situation very well. He had a problem with George and everyone knew George had a problem, but everybody thought that his ability would overcome everything. It was a brave decision, but that was Tommy. He didn't shy away from it.'

Docherty admits, 'There was a bit of ego about [Best's return]. I wanted to be the man who handled George Best, but I couldn't.'

Best walked round an empty Old Trafford after United's 1–0 win, acknowledging that 'I was never going back', and duly failed to report for training that week. 'It had always been a family club,' he wrote. 'Now the wide boys were moving in. And there was Tommy Docherty. This man had promised me one thing and then gone away and done something else entirely. I couldn't work with someone like that.' A long-running saga had reached its conclusion, save for the sequels in such places as Fulham, Fort Lauderdale and, significantly for Docherty, Dunstable.

Having edged past Plymouth, a fourth-round defeat at Ipswich left United to concentrate on an increasingly harrowing fight for survival. Not once between the start of 1974 and the end of the season would they lift themselves out of the relegation places. Defensively, things weren't so bad. Only once in the final fourteen matches did they let in more than a single goal, yet only bottom-placed Norwich scored fewer than United's thirty-eight. At least Stepney would not remain leading scorer, although no one managed more than the meagre six of McIlroy, who did not feel like he got back to full fitness after his car crash until late in the season. Macari scored five, and Jim McCalliog, a £60,000 deadline-day signing from Wolves who inherited the penalty duties, netted four times.

'The year we went down, we didn't score in about 17 games,' says Brian Greenhoff, who was playing his first season of League football 'That was the problem. Our defence and our general football towards the end of that season were good. The first couple of games I played, we played defensively and then we opened up. But when you can't get goals, it gets difficult.'

Failure to find the net against Leeds in front of a 60,000 Old Trafford crowd in February left United bottom of the table and six points adrift of West Ham, who occupied the all-important 19th place. In the days of only two points for a win, it looked increasingly like a lost cause, even with fifteen games to play.

Busby certainly appears to have decided that all hope had gone. Docherty had recently spent £50,000 on a former Chelsea charge, Brentford left-back Stewart Houston, but his suggestion that United invest £400,000 in an unsettled Peter Osgood was rebuffed because Busby felt the money would be better saved for rebuilding in Division Two.

Docherty stated after the Leeds defeat, 'Away from home we have had to play it a bit tight. Now we must go out and win every game.' A year later he would remark, 'We played far too defensively last season. When I finally gave the lads freedom and told them to attack, it was a month too late.'

It was around this time that Busby, as he would recall, approached Docherty and suggested, 'Let's go out with dignity, Tommy.' Docherty adds, 'Matt could see we were sinking, the question was how you put the ship back on an even keel. He said to me once or twice, "If we are going to go down, let's go down with a bit of class and style."'

There was no immediate impact on the scoresheet following the Leeds match. After Greenhoff and Houston scored from a distance to complete a recovery from 2–0 down at Derby, there followed a sequence of five games in which United scored only once while conceding just two goals – hardly thrill-a-minute football. One notable incident, however, occurred during the goalless draw against Wolves when Stepney had a penalty saved by Gary Pierce to mark the end of his spot-kicking duties. Another 0–0 draw, at Manchester City, was notable for the sending off of Macari and Mike Doyle after an altercation in which the United man threw the ball in his rival's face. When both men refused to leave, referee Clive Thomas took the teams off the field and spoke to both managers in the dressing-room, before the game resumed after a seven-minute break. This was hardly the 'dignity' of which Busby had spoken.

The following game, a 3–1 win at Chelsea, is often cited as the one that heralded the new approach. It was also significant for the move of Greenhoff into central defence after Steve James took a kick in the mouth. Greenhoff would eventually settle there for United and earn England caps in that position. At 20, he was one of the new faces cited by chairman Louis Edwards, who said after the match, 'We are resolved to stick by the young players Tommy Docherty is developing. Aren't they marvellous?'

For his part, Greenhoff remembers the thrill of being a young player under the man who had taken him and his father out to dinner several years earlier when he was a Barnsley schoolboy. 'The deal he offered me to sign for Rotherham was better than United, but you can't turn United down,' he says. 'When he came to United he recognised me straight away and I thought, "I am never going to get a better chance." His arrival excited a lot of people, especially the younger players.'

Meanwhile, Edwards's comment that 'we shall not believe we are relegated until the last kick' gained extra credence with a run of four wins and a draw. United rose from bottom to 20th position with four games to play and had writers such as David Lacey saying, 'They have shed, for good one hopes, the dour, desperate image which was so tarnishing the club's reputation.'

But one point from matches at Southampton and Everton brought United into their final home game needing to beat neighbours City to have a chance of staying up. Even then, it would need Norwich to take points off Birmingham to keep alive United's hope of survival until their season finale at Stoke.

A crowd of 56,996, a mixture of suffocating anxiety and pent-up aggression, saw Morgan threatening for the home side and McCalliog forcing full-back Willie Donachie to head off the line. Any lightening of the mood by news of Norwich's goal was replaced by further depression when Birmingham rallied to lead 2–1 at half-time. Defender Colin Barrett cleared off the line from McIlroy's shot, but the further the game advanced the more City appeared likely to score.

Dennis Tueart, FA Cup winner with Sunderland a year earlier, shot twice from long range before, with seven minutes to play, came the moment that remains ingrained in football legend. The barrel-chested figure of Francis Lee drove diagonally across the penalty area and, after he scuffed a shot across goal, Law back-heeled the ball into the net. It was an act of such nonchalance that it screamed disinterest, even reluctance, knowing what it would mean to the club he loved and had been driven out of. Any notion of enjoyment at personal revenge was dispelled by the vacant stare on Law's face as teammates tried to cajole a smile.

As attention focused on the scorer, streams of fans emerged from both ends of the ground, with no apparent idea of what to do once on the pitch. Sheer numbers, however, were enough for referee David Smith to meet with both managers while the players stood watching the scene. Once the game was ready to resume, a shell-shocked Law allowed himself to be substituted. Before long, smoke was belching from in front of the Stretford End and then, as Houston carried the ball forward, he was almost tackled by a lone spectator galloping towards him in black Oxford bags and grey jacket. That empowered a few more intruders, one of whom Buchan guided away. But as City attacked, the dam broke, waves of spectators pouring on from both ends. Some players ran for cover, others walked bemused through the crowds. An appeal from Busby proved futile and Smith abandoned the game, with the Football League quickly deciding to allow the result to stand. If the United fans' intention had been to get the game abandoned and replayed, even that would not have saved them. Birmingham's victory had seen to that.

Docherty delivered champagne to the City dressing-room, while newspaper offices began to prepare headlines such as the *Mirror*'s, 'MOB LAW – United down in disgrace,' and others pondered whether Law had been deliberately trying not to score. Saying he felt 'sick about it all', he had even been found sitting in the United dressing-room with his head in his hands.

According to Jimmy Greenhoff, signed by United in late 1976, Docherty would recall Law's ordeal with enough sympathy to ensure that he was not put in a similar position when United visited his former club. 'I don't think the Doc ever forgot that day. He said to me, "You're not playing today, son." I thought, "Why is he leaving me out against Stoke at Victoria Road?" but he said, "You are not sending them down."'

For his own part, Docherty recalled the pain of relegation by explaining, 'For the first and only time in my life I knew what depression was . . . I had no enthusiasm for anything. I felt like an empty shell.'

A season and a half into the job, Docherty had every reason to believe that his time at Old Trafford might be up. McGuinness and O'Farrell had been squeezed out after approximately the same amount of time because they'd failed to bring back the glory days. Docherty had led the club into the Second Division for the first time since 1938.

Yet Busby assured him that he had the support of the board, stating publicly, 'I believe in Tommy Docherty, that he's capable of making the club great again. Whatever happened this year, I've never seen a player not try. Tommy's made it a happy club again.'

According to Blunstone, thoughts turned quickly to the following season. 'When we went down, we were really flat,' he says and proceeds to give his version of a meeting a few days later when Docherty asked his staff for their thoughts on the approach to Division Two. Recognising that 'we had no Nobby Stiles type in midfield', Blunstone asked his boss, 'What is the best team you have ever managed?'

'Chelsea,' Docherty replied.

'And what system did they play?'

'4–2–4.'

'Correct,' Blunstone continued. 'Why don't we play that?'

'Because,' came the response, 'there are no wingers around!'

Blunstone continues, 'I said, "Don't tell me that. Of all the teams in this country there must be two wingers out there somewhere." And I knew that we had Jimmy Nicholl and Arthur Albiston coming through who could play as overlapping full-backs to support them.'

Crerand had also had such conversations with Docherty, urging him to follow his natural preference for 4–4–2 instead of the 4–3–3 he felt he was lumbered with because of Ian Storey-Moore's injuries. Faced with life in a lower division and the opportunity to rebuild, Docherty was prepared to rethink. It would take a while to find the players Blunstone knew were out there, but the Doc was ready to give his team wings.

14

TRIUMPH AND TANTRUMS

'There was so much politics at Old Trafford, Henry Kissinger wouldn't have lasted 48 hours.'

If the residents of the Second Division had been wondering what the new kids on their block would be like, the answer arrived on the opening day of the 1974–75 season. On the field, a young Manchester United team that included only one European Cup veteran made clear its intentions by strutting to a comfortable two-goal victory. Away from the action, the self-styled 'Red Army' intimidated and terrorised Orient fans in their own home, battled with police and, by the end of the day, appeared to have overrun East London. The rest of the division held its breath and thought, 'There goes the neighbourhood.'

Anyone living close to Brisbane Road awoke to find that United fans had been arriving since the dead of night, sleeping in gardens and doorways. Those travelling later interrupted their journey to battle with Arsenal supporters at Euston station. By the end of the day twenty-seven United fans had been arrested, two policemen reported injured and a London Underground train damaged. 'This football madness must be stamped out, and quickly,' Hector Monro, the minister of sport, declared. 'With jail sentences if necessary.'

Pitch invasions and fighting had prefaced the entrance of the United players, with railings uprooted for use as weapons and glass thrown into the goalmouth. A sun-kissed all-white kit gave Tommy Docherty's players an angelic appearance at odds with the apparent devilment of their followers.

There were still important component parts of the team to arrive – notably, those wingers – but the United line-up was fundamentally that which would serve them well for the next couple of years. Willie Morgan led them out in spite of a nasty injury he'd received to his left eye while playing tennis during the summer. Doctors would report no permanent damage, but his sight would become a factor in events later in the season.

The man Morgan was feeding from the wing was Stuart Pearson, the young centre-forward who had made an impact on Docherty at Hull City and had arrived on a £200,000 transfer. Pearson would be the fulcrum of the attack Docherty was to build; he was a player to whom the ball stuck and who could either hold up possession or quickly bring colleagues into the game. A compact package at 5 ft 10 in., he would score his share of goals, too, without ever being an out-and-out poacher. The amount Docherty paid included £33,000-rated Peter Fletcher, who had managed only seven first-team appearances.

Also gone was Brian Kidd, with whom Docherty had become increasingly impatient, selling him for £85,000 to Arsenal. It left goalkeeper Alex Stepney as the only survivor of 1968 in this line-up: Stepney, Forsyth, Houston, Greenhoff, Holton, Buchan, Morgan, Daly, Pearson, Macari, McCalliog. Sub: McIlroy. 'We had a good young side,' Jim McCalliog recalled. 'He was buzzing, was the Doc. You could feel it.'

Lou Macari remembers, 'We'd had a tough couple of years, but Doc had a way about him of convincing and cajoling people into believing there were better times ahead. He said we'd bounce right back. We didn't know if we would because we knew nothing about that division.'

As police bordered the playing area, United were a class above their opponents, sweeping the ball across the pitch as though it was a training session. Morgan opened the scoring after 28 minutes, and the surprise was that they did not make the game safe until Stewart Houston climbed to head in Alex Forsyth's free kick with 17 minutes remaining.

Of course, discussion after the match centred on United's fans. While Orient manager George Petchey likened them to 'Hitlerites', Docherty did himself few favours with a clumsy, if well-intentioned, defence. 'Their support can be an embarrassment at times,' he said, 'but I'd rather have them as an embarrassment than not at all. They are so biased . . . it's like having 50,000 Bill Shanklys.' His comments provoked *Daily Express* cartoonist Giles to depict a group of locked-up yet smug-looking United fans pointing at some bruised policemen and asking, 'If Tommy Docherty is speaking up for us what are the Fuzz beefing about?'

The march of the Red Army around the provincial outposts of Division Two – stopping little short of rape and pillage, judging by the media reportage – would be as much a feature of United's season as the team's mostly untroubled pathway to the title. 'The greatest period of off-the-field anarchy' in United's history is how authors Richard Kurt and Chris Nickeas describe it. The bigger clubs in bigger towns would often front up, creating full-scale battles at places like Sheffield Wednesday, while the smaller towns cowered behind boarded-up shop windows. 'There is certainly concern that we are to be the next victims,' said Cardiff City secretary Lance Hayward before United's second away game. 'We are taking every possible precaution.'

Docherty banned 18-year-old son Tom from away games, although he insisted, 'The troublemakers are a minority. But because of the size of our following, that minority is larger than any other. The ultimate solution to the problem lies within the courts.'

At the instigation of either Docherty or Stepney, depending on which account you believe, United invited fans to Old Trafford one Sunday morning to meet the squad. The naive hope, according to Stepney, was to let them know that they were letting the club down, although it appeared to be more about being seen to be making an effort to deal with a problem largely beyond the club's control. 'They are bad news,' captain Morgan told a BBC crew. 'It is getting us a bit down now. We want them to stop it, and if they won't stop, we want them to go away and support somebody else.'

Some hope. As the notoriety grew, the 'hooligan' element took greater pride from their exploits and attracted more to their number. As Kurt and Nickeas note, 'The paradox, of course, is that the Red Army grew to gigantic strength and power almost in inverse proportion to the status of the first team.'

United historian Michael Crick attended every United away game at that time and argued, 'I don't think it was really true that the hooligan element was very small,' suggesting that it was 'perhaps a majority of away fans'. Writing in 1997, Kurt and Nickeas concluded, 'There are plenty of forty-something blokes who, basing their judgements on football as an all-round emotional experience, will happily cite 1974–75 as their favourite season ever.'

The football, for the most part, also made it a memorable time for United fans. According to Brian Greenhoff, 'the boss made it clear we would never play defensively again', and there were no complaints about the way in which they won twelve and drew three of their first sixteen games. One report after a victory at Fulham began, 'If entertainment is the name of the game then Manchester United are God's gift to the Second Division.'

The fast start was achieved despite the intermittent presence of Pearson, suffering a hamstring injury, and a reliance on Daly's penalties for five goals in the first seven matches. It earned them a five-point lead over the only team to beat them in those early weeks, Norwich City. Ted MacDougall, scoring regularly since his transfer from West Ham, grabbed both the home team's goals, prompting Docherty to sneer, 'I still think he can't play.' A bit of charm and grace in defeat might not have gone amiss, especially as United's fans were in danger of losing any goodwill that the club was garnering through its refreshing style of play.

'They were one of the most attacking teams in the country,' says Graham, whose exile meant he played no part in what he called 'a very exciting time for United'. According to Sammy McIlroy, 'The accent was to be on attack, attack. We would revert to the recognised Manchester United style of play: going for goals, entertaining and believing that the results would come.'

Docherty dismissed those who suggested United would struggle in the mud and cold of winter, the traditional barb thrown at any footballing team in the days of pitches like paddy fields. 'We are capable of varying our game to suit the conditions,' he said.

Amid the good start to the Division Two campaign came another of those nights still remembered down the decades. When Manchester City arrived at Old Trafford in the third round of the League Cup they were greeted by what Kurt and Nickeas recall as a 'hyperventilating, rip-roaring, white-noise-blasting' crowd of 55,225. This time they were behind fences installed in the wake of the recent pitch invasions. City's Rodney Marsh had two goals ruled out for offside before Daly converted a penalty after seventy-eight minutes to win the game.

Other matches followed that can take their place alongside any United game in the Premier League era for sheer excitement and tribalism. On the final day of November, the visit of second-placed Sunderland drew a crowd of 60,585, the nation's biggest of the season. Pearson gave United the lead after deftly controlling Macari's pass, but Sunderland led 2–1 at the interval. United equalised when Pearson turned his defender this way and that before delivering for Morgan at the far post, and the winning goal came amid tumult when Daly's right-wing cross was turned in by McIlroy. Sunderland defender Dave Watson recalls, 'I still remember what a great game it was and that we were unlucky to lose. It was back to front: defend, attack, defend. A real English game and a fantastic occasion.'

Even in clips of the game available on the Internet or DVD, the noise and fervour of Old Trafford leaps out and assaults the ears in a way that the more sedate atmosphere of the all-seater modern game rarely achieves. United fan and author Jim White recalls, 'The crowd was all part of the experience: the surges, the songs, the camaraderie combined into a thrilling sense of empowerment.' Or, as Kurt and Nickeas, put it, 'Years later, players still marvelled at the blood-boiling excitement of being in the midst of such a maelstrom.'

A week later came total mayhem, on and off the pitch, at Sheffield Wednesday. Hillsborough would eventually see a much darker day, but, with 20,000 United fans spread around the ground, a final tally of three pitch invasions, 106 arrests and 51 injuries seemed bad enough. Keeping tally of the goals was almost as tough. United, leading via Stewart Houston's free kick, collapsed to 3–1 down in the space of 11 minutes as Wednesday surged through the soft centre of their defence after Holton suffered a broken leg. Macari had an easy task for United's second, and Pearson stabbed in after Forsyth's low cross on the run. David Sunley restored Wednesday's lead, but, with police surrounding the field and less than ten minutes remaining, Forsyth's free kick ricocheted around the box until Macari made it 4–4.

It was then that Docherty admitted to seeing promotion on the horizon. 'No other team would have come back against Wednesday the way we did,' he declared. 'I have not said it before, but now I'm sure: we'll be in the First Division next season.'

Sir Matt Busby announced, 'The club is smiling again. The past few years have been like a nightmare. We are back on the right lines again and I've got this feeling deep down that we are going to be OK for a good few years.' Such was the optimism around the club that Frank Blunstone turned down the chance to return to Chelsea as manager in place of the sacked Dave Sexton, putting 'job satisfaction and family happiness' ahead of £15,000 a year.

Martin Buchan, however, says that the season was not always the breeze that some remember. 'We got a good start and never looked back,' he recalls. 'But when Lou Macari said to me recently that Division Two was a piece of cake I wondered if we were playing in the same games. I told him, "If I knock the ball up and you don't fancy chasing it you leave it. If someone knocks the ball past me I can't assume it is going to the keeper." As a defender it wasn't such an easy ride as Lou thought. You couldn't relax at the back. But the season got us into winning ways.'

There had been little opportunity for Docherty to swagger during his time at United, but what he saw now had put the strut back in his stride. Yet, as was so often the case in his career, conflict was walking alongside him.

Morgan would argue later, 'He's humble in bad times but prone to destroy when things are going right. When he arrived at United he was terrific. We were under pressure from relegation and he handled everything right. But it seems he could just not cope with success.' Journalist David Meek saw things differently, claiming that 'he took success in a quite-level headed way and knew enough about football that your luck could change overnight'. Yet Stepney said that Docherty displayed 'the aloofness of a game-cock' and distanced himself from Busby, which eventually seemed like a fatal error.

The relationship with Morgan, his club captain, became particularly complex – just as it had been at Chelsea with Terry Venables* – planting a seed of mutual contempt that would eventually achieve full bloom in the law courts. The skipper was clearly angry when Docherty substituted him at Portsmouth, as he had at Norwich a couple of weeks earlier, and Greenhoff recalled him sitting in a Southsea nightclub deriding his manager. Two games later, Morgan made way for Pearson to score the only goal against Southampton. 'I was so sick that I got changed and went straight home without

---

* Docherty, as we have seen, was prone to switch club captains like he changed his socks: Malcolm, Tambling, Venables and Harris at Chelsea; Charlton, Graham, Morgan and Buchan at United.

waiting for the end,' he said. 'I didn't do it to cause any trouble. It was a spontaneous reaction and I apologised for it afterwards. From then on it seemed to be a matter of having a bet each game on the time I was going to be pulled off.'

Morgan would be substituted on a further five occasions before the end of the season, by which time the Division Two trophy was being delivered to Old Trafford – but not into his hands. In January, Docherty replaced Morgan as captain in the same abrupt manner in which he'd given him the role. At half-time in an FA Cup third round replay at Walsall – where two extra-time goals by the prolific Alan Buckley clinched a 3–2 upset – Docherty was said by observers to have prevented Morgan offering advice to Forsyth, snapping, 'You've got your own troubles without telling him how to play.' Morgan apparently told Docherty there was no point in him being captain if he was to be subjected to such treatment and received an apology in front of the team. Yet it was Buchan who led them out in the next match.

The Docherty–Morgan relationship would descend into a litany of grievance and accusation. It emerged that Docherty had reportedly told an October board meeting that the winger had asked for a transfer and recommended they refuse it. Morgan would deny having made such a demand. Morgan claimed that Docherty wanted him to play in the team despite doubts about his full recovery from his eye injury because the attention he attracted took pressure off his colleagues. Yet Docherty offered Morgan's eyesight as a reason for his intermittent presence in the team during the second half of the season.

After losing the second leg of their League Cup semi-final against Norwich to a headed Colin Suggett goal, following a 2–2 draw at Old Trafford, Morgan claimed that Docherty shook the hand of every player as they entered the dressing-room, but 'when it came to my turn he just turned his back on me'. Dropped again before a game against Hull, Morgan was said by his manager to have been giving '25 per cent effort'.

Morgan's seemingly inevitable exit from Old Trafford was hastened two weeks later with the debut of Steve Coppell, an energetic right winger signed from Tranmere for £40,000, plus another £20,000 after twenty first-team appearances. 'Willie was never the same player after he injured his eye,' Docherty asserts. 'I signed Stevie Coppell to replace him eventually, but he came in and just took off. Willie was seeing things a little bit late.'

Docherty signed Coppell on the recommendation of Busby's former assistant, Jimmy Murphy, who still undertook scouting duties for United. 'Get him as quick as you can. He is different class,' Murphy had told him. Having been playing part-time while studying for an economics degree at Liverpool University, Coppell was earning only £10 a week. But when Tranmere general manager Dave Russell invited him to meet Docherty he instructed him to say he was on £30.

'I am introduced to the Doc, who is his usual ebullient self,' Coppell recounts, 'and he says, "People whose opinion I respect say you are a good prospect. What are you earning?" I told him £30 a week and straight away he came back and said, "We'll double it." To this day I think he said it for effect and whatever I'd said I was on he would have said that.

'It was massively daunting meeting him, but he was a very likeable bloke. I thought driving over if that I agreed terms – and I knew I would because when you are a student on £10 a week even £12 is a lot of money – I would finish my second year at university and put the third on standby. I mentioned this and he said, "Don't you dare. Football can chew you up, spit you out and leave you on the pavement. If you get your degree it is with you for life. You are going to stay on. We'll work around you." I didn't really have a say in it.'

Listed in the programme against Cardiff as 'Kopel' and late for the pre-game lunch after losing his way to the ground, Coppell had to borrow a pair of boots from Pearson because Tranmere had sent his to Aldershot. 'I was frightened to death to speak to any of the players,' he recalls. United had suffered the winter slump that Docherty insisted wouldn't happen, winning only two of eleven games in all competitions since Christmas, and the fans clearly didn't believe that taking off Morgan, one of their favourites, after a goalless hour was the solution. With the boos having barely died down, however, Houston put United ahead from a corner while Coppell was still making his way into position. Then the new boy's first touch set up a second for Pearson. Coppell also, somewhat fortuitously, laid on the final goal for Macari in a 4–0 win.

Coppell had read the speculation about Morgan's future but was not at the club often enough to notice friction between him and

Docherty. Meanwhile, the manager stated it would be down to the players to prove who deserved a place in the team, although Coppell was retained for the rest of the season.

Whereas Morgan's style could be somewhat more languid and thoughtful, also lending itself to a central midfield role, the 19-year-old Liverpudlian was direct and without frills. 'Doc kept instructions to a minimum,' he remembers. 'He told me to just take people on and it didn't matter if I lost it nine times because on the tenth we'd score.'

Buchan argues that there was considerably more to Coppell's game than 'knock it past him and run', as the player himself describes it. 'I was fortunate to play with Best, Law and Charlton, but they were part of the team of the late '60s,' Buchan says. 'Under the Doc, Stevie was the best player I played with. He had everything: intelligence, pace, he was brave, could score goals, make goals and worked his socks off.'

Coppell was part of an approach endorsed by Nottingham Forest manager Brian Clough after United's 1–0 win at the City Ground. 'I have seen enough of the other promotion-chasing clubs to know that United are playing at least 30 per cent more football,' he said.

It was a late-season visit to Old Trafford by York that saw Docherty finally unleash a true 4–2–4 formation. Greenhoff's return to the centre of defence for the injured Steve James created a midfield vacancy that was given to Morgan, albeit on his unfavoured left flank. But it was still only a taste of what was to come in the next two seasons and was not to offer a long-term lifeline to Morgan.

The inevitable end of a United career notable for being the longest by anyone at the club without winning a major honour would come amid more acrimony and contradiction – surrounding United's long summer tour to the Far East and Australasia. According to what Morgan told Jim White, Docherty had informed him that he didn't need to travel with the team and should instead take his family on holiday. Lo and behold, a headline then appeared in the Manchester *Evening News* claiming, 'MORGAN REFUSES TO GO ON TOUR'. There was no possible reconciliation now, and Morgan would return to his former club, Burnley, for £30,000. Says Docherty, 'Willie wanted a free transfer, but the board said no. Matt said he thought I was wrong letting him go.'

Morgan did not go quietly, recounting in a subsequent interview an incident earlier in the season, when he claimed that he and Stepney had been asked by Docherty to speak up against the treatment of players by Tommy Cavanagh in order to provide a reason for his dismissal. Docherty knew neither was the biggest fan of their coach but had apparently misjudged their likely complicity in his scheme. 'We were astounded and both stuck up for Cav,' said Morgan. 'That gave me an insight into Docherty's methods.'

Another accusation levelled by Morgan was that new skipper Buchan's relationship with Docherty ran no more smoothly than his own. Claiming Docherty tried to transfer Buchan on three occasions, he also described a practice match in which Docherty sent Buchan off for questioning the effectiveness of his 'ranting and raving'. He said that the pair had 'repeated verbal clashes in the dressing-room'.

Buchan agrees that 'it wasn't a cosy relationship; we didn't discuss selection and tactics like a cricket captain' and recalls the discussions he'd had earlier over the position in which he was playing. 'He was playing me at left-back. Defensively I was good, but going forward down the left, Ryan Giggs I was not. I said, "If you want to play me at full-back, play me on the right, then I can get forward and get a cross in. I'll do a job for you." I wasn't happy about being expected to go forward like a left winger.

'We did have a bit of a set-to at Ipswich at half-time. He said, "Do you want a move?" so I said, "If that's what you want, get me a move." Next week I was told QPR wanted to sign me and he asked me if I wanted to go. I said, "Yes." I didn't want to, but I wasn't going to back down. I never heard any more about it. I think wiser counsel prevailed and I was back playing in the middle.'

Meanwhile, former captain Graham, who had 'no intention of falling out with Tommy as he tried to needle me', was eventually transferred to Portsmouth in exchange for Ron Davies. The ex-Wales centre-forward, playing eight scoreless League games as substitute, made no more impact than Chelsea's Tommy Baldwin, signed on loan for a couple of matches as cover for Pearson.

McCalliog was sold by Docherty for the second time in his career, to Southampton for £40,000 as the transfer deadline approached. Although the midfielder said he had no regrets about the move, and would be haunting his old boss once again the following year, he maintained he enjoyed a good relationship with Docherty and that it was actually Cavanagh with whom he had fallen out.

Cavanagh could be something of a lightning rod in his own right. A much-travelled player who had been in Preston's reserves during Docherty's spell there, he had managed briefly at Cheltenham Town and coached at Huddersfield and Nottingham Forest before being recommended to Hull by Docherty, who then also asked him to help out with his Scotland squad. He'd been named first-team coach soon after Docherty's arrival at Old Trafford. Former Forest player Storey-Moore recalled that none of the players at that club had ever known training as tough as that instigated by Cavanagh, while Daly claimed that few of the United players liked him, describing him as an 'abusive, aggressive type of chap'.

Cavanagh's preferred approach with any young player elevated to train with the first team was to rebuke them unmercifully for any little mistake. The shouting stopped when they were a little older and Cavanagh was satisfied that they'd passed their initiation and proved they had a temperament capable of taking stick from big crowds.

One of the most famous Cavanagh stories from the time emanates from the start of the 1975–76 season, when Docherty decided to make Irishman Paddy Roche his first-choice goalkeeper and ordered Stepney to train with the reserves, only for the veteran to be recalled when Roche had to return to Dublin following the death of his father. Arriving to find that all the training gear was already taken, Stepney took the field in a scruffy collection of equipment, only to be berated for his appearance by Cavanagh, whose sergeant-major bearing could not abide untidiness. Stepney admitted to being so enraged that he grabbed his coach by the throat, although the watching United players understood the source of his anger. According to Macari, Cavanagh was carrying the can for Docherty, 'whose treatment of Alex had ultimately fuelled the violent response'.

There are two elements to Docherty's propensity to lock horns with his players. First, is the lack of sensitivity it is claimed he displayed towards players for whom he had no long-term use. Compare, for example, the way Graham was treated by Bertie Mee and by Docherty when each considered him surplus to requirements. 'He seemed to like to puncture people who got above themselves,' said Graham. Or consider the allegedly duplicitous manner in which Docherty dealt with Morgan and Law. If you accept the players' version of events it is difficult to find an excuse for Docherty in those cases. You certainly won't find one in the pages of Law's autobiography, where he writes, 'It soon became apparent that Docherty was not a popular figure at Old Trafford, basically because the players did not trust him, and therefore felt insecure.'

Docherty puts criticism of the way he dealt with players down to the natural disappointment and anger of those who know they have no future at a club. 'When you let players go they don't like you,' he says. 'That is understandable. The ones you bring in and give a chance to, they love you. There is never a right way or a nice way to get rid of a player. Players will always have their gripes – and quite rightly – if they didn't think they got a chance. It happens in any walk of life.'

Author Michael Crick argues that it was a case of older players 'rumbling' Docherty, meaning that he could no longer afford to have them around, while McIlroy's summary was, 'If he liked you, and you got along together – which usually meant doing things the way Doc demanded – then all well and good; if you crossed him, then watch out for trouble.' McIlroy felt there were only two ways to deal with Docherty. 'You either keep quiet,' he said, 'or you blast it out with him.'

Buchan fell into the second of those categories. 'I was brought up to stand up for myself,' he says. 'If I thought I had a case I would fight. You have got to have faith in yourself and your ability – and there was a bit of Scots bloody-mindedness!'

One of the relationship breakdowns that would prove ultimately most injurious to Docherty's Old Trafford career was that involving assistant manager Paddy Crerand. As Graham put it, 'They soon fell out and there was an atmosphere whenever they were together.'

Signed from Celtic in February 1963, Scotland wing-half Crerand continued to enjoy a close relationship with Busby even once one had left the managerial seat and the other retired from playing. Busby saw Crerand as a future United manager and Docherty's appointment of him as his assistant was an acknowledgement of that, although Docherty would later say that he wished he'd put Bobby Charlton in the role.

Crerand was one of those who initially welcomed Docherty's arrival as 'a breath of fresh air for a club that had been stagnating'.

Yet, as a Gorbals product himself, he also remained wary of a warning from his former Celtic boss Jock Stein, who called Docherty 'a Glasgow corner boy'. Unhappy with the treatment of Law, Crerand found his trust in Docherty dissipating throughout the relegation season. By the beginning of 1974–75, he said it had 'completely evaporated'. Docherty, he believed, had little faith in his ability and gave him increasingly menial tasks, rarely tolerating his presence at United games. When Crerand was around, such as during a League Cup defeat to Manchester City in late 1975, he was ordered out of the dressing-room. Most damaging of all, Crerand believed, were stories that Docherty was supposedly feeding to Busby about his professionalism, accusing him of drinking and lack of punctuality.

The second aspect of Docherty's relationship issues – perhaps less harmful in the long run than the irretrievable breakdowns with those such as Venables, Morgan and Crerand, but no less a characteristic of his managerial career – were the frequent rows and reconciliations with players who continued to play good football under him and ultimately outlasted him at their clubs: men such as Osgood and McCreadie, Stepney and Macari.

'He took a dislike to everybody at some time or another,' said Macari. 'Most of the time it would blow over in a day or two, then you would be back onside. Other times it didn't. It was Jekyll and Hyde stuff. Confrontation was a technique he was fond of, particularly with the more established players.'

Brian Greenhoff suggests that such incidents are merely the reality of football life, to which the likes of David Beckham, Jaap Stam and Roy Keane would attest. Not every bust-up is caught on camera in the manner of Roberto Mancini and Mario Balotelli on the Manchester City training ground. 'You would see the odd fall-out, but you tried never to get involved in it,' Greenhoff says. 'I am sure it happened with Alex Ferguson. You have a row, but the players go out and do what they have to do and managers don't hold grudges. If Tommy Cav or the Doc had a go at me, I wanted to go out and prove them wrong.'

Buchan adds, 'Doc was very pragmatic. He wasn't there to be popular; he was there to do a job. He was a bubbly, irrepressible character and he was good with players. He talked their language. The only 11 happy players you ever have are those in the first team. Some are unhappy because they are dropped; some will be unhappy because they are injured and frustrated. It's the same at any club in the world. If you are not in the team you are not happy. I think people tend to go overboard on that subject.'

Brian Clough understood the situation Docherty faced, saying, 'Tommy upset a lot of players, but which manager hasn't? Every Saturday the reserve team is upset because they are in the reserves.'

Brawling baseball manager Billy Martin, who was leading the New York Yankees back to the pinnacle of their sport as Docherty was reviving United, would have empathised with his Old Trafford counterpart. Infamous for battles with his players, which often descended into physical confrontation, he understood that there would always be some players on his team who loved him and some who hated him. 'The manager's job,' he stated, 'was to keep everyone else from going over to the side who hated you.'

Docherty insists the matter of mutual affection was an irrelevance to him when it came to performance. 'It really didn't matter if they didn't like you, as long as they could play and would play for you. If your opinion was that he wasn't good enough, you got rid of him. And if he was good enough then it didn't bother me if he didn't like me.'

Macari learned quickly that his best way of dealing with Docherty was to be similarly unconcerned about the state of the relationship. 'The Doc was a laugh a minute,' he says. 'But what I found strange was when there was a confrontation. You'd paid the consequences and you'd be thinking, "Blooming hell, I have dropped a bollock here," and be worried about meeting him again. But next time you saw him, maybe two hours later maybe two days, it was if he'd forgotten the issue. You'd clashed, but very quickly he was back in your camp again.

'I accepted that. All managers are different and I never believed you should be standing in judgement of them. You do what you are told. I had no problems, but it wasn't the same for every player. Over a period of time he fell out with people I could never imagine – Willie Morgan, for example. They were the best of pals, wining and dining together, and had a good captain–manager relationship. It made me think my little tiffs had been nothing. There are lots of people in the game who, once Doc has crossed them, are not going to forget, but I couldn't take that approach because I was aware he was entitled to fall out with me.'

Macari had begun the season disgruntled with Docherty for using him only as injury cover for Pearson and had been further antagonised by his manager telling him he couldn't co-promote a boxing bill at Salford Rugby League club 'without the permission of my directors'. Over the second half of the season, though, Macari settled into the goalscoring midfield role he favoured. His eighteen goals included seven in the run to the League Cup semi-finals, while his total in the League was bettered only by Pearson's seventeen.

He'd scored in three consecutive games and left himself poised for a recall to the Scotland team when United visited Southampton early in April, knowing that a win would clinch promotion with three matches to play. After seventy-six minutes, Macari scored the only goal of an ill-tempered game in which Peter Osgood was booked for one tackle, almost broke Macari's leg in another and elbowed debutant Jimmy Nicholl. 'I was so angry after that tackle,' said Macari, 'that it was a case of me getting sent off or scoring a goal.'

After victory over Fulham, the Division Two title was secured with a draw at Notts County, although United lost a two-goal lead while fighting flared around the ground. 'These hooligans were shocking,' said Docherty. 'The team have admitted that their performances are being affected.'

When the trophy was presented before the last game of the season at home to Blackpool, United's players seemed torn between full-blown celebration and a more sheepish acceptance that they should never have been contesting such a prize. Their performance was triumphant enough, a 4–0 win seeing them finish three points clear of second-placed Aston Villa, who had beaten also promoted Norwich in the League Cup final.

A brief, exciting and fondly remembered episode in United's great history was over, much to the relief of Docherty, who never subscribed to the notion of it having been 'the making' of his side. He refused to accept that the process of revamping his team was easier for being carried out in a winning environment. 'I can't say I have been grateful for our year in the Second Division,' he said. 'I would have much preferred to have plodded along in mid-table.'

What was it about bloody tours? From clashes with officials in Bermuda to food fights in America, you knew to expect drama when Docherty led his team on off-season jaunts. Having already created a stir with the absence of Morgan, Docherty returned from Australia with further damage done to the accord of a squad who had questioned the wisdom of the trip in the first place. 'We wondered why we were going away for thirty days and playing an eight-game tour,' says Greenhoff. 'But they obviously wanted to keep us fit.'

Problems began when those who joined up with the squad late after playing for Scotland – Macari, Forsyth, Houston and Buchan – were told that their laundry had to be paid for out of their £2 per day spending money. After Docherty dug in his heels, it was the arrival of Busby on the scene that resulted in an increased allowance of £6.

Money reared its ugly head again when Docherty invited Coppell, McIlroy and Greenhoff to help him form a head-tennis team for a much-anticipated tournament in Perth. Each man would pick up A$150, but the inexperienced trio all appeared unaware of the tradition of donating such earnings to the players' pool. The senior players were quick to highlight the rule when they found out about the deal.

Coppell explains, 'I thought nothing of it. I hardly ever spoke to any players. I was still frightened to death and only met them on match days. Going away was a chance for me to get to know everyone. We had some kind of meeting where Lou and Martin piped up, "This is out of order. You are representing the club. The money should be split." I said that it seemed fair to me to split it among the squad and the meeting closed.

'I was in the lift and the Doc got in. "You little shit," he said. "When you are in that situation you back me 100 per cent or you are on the next plane home. When I say do something you do it, and if you don't you'll never play again." I was totally stunned. I didn't really want to do the head-tennis anyway and next minute I get this barrage of abuse. He had settled down next time I saw him, but I saw a side of him I'd not seen before. I knew I didn't want to get on the wrong side of him.'

Greenhoff recalls, 'I wasn't happy about it and the Doc wasn't happy. The senior players were never going to get the money off him, but I remember me, Stevie and Sammy being threatened with expulsion from the players' pool. It was all very petty. It was worth about $40 each to them. I was on about £80 quid a week and they were on £200 and they wanted to take $40 dollars off a kid. I found it very poor.'

Before the end of the tour, the players demanded to meet with Docherty. 'It was like something from a third-rate Western film,' was Stepney's description. Eyewitnesses recall the manager sitting at a table in front of his players and responding to their grievances with criticism and insults while working his way through a bottle of brandy. There were threats of careers at United being terminated and Coppell recalled being called 'a cunt'. Full-back Arthur Albiston, one of several inexperience players on the tour, had been spared by Docherty, who told him he was too young to attend the meeting.

According to Greenhoff, 'the tension lasted for three or four days and then we got on with things', which would include returning to make a storming start to their First Division campaign. It offers evidence of several things, not least the lack of today's around-the-clock media scrutiny, which probably would have kept such a potentially explosive pot boiling for much longer. As David Meek explains, 'In those days, as the local reporter, you didn't look for the seamy side. I knew he had fallen out with a few, but you didn't write much about it. It wasn't seen as the task of the local reporter.'

Also, it says much of the professionalism of the players that such matters could be so quickly put behind them. And does it not suggest that there must have been something about Docherty that, despite the chronic aggravation, kept his players performing to such a high level? Something beyond the 'I'll show you' mentality he instilled in those he had taken to task?

For some, it was the sheer humour of the man. 'Normally when a manager falls out with the players he is probably on the slippery slope to getting the sack,' ventures Macari. 'But it was great to be part of United at that time, on and off the pitch. There is nobody in football now who manages the way he did. He was the life and soul of the party and, no matter what people say about him, he is funny. There was always a great atmosphere in the camp.'

Docherty tolerated pranks such as Macari locking Daly and Roche in their Belgrade hotel room for 24 hours without a phone or food, while Jimmy Greenhoff describes the laughter that would break out in the dressing-room not long after Docherty's arrival, in contrast to the silence that existed under successor Dave Sexton.

Docherty could be so many different things – good and bad – to different people, but few doubt his love of the game, a fervour that transmitted itself to his players. 'He probably never became in his career what he should have been,' says Graham, 'but you couldn't doubt his passion. It was his biggest asset. He loved football. People who played with him at Arsenal always spoke about his unbelievable passion. Enthusiasm just gushes out of him.'

Coppell states, 'I had nothing but respect for him – he was always surprising. At half-time he would come in and bollock you even though you were winning, and when you were two down he would just tell you to keep playing the same way and you'd get a result. It was not logical, but it seemed to work. He had such energy, even when he played five-a-sides. And he used to have a drink occasionally and he'd always throw the dregs on the carpet. He and Tommy Cav would have a glass of wine and they would sprinkle the last drops on the floor. I don't know if they thought it was good luck, but it seemed to suit him. "I don't give a shit. I am just going to do my own thing."'

Bobby Charlton declared, 'Whatever else was said about Tommy Docherty, there was no question about the fact that he knew the game,' while winger Gordon Hill, whose first of three stints under Docherty would begin in November 1975, says, 'Having played at the top level, he understands where you are coming from and you can understand him. He hated to lose. In one Friday training session he nearly broke my neck; he came in to tackle me from behind and just blind-sided me. He said sorry and there was never any malice about it.

'We stayed at Mottram Hall before some FA Cup games and one time we stayed on the Saturday night and went for a walk on Sunday. The waiters there offered the Doc a game. There was a cow pasture there so they put a couple of coats down. Cav, Frank, the boss and some others were playing and some of us were sitting on the fence watching. The waiters were Italian and Spanish and, I am not kidding you, the Doc kicked the shit out of them. The day before, we had been playing in front of 50,000 and now the Doc was taking it just as seriously. Afterwards he said to them, "Don't spit in my food."'

Brian Greenhoff insists, 'I have always had nothing but respect for him. Everything I achieved in football came from when he took me under his wing. One or two players had problems with him, but I didn't. He was never anything but totally honest with me and that got the best out of me.'

Nowithstanding the strange story of Docherty's attempt to be rid of Cavanagh, he seems to have had a working relationship with his support staff that helped maximise the potential at their disposal. 'He had a perfect sidekick in Tommy Cav,' Greenhoff continues. 'They could bounce off each other. Sometimes he would wait for Cav to come in and bollock somebody and he would let him do it. Then he would calm it down. It is how you go about getting the best out of some players.'

Hill adds, 'There was a good relationship between TD, TC and Frank at that time. The boss told them exactly what he was looking for and they understood what they were trying to achieve. They were a nice little team.'

Docherty was not one to rule Old Trafford with an iron fist. 'Strict discipline was not something that was instilled at United,' according to Macari, who frequently found himself thinking, 'That would never have been allowed at Celtic.'

But, Hill says, 'When he kicked you up the arse, my God, you knew it. He used to come in after we'd lost and was very humble. He didn't rant and rave. He would walk around saying, "I cannot believe you have given that game away." It was positive. It was not, "You're fucking shite, the lot of you." If it got to a certain point then Frank or Tommy Cav would step in and soften the blow. That would stop the boss from really going mad, but he knew you didn't need to tell a pro he'd had a nightmare game.

'In those days you knew largely what the opposition would do and the boss's strength was using that to plant confidence in you. He'd say, "Gordy, that defender can't play. If you go at him once and beat him he will be so careful that you'll have beaten him for the whole game." They did their scouting, but they wouldn't sit on a computer. They would watch a game and look at the form and then they brought it in when they talked to you about your own game. After training on a Friday we'd sit there for about half an hour to an hour going over it.'

Buchan explains, 'You knew what was expected of you. Doc would run through the opposition in an almost comical way: "That right back, I have seen the *Queen Mary* turn quicker." But he would get across what you needed to know. It would be serious and with humour at the same time.'

Now, the First Division would be a brighter place for the return of those Docherty traits to the top flight. 'This is only the beginning,' he promised as he contemplated what lay ahead. 'Give us two years and we will be back in business again, competing for major honours.' It would take half that time.

15

RETURN TICKET TO WEMBLEY

'The feeling of losing the Cup final must be worse than dying. At least if you're dead you don't have to read about it in the papers the next day.'

Martin Buchan states it unequivocally. 'Those two years under the Doc back in the First Division were the happiest of my playing career.' Many of those who packed out United's matches during that time – even if they continued to watch throughout the Alex Ferguson era – hold equally fond memories. Old Trafford, birthplace of the 'Busby Babes', Bobby Charlton's 'Theatre of Dreams', was witnessing something special once again.

'There was some trepidation going back in to the top division,' Buchan continues. 'But you felt you could give anybody a two-goal start at Old Trafford and beat them. We used to train at the stadium on Friday then go up to the old boardroom and have a pot of tea and Tommy would give us his team talk. Nobody would rush away and you could almost touch the players' anticipation. It was the place to be.'

Steve Coppell remembers, 'Tommy Cavanagh used to stand in the changing-room and say, "Shut the door. We've got to keep the energy in the room. The boys are buzzing." Everyone was so raring to go that we would play at a high tempo and, more often than not, we'd beat teams.'

Yet as United's return season in Division One approached, Tommy Docherty was either up to his old tricks or suffering from an attack of modesty, even stage fright. 'I don't want to put too heavy a burden on the players, the club or myself,' he said. 'I'll be happy if we go through the season without too much pressure on us, never looking like winning anything and never being in danger.'

His ego boosted by United's Division Two success, it is hard to imagine Docherty being truly daunted by what lay ahead, honestly desirous of a low-key campaign. Besides, the combination of the biggest club in the country, one of football's most outspoken managers and a vibrant young team were hardly the components of a quiet life. As early as the first six games of the season – five wins and a draw – it was clear that his comments could be disregarded. Momentum was building on a wild ride that at one point promised to bring a League and Cup double to Old Trafford, a feat beyond even Matt Busby. United were on top of the table as late as the end of January, just as a thrilling FA Cup run was gathering speed.

Docherty began the season with an extended contract that took him to the end of 1979 and made him the nation's best-paid manager at a reported £25,000 per year. 'We felt we had to make some move towards recognising what [he] has achieved so far,' said chairman Louis Edwards.

'The financial part of it is very satisfying,' Docherty responded, 'but the main thing is the confidence the board has shown. This gives me the time necessary to complete the team rebuilding and make United a force everybody will respect.'

The most significant summer signing had not exactly set Stretford End pulses racing. Tommy Jackson, a Northern Ireland midfielder, was acquired from Nottingham Forest on a free transfer, mainly to skipper the reserve team. But when United – fresh from seeing Jim Holton and Lou Macari sent off in pre-season games in Denmark – re-entered Division One with a 2–0 win at Wolves, Jackson was in the number-four shirt. He would retain it until Docherty finally completed his winged vision in November.

Even playing with less natural width than he desired, United were announcing their return in scintillating fashion. 'Back where they belong,' was how the BBC's Barry Davies described it at the first home game, also noting Old Trafford's new restaurants and executive boxes. Still sporting summer tans, United kicked sand in the faces of a Sheffield United team that had no answer to wave after irresistible wave of attack, Stuart Pearson scoring twice.

United led the table after their unbeaten six-match run. The final game of that sequence was a 3–2 home victory over Tottenham in which Docherty made his first unenforced change of the season, dropping right-back Alex Forsyth for young Irishman Jimmy Nicholl.

Frank Blunstone recalls, 'Tommy said, "I'll put Forsyth in the reserves and see how he does." You can tell a lot about players in the reserves. Some don't bother their arse and some will give you the same as playing in a Cup final. We were sitting in his office later and there was a knock on the door. Forsyth is there saying, "Why am I in the fucking reserves tomorrow?" Doc answers, "Because the A team haven't got a game." Alex went off with his tail between his legs. Tommy wanted to shake him up and he did all right next day. He said, "I told him, didn't I?" Sometimes players came out from seeing him wishing they hadn't gone in.'

As United travelled to face unbeaten Queens Park Rangers, Busby enthused about the 'rehabilitation' under Docherty, named Manager of the Month for August. 'A lot of new young blood has been brought in,' said Busby. 'Not only are they winning, but the way they are playing is so pleasing it makes us feel that once more we have a young team capable of bringing honour to the club. They are constructive, penetrating and attractive.'

Cavanagh claimed that 'the greatest club in football have got back their self-respect – and it's down to the Doc', and further praise was forthcoming even after a 1–0 defeat at Loftus Road. Writer David Miller argued that 'United's performance was one of the most significant I have seen in the past ten years', his statement founded upon the fact that they 'attacked flat out', recalling 'the spirit of the Fifties'.

It was a similar story at Manchester City a couple of weeks later when the two teams shared four first-half goals in an exhilarating 2–2 draw contested against an ear-splitting background of noise. Another two weeks on, United won at fourth-placed Leeds as Sammy McIlroy lashed in two goals. 'We have a terrible affliction, you know,' beamed Docherty. 'We play football.'

Yet there were signs of vulnerability that Docherty intended to eliminate. After defeat at West Ham cost them the First Division leadership, he finally executed his plan to place Paddy Roche in goal instead of Stepney, who had cost United a game at Derby by dropping the ball at the feet of Charlie George and whose mix-up with Buchan had led to a goal at Upton Park.[*] According to Stepney, Docherty told the remaining hero of 1968 to 'finish your time in the reserves' and then ceased to speak to him.

Norwich were beaten in Roche's first game, but it was the Irishman's second match, at Anfield, where he suffered the defining moment of his ill-fated United career. Ian Callaghan delivered an inswinging, diagonal cross from the right and Roche, climbing over Greenhoff's shoulders, tried to clasp the ball to his body. 'It was an easy header for me,' says Greenhoff. 'He should have left it.' To Roche's horror, the ball fell from his grasp for Steve Heighway to score a simple goal. The feared duo of Kevin Keegan and John Toshack each set up the other for further goals in a 3–1 victory.

Four days later, Roche was not the only one to blame as Manchester City exacted revenge for the previous season's League Cup defeat with a 4–0 thumping in the fourth round at Maine Road, although he did let one goal slide under his body.

However, the day was not a disaster for Docherty. Having failed to get Huddersfield to part with 18-year-old Martin Fowler, he'd instead completed the £80,000 transfer of 21-year-old Millwall winger Gordon Hill, a favourite at The Den who had earned himself the nickname 'Merlin'.

'We'd already bought Steve Coppell,' explains Blunstone, 'and Bill Foulkes suggested we look at this winger who had been on loan with him in Chicago in the NASL. Signing Gordon meant we could go to a real 4–2–4, and people loved it.'

Hill, who even now refers to Docherty as 'the Boss', adds, 'I had known about him because I used to go to watch Chelsea and he'd had a very successful team. He had a self-destruct button, but at United you thought this might be where he is going to stay for some time.'

Saturday, 15 November saw Hill's debut in a 2–0 win against Aston Villa. It rounded out the vision Docherty had for his team, with Coppell and Hill patrolling the flanks either side of midfielders Daly and Macari. 'I have completed the jigsaw,' he announced. The uniqueness of the formation at that time in English football should

---

[*] Stepney had also been involved in a bizarre incident during an early season win at Birmingham, where he was replaced in goal by Greenhoff after he suffered a locked jaw while shouting at his defenders.

not be underestimated. Few teams had either the personnel, or the balls, to contemplate such a move. Those who had one attacking wide man would usually balance it by having their midfielder on the opposite flank playing a deeper and more central role.

Docherty, having already encouraged the speedy Coppell's direct style, sent out Hill with simple instructions. 'Go out and create as much as you can,' he told him. 'Get crosses in and score goals. That is why we signed you. If you can't get back, don't worry. I didn't buy you to play as a defender.'

Buchan ventures, 'Hilly probably had more talent than Steve, but he could be frustrating at times. He came out with breathtaking bits of skill and scored a lot of goals for a winger, but I felt he could have scored a few more.'

Hill, who says Docherty's confidence was 'a reassurance', adds, 'He always said he didn't mind them scoring one as long as we scored two. I loved that. I loved the entertaining way he had Chelsea play. They might have been beaten 4–3, but people went away saying what a great game it had been. I also got a lot of inspiration from Frank Blunstone because he was an England winger. He said, "If you are causing them problems then they are not attacking our goal."

'They had done their homework in putting us all together. They had a great worker in Stevie Coppell, who would save you twenty goals and score five, while I would score you twenty goals and not even defend five. The Boss would say, "Give the ball to the two chookies and let them do the damage." You can't fault him for the way he wanted his teams to play.'

As Hill was settling into the side, Roche's days were drawing closer to conclusion at Highbury, where Alan Ball gave the home team the lead in 12 seconds. After 25 minutes, Roche went after – and missed – a Sammy Nelson free kick, leading to a second goal. With Pearson having pulled one back and the game approaching its conclusion, Roche pawed a George Armstrong corner into his own goal. A popular teammate, he now had the United fans on his back and Docherty had no choice but to revert back to Stepney, who immediately kept a pair of clean sheets.

It was United's attacking play that once again earned the plaudits as they reprised their early season demolition of Sheffield United with a 4–1 win at Bramall Lane, where Pearson netted twice and

Hill scored his first United goal. The winger was on the scoresheet in three of the next five games as United returned to first place.

With his team picking up points and pleasing the eye, Docherty was ready for some evangelism, especially after a 3–1 home win against struggling Birmingham. The visitors' resistance was broken by a Forsyth half-volley before Hill set up Macari and a defensive lapse gave McIlroy an easy third. Birmingham's stubbornness spilled into violence when full-back Archie Styles earned a sending off by hacking at and stamping on Coppell. Speaking to the television cameras, Docherty complained, 'If the referee had booked or sent off everyone he could have, they'd have ended up with about five men. We are not only trying to play attractive football, we are trying to clean up the game by the way we play.'

Docherty apologised publicly to Birmingham the following day, admitting he had 'overreacted'. However, the state of the game was becoming a common theme of his. Earlier in the season, as England reflected on failure to advance from their European Championship qualifying group under Don Revie, he had stated, 'There will be no sympathy for players and managers from the public until clubs realise that their paramount duty is to please the fans. We have to stop strangling our domestic game with caution.'

A few months earlier, he'd commented, 'I am concerned about the way football is going. Dangerous play, such as tackles from behind, is creeping back into soccer . . . I am not pleading for a namby-pamby type of game, I was a very physical player myself, but times are changing and I honestly believe that fans want to see creative, skilful soccer allowed to flourish.'

Docherty, of course, had been less idealistic when United were in peril two years earlier, but now he had first place in the table to lend weight to his romanticism. *Evening News* reporter David Meek even called this United side 'the best combined footballing team that they have perhaps ever produced'. A critic of the early style of Docherty's team, Meek admits, 'I completely changed by my tune from the Division Two campaign onwards. They brought back playing with wingers, which was not fashionable, and it was innovative football.'

Meanwhile David Miller of the *Daily Express* placed United in a wider context by writing:

The Red Revolution, the transformation of Manchester United in 18 months from relegation back to the First Division leadership, is not only one of the most exciting phases of their colourful history but a tribute to the former Jekyll and Hyde – Tommy Docherty. United's example of playing with two conventional wingers, Steve Coppell and ex-Millwall star Gordon Hill, is the most significant development of this season as English soccer tries to get back on the rails.

Docherty explained that one of the advantages of wingers was that it helped prevent full-backs from acting as additional attackers, a development in English football in which he had played a major part. Coppell explains, 'It was a small, quick, fiery team. The way we played was to get the ball out wide, get crosses in and get people in the box. From what I have been told, Doc's football philosophy was born out of the Preston team he played in with Tom Finney. I think it was an expression of that style, which he fine-tuned and upped the tempo on. People thought he would be more conservative in Division One, but if anything he was even more full-on. He wanted us to be quicker, even more ruthless getting at teams.'

Hill recalls, 'He wanted us to get the ball up, knock it wide, get to the bye-line and cross it. That will always be the most dangerous ball. Defenders could kick the shit out of you, but we overcame that with players like Lou Macari, who I have so much admiration for. And can you imagine what our players could have done today on these pitches with these balls? We got it out wide because that was the only part where there was any grass. The style of football United had been built on, and are still playing; their never-say-die attitude; the way they can play at 100 mph – that was us. The Doc wanted his teams to entertain and play open, flying football. He wanted them to attack and be sophisticated enough to defend.'

Blunstone believes Docherty achieved his aim of replicating the style of his Chelsea team of the 1960s. 'It was very similar,' he says. 'It was 4–2–4 when we were attacking and 4–4–2 when defending. Hilly liked to have a strike at goal and nine times out of ten he hit the target.'

Docherty recalls, 'They blended beautifully. After I saw Brazil play I wanted 4–2–4 so the midfield four were all creative players and we encouraged the full-backs to get forward. I used to be excited on a Friday night because I loved to watch them play. I was a fan. I'd been brought up with wingers.

'I wouldn't have got in my United team. I wasn't good enough and we didn't have a ball-winner. When we lost the ball we attacked the opposition player and the ball to make them do things hurriedly and make a mistake. We were like flies round a sugar bowl. Ours was a young man's game; you worked twice as hard when you didn't have the ball. Coppell was ideal for it, although Hill was different. He was an entertainer, a goalscorer.'

Despite Docherty's insistence on perpetual motion, United's players bear none of the accusations – as at Aston Villa – of pushing too hard to achieve it. Pearson explained that 'the training was spot on; we never left our legs on the training pitch' and recalled frequent days off and considerable care over the state of players' bodies.

Greenhoff continues, 'The Doc decided we were going to be "up and at 'em" and he had the quick players to do it. We didn't have anybody in midfield who could tackle, but what Lou was good at was pinching the ball.'

Having seen his position at centre-back further cemented when Holton suffered another broken leg in a reserve game, Greenhoff believes his move into the back four had been because of Docherty's desire for an expansive game. 'It just seemed to happen. I think they wanted someone who could come out with the ball. I wasn't the greatest defender; I used to make a nuisance of myself, and I was lucky to have a fantastic player alongside me. Everybody had 6 ft 3 in. centre-forwards so I wasn't going to win much in the air, but Martin was covering for me. The longer we played alongside each other, the better we got. People said we played an offside trap, but we just practised attacking the ball. If it was knocked out we all came out together. If attackers were too lazy to come with us and got caught offside that was their fault.'

Docherty adds, 'I found Brian's best position by accident. He was good upstairs and good on the ball. We started playing football from the central defender positions, knocking the ball about and playing one-twos. Mind you, you never asked Brian what was wrong with him because he was a hypochondriac. But if it hadn't been for injury I would never have thought about him as a centre-back. Buchan wasn't a great tackler – OK in the air but not great – but so quick and could read the game. He used to run alongside people and just overtake them. It was like a challenge to him to see if he could leave it to the last minute, but when he made up his mind he got the ball.'

If United's approach appeared to lend itself more to the on-the-day nature of knockout football than the week-in, week-out consistency required to win the League, a run of four games without maximum points during February bore this out. A goalless home draw against Liverpool cost them a chance to steal a significant march on the title favourites, although a 4–0 victory over West Ham at the end of the month left them level on points with the Anfield side and QPR. But with United safely through to the quarter-finals of the FA Cup, the remainder of the season was always likely to become a battle of priorities.

Having beaten lower-division opposition in Oxford, via a pair of Daly penalties, and Peterborough, United had faced their first significant test at Leicester in the fifth round. After leading at half-time through Macari and Daly, they spent most of the second half defending, although Leicester manager Jimmy Bloomfield was gracious enough to talk about a 'victory for football' after the game rather than dwelling on United's good fortune in a 2–1 victory. Whether it was genuine admiration, pure ostentation or the effects of Valentine's Day, Docherty's response at the final whistle was to race towards Stepney for a very public embrace. Stepney, like a child avoiding a kiss from a lavender-fragranced aunt, wanted no piece of it, although he did admit that Docherty's apparent reconciliation eased the remainder of their time together. In fact, he always felt that Docherty actually wanted to like him, but his links with United's glorious past kept getting in the way.

The sixth round paired United with Wolves, lying just off the bottom of Division One, for one of the most dramatic episodes of the Docherty era. He had already upset the Midlanders in November, when opposition centre-half John McAlle accused Docherty of bad-mouthing him to referee Kevin McNally at half-time. McAlle was subsequently sent off following a 57th-minute foul on Pearson. 'I waited for Docherty after the match and called him a bastard,' McAlle said. Docherty accepted that he had been to see the referee, but denied that he'd mentioned the Wolves defender, who had already been booked.

The 59,433 inside Old Trafford for the quarter-final quickly saw the best of Daly, all poise and balance as he stepped through challenges to force a low save from Phil Parkes. Pearson lifted the ball against the bar and Parkes made a double save to keep the game scoreless at half-time. Against the run of play John Richards gave Wolves the lead, but United forced a replay when Daly drove into the box and shot across Parkes.

Wolves struck twice in the first 21 minutes of the replay, through Steve Kindon and Richards, and Docherty's 31st-minute substitution of Macari by Nicholl was caused by the midfielder's lingering groin injury rather than a tactical rethink. Within five minutes, Pearson had headed in from Hill's corner, but it was not until fifteen minutes from time that Greenhoff levelled the tie. Having not led throughout 180 minutes of football, United took a decisive advantage when McIlroy ran through to score six minutes into extra time.

The semi-final draw paired United with League champions Derby, leaving Second Division Southampton to face Third Division Crystal Palace at Stamford Bridge. The general consensus was that the winners in Sheffield would have one hand on the trophy. Docherty displayed his contrary nature by warning his players not to indulge in any predictions and then promptly announcing, 'This is the first time the FA Cup final will have been played at Hillsborough.'

Docherty approached the game like the final itself, even marching his players out of the hotel in which they'd planned to stay in the Derbyshire town of Buxton after discovering dirty bedrooms, diverting them instead to the favoured Mottram Hall. Macari was not considered fit enough to play and the ever-willing David McCreery received confirmation of his place on the morning of the match.

The first Saturday of April 1976 will be forever remembered by United fans as Gordon Hill's day. It was the winger who ensured that United would advance to Wembley as favourites to win their first trophy since their European Cup triumph eight years earlier. According to Macari, 'This match summed up Manchester United under the Doc for me: great football played on the deck at good pace with a pair of wingers causing havoc. Gordon Hill never played a better game in a red shirt.'

It was the kind of performance that prompted Coppell to say in later years, 'Gordon was one of the best players I have ever seen, as he was very intuitive and had a very handy knack for getting goals.' That knack took only 12 minutes of an impassioned afternoon to manifest itself. Coppell had already stabbed over from close range when Hill, slightly right of centre and just outside the penalty area, took a couple of touches to tee up an unstoppable curling left-foot shot. What is often overlooked in the memory of Hill's finish is a build-up typical of this direct, fast-paced United team. Greenhoff seized on a misplaced pass, driving it low to Hill, who laid the ball off to Daly on the left and cut inside to be well placed to receive the return pass. It was simple and beautiful.

Derby, unable to reproduce the form of their strong challenge to defend the League title, did little to justify the boast of Welsh winger Leighton James, a £330,000 signing from Burnley, who had told United players outside the dressing-room that it was 'not worth turning up'. James was subdued by Forsyth's strong tackling, while Scotland international Bruce Rioch made his presence felt more by physical assaults on McIlroy and Pearson than with the ball. Derby's best chances fell to their rangy centre-forward, Roger Davies, but twice he was denied by Stepney.

Rioch admits, 'They had a fit, young, mobile team and they didn't allow us to settle. They set about getting around us and were able to get close to us and niggle us, denying us the time and space we wanted. They deserved their victory.'

That result was secured six minutes from time after Coppell was upended just outside the area by Steve Powell. Hill stepped forward and, with the help of a deflection, drove the free kick inside keeper Graham Moseley's left post. '[Hill] won us the semi-final himself,' said Forsyth. 'Give Gordon a bit of space, he would destroy you.' The fact that it was Hill and Coppell who had made the decisive late contribution was significant, given that both had been feeling weary-legged after Docherty insisted on taking them rabbit shooting the day before the game.

With training reduced to accommodate their remaining games, United had in the meantime maintained their title challenge with a typical 4–3 romp at Newcastle and a 3–0 home win over Middlesbrough, leaving them second with six games to play. But with Wembley secure and injuries denying them Pearson, Coppell and Daly for varying lengths of time, three of the next five games were lost, leaving United to settle for third place. 'We got one or two injuries and that is when you notice not having a big squad,' says Greenhoff. 'We got caught out.'

Hill confesses that the thought of playing at Wembley was difficult to put to the back of his mind during League games. 'You wanted to win,' he says, 'but it was difficult to make yourself play too hard.' Others, such as Buchan and McIlroy, insist that they played as keenly as ever, both in pursuit of points and also to ensure that they kept their place in the team for Wembley.

Then there were the inevitable off-field distractions, as much a part of FA Cup finals in the pre-Premier League era as someone in a white suit leading the community singing. A visit to a shoe factory; fittings for suits; the recording of a single, 'Manchester United', that reached the heights of number 50 in the charts; squabbles with newspapers unwilling to put their £250 into the players' pool for interviews; bickering about whether money could be individually earned or entirely shared – all were part of the backdrop to a fading League campaign that Docherty was powerless to restore. According to Daly, the Wembley build-up was a 'load of shit' that 'got out of control'.

Whatever the reason for performances such as a first home loss of the season against Stoke, the FA Cup was a formality, wasn't it? Certainly according to most experts, who offered little hope to a veteran Southampton team whose Division Two promotion push had come up short. The Saints had earned their place at Wembley by overcoming only one top-flight team, Aston Villa, and had concluded their journey with a 2–0 win at Stamford Bridge against Palace in the 'other' semi-final. That result denied the media the headline-grabbing prospect of the Doc versus Big Mal, and the sight of Palace boss Malcolm Allison in his lucky fedora hat leading out his team alongside Docherty. Not that the opposition were short of characters. In a team led by former guardsman Lawrie McMenemy, England forward Mick Channon was partnered by Peter Osgood, signed from Chelsea two years earlier for £275,000, while Jim McCalliog, twice sold by Docherty, supported them from midfield.

'You can't take anything for granted,' notes Greenhoff. 'When you looked at the Southampton team you saw a lot of good players. As a defender, you know you're going to have a hard game against Osgood and Channon. We did think that if we got into them for 15 minutes and scored we would win, but the longer the game goes on, you get nervous about it. It only takes one deflected shot.'

The combination of off-field activity, specialised preparation such as additional massage sessions and their stay in a Hertfordshire hotel meant there was a limit to how much Docherty could maintain a semblance of normality. He did, however, avoid further unsettling his players by keeping quiet his signing of Burnley centre-half Colin Waldron – another young player he'd had at Chelsea – on a free transfer.

Docherty's pre-game message urged his men to believe in themselves, that if they played as they had all season victory would be theirs. Yet Buchan reveals, 'I had misgivings because I could see that some of the younger lads got carried away with the player pool. A lot of them thought they just had to turn up to get their medals. Southampton had a very experienced side. They weren't mugs.'

On a typically sunny Cup final day, Docherty, in brown jacket, tan trousers and shirt – set off by a brown and tan tie – looked like *The Sweeney*'s Jack Regan on a night out as the teams emerged from among the Saints fans cramming Wembley's tunnel end. Meeting the teams before the game, the Duke of Edinburgh enjoyed his brief chat with Docherty, putting a friendly hand on his arm as their conversation ended. Docherty helped introduce the following team to the Duke: Stepney, Forsyth, Houston, Daly, Greenhoff, Buchan, Coppell, McIlroy, Pearson, Macari. Hill. Sub: McCreery.

United's hopes of dulling the yellow-shirted underdogs' spirit with an early goal could have been fulfilled when Saints goalkeeper Ian Turner spilled a left-foot shot by Coppell, but not quite close enough to Macari or Pearson. Hill attacked veteran right-back Peter Rodrigues to set up a shot for Pearson, again saved uncertainly. He also had his own attempted lob snuffed out by Turner after 13 minutes.

As Greenhoff had feared, the longer United went without making territorial advantage count, the more Southampton's confidence grew, with McCalliog threading a pass for the charging Channon to force a save. 'The first 15 minutes was tough,' said McCalliog. 'It looked like they were going to get a few goals, but I think the longer the game went on, the more I came into the game, then the more we controlled it.' Frustration grew throughout the ranks of Docherty's team. On a pitch that looked uneven and thin on grass in some places, indicating the start of what was to be a famously hot summer, United's passing, usually swift and assertive, became stilted. Hill drifted to the margins of the game, while Coppell, looking like an urchin in oversized shorts, was forced to carry the burden of the attack against the streetwise Southampton back four.

The closest United came to a goal was on the hour, when Pearson flicked on Hill's right-wing corner and McIlroy, stretching at the far post, headed against the bar. But now Southampton were creating their own chances, with the threat of Channon growing and openings falling to midfielder Nick Holmes and Rodrigues. From McIlroy's miss, Southampton launched into an attack that ended with Channon wandering across the box to shoot just over.

After 67 minutes, McCreery was sent on for Hill, who admits, 'I was having an absolute nightmare. They held the card up with my number and I looked at the boss and said, "Me?" and he said, "No, all fucking 11 of you!" Even then he was able to have a joke.'

But it was gallows humour. As when Chelsea flopped against Tottenham nine years earlier, Docherty was forced to watch his players fail inexplicably to achieve their potential. 'We just didn't perform as well as we should have done,' is all Hill can offer, still bemused by events.

'It was massively disappointing,' says Coppell. 'We were built up too much. We created nothing as an attacking force and Southampton had some terrific players who could get themselves up for a day. They stifled us. Our key players never got going.'

Unsurprisingly, Docherty prefers not to believe his team took their task lightly, saying, 'We were beaten on the day by a better side. We didn't play anything like we could, didn't create anything. We were just not good enough, because of nerves on the day or whatever.' Hill, however, does accept Buchan might have been accurate in his observation, saying that 'maybe we were overconfident and some of us went through the motions'.

Southampton's lightweight midfielder Bobby Stokes had already attempted a couple of long-range efforts when, with seven minutes remaining, he created his own piece of FA Cup history. McCalliog knocked a bouncing ball forward and Stokes, coming from what United believed was an offside position, hit a first-time shot with his left foot from the edge of the penalty area. Referee Clive Thomas chose not to whistle and the ball bounced past Stepney's left hand, just inside the post.

Docherty had lost his third FA Cup final – and was still without a win in seven visits to Wembley as player and manager. After a generous embrace with McMenemy, he appeared shell-shocked as he ambled out to the pitch, puffing out his cheeks and looking around for someone to commiserate or congratulate. One by one, he went to his heartbroken players and hugged them. Finding Greenhoff on his knees sobbing, he placed a fatherly hand on the player's head.

McMenemy would praise Docherty for his generosity and grace, as did several newspapers and their readers' letters columns. When the Southampton manager said, 'It would be utterly wrong to suggest this was simply a defeat for flair by organisation and that our victory [will] turn English soccer in the wrong direction, away from United's exciting leadership,' he was not targeting his opposite number. Docherty made no such arguments. Nor did he question himself or doubt his players. Fate – including the referee's failure to spot an offside – was, he believed, to blame. Nothing could change it.

In the Wembley dressing-room he battled to show a brave face. 'Don't worry,' he told anyone who would listen. 'We'll be back next year and we'll win it.' When he saw his oldest son at the Russell Hotel after the game, he promised, 'I'm going to win this next year,' leaving Michael in no doubt about the depth of his conviction. And when United were welcomed back to Manchester by 20,000 fans in Albert Square the following day, he took the microphone to repeat his guarantee.

'It was tongue in cheek,' Docherty now admits. 'That was hope rather than expectation. But I felt I had to say it. Some people probably thought, "Big-mouth twat."'

Among players, views differ on how much belief in United's destiny actually existed. Coppell remembers thinking, 'Blimey, fancy putting that expectation on us.' But he adds, 'Doc made a commitment and the crowd loved it. It was a big call to make but that was the Doc.'

McIlroy would recall that he was without 'any deep feeling of conviction' that he would be back at Wembley, fearing instead he might have blown his only opportunity. Hill, by contrast, adds, 'There were tears from everybody, but we had that "we'll be back" attitude. Everyone knew we would be.'

After completing the season with a morale-lifting 2–0 victory over Manchester City, Docherty received a small tangible reward for United's efforts. He was given the First Division prize in the

Bell's Manager of the Year voting, with Liverpool's Bob Paisley having won the overall award for leading his team to the Championship and UEFA Cup. Next season Paisley and Liverpool would chase an historic treble – and find Docherty barring their way.

While the West Indies cricketers were bouncing the living daylights out of John Edrich and Brian Close at Old Trafford's cricket ground – one of the defining images of the sporting summer of '76 – the Docherty and Crerand partnership across the road was finally approaching close of play. The European Cup winner had erupted in rage at a civic function following the FA Cup final, allowing his grievances to pour out and admitting that it almost became a 'fist fight'. Then he had shown up for pre-season training and found that no kit had been laid out for him. Saddened and angered at feeling unwanted by the club that meant so much to him, he accepted that 'my position had become untenable'.

The stories placed in the press cited Crerand's desire to be a manager in his own right as the motivation for his departure to take charge of Northampton. Docherty spoke highly of his colleague and declared him to be prime managerial material. It was all a sham, designed to save the face of all.

Docherty, who had earlier told the United board that he 'made a mistake in appointing Pat as my assistant' and demoted him to the youth team, had already angered Crerand by telling Jock Stein that he couldn't recommend him to be his number two at Celtic. Docherty saw it as an honest assessment, Crerand as sabotage. Docherty then declined to give Northampton general manager Dave Bowen a glowing report of a man of whom he said, 'We just weren't compatible in terms of our working practices.' His explanation years later was that he didn't believe in giving someone a positive reference as a way of getting rid of him.

Crerand, who once told author Jim White that he would 'rather go to the dentist than talk about Tommy Doc', had realised he was engaged in a losing battle. 'Docherty was a wily character well versed in football's politics,' he would state in his autobiography. 'He could be charismatic and he made sure that he had the chairman, Louis Edwards, on side.' He also commented that 'Docherty was popular with the fans because they liked the type of football the team played', which supporters of the Doc could point out was surely more important than anything that went on behind closed doors.

Blunstone, promoted to assistant manager in place of Crerand, adds, 'I thought Tom and Paddy were quite close to start with. But sacking him was the worst thing he could do.' Cavanagh then felt slighted at the new appointment, although Blunstone argues, 'Tommy asked me to be assistant because I was still handling the reserve team and youth team and therefore I was there at the club when he was away with the first team.'

United's usual pre-season travelling offered the opportunity for the latest fall-out with Macari, who claimed, 'I am being victimised,' after being substituted before half-time at Red Star Belgrade. Docherty responded with, 'This is not the Lou Macari Football Club,' before calling the incident 'a storm in a teacup'.

Meanwhile, Jimmy Nicholl was told he was now first-choice right-back, while the unfortunate Holton was informed that he had no future at the club. His time had been and gone. The man whose battling qualities helped shape Docherty's pre-relegation backyard fighters would have seemed out of place in his exciting new creation – like a bearded prog-rocker in one of the punk bands capturing headlines in the music press that summer. Once again, Docherty's verdict was delivered swiftly and in cold blood. No wonder David Meek commented, 'Docherty is not a very sensitive soul when a player's usefulness to him is over; he is downright ruthless and cruel.'

With so much emphasis placed on returning to Wembley, perhaps it wasn't surprising that United made a slow start in the League, winning only one of the first five games. Then came a sequence of three victories, the second of which – at Maine Road – was one of those games beloved by compilers of the decade's greatest games. Dennis Tueart headed City into the lead before Steve Coppell shot home after 15 minutes. Michael Docherty was lining up against his father's team, having become another victim of Burnley's post-Jimmy Adamson purge, but was powerless to halt the surging Gordon Hill, whose 26th-minute cross was diverted in by David McCreery. A marvellous third goal – Macari outside of the boot, Hill first-time cross, Daly swift finish – settled a 3–1 United win. When they followed it up with a 2–0 success at struggling Leeds, they were top of the table. But then came a miserable run of eight games without a win, the first seven played without Buchan, who had injured a thigh muscle playing for Scotland.

According to Blunstone, Docherty wasn't one to spend too long fretting over setbacks. 'Tom couldn't give two hoots,' he chuckles. 'His attitude was to have a drink, laugh it off, forget it and start again on Monday. I think that makes the players more relaxed. He'd be cracking jokes with them.'

Coppell recalls that his first season as a full-time professional revealed more of Docherty's methods. 'I had rarely trained a full week apart from university holidays. Sometimes if we won on a Saturday he would say, "I will see you Thursday." I was a full-time professional footballer. What do you do between Saturday night and Thursday? Or sometimes you would come in on a Friday and Doc would say, "Right you have done enough this week, just have a bath." I am thinking, "I am a full-time pro, this can't work," yet on Saturday we would be like whirling dervishes.'

Not so much, however, during the poor sequence that began with a 4–0 hammering at West Brom. Docherty claimed he could have avoided the result by assigning McCreery to man-mark playmaker Johnny Giles, but that was not the way his teams played. Hill adds, 'More experienced teams would have shut things up and played it tight to get a few results.'

United could have done with a helping of pragmatism as they slumped to 17th position by Christmas, before vast improvement in the first three months of 1977 lifted them to the fringes of the title race. Yet it was the cup competitions that would define their season.

In the League Cup, they reached the quarter-finals before losing 3–0 at home to Everton, having achieved their biggest victory under Docherty in the fourth round, Hill grabbing a hat-trick in a 7–2 win against Newcastle.

The early season excitement, though, was provided by United's return to Europe for the first time since their European Cup defence ended in the semi-finals in 1969. Ajax, runners-up that year before winning the tournament three times from 1971 to 1973, provided their first opposition in the UEFA Cup. Docherty warned that the behaviour of United's fans would make them much-scrutinised travellers and told his players that the team's revered European reputation was not to be tarnished by on-field behaviour.

According to Greenhoff, United's intention was to approach the games like any League contest. 'Our best chance was to have a go and attack. We were not much good at the negative game.'

Holland's stylish defender, Ruud Krol, scored the only goal of the first leg in Amsterdam, but United were heartened by Macari hitting the post and claims that a shot by Stewart Houston had crossed the line. Two weeks later, Macari levelled the aggregate scores after 43 minutes and, with an hour played, Docherty sent on young full-back Arthur Albiston for Gerry Daly and moved Greenhoff into midfield. Five minutes later, Greenhoff was involved in a move with Coppell that set up McIlroy for the tie's winning goal.

Juventus were United's opponents in the second round, inevitably throwing Docherty's mind back to his traumatic experience when Chelsea had faced Roma 11 years previously. While no one was throwing tomato soup at the chairman this time, Macari was able to say, 'I have never seen a more cynical display from any team.' The Turin giants' line-up of Italian internationals included fearsome figures such as Claudio Gentile and Marco Tardelli, both of whom made their mark on Coppell. The young winger had his toes stamped on and his torso pinched by Tardelli throughout the first leg, before having his testicles mangled by Gentile in the return.

United travelled to Italy with a 1–0 lead, courtesy of a Hill screamer. Nicholl delivered a diagonal cross, Coppell helped it on with his head and Hill volleyed the ball triumphantly past Dino Zoff. Or, as BBC commentator Barry Davies put it, 'First time. Left peg. Woof!' Juventus had overturned the same deficit against Manchester City in the previous round and United proved no more able to survive than their neighbours, losing 3–0 after Roberto Boninsegna scored two close-range goals.

Out of Europe and in the midst of a poor run in the League, Docherty made the final significant signing of his United career: one that was a good deal more intriguing and greater in consequence than his transfers of earlier in the season. Following the arrival of Waldron – who played only three League games before being reunited with former Burnley boss Adamson at Sunderland – Docherty had signed Middlesbrough winger Alan Foggon for £40,000. After three appearances as a substitute, he too was on the way to Sunderland, where Jim Holton also ended up after a £40,000 transfer (although he was soon shipped on to Coventry).

Docherty's preoccupation with wide men manifested itself in the £30,000 signature of Tottenham's Chris McGrath, a deal concluded shortly after United announced a record profit for a British club of £301,438 – built largely on the back of £1,300,000 in gate receipts. The manager insisted he was not about to spend all of that money and, in fact, remains proud of the fact that, despite his reputation as a big-spender, he balanced the transfer books at most of his clubs. 'I treated the club's money like it was my own,' he says. On this occasion he declared, 'The days of the big deals are over for this club and we are one of those who can afford them. It is stupid these days to pay £200,000.'

The sum of £120,000 was apparently deemed acceptable, though, especially when it allowed United to capitalise on Stoke City's financial needs to secure Jimmy Greenhoff, older brother of Brian. Greenhoff major had been part of Don Revie's dominant Leeds team of the late '60s, winning medals there without ever commanding a regular place. After one season at Birmingham, a £100,000 transfer to Stoke in August 1969 had seen him become a folk hero at the Potteries, his skilful forward play helping the club to two FA Cup semi-finals and victory in the League Cup.

As recently as October, Docherty suggested that Revie, now England manager, should pair United's Stuart Pearson and Greenhoff in the World Cup qualifier against Italy. 'They would cause a lot of trouble,' he said, adding that Coppell and Hill should flank them. Perhaps Stoke manager Tony Waddington had been paying attention, for when the roof blew off the club's Butler Road stand and funds were needed to cover the uninsured damage, he contacted Docherty to see if he wanted to make his dream forward line a reality.

'I had become a bit of a hero and I had this rapport with the supporters,' Greenhoff told Sky Sports' *Time of Their Lives* three decades later. 'I had decided I was going to end my career there.' When Waddington invited Greenhoff to join him on the Victoria Ground pitch, the Stoke captain assumed it was to discuss team selection. 'But he started talking about the stand and insurance and said, "Jimmy, we have to sell someone. We're going to sell you."' Waddington told him that Docherty had always said, 'If ever you get rid of Jimmy I want him.'

A gloomy Waddington informed reporters, 'It is impossible to explain this deal in any terms other than economics. We had a gate of 16,000 last week and we cannot survive on those terms.'

Greenhoff left behind the promise of a testimonial game for the prospect of winners' medals, saying, 'I've got a great move.' Docherty responded, 'It's a big financial sacrifice to make, even when joining a club like United. It's a tremendous decision, particularly when players are being slagged off for being greedy and selfish.'

As an experienced player, Greenhoff was wary of Docherty's reputation and it took three meetings before he agreed to the transfer. 'At my age, 30, I didn't want to be going there and then out the door the next year.'

Aware of Stoke's plight, Docherty was cheeky enough to ask Waddington about Peter Shilton, and discussions about the England goalkeeper continued over an extended period. In the end, a £275,000 fee was tentatively agreed, but a wage demand thought to be around £50 per week higher than Docherty's best-paid player proved beyond United. Even now, Shilton remains the player Docherty most regrets not being able to sign. 'Having him in goal would have won us the Championship,' he insists. 'Look at what he did for Nottingham Forest.'

For now, though, Docherty was excited enough about the man he did acquire. And no one was more pleased to see Greenhoff turn up than reluctant striker McIlroy. He had already told Docherty he felt he was not playing well and wanted to move into midfield. 'The Doc gave me a fair hearing,' he remembered. 'But he also pointed out that the team was going well and he wasn't prepared to drop someone else just so I could feel happier about my own game. He was satisfied with the job I was doing.'

With Greenhoff ready to team up with Pearson, however, McIlroy was finally to partner Macari at the heart of United's midfield. 'They were both great players,' says Hill. 'Louey had such an engine and just used to keep going. Sammy was exactly the same. Those two were our heart.'

All of which left Gerry Daly as the odd man out. Omitted from Greenhoff's third game – in which McIlroy scored the only goal in a 3–1 defeat at Arsenal – he would start only one more match and in early March was transferred to Derby for £175,000.

It was a spectacular fall from favour for a player so synonymous with United's style and success over the previous couple of years

– although hardly an isolated milestone on the path of disharmony that Docherty's career often followed. One newspaper story attempted to create a dispute over whether the dropped Daly had asked for a transfer, while Docherty said publicly he'd received an offer he couldn't refuse, which was consistent with the financial caution he'd expressed earlier in the season.

Daly's first response when presented with the move was to turn it down, even when the manager told him he saw no way back into the first team. Busby urged him to stay, warning him cryptically, 'There's something going on. We can't tell you what it's all about.' Having agreed to discuss the deal with Derby manager Colin Murphy at The Belfry, the meeting degenerated into further confrontation with Docherty. Like so many before him, Daly – who enjoyed playing under Docherty and liked him as a man – struggled to make sense of his boss's apparent change of opinion about him.

Daly says he has made his peace with Docherty in recent years but 'didn't trust him and didn't believe a word that came out of his mouth'. He recalled his manager telling him that no matter how well he played, he would never get out of United's reserve team.

Perhaps United's finances really did mean they couldn't afford to carry a substitute who could command such a large transfer fee, despite the varied options he offered off the bench or in the event of injury. Yet Blunstone suggests that Docherty had doubts about Daly's ability to continue to perform at the required level, questioning his lifestyle and calling him 'a good player, but inconsistent – a bit airy-fairy'.

Jimmy Greenhoff scored his first United goal, a long-range lob, in the 4–0 Christmas victory over Everton, which broke United's grim winless streak. Clearly benefitting from his new partner's presence, Pearson also scored, following up with five in the next five League games.

A 1–0 home win against Walsall in the third round of the FA Cup achieved revenge for two years earlier and began a fifteen-game unbeaten run, carrying them towards the top of the table and just one game from a return to Wembley. The first League match of that sequence, a 2–0 home win against Coventry, was notable for Buchan giving Hill a very public slap on the back of the head for not covering back.

The fourth round of the FA Cup sent QPR, a poor imitation of the title-challenging team of a season earlier, to Old Trafford, where a crowd of 57,000 saw Macari round off a good move with a 16th-minute winner. A month later, seven days after Jimmy Greenhoff's hat-trick against Newcastle, a delicious opportunity for revenge arrived in the shape of a fifth-round tie at holders Southampton. Docherty played down that factor, preferring to say, 'The lads just want to get to Wembley to make up for last year.'

Unable to use their Cup triumph as a springboard for promotion, the Saints were even heavier underdogs than ten months earlier. But twice United were pegged back in the first half after goals by Macari and Hill, while Stepney had to perform well to ensure the tie continued at Old Trafford.* United dominated the first half of the replay, only to find themselves still level at half-time after Jimmy Greenhoff's header was cancelled out by full-back David Peach's penalty. But it was Greenhoff who hooked in the winning goal after 69 minutes to secure a quarter-final against Aston Villa.

Any raised eyebrows Docherty had caused by his signing of an uncapped 30-year-old were now firmly back in place. 'When you knocked the ball up to Jimmy it just stuck,' he recalls. 'Pearson and Greenhoff weren't big lads, so we went down the line and hammered hard and low. If it was wet it was lethal. It could go all over the place, so all our crosses were violent.' Greenhoff even remembers jumping out of his skin when Cavanagh screamed 'Violence!' in his ear, referring to the preferred United method of crossing or finishing.

Buchan recalls, 'As a defender you could close your eyes and knock the ball forward and Stuart or Jimmy would get on the end of it,' while Coppell would come to describe Greenhoff as 'the best player I ever played with'.

Hill asserts, 'Jimmy was the best uncapped player I have ever seen, and most players around that time thought so too. He and Stuart seemed to have a sixth sense about what each other would do.' Pearson explains, 'We knew where each other were going to be,' adding, 'I played for England with Mick Channon and Kevin Keegan, and Jimmy was better than them.'

According to Blunstone, 'We thought Jimmy and Stuart would

---

* The match was discussed a month later in the House of Commons when Southampton MP Bryan Gould cited the 'shameful and sordid behaviour' of United's fans as he called for new measures to combat football hooliganism.

work well together. Stuart was aggressive and Jimmy had that touch of class.' Of course, their effectiveness depended initially on the service they received, with full-backs Nicholl and Arthur Albiston having been developed with an emphasis on their attacking contributions. 'Tommy wanted me to encourage them to go forward,' says Blunstone, 'to overlap and be a part of the attacking build-up.'

'The full-backs gave us good service,' says Pearson. 'Jimmy and Arthur were sound defensively, but they were a more attacking style of full-back and they would always play it into our feet.'

Aston Villa arrived at Old Trafford for the sixth round of the FA Cup in the midst of a three-game epic against Everton in the League Cup final, in which they would eventually prevail. They showed little sign of being distracted, though, when forward Brian Little scored from 30 yards, although Stewart Houston equalised with a 25-yarder of his own. A reshuffle caused by Brian Greenhoff's groin strain didn't aid United's quest for fluency, but Macari secured victory inside the final 15 minutes with the game's third goal from distance.

By the time United attempted to expand their on-field reputation with a semi-final against Leeds, the club's image had been tarnished once again by hooliganism, this time at Norwich. The club's followers had continued to attract unwanted headlines over the previous couple of years, although not at the same rate as their season in Division Two. They had even won universal praise for their conduct in defeat at Wembley. Yet Manchester United Supporters' Club chairman David Smith was forced to call events around Carrow Road 'the worst exhibition of wanton, all-out destruction I have seen' and said that some perpetrators were 'out to pillage everything'. A stand was damaged, missiles thrown at police and opposing supporters, windows smashed around the city, and cars overturned and dumped in rivers.

'That day it was frightening,' is Docherty's recollection. 'I came on to the pitch before the game and tried to cool it down and a slate whizzed just past me. If it had caught me it would have cut my head off. I just shot off as quick as I could.' An emergency session in Parliament led to United fans being banned from buying terrace tickets at away grounds, although many still found a method of securing their places.

Docherty said he was pleased to have avoided Liverpool or

Everton in the semi-final draw, preferring to play a Leeds side that had discarded many of its old faces as manager Jimmy Armfield led them into a period of transition. United's players were the first to leave their dressing-room. As the Leeds players lined up alongside them in the Hillsborough tunnel, Joe Jordan and Gordon McQueen looked down at the likes of Coppell, Macari and Hill. Up went a shout: 'Come on, lads. We've only got to beat a bunch of fucking midgets.'

United proved that size wasn't everything. They tore into their opponents and appeared to have the tie won inside a quarter of an hour. After eight minutes, Houston helped on Hill's corner and Greenhoff scored; six minutes later, Hill linked up with Pearson and let fly with a shot that rebounded off Paul Madeley for Coppell to shoot home on the volley. United could have put the game away for good, but were responsible for giving themselves a nervous final 20 minutes when Nicholl needlessly fouled Jordan and Allan Clarke converted the penalty.

But United were not to be denied, and the destiny to which they believed they had been bound all season was a reality. Tommy Docherty was going back to Wembley for the eighth time. Things would be different on this occasion. In fact, before too long, nothing in his life would ever be the same again.

16

THERE'S SOMETHING ABOUT MARY

'Football management is like nuclear war. There are no winners, only survivors or casualties.'

'If I look you up on the Internet am I going to find a hundred people who want to kill you?' The question has been posed to me by Tommy Docherty's wife, Mary, as she delivers a tea tray to the living room of their home on the edge of the Derbyshire Dales. While she has been brewing up in the kitchen, Docherty and I have been discussing his possible participation in an interview for this book.

'She's my minder,' Docherty explains with obvious affection. 'And my manager.'

'He's too generous to people,' Mary fires back. 'He'll talk to anyone and sometimes it can backfire on him.'

As the world knows, Docherty loves to talk. It is how he has made his living since leaving football. But having agreed for me to come and visit, I know that to get him to spend time discussing his life with me it is Mary who has to be convinced. Replying to a further question about my journey, I explain that I came off the motorway and drove through the countryside to reach their house in the village of Charlesworth.

'At least then if you threw me out I would have had a nice drive.'

'Well, it was a possibility,' she admits.

Spend even a short amount of time with the Dochertys and it is impossible not to recognise the love that bounces between them. It seems like they both know he could not do without her, and each revels in their role in their relationship. They are as happily affectionate as newlyweds. 'They think the world of each other,' says broadcaster and friend James H. Reeve. 'They are like a couple of teenagers.'

It is also impossible for someone of my age to see them together without visualising those pictures of them sitting side by side on a sofa in the summer of 1977, appearing shell-shocked after declaring to the world their love for each other. It was a revelation that altered the course of their lives, Docherty's career and the history of Manchester United. That it should come within days of him winning his first major trophy in three decades in the professional game is entirely in keeping with the often-frenzied narrative of Docherty's story.

In the course of writing this book I have heard it suggested that United might have tolerated their manager's relationship with Mary, then the wife of the club's physiotherapist, had he agreed to maintain its clandestine nature. Perhaps that was what Sir Matt Busby was hinting at when he reportedly said to Docherty, 'You're a bloody idiot. Why didn't you tell me? We might have been able to do something.'

But no longer would that have been acceptable to Docherty, and never has there been a moment's doubt about the course of action he chose. 'Mary is worth one hundred Manchester Uniteds,' he declares.

Any regrets lie down a different path. 'The best thing that has ever happened to me was her, by a long way,' he says. 'But with hindsight, if I could have my time again, I would never have gone to Manchester United.'

As United's second consecutive FA Cup final grew nearer, Docherty's future was already the subject of speculation. In March, stories emerged of an approach by Derby County. According to a 'friend', he had unresolved issues with United and problems in his relationship with Busby. Some suggested Docherty was behind the story, agitating for another improved contract even though he still had fifteen months to run on the current one. In April, another report claimed Derby would offer him £28,000, more than half again what he earned at Old Trafford. But, as he reflected in his autobiography, 'I wanted time to finish the job I set out to do.'

Before the semi-final against Leeds, Docherty came out and said he wanted a contract that offered him security of tenure rather than vast sums of money. 'I'll honour [my] contract and see it through.

If the board want to do something about it, marvellous. If not, well, I'll just have to get on with it.' Noting, accurately as it turned out, that 'there are a few people around who would like to see me leave', he added, 'The board could have stopped all this speculation and done something about it.'

With a return to Wembley secured, the *Sunday People* claimed that Docherty would have been fired had United lost the semi-final. Busby and the board were reported to be angry at the public nature of the contract debate – a conjecture repeated by other reporters – while some at the club still held the departure of Willie Morgan and Paddy Crerand against him. But when Louis Edwards entered the arena it appeared that a new four-year agreement had been reached, although fixtures and Easter had prevented it being signed. 'If I have my way he will be with us for the next 40 years,' the chairman said.

On the field, United's slender Championship hopes vanished in a 4–0 loss at Queens Park Rangers, before Cup final opponents Liverpool took a significant step towards wrapping up the title by beating United by a single goal. The game at Bristol City had serious Wembley ramifications when Stewart Houston cracked and dislocated his ankle jumping for a ball, but it was another incident that captured more headlines. Sammy McIlroy and Bristol midfielder Gerry Gow were sent off after a clash, and Docherty appeared to make his views known to Gow, the enforcer in his team, who then had to be restrained from going at the United boss. Rival manager Alan Dicks described Docherty's behaviour as 'bad for football', although Docherty argued that McIlroy had been the subject of his ire. Turning his attention to more important matters, he informed Arthur Albiston immediately after the game that he would play in the final.

Wembley week arrived, although not without further drama in the meantime. Docherty said he was 'lucky to be alive' after a car with a trailer jack-knifed, crossed the central reservation of the A74 and hit his car as he was driving back from Scotland. Seven days later, in a separate incident, he was banned from driving for six months after admitting doing more than 50 mph in a 30 mph zone.

United had one last League game to fulfil, at West Ham, five days before facing Liverpool. The perils of a match so close to the final were highlighted after Martin Buchan injured knee ligaments when Trevor Brooking fell over his leg. 'We were staying down there all week and on Tuesday morning my knee had stiffened up badly,' Buchan recalls. 'I said to the Doc, "You might as well give me my train ticket back."'

Never one to snub his nose at superstition, Docherty had booked his team into the Selsdon Park Hotel in Surrey, where Southampton had been based a year earlier. In an effort to ensure further differentiation from the disappointing events of 12 months earlier he also ordered no commercial activity during the week. According to Steve Coppell, he had, though, earlier manoeuvred himself into an advert for Gillette previously intended for his young winger. After sharing the gig with Docherty and Gordon Hill, Coppell noted, 'Doc inevitably was the star of the show and it was his car boot which was full of razor blades rather than mine.'

Docherty's greatest concern during the build-up to the game – from a football perspective anyway – was Buchan's battle for fitness, although he was far from pleased by the FA's intention to stage a replay, if required, on 27 June, more than six weeks after the first contest. Rival manager Bob Paisley, whose Liverpool would play in the European Cup final in Rome four days after Wembley, commented, 'I am not intellectual enough to express my disgust at this stupidity.' Docherty's own suggestion was the Saturday after the original game, adding, 'Let's face it, the Home Internationals are a bit of a joke.'

Buchan came through a cursory fitness test on Friday morning. 'It consisted of me standing in goal in five-a-sides and kicking the ball off the line,' he remembers. 'I played the next day with strapping and after about five minutes I had a 50–50 in the centre circle with a certain gentleman called Tommy Smith. I came through that and thought, "I'll be all right here."'

A relieved Docherty prepared to deliver his eve-of-game address. He concluded an impassioned speech by promising his players they could share £5,000 out of his own pocket if they won, a typically impulsive gesture that he never truly believed would make one jot of difference to the outcome. Docherty was more fearful of the result than he had been a year earlier. 'I thought we would beat Southampton, but I wouldn't have put tuppence ha'penny on us beating Liverpool,' he recalls. 'But I am a great believer that if your name is on the Cup you win it.'

Coppell explains, 'It was different this time mainly because we were underdogs. Their team was one hell of an outfit, and they looked red-hot and so controlled. On our day we could beat anyone, but this Liverpool team was becoming a machine. Doc always used to tell us to enjoy it, but this time we were all aware we had jobs to do.'

Buchan might have been taking a risk with his fitness and Hill had been troubled by his knee, but, for once, Docherty appeared to have achieved emotional harmony within his squad. Even Stepney, grateful for the support Docherty had given to his testimonial season, felt newfound warmth towards his manager. 'My relationship with the Doc stabilised,' he would say. 'My feeling towards [him] had mellowed.'

Meanwhile, Docherty had been speaking at length about the significance of his fourth Cup final. 'I'm not being haunted by the thought of losing again,' he said, although he admitted, 'I want a major trophy for peace of mind.'

He suggested that United's return to Wembley was a reward for the patience he had developed over the previous decade. 'People won't accept that I've changed since the days when I turned Chelsea inside out. [Earlier this season] I looked hard at the team we'd got and considered whether I ought to strengthen it. But the more I considered, the more certain I became that there were very few players better than those we already had. Jimmy Greenhoff brought a little maturity because that's one commodity with which you cannot endow players.'

He concluded that 'losing the Cup final was a very sobering experience and I believe we've come out of it all as a better side'. And although the nation might have been intrigued by Liverpool's quest for the treble and supportive of their bid to become the second English team to become champions of Europe when they faced Germany's Borussia Moenchengladbach, a great deal of goodwill rested with Docherty's side. 'I think it was because of the way we played and the way we took defeat a year earlier,' he suggests. 'It was a young, inexperienced team and people respected them.' Typical of many was the view expressed by Arsenal captain Pat Rice, who said United deserved to win in recognition of what they had brought to English football.

Having felt relaxed enough to allow television cameras into the hotel on the eve of the game – capturing Hill being massaged by physiotherapist Laurie Brown while he read the latest on his manager in a newspaper – Docherty spent next morning in a state of distraction. He read the papers and compulsively checked on his Wembley suit: anything to make time pass. 'I'm bricking it,' he confided to Tommy Cavanagh. But, describing his team as 'a coachload of excitable schoolboys' a year earlier, he sensed a mood of intent once they got to Wembley this time. Offering a final reminder to his team to play their usual attacking game, he concluded, 'These are the good old days. Just you wait and see. We let ourselves down last year. Go and win it for the fans.'

According to Docherty, the feeling of helplessness experienced by all managers once their teams head to the field is more acute at Wembley than anywhere. 'You feel detachment because you know there is little you can do.' Docherty – grey-blue suit, red shirt, silver patterned tie – chewed and chatted to Paisley as they went through the traditional march towards the Royal Box side of the ground, where 'You'll Never Walk Alone' fought for attention with the national anthem as the Duke of Kent arrived to meet the teams. Freshly brushed, fashionable pageboy haircuts dominated the United line-up, barely an ear on view, before they shed their black tracksuit tops and tore into Liverpool with typical exuberance.

Within three minutes they had pieced together a pair of high-speed moves offering the perfect snapshot of Docherty's United, a team that Macari describes as 'Doc's final creation, and possibly his finest'. Stepney's quick release found Coppell, who raced down the right and laid off to Jimmy Nicholl. The full-back's first-time clip into the box was flicked on by Jimmy Greenhoff before running away off Stuart Pearson's shins. Then Coppell linked with Nicholl and Greenhoff on the right before nodding into the path of the onrushing Macari, who shot into the side netting. It was all United in these early stages, Greenhoff's neat touches and Pearson's short-striding runs and close control providing the focal point.

Ray Clemence dealt with a dangerous cross by Hill and a shot by Pearson, but as half-time approached it was Stepney who went into action to save Ray Kennedy's header. Defensively, Albiston had coped well, right-back Nicholl had proved a stubborn opponent for the leggy Steve Heighway, and Buchan had come through without further injury. 'We're doing very well, but to win this, we have to do even better,' Docherty told his men. 'Let's get forward in numbers, put them under pressure.' Pearson and Greenhoff were ordered to work even harder to drag their markers around the pitch. 'Do that and we'll get one,' Docherty insisted.

Liverpool began the second half with momentum at their backs, even if the breeze was behind United, but it was United who struck after 51 minutes. McIlroy headed on a bouncing ball and Liverpool's hesitation allowed Greenhoff to nod it forward into the path of Pearson. Shaking himself free of full-back Joey Jones, his fierce right-foot shot beat Clemence low at the near post. But the lead lasted only two minutes, Jimmy Case taking a couple of touches to control Jones's pass before turning to send a trademark strike past Stepney from the edge of the box.

Three minutes on and United were in front again. Macari's flicked header sent the ball into the penalty area, where Greenhoff tussled with the formidable Smith and saw the ball run back to Macari. His shot hit Greenhoff in the midriff and flopped over Clemence into the net. Both United men ran away thinking they had scored, although replays clearly indicated that Macari's effort would have missed the target.

Without David Fairclough, whose vital goals off the bench had earned him the label 'Supersub', Liverpool appeared to lack the ability to change the direction of the game over the final half-hour. In fact, they replaced their only out-and-out goalscorer when David Johnson made way for midfielder Ian Callaghan. He sent in a series of crosses that produced no end result and it was not until 12 minutes from time that Stepney had to save twice in quick succession from Case. For the second year running, McCreery replaced Hill – who earned a word of praise from his manager – and Liverpool prepared a final assault. With two minutes left, Kevin Keegan, playing his last domestic game before a transfer to Hamburg, set up Kennedy, who clipped the bar after squirting clear of Nicholl. 'Liverpool have won on points, but United are going to win the Cup,' Jack Charlton told television viewers just before Buchan headed away from Keegan and celebrated referee Bob Matthewson's final burst on his whistle.

After eight visits to Wembley, including three losing FA Cup finals, Tommy Docherty was a winner. As evidenced by the pre-game support from neutrals, there were few who begrudged him his glory. In the *Daily Telegraph*, Donald Saunders argued that United 'continued to set an enterprising example' and added that they were winning 'badly needed converts over to their faith, which many believe alone offers English football salvation'.

Docherty hugged Cavanagh and Paisley almost simultaneously before, for the second year running, going round his players embracing everyone – this time in triumph. Having consoled his opponents, Docherty was up front and centre as United paraded the cup around the pitch, only rarely relinquishing a grip on the trophy. Grinning widely, he posed for pictures with the lid of the cup on his head before reluctantly heading off for the post-match interviews.

When he met ITV's Gerald Sinstadt there followed an exchange that smacks you between the eyes when you know what happened next. Having been told by Docherty that getting to Wembley was easier than winning there, Sinstadt ventured, 'You left your wife behind this time. Is she going to be able to come again?'

Docherty was visibly startled and blurted out, 'I thought you said, "You left your wife," there,' and added that she had made a late decision to travel to London after all. He concluded, 'Maybe she's been the jinx all along. That's her finished with football.'

It is a jarring, uncomfortable conversation to watch now in view of what was lurking around the corner.

On what should have been one of the happiest evenings of his life, Docherty was moody and subdued. It was so obvious that various people approached him during United's victory banquet at the Royal Lancaster Hotel to ask him what was wrong. Agnes recalled her husband being distant, desperate not to be in her company and unwilling to communicate. Docherty would admit, 'I treated her badly. I was off-hand, brusque, irritable . . . Agnes responded with tender concern. She believed my work had brought me to the verge of a nervous breakdown.'

Quite simply, his life was at a crossroads and the route he was to take was weighing heavily upon him. 'I knew that Mary and I were going to be together,' he explains. 'I didn't know what would happen. Even after winning the Cup I never thought of life continuing the same at Old Trafford. I knew our story had to come out because someone would have seen us eventually. If they had already then they hadn't told anyone about it.'

After a long pause, he continues, briefly slipping into his frequent habit of speaking in the second person, almost as if to depersonalise certain issues. 'There was the prospect of telling your immediate partner what you were going to do, which wasn't easy, and then going to the club and telling them what was happening. I was due to sign a new contract so I needed to tell them.'

The story he had to relate – or the outline of it at least – was that he and Mary, whose husband, Laurie, had been appointed club physiotherapist in 1970, had met in the summer of 1973 and had shared pleasantries and small talk over the course of subsequent meetings. He'd even jokingly asked her a couple of times if she would ever consider going out with him. A couple of years later, Docherty paid a visit to Brown during a stay in hospital and, after visiting hours, ended up sharing a drink with Mary in a nearby pub. 'We began talking about our lives,' he recalled. When they saw each other a week later both remarked how much they'd enjoyed their conversation and that they should do it again. Each confided in the other that their marriages were stagnating. Explaining that Mary 'helped me put things in greater perspective', Docherty sensed a deepening friendship and admitted that 'eventually what for some weeks had been inevitable did happen'.

He would later tell the *Daily Mirror*, 'Towards the end of 1976, we began to realise that the bond between us was stronger and more powerful than an everyday friendship. Quite simply we were in love – deeply and irretrievably in love.'

With Mary, 18 years younger than he was, he realised there existed the prospect of something more than 'going through the motions of marriage', describing their feelings as 'something we could not avoid. You don't consciously try to fall in love. It just happens.'

Events were brought to a head by knowledge that a Sunday newspaper, the *Sunday People*, was about to break the story of their affair. 'I don't know who told the newspapers about Mary and me. All I know is it wasn't us,' he wrote later. 'It rankled to see our relationship the subject of sullied copy in some newspapers.'

On the Thursday before publication, Docherty told Agnes that he had set up a home with Mary and was moving in with her. According to Agnes's version – disputed by Docherty – he called her again the following day to say he had changed his mind, before doing a further about-turn the next morning. At that point Agnes gathered the three youngest children together and broke the news to them.

Docherty says that Laurie Brown had known for a while, commenting on one occasion that 'he used to babysit for us'. In another account he said that Brown knew about the initial drinks date and some subsequent dinners, which suggests that he didn't know the full extent of the relationship – although it would have taken someone very trusting or naive not to have suspicions had that been the case. Brown said he 'didn't have an inkling'. Perhaps the oddest part of all was that Docherty and Mary were moving into the 'granny flat' annexe of the Browns' family home, from where she could still carry out various maternal duties for her two daughters, Jane and Helen, seven and four at the time. Agnes would later claim that their home-building had taken place while she'd believed her husband was absent from their house in Hales Barn, Cheshire, visiting his mother in Scotland.

The *Sunday People* duly ran their story on Sunday, 19 June, four weeks after the FA Cup final, under the headline, 'THE DOC RUNS OFF WITH TEAM WIFE'. Docherty had chosen to cooperate with the newspaper, in return for a sum that has been variously reported as anything between £5,000 and £25,000, and had told them:

> We are in love. We've got something special going for us and we've decided we would like to spend our future together. We haven't rushed into this. There's been a lot of soul-searching. The bond has grown between us over the last three years and we've decided to bring our relationship into the open rather than live a lie. I believe that what has happened between Mary and me will be understood and accepted. It happens, after all, to other people every day.
>
> This has nothing to do with football. It is a private matter and I've always believed in keeping my public and private lives separate. I shall continue to devote my time to keeping United a top team.

Once the story had broken, the couple spoke later that day to more media, hoping it might dissuade them from camping outside day and night. 'I know it sounds corny, but I'm in love with him,' said Mary as reporters and photographers squeezed into their living room. The *Daily Mirror* placed its front-page picture of the couple directly under an exclusive shot of runaway 'Great Train Robber' Ronnie Biggs, wearing an England shirt on a Brazilian beach with his young girlfriend on his arm. It was hard to tell who the paper considered the bigger rogue.

Docherty stated optimistically, 'We hope this will be the end of it and Mary and I can get on with our lives.' To his mind, that included continuing to work at Old Trafford alongside Laurie Brown. 'We both have a job to do,' he said. 'I think we can still work together.'

That hope had arisen from a conversation with director Martin Edwards. With chairman Louis away, Docherty had called the younger Edwards to explain his domestic situation before it became public knowledge. According to Docherty, he received assurances that the club would view it as a 'private matter'.

As hard as it seems to believe, there was genuine shock in all corners of the club at the revelation of the affair. Crerand recalled being tipped off by a reporter and breaking the news by phone to Busby, who answered from his holiday home in Ireland with the comment, 'What's he done now?'

Skipper Buchan recalls, 'I was shocked. I thought I knew most of the things that were happening in and around the club, but I certainly didn't know that.'

Coppell remembers being amused by the apparent absurdity of the news. 'I could not believe it,' he says. 'It came on the radio and, let's be fair, Doc is rough and ready at the best of times. I had met Mary a few times. Laurie was a good bloke, put upon sometimes and a different character to Tommy Cav and the Doc, both massively gregarious. Laurie was quiet, an Aberdonian, and when he spoke he had a lilt in his voice, like singing. Mary looked distant and I knew she was into horses. Football wasn't really her world; she just tolerated it. I burst out laughing. It couldn't be.'

Hill reiterates that the players had no idea what was about to transpire: 'Sammy Mac and I were taking separate holidays in Ibiza. I ran into Sam on the beach and we said, "What are you doing here? Grabbing a few days' break?" and the like. Then Sam said, "You won't believe what has happened. Look at this." He had got an English paper. "He has been having an affair with Mary Brown."

'I said, "You've got to be joking," and I asked Sam what it meant because he knew the score at the club. He said, "They are very, very religious at United. That is a no-no. They will get rid of him now.

270

He is tarred." I said, "Get out of it; we have just won the Cup." I couldn't believe it.'

Brian Greenhoff confirms, 'I hadn't heard anything about it and I've never spoken to a player who had. We were gobsmacked. You were thinking, "Is nobody on the board having an affair?" It could have been anybody in the office. I didn't know what to expect.'

Even those who worked closest to Docherty were in the dark, although Frank Blunstone says that the announcement explained some strange behaviour over the previous year. 'He'd come in one day and said, "I think we ought to come in on Sunday." I asked why and he said we'd have a drink and a chat about the game. I said, "I don't agree with it, but you are the boss." Sunday morning we turn up: no sign of Tommy. We sat around waiting. Next day I asked him, "Where the bloody hell were you?" He said he got caught up with the press or something. He said we'd do the same again next week. Next week, same again. I said to him, "I am not coming in again." Of course, we later found out he was going out with Mary. He was getting Laurie to come in, but he couldn't just get Laurie in on his own, so he got us all in.'

The story meshes with the accounts given by both Brown and Agnes. Meanwhile, Brown told reporters that he expected to be leaving Old Trafford. 'I have lost my job, my wife and two smashing kids. I have not been sacked, but could you work with a boss who has stolen your wife?'

Having met with Louis Edwards, Docherty announced, 'There is no question of me leaving the club. They want me to stay. The board have been absolutely marvellous.' Later, he even told a story of Derby chairman George Hardy calling Edwards in his presence to ask about his availability, to which Edwards responded, 'It's an unfortunate situation, but it's a 48-hour story. It will blow over and there's no way Tommy is leaving Manchester United. He's doing a great job.'

But while Docherty was away escaping the media attention – first with the United youth team in Portugal and then in the Lake District, staying at a friend's hotel with son Michael's family – his future was being discussed at some length. Cavanagh had even warned him that those he referred to as 'the junior board' had been 'stirring things up'.

On 29 June, Docherty was recalled from the Lake District to attend a meeting with the board, staged at the chairman's home in

Alderley Edge. Also present were Martin Edwards, Busby, vice-chairman Alan Gibson, directors Bill Young and Denzil Haroun and secretary Les Olive.

'Under the circumstances we think it would be in the best interests of everyone concerned if you resigned,' the chairman told him, citing a breach of the club's 'moral code'. Docherty, who had never heard of such a code, refused, arguing that he should be judged on his ability to do the job, not his private life. He recalled Edwards's reply as, 'In an ideal world. But, as you know, we live in a far from ideal world.'

What happened next offered Docherty a suggestion that perhaps there were other forces at work, that certain people had been waiting for any excuse to get rid of him. According to him, Martin Edwards said that the board believed he had been selling Cup final tickets. Docherty readily admitted to that, pointing out that he had done so ever since he had been at the club and had often undertaken the task on behalf of Edwards's father and other senior figures at the club. He had apparently done it so openly that he'd even had Stan Flashman, the infamous king of the ticket touts, in the boardroom, where a barman remembered wanting to punch both of them as they concluded their business.

Docherty knew he was fighting a losing battle. With 18 months to run on a contract worth £18,000 per year and a four-year, £25,000-per-season deal sitting unsigned, he turned his thoughts to ensuring a decent pay-off from the club to whom he had delivered the FA Cup 44 days earlier. (Ultimately, it would emerge during court hearings over maintenance payments to Agnes that his settlement had been in the region of £50,000.)

According to Docherty, an alternative discussed was United giving Derby permission to negotiate a deal for him to go to the Baseball Ground, which had the potential to save face all round. Later that evening, though, he received a call from Louis Edwards saying that the directors had reconsidered and dismissed that option.

It was not long after the board meeting that word began circulating that Docherty had been asked to resign. There are various accounts stating that Docherty had been suspended while the board considered their next steps, although United denied it at the time and released a statement saying, 'The situation regarding the manager and other members of staff was discussed. There is no change in their positions at the club.'

All the while, the players were waiting anxiously to see if they were to lose their boss. 'I thought he would keep the job on the back of winning the FA Cup,' says Coppell. 'Being pragmatic, this was a privately owned company and he was delivering the goods.'

On 4 July a further board meeting was staged. Docherty was asked to attend and recalled being in there for less than two minutes. The statement emanating from the meeting was unequivocal. Olive announced, 'A meeting of the directors has decided unanimously that Mr Docherty is in breach of the terms of his contract and his engagement is terminated forthwith.'

Wondering whether the club had even breached the Industrial Relations Act by giving him no formal warning, Docherty told reporters, 'It has nothing whatever to do with my record as a manager. They can take my job away, but they can't rob me of my ability. I refused to resign because that would have been the easy way out.' Calling it the 'the most shattering experience of my life in football', he added, 'I am terribly disappointed in Manchester United. During the past two weeks I have been treated like an animal. I have been punished for falling in love. It's as simple as that.'

Asked for his reaction to Docherty's sacking, Brown said he took no joy in it. 'Jobs are ten a penny,' he answered. 'What I want most of all is my wife and family back together with me.' Speaking to author Sean Egan decades later, Brown said that Docherty's habit of making him work on Sundays so that he could see Mary made him a 'bit of a mug'. He was angered by Docherty's position that 'I was sacked for love and all that crap'.

Only once did Brown claim a small piece of retribution. Docherty had been driving away from home when Brown gestured to him. Docherty wound down the window to see what he wanted and Brown hit him, explaining later that he had been angered by his comment that he would be all right for money. When Docherty cleared his office at Old Trafford, he did so with a black eye as well as a heavy heart.

Brian Greenhoff says that the outcome didn't surprise many players. 'We were really disappointed it happened, but something had to give.'

Macari, though, was one of those taken aback. 'That couldn't happen, not with the relationship he had with the chairman,' he declares. 'Doc used to call him "Big Chop Souey" because it rhymed with Louis. He did it in front of him and the chairman loved it, and he loved Doc's company. Because of that I never considered he would be out of the door. We'll never know what that team might have done because competition was so fierce. But when someone tells you things and they start happening, like going back to Wembley, you believe in them even more.'

Hill says, 'Doc had put his mark on something. He had put his team together and we were getting ready for Europe and the League. We were flying.'

Coppell remembers that 'we went into the summer feeling pleased with ourselves and looking forward to next year' and points out, 'Around that time they were allowing home clubs to keep their own gate money. Looking at the economics, it was only a matter of time before United, with our crowds, became dominant.'

Club captain Buchan, who admits that 'I don't know what the thought process was to sack him', acknowledges that 'managers come and go' and that his job was to play for whoever was in charge. But he adds, 'I will go to my grave wondering what would have happened if the Doc had stayed. We had a decent team and the confidence of winning a major trophy. You never know who he might have been able to bring in. It was well documented that he was after Peter Shilton. We'll never know how good that team could have been. It was building its own momentum.'

So what exactly happened between the first assurance given to Docherty that his job was safe and the ultimate decision to fire him? Theories are as abundant as those about the Kennedy assassination. Three and a half decades later, Docherty has heard them all. He gives credence to little bits of all of them without knowing, ultimately, which was the overriding factor.

'I am told that the directors' wives had a big say, but that's just hearsay,' he explains. Conceding that 'it could be a contributing factor', he also suggests that the wives knew little of what really went on around the club. 'I had seen a lot of things going on while I had been on tour,' he notes.

Their influence was, however, the aspect upon which the newspapers initially focused, with one headline reading, 'CLUB WIVES OUST DOC'. There is no direct evidence to suggest that

Lady Jean Busby or Muriel Edwards had been sharpening their husbands' knives. Yet, with no quotes – even from unnamed insiders – to support the notion, the story stated, 'Directors' wives at the club, which is proud of its family image, helped force him out. They acted from shock and embarrassment over his love affair.' Alex Stepney agreed in his autobiography that the directors' wives would have been 'leading the attack' against Docherty.

Tied into all of this is the club's strong Catholic background and, at the time, its powerful public image of morality, personified by Busby. 'I think Matt had a big say, being a Catholic,' Docherty says. 'I think maybe he was disappointed in me, being a Catholic as well.'

David Meek, however, believes it was far more straightforward. 'He gave the club little option but to ask him to go,' he asserts. 'It was something he brought on his own head. It was not about personal vendettas or people not liking him. It was just an impossible situation. Louis Edwards kept saying it was a private matter, nothing to do with the club, but the penny finally dropped. I am sure Matt was more puritanical and felt that the name he had spent so many years building up would be damaged if Tommy stayed.'

The club's attitude towards the wronged Laurie Brown is obviously significant. Earlier on the day of Docherty's dismissal, he met with the board and told them that he intended to remain in his job and later explained that the directors appeared united in their desire for him to do so. The board may simply have felt unable to inflict a further blow upon an already wounded man, or perhaps they feared that Brown, if sacked, would accept an offer to tell his story to the press and bring all sorts of skeletons out of various cupboards. Docherty, for instance, would claim after Busby's death that he had a 'lady friend' whom he visited on trips to London.

Authors Richard Kurt and Chris Nickeas write, 'If, in brutal terms, the exchange United made of Brown for Docherty damaged our playing prospects, it did safeguard the club's soul. That is far more important, just as style means more than success on the field.'

There is, however, a strong whiff of hypocrisy blowing through such a stance. Busby knew exactly what type of character he was appointing when giving Docherty the job. He hired someone he was confident would, wherever possible, uphold the attacking traditions of United on the field. Equally, he knew Docherty had a way of dealing with people and tackling his profession, and life, away from the pitch that might upset some more delicate sensibilities.

The influence of Busby creates a wider tapestry upon which those peripheral characters on the 'junior board' come into view. Docherty recalls Busby saying to him before his fateful meeting with the directors that he 'could have spoken to people'. Ultimately, though, Docherty believes that even Busby's support would have made little difference. 'Matt had some influential friends in Manchester who this wouldn't have gone down well with,' he says.

Stepney contends that 'a lot of resentment' had built up among the 'hangers-on' over Docherty's treatment of so many United family favourites. 'He should have remembered that in many respects Manchester is like a village,' he said. 'Docherty's habit of taking a few drinks on board and talking about Manchester United to all who cared to listen began to rebound on him.'

It emerged within days of Docherty's departure that private detectives had been compiling a dossier on his activities for two years. This included accounts of Cup final tickets finding their way onto the black market, incidents in hotels during tours, and allegations from parents that he had slapped an 11-year-old boy, an incident that led to an out-of-court settlement. Chris Moore, the director of a Stockport-based agency, said, 'I can't deny an investigation was made. These investigations were into a lot of things. I'm not going to break confidences.' It is reasonable to surmise that such an investigation would also have discovered the relationship with Mary, which may have been how it reached the attention of the newspapers. According to the *News of the World*, this operation was being carried out not on behalf of the directors, but local businessmen. Those 'junior board' members again?

There had always been influential United supporters opposed to Docherty's presence at Old Trafford. As early as his third month in the job, a group of seven men, including an MP and a QC, proposed a takeover of the club in which Frank O'Farrell would be reinstated as manager.

Meanwhile, even if Busby himself had not been sending gumshoes on Docherty's trail in the manner of a paperback thriller, he had, according to many, lost his desire to support his manager any longer. Nightclubs such as the Playboy Club and the Cromford Club were the settings for the likes of Busby, Morgan, Law and Crerand to get together with well-known local bookmaker Paddy McGrath – who had a business interest in those venues – and share their dissatisfaction with Docherty.

In the end, many wanted him out simply because he was 'disliked', although Macari is one who refuses to believe chairman Edwards was among them: 'I don't know who else had a say, but it couldn't have been Louis who was responsible for Doc being sacked. He loved him.'

Another interpretation of 'disliked', of course, is those Docherty had upset during the course of his Old Trafford career. 'He never got the sack for running off with Mary Brown,' says Blunstone in a conspiratorial whisper. 'I know he didn't. He got the sack because he fired Paddy Crerand, who was very popular down there and had a lot of friends. When Doc got rid of Paddy they couldn't sack him then because results were good. They waited until they had something. As soon as he stepped out of line, "bang," they had him. That is a fact. If he had kept Paddy there he would have got away with it. They would have got rid of Laurie instead because you can always replace a physio.'

Docherty, who echoed Macari's belief that his close relationship with Louis Edwards would keep the chairman on his side, ponders, 'Maybe some of the players I had got rid of had said things and had been stirring things up and there were repercussions involving people like Paddy, Willie and Denis. Getting rid of Paddy probably is one of the reasons. I know Matt wasn't happy when Pat was no longer assistant manager.'

Docherty also relates a story that hints at the growing distance between him and Busby and offers a further suggestion of hypocrisy. 'We were away a few nights in Spain,' he explains. 'Big Louis loved a night out, a nice cigar and a glass of champagne. He said, "Tom, what are you doing tonight? Come to my suite for a drink. I have invited some of the lads." Later, Matt found me and said, "Tom, I believe some of the players have gone to the chairman's room for a drink." I said they had and that I was going too. He said, "Do you think it's a good idea?" I said, "You are playing golf with them in the morning." It was all right for him to play golf but not for me to have a drink with them and the chairman.'

In his 2006 autobiography, Docherty even reprinted a letter he'd received shortly before his dismissal from friend and former United manager Frank O'Farrell, warning him about 'the Knight'. O'Farrell wrote, 'He must be suffering torment at not being able to get rid of you as is rumoured he had been trying to do.'

Daily Mirror writer Frank Taylor greeted Docherty's dismissal by stating, 'Rumours that the Doc was going to get the chop soon started because he wasn't in the old tradition of the gentleman manager.' Yet Docherty's supposed 'crimes' were as old as the game itself and not a total surprise to Busby, who appears to have been happy to tolerate them while the team was regaining its place in English football's upper echelons and doing so in a style that reflected his own football philosophy. So if even Busby was ultimately determined to be rid of Docherty, what pushed him across that line?

Maybe the weight of Docherty's foibles and failed relationships with Busby's pals eventually outweighed the benefits – especially as the club was now safely back in the big time. In some respects, the Doc's job had been done. Someone else, someone safer, could take over. Brian Clough had been the victim of a similar set of circumstances four years earlier when Sam Longson and the Derby board found they could no longer tolerate the unique personality of their Championship-winning manager and accepted his impulsive offer of resignation.

Or perhaps it was simply the 'scandal' of Mary Brown. If so, then former United player Eamon Dunphy believes that is where the hypocrisy is at its most extreme. 'The myth of United's integrity suited Matt Busby,' he says in his examination of Old Trafford under Busby, *A Strange Kind of Glory*. Busby would even use it to temper players' wage demands.

Dunphy contends, 'The hypocrisy of Docherty's years at Old Trafford, ironically reflected in the furore surrounding his demise, is extraordinary by any standards. When United's board of directors – the same men now lauded for upholding decent standards – had sacked McGuinness and O'Farrell nobody mentioned integrity and tradition.'

Whatever the role of the United wives, the 'junior board', Busby or his acolytes, one thing is worth stressing: the summer of 1977 was not the ideal time to get caught on the wrong side of the morality divide. It was the year of England cricket captain Tony

Greig shocking the establishment by recruiting players for Kerry Packer's World Series Cricket, which would fight with traditional Test matches for players and fans. Only a week after Docherty's dismissal, Don Revie declared that he was quitting his job as England manager to be paid a fortune in the United Arab Emirates. And in the wider community, shocked royalists had been choking on their ham sandwiches at street parties as the Sex Pistols hijacked the Silver Jubilee by taking 'God Save the Queen' up the charts.

The royal family, loyalty to country, honour above money, sense of sportsmanship: these were the British, especially English, traits that people identified with and fell back on when the outside world encroached too much – as it had in recent times through the unions, the IMF, inflation, terrorism and hooliganism. Woe betide anyone who chipped away at people's pillars of normality and comfort, of which fidelity was most certainly another.

Without the benefit of knowing that they would still be together more than three and a half decades later, the story of Tommy Docherty and Mary Brown was seen as some kind of sordid fling, resulting in Docherty 'running off' with someone else's wife. That wouldn't do at all. The innuendo and bird-chasing of the *Carry On* films was one thing, the lowbrow smut of *Confessions of a Window Cleaner* and its sequels another. But real life, with all its passion and heartbreak and complications, as presented a year earlier in the groundbreaking *Bouquet of Barbed Wire*, was something to be kept behind closed curtains. People watched ITV's controversial series in their millions, but almost as a window on another world. Britain remained more at ease confronting its own sexuality through the seaside postcard than via the reality of a steamy drama that seemed almost Continental in its earthy portrayal of real physical and emotional relationships.

Only days after the Docherty revelations, the National Association of Schoolmasters and Union of Women Teachers launched a much-publicised attack on certain programmes shown on British television, citing shows such as *The Sweeney* and sitcom *The Many Wives of Patrick*. Their report to the Home Office stated, 'It must be a source of concern that programmes are broadcast which are either immoral in their outlook or confirm immoral attitudes,' before going on to claim that children were being confronted by 'false and undesirable standards'.

In such an environment, there was no shortage of writers lining up to comment on the 'Mary Brown Affair'. The influential Jean Rook, the 'First Lady of Fleet Street', accused Docherty of 'tasteless gall' in talking so publicly about the relationship – although she might have held a different view had he selected her own newspaper in which to break the story in the first place. She argued that Docherty's wife, Agnes, had been 'kicked in the teeth' by Mary's declaration of love for her husband and concluded, 'Mr Docherty, who will never walk alone while his wife is still living in their present home while he is setting up another with Mrs Brown, says: "This sort of thing has been happening since Adam and Eve." It has. Mr Docherty is just one of teams of middle-aged men who have played precisely the same shots since the kick-off of time. He should get on with his little game and keep his goal mouth shut.'

The news of Docherty's sacking was welcomed by writer and campaigner Mary Kenny. 'I'm glad Tommy Docherty has been sacked,' she wrote. 'This is a man whose personal example must be widely influential with a lot of people, and in walking out on his wife and four children – with a woman who herself has a husband and two young children – he has given them a rotten lead. If we have any vestige of respect left for the family and for family responsibilities, then society must insist that he pays the price.'

It would be too easy to say that opinion on the Docherty firing was split strictly along gender lines, but *Sunday Express* editor John Junor offered a view more in line with Docherty's when he asked, 'How can the sacking be justified? How can who he sleeps with have any bearing on his efficiency as a football manager? Would Manchester United be likely to score more goals if he sat watching the telly every night with his own wife?'

Docherty's anger with the 'moral code' argument would intensify years later when Martin Edwards, having inherited the chairman's position from his father, was the subject of tabloid revelations about his private life. 'The attitude of people to the alleged indiscretions of prominent figures today is totally different now to the attitude of certain people towards me in 1977 for leaving my wife for another woman,' he said.

Yet the impossibility of Docherty's situation in the 1970s does not assume that he would have 'got away with it' amid the greater ambiguities and tolerance of the twenty-first century. To suggest he was merely the victim of a morality struggle within Manchester

United or of the age is too simple. He is perfectly entitled to ponder, 'Whether it would have happened today I don't know,' but it's too easy a supposition to say that everything would be different.

At the time, David Miller pointed out, 'Docherty was not a run-of-the-mill employee, but the prominent chief executive of a famous, revered institution, and necessarily his private life is of public concern. It would even be different if the Other Woman were the wife of any other club's physiotherapist.'

There is barely a celebrity who has not been caught with his trousers down. It ruins few; it even enhances the profile and reputation of some. Yet when it is a colleague who has been the unwitting victim, when that romantic concept of dressing-room unity in which we all like to believe has been torn apart, we can still be almost Victorian in our reaction. Look at the vilification that greeted former England captain John Terry when he was alleged to have slept with a recent girlfriend of Wayne Bridge. The story of a manager sending the physiotherapist off on weekend errands while he was seeing his wife would probably be too much for most Premier League clubs even now.

In conclusion, as you would expect with a complex, contradictory character like Docherty, his departure from Manchester United involved multiple complicated factors, as had his exit from Chelsea. Few of them were visible to the United fans, most of whom were left mourning what they feared was the end of an era. 'On the terraces,' writes Jim White, 'nobody could believe it. All the foot soldiers of Doc's Red Army saw was a team playing with verve, skill and a complete lack of fear. They had no idea what was going on behind the scenes and, frankly, few cared.'

United historian Michael Crick summed it up by highlighting the affinity between fans and manager: 'To those on the Stretford End, the street-fighter Docherty was one of the lads. Ticket dealing and running off with a colleague's wife were something they might do themselves. It is his exciting young team they remember.'

Docherty's rebuilt team achieved much and had the potential to realise even more. He'd once called the United job 'the one I really wanted, the top job' and said 'I'm not about to let go of it', yet when he looks back at those days any regret is less about what he left behind at Old Trafford than what he gave up to go there in the first place.

'I have thought about it a lot and the real thing to come out of United was meeting Mary, but outside of that I should have stayed at Scotland,' he says. 'I do regret leaving, with hindsight – even with all that our team achieved at United. I always felt like I had unfinished business. If United hadn't come in for me I would have seen out my time with Scotland at least until after the '74 World Cup. I would probably have gone back into club management eventually, but it would have depended on how we were going with Scotland. We had a good team, and if we were still doing well, you don't know. But to come to United, well, the politics was unbelievable. I should not have gone there.'

17

COURTING DISASTER

'In football, when one door closes another one slams in your face.'

Michael Docherty's voice trails off in mid-sentence and words give way to tears. A long pause and some deep breaths later, he apologises and continues to talk about the father he 'loves to bits'.

It is more than three and a half decades since the decision that shattered Tommy Docherty's professional career and sent his personal life down a path that no family ever expects to travel. It was a choice that has brought much happiness into his life and has found him surrounded in his advancing years by a second family that he adores. Yet it has also caused heartache: the loss of husband and father suffered by his first family and a deep rift that has never healed. Docherty accepts he was the cause of such hurt, yet he is more reluctant to acknowledge his own pain at having lost all contact with three of the four children he had with Agnes, who died in 2002.

It is Michael, his eldest son, who has found himself crossing the Docherty family divide, he whose tears prove that the wounds of 1977 still cut deeply. And it is Michael who suggests that his father's pain is greater than he would ever admit.

'Obviously for Mum it was a very difficult,' he says. 'For their own reasons my brothers, Tom and Peter, and my sister, Catherine, don't speak to Dad. Tom never has from day one, and Peter similarly. Peter was only 12 when the break-up happened. He grew up with the ignominy of everything that went on; he was bullied at school and fights ensued. He got into all sorts of trouble because of this. I can understand the difficulty of that. I have tried to mend that, but they have chosen not to make contact with Dad.'

It is in recounting the effort of trying to keep the family together that Michael succumbs to his emotions. 'I always tried to keep Mum and Dad on a level footing,' he says haltingly. 'Mum didn't speak to me for two years because I knew what was going on and didn't divulge it. I met Dad on a couple of occasions in a couple of different venues, purely for a chat; there was no subterfuge. He told me he thought he was going to lose his job. After two years, Mum spoke to me again. She apologised to me for putting me in a position I shouldn't have been in.

'I tried in the early years to get us all to the situation where we met as a family. But Tom has never batted an eyelid and actually I think Dad admired him for that. I understand completely where it is coming from. Peter is a great kid; he was the one who was hurt most. Catherine and I were older, more aware. I was a target because I was a good player at the time. I got followed by the press and I got offered money by newspapers. I told them where to go. I wasn't interested.'

Docherty senior states, 'Michael has been great. He always said, "Dad, I love you to bits and I love my mum." He has been great to me ever since. The others I never speak to and Michael doesn't see them a lot because they think he is wrong with the attitude he has taken. He has not taken sides. And he loves Mary to bits as well.'

At the time of our discussion, Michael was preparing for his own second wedding. According to Docherty, 'He was asking if we were going. But we went to a party about a year and a half ago and the family were there. Before that I hadn't seen them for about ten years. We didn't speak to each other, but if looks could kill . . . So Michael said to me, "If you want to come to the wedding you're welcome but if you don't want to I will understand." So I said, "No, we'll do something another time."'

Docherty's own second marriage took place in 1988. As well as Mary's two daughters with Laurie, they have two of their own, Grace and Lucy. At the time of writing there are four grandchildren from his marriage to Mary. Docherty puffs with pride when he speaks of them all.

Yet when questioned about the pain of being a father estranged from three other children, he shrugs and says, 'I got used to it. It must have been difficult for me at the time, but it doesn't bother me now. I got over it very, very quickly. That is life I suppose.'

Without someone sitting across from him in interrogation he was a little more candid in discussing the subject in his 2006 autobiography, where he admits, 'The one thing that did get to me was the feelings of our children and their reaction to my leaving home.' Recognising that they 'never accepted me leaving their mother', he concludes, 'There has been much pain in that respect, for everyone concerned. I still live in hope the day will come when old wounds may be healed.'

It's hard, therefore, to believe that his apparent acceptance when questioned directly – which can appear to border on indifference – is anything but a defence mechanism. Michael certainly believes so. 'He is a very deep man,' he says. 'I am probably the closest person to him other than Mary. He divulges very little and keeps everything close to him. But I am sure that he hurts because he doesn't have the apparent love of his children.'

In one interview, Docherty admitted, 'People get a lot of joy out of seeing you suffering, so you don't let them see that.' On another rare occasion, he elaborated by saying, 'People who think I am not serious enough don't really know me. If I didn't have a sense of humour I'd be dead by now. Of course I have been hurt. You laugh and joke and the pain goes away for an hour. But it comes back the next morning.'

An insight into the distress of Docherty's family was offered in 2008, with the publication of a book compiled by his journalist son Tom, based on his mother's notes and diaries. Entitled *Married To a Man of Two Halves*[*] and published posthumously under Agnes's name, it is her account of her years with Tommy and the story of their marriage break-up. In his introduction to the book, Tom outlines the pain of the course his father chose. 'He's still alive and yet I think of him in the past tense,' he writes. 'But mostly not at all.' He describes his father as a 'fleeting presence' during his childhood, adding that 'his job consumed him to the exclusion of any affection'.

Inevitably, given the nature of the book and the complexity of emotions in the relationships involved, Agnes's account veers between bitterness and an apparent need to demonstrate a love for

---

[*] The paperback edition the following year was renamed *Dear Tommy*.

Docherty that no other woman could possibly match. The result is a mostly uncomfortable read, but it does contain further serious allegations about Tommy as a husband. The most damning is the assertion that Docherty used his frequent scouting and educational visits to Germany in the mid-'60s to nurture an affair with a woman in Munich. Agnes claims that Docherty admitted to the relationship. The timing, as Chelsea progressed towards the 1967 FA Cup final, could not have been worse for her, coming as she was preparing for a serious operation to correct a chronic spinal injury, the outcome of which was far from certain and which even threatened her ability to walk. She says that Docherty's mistress, whom she identifies as a married woman named Maria, even became pregnant by Docherty, although she never had the baby.

'No, that's not true,' Docherty replies when I ask him about the pregnancy. 'To be quite honest with you, I didn't even have that relationship.'

Docherty claims to be unmoved by the content of the book and uninterested in discussing it because all he knows of it is what he has been told. 'I swear on the Bible I have never read it,' he says. 'Michael said, "Dad, Tom has written a book – don't read it; it's a load of rubbish." Maybe because I haven't read it I don't feel too badly about it.'

Endeavouring to create a new life outside their fractured family relationships, Docherty and Mary prepared to move into a cottage in Derbyshire, with the redecoration funded by the money she earned from telling her story to the *Sunday People*. Insisting that she was not the 'wicked woman' she had been portrayed as, she said, 'Now all Tom and I want is to be left alone. I am very much in love with him and I believe he is with me.'

Meanwhile, Docherty had a post-United career to piece together. 'I was never going to sit and mope,' he explains, 'so I just tried to get on with my life. My view was that there were worse things happening to other people.'

Given their very public interest in Docherty before he departed Old Trafford, it was no surprise that Derby were favourites to become his next employers after Colin Murphy was fired. Murphy had been unable to keep the club at the elite level achieved by title-winning managers Brian Clough and Dave Mackay, and the club had picked up only two of the possible first ten points of the new season.

First, though, Docherty had flirted with – but failed to keep a date with – a club in the United Arab Emirates who were said to be offering £50,000 a year. Then he accepted a £20,000-a-year offer from Norwegian champions Lillestroem, who threatened to sue for compensation when Derby announced him as their manager in mid-September. 'He has broken the trust between us,' said chairman Eimar Kroken, who accused Docherty of having two contracts. Docherty insisted his agreement with Lillestroem had been provisional and based on the absence of any suitable offers from England.

After MP Tom Hendry, a mutual friend of Docherty and Derby chairman George Hardy, set up a meeting, that offer quickly materialised. 'We see this as the start of a new era,' announced Hardy. 'Tommy will bring three major qualities: 100 per cent knowledge of the game, a financial brain and an insight into human nature.'

Docherty's response was, 'It's another challenge, another chance for me to rebuild a club. I thrive on that sort of situation.' It was impossible, though, for people not to compare his sickly new home with the apparently healthy one he had left behind.* 'It's a different situation from the one I had when I went to Old Trafford,' he continued. 'I had to get rid of a lot of players. But that's not the case at Derby. There are so many good players there already and good teams don't become bad teams overnight. I am sure I can get the club out of trouble.'

Docherty evidently saw no irony in declaring that his players would be judged as much for their off-field conduct as on-field performance. In what sounded very much like a 'moral code of conduct' he declared, 'I'm not just interested in what happens for 90 minutes on the park. As far as I'm concerned a player's responsibility does not end with him putting in his lot in a match. We've got to put things right on the field, but we must remember that we represent Derby off the field as well.'

Once outgoing manager Murphy and his assistant, the future

---

* Having appointed Dave Sexton to succeed Docherty – as he did a decade earlier at Chelsea – United were among the pace-setters in the League and in the early stages of a European campaign.

Crewe manager Dario Gradi, decided not to remain at the club in reduced capacities, Docherty brought in a trusted lieutenant when he appointed Frank Blunstone, whose energy and enthusiasm he felt could galvanise talented players who were underperforming. 'I didn't have to leave United,' Blunstone explains. 'I knew Dave Sexton and had worked with him. I don't think Tommy Cavanagh got on very well with him because they were both coaches. Dave wanted us both to be assistant manager, so I decided to go and work with Doc again.'

Despite his earlier suggestion of sticking with the current players, Docherty was soon wheeling and dealing. The reality of life at the Baseball Ground was that he would have to sell to fund new recruits. Archie Gemmill, whom Docherty said he 'never warmed to', joined Clough at Nottingham Forest, although Docherty ensured that Gemmill made it known he'd wanted the move in order to prevent the crowd blaming the new manager for releasing a popular player. He received £100,000 plus goalkeeper John Middleton for the midfielder, but his board voiced their discomfort with selling to Clough and their local rivals.

Former Charlton striker Derek Hales returned to London to join West Ham for £110,000, and by the end of the year full-back Rod Thomas had departed for Cardiff, goalkeeper Graham Moseley for Brighton and former Sunderland FA Cup winner Billy Hughes had joined Leicester. Gerry Ryan and Francis O'Brien had arrived from Irish club Bohemians, while Docherty attracted the disapproval of Sexton, who accused him of being 'sneaky' in trying to tempt away a Manchester United man. 'He is using back-door methods to approach one of my players,' Sexton complained. 'He used the same method to get Frank Blunstone.'

Docherty's most significant moves came within a few days of each other. In late October, he acquired Scotland midfielder Don Masson, a stylish and tenacious playmaker who had done much to propel Queens Park Rangers to the brink of the title two seasons earlier. Masson arrived in a £175,000-rated exchange for Wales winger Leighton James. Gerry Daly, aware that Docherty's comments over the years had earned him a reputation for disliking the Welsh,*

---

* Docherty was still nourishing that reputation during the 2012 Olympics when calling the Welsh players in the Great Britain football team 'a disgrace' for not had warned James that he 'might as well put his house up for sale' when their new boss arrived. 'I don't think he treated any of the players well,' said James recently, explaining that Docherty had been the only manager he ever retained 'animosity' towards.

Docherty followed up by buying Masson's Scotland captain and midfield partner, Bruce Rioch, for the second time in his career, paying £150,000 to bring his former Aston Villa player back from Everton a year after he'd left the Baseball Ground.

Masson expressed his excitement by saying, 'I can't wait to play for the Doc because he makes you feel ten feet tall.' The former Notts County man was looking forward to a return to the Midlands, as was Rioch, who explains, 'My wife and I both wanted to move back. I was happy playing for Derby and living in Sutton Coldfield, where I'd moved when I went to Villa.'

Docherty's spending continued with the signature of Luton defender Steve Buckley, persuading his board to raise their offer to £160,000 to beat off Aston Villa's interest. He could not, though, secure funds to compete successfully for Scotland centre-half Gordon McQueen, who would join Manchester United from Leeds for £500,000.

The new manager's impact on results was initially impressive. After losing to champions Liverpool in his first game in charge, Derby won three in a row, repeating that feat in late November and pulling themselves into tenth place by the start of 1978. But they won only five of the final eighteen matches and ended disappointingly, although at least safely, in twelfth position. United finished only two places and one point ahead of Derby and Docherty continually claimed to be happier at the Baseball Ground than Old Trafford. But it was impossible for him not to have looked at his old club and wondered what might have been, even criticising Sexton for tearing his team apart.

'He had left one of the greatest clubs in the world,' says Rioch, 'which I thought was grossly unfair. After Manchester United, there are not many clubs you can go to. It must have been a huge blow to him. He had a young, vibrant side there and he must have looked

---

singing the national anthem. He added, 'I'm Scottish and I loved beating England. But when I did National Service they didn't ask if you were Welsh, Scottish or English. You were all in it fighting together.'

at our 30-year-olds and decided he had to change them.'

Son Michael suggests, 'He was disappointed because he laid all the groundwork at United. He said to me after that, "There is only one way for me and that is down." Without a shadow of doubt he was never the same again after United. That was the zenith of his career and everything after that was a no-no. He'd basically had the world in his hands at Old Trafford and he knew it. He blew it, if that's how you want to look at it. He put his career behind love and marriage. But he doesn't regret it.'

As usual with Docherty, even an unremarkable mid-table season had not been without its share of soap opera.

Daly, sold to Derby by Docherty, found himself on the transfer list in late November, with his manager saying, 'I don't mind if a player hates me if he does his stuff on the field, but he has started messing us about.' But Daly had already warned Docherty that he wouldn't force him out of Derby as he had from United and would end up outlasting him at the Baseball Ground.

Early in the New Year, Docherty was in hot water for accusing Lawrie McMenemy on national radio of talking 'a load of cobblers' after the Southampton manager defended the permanent appointment of Ron Greenwood as England manager ahead of Brian Clough.

Rioch, sent off at QPR on Boxing Day along with teammate Charlie George, was in trouble with his boss in March when he left the field without permission before half-time against Newcastle. Docherty conceded that a groin injury necessitated his withdrawal but argued, 'He didn't signal to the bench, so we couldn't get the substitute warmed up.' Initially fined a week's wages, Rioch was also suspended for two matches, although that was reduced to one.

'We had one or two dust-ups,' Rioch remembers. 'I had changed since Villa. Instead of being 21 and going with the flow I was 28 or 29, with my own opinions. I was strong-minded and thought I knew a bit about football. It was mostly my fault. He had the difficult job of turning the club around. A lot of the top-class players were leaving and others weren't happy. The standard wasn't as good as previously, and when I walked off I was at the point where I was pissed off with it all. I was injured, but it was the wrong thing to do.'

There was even an unseemly confrontation at Derby's next game, at home to Liverpool, when Docherty and Rioch got into a slanging match outside the dressing-room and continued their argument in the street. Rioch, described as 'ashen-faced' after the incident, told reporters, 'Docherty has just told me he will put me out of the game.'

He explains, 'Doc tried to poke me on the chest. I said, "Don't you dare poke me or I'll break your fucking finger. The only man who can poke me is my dad." It might have been then that I said to him, "You'll be gone before me because I have got a contract for another three years and you won't make another three years here."'

With the World Cup finals in Argentina looming, the Glasgow *Evening Times* accused Docherty of destabilising Scotland's chances with his treatment of the national captain. 'The trouble with the Doc,' Hugh Taylor wrote, 'is that he is a dramatist, sees everything larger than life and can't keep out of the headlines.'

In May 1978, with the anniversary of his United departure approaching, he created even more of them by teaming up with the *Daily Mirror* on a series of first-person articles. Over the course of four days he revealed the chronology of his relationship with Mary, how he had broken the news to his wife, and the events leading up to his sacking. 'In telling my side of the story I do not ask for public sympathy, approval or support. I do not need it,' he stated. 'But I hope when you read what follows you will at least begin to understand what I mean. And how I feel.'

Even this, however, was not a simple matter of 'setting the record straight', as journalist Norman Giller recalls. 'We wrote a book together called *The Rat Race*. It was the story of Tommy's love affair,' he explains. 'But before we went to publication he took my manuscript to the *Mirror*. So I sold my version of it to *The Sun* to try to salvage something for myself. It finished with him sending me a telegram saying he was suing me.'

Giller issued a counter-action and the matter was eventually resolved with Docherty making an out-of-court payment to his ghostwriter. 'We had a big falling-out,' says Giller, 'but, typical Tommy, a few months later he was back at QPR and we were pals again.'

As Docherty's first season at Derby concluded, he was having second thoughts about both Rioch and Masson and made them available for sale. 'I thought they were super signings,' he said. 'But I am realistic enough to admit they have turned out to be poor investments.'

Before he left, Masson was twice fined by Docherty, first for not turning up as a standby player against Arsenal and, after returning from Scotland's disastrous World Cup campaign, for 'unprofessional behaviour' in writing that he didn't want to play for Derby again. After Masson had reportedly refused terms offered by Norwich, Docherty warned, 'Unless he wakes up to the facts of life at the age of 32 he will jeopardise his own future.'

Masson would return to Notts County for a bargain £30,000 in September, while Rioch would remain at the club throughout the 1978–79 season, playing only seven League games and being loaned to Birmingham and Sheffield United.

The early weeks of the new season saw striker John Duncan arrive from Tottenham for £150,000 and defender Aiden McCaffrey from Newcastle for £60,000. Colin Todd was sold to Everton for £330,000 and Gerry Ryan to Brighton for £80,000 as Docherty continued to give the club the makeover he'd originally felt would be unnecessary, racing past 30 transfer deals since arriving at the Baseball Ground. 'Everyone at this club is available,' he declared. 'The only problem is for managers to come up with the right price.'

Sometimes, though, the right price was not enough. The success achieved by Clough in leading Forest to the League title and League Cup in their first season back in the top flight had increased the pressure on Docherty among the Derby directors, who were even angry at him for allowing his team to be the opposition for Forest's joint benefit game for Clough and assistant Peter Taylor. Late in the year, the apparent jealousy of the board prevented him selling George to Forest. Docherty was an admirer of the former Arsenal man and had even spoken up for him when he refused to play for the England B team, claiming it was like asking Johan Cruyff to try out for Lincoln. In return, George, not noted for harmonious relationships with managers, said, 'Tommy Docherty and I understand each other. If we fell out we'd both be the losers.' Even so, Docherty felt the money the ex-Arsenal man would generate was too good to pass up. He was prevented from sending him to Derby's near rivals by what he felt was the 'small-mindedness' of the directors. Instead, George was sold to Southampton for £400,000.

Docherty's activity in the transfer market appeared even more frantic than normal. Centre-back Steve Sims was purchased for £250,000 from Leicester, only for him to fail Derby's medical.

Docherty spent £12,000 to buy former Chelsea defender David Webb from Leicester and in January paid £275,000 for the big, blond Chelsea stopper Steve Wicks, having just spent £50,000 on Sunderland striker Roy Greenwood. He also managed to get into another public row with Sexton over United's refusal to sell David McCreery. 'Too many of our staff and players have gone to Derby,' Sexton complained.

Docherty had already raided his old club for one of his favoured sons, having paid £250,000 for winger Gordon Hill late in the 1977–78 season. 'It's a lot of money for a club getting gates of 20,000 but we are getting a natural entertainer, a goalscorer, a character,' Docherty explained.

Hill brought with him tales of a 'vendetta' against him by some United players and accusations by Sexton of being a 'selfish player' whom teammates found it hard to accommodate. They seemed to have had no such problem under Docherty. Hill recalls, 'I fell out with Dave Sexton. He was trying to stamp his football on the club and change a winning team. He brought in Joe Jordan and Gordon McQueen – lovely guys, but Leeds-type players. At half-time in a reserve game they said they'd accepted a bid from Derby, and I met the Doc at Mottram Hall with Stuart Webb, the secretary, and done the deal. I didn't see Dave lighting it up at Old Trafford. There is a special rapport you have with United supporters. Sir Matt had it and TD had it. Sexton didn't.'

But Hill discovered that Docherty was different to the effervescent character he'd worked for at United. 'He was much more subdued. I felt the drive was still there, but he was more placid, a bit mellow. His dream job was United. That left a dent in him. Derby had been a high-flying side, but they were just coming off that.'

Failure to win any of their first five games of 1978–79 set the tone for another disappointing season. Derby never rose above halfway in the table and were beaten 3–0 by Preston in the third round of the FA Cup. They managed a miserable return of three victories in their final twenty-five games and sank to a final position of 19th. After a home defeat against Ipswich, watched by the club's lowest crowd for ten years, fans stayed behind to chant, 'Docherty out!' Although Derby never slipped into the bottom three, it was not until a 0–0 draw at Old Trafford in the penultimate match that they were safe from relegation.

Having fielded thirty-one players in League games the previous season, Docherty used twenty-nine in this one, prompting journalist and Rams fan Paul Rouse to look back on the club's decline several years later and write:

> The man who really set the ball rolling was Tommy Docherty. The man with more clubs than IQ points soon began to weave his familiar magic at the Baseball Ground, ripping the heart out of a good, if ageing, side to the point where he was buying and selling faster than a currency trader on Black Wednesday. Far from being able to get to know each other on the training ground, most players met for the first time in the tunnel, and stood more chance of being featured on *Blind Date* than *Match of the Day*.

According to the man who observed him at work most closely, it was a pale imitation of the Docherty of Chelsea and Manchester United who stumbled through the season. 'Derby was a waste of time,' says Blunstone. 'He had gone. Yes, he had taken a knock, but also when it came to Derby he wouldn't come out to training with the players. I used to say to him, "You've got to come out, even just for a while." At United he would be there playing in five-a-sides, but you couldn't get him out at Derby. It seemed to me he had hit the bottle badly at that time and was drinking more and more. He was in trouble.'

Rioch witnessed Docherty's old inability to rub along with experienced players with strong opinions. 'Maybe it's a control thing,' he suggests, 'not wanting players to disagree or make their points back. Sometimes senior players don't allow you to have that control. I don't think I made it easy for him; a few of us didn't. A few weren't keen on playing.'

Blunstone concludes, 'The team had gone over the top and no one had got rid of them. I thought McFarland, Todd and George were past their best. Someone like Alex Ferguson would have pushed one of them out every year. At Derby, they all grew old together. They had sussed out Tom and they took advantage. It was a bloody hard job and I didn't enjoy it. Tom wasn't going to last much longer.'

Docherty was hardly in the best state of mind to tackle the difficult task at the club, given the tornado of off-field events in which he was caught up throughout the season.

In early summer, he'd found himself being interviewed by the Fraud Squad as part of a corruption investigation. The interview centred on a £1,000 payment he was reported to have received in connection with George Best's appearances for non-League Dunstable in 1974 after Best had ended his Old Trafford career. Detective Chief Superintendent Ken Forster of Manchester CID stated, 'Inquiries by Fraud Squad officers into allegations of bribery and corruption have now been completed. A file is being prepared and will be sent to the Director of Public Prosecution for him to decide whether or not an offence has been committed.'

In the end there was no criminal case to answer, but the incident added to the reputation of Docherty as a wide boy. It was claimed that Dunstable had given him the money in order to secure the participation of Best, who was still officially registered as a United player. Dunstable manager Barry Fry would subsequently say that he had no doubt that the money was for Docherty's personal use.

In October, Docherty ended up in Chesterfield Royal Infirmary with broken ribs and head injuries after crashing his car near Buxton while returning from work, hitting two trees and damaging a wall. Police reported that no other car was involved but said that the incident occurred on a 'notorious stretch for mist and fog'. Docherty was charged with careless driving and, with two endorsements for speeding on his licence already, was subsequently banned from driving for four months, despite his plea that it could affect his job.

November saw the episode that Docherty regrets more than any other: his libel action in court against Willie Morgan and Granada Television. 'I had never taken offence at anything similar before,' he says of Morgan's description of him as 'the worst manager there has ever been' on the station's *Kick-Off* programme early in 1977. But having seen a tape of the interview and been refused an apology, Docherty was encouraged by a legal firm to take it further, as it could be detrimental to his career. If every manager sued every former player who made such comments the legal profession would be even wealthier, yet Docherty took the advice and went to court. 'I should have been more patient. People had often said to me I was a bad manager and I'd say, "That is your opinion." I trusted the advice I was given and I was probably after a few quid as well.'

Morgan had spent considerable time and money preparing his defence against Docherty's charges. Despite the protests of

Docherty's lawyers, he had even won a six-month adjournment earlier in the year in order to continue his groundwork. Now, Laurie Brown, Ted MacDougall, Paddy Crerand and Denis Law were among those lined up to testify on Morgan's behalf.

The case began in the High Court in London on 13 November and Docherty spent most of the proceedings defending his reputation as a manager. Among the financial issues discussed were the payment from Dunstable, the sale of FA Cup final tickets – described as 'ludicrous' by Docherty's barrister, Peter Bowsher QC – and the £5,000 bonus he had promised his team for beating Liverpool at Wembley. Martin Buchan tells the story of Docherty handing him the money to share among the players in the days after United's triumph, but as the skipper was about to go on summer holiday Buchan advised that it could wait until the start of pre-season training. Of course, Docherty was gone by then, and the money with him.

Docherty spoke of the success he'd achieved in rebuilding United on the field, explained to the court the circumstances of his dismissal and set about refuting each of the accusations levelled at him by Morgan's team. As well as the money matters, he denied singing an obscene song about Morgan in front of nuns and priests at a dinner and putting Denis Law on the transfer list after telling him he had a job for life. He also said he was considering legal action against United chairman Louis Edwards for commenting that 'we wanted a gentleman as well as a good football manager' when appointing Dave Sexton. But it was the Law episode that proved his undoing.

Docherty had told the court that he'd given Law plenty of warning of his free transfer, which he described as a 'golden handshake'. But in cross-examination, John Wilmers QC, defence counsel for Morgan, suggested Law had not agreed to such a move.

'Law protested and you agreed to take him off the list?' he asked.

'Yes,' Docherty replied.

'But the next day, when Law had travelled to Scotland to visit his sick mother, he heard on television that he was on the list?'

Docherty acknowledged that he had given the news to the media.

'No decent, competent manager would dream of treating a man like Law in that way,' Wilmers continued.

Docherty conceded, 'It was the wrong thing to do. It was very wrong.'

The following day, the third of the case, Wilmers referred back to the previous day's proceedings and asked Docherty, 'You told a pack of lies to the jury about this, didn't you?'

'Yes, it turned out that way,' was Docherty's damning response.

With that, the court took a break and the judge, Mr Justice O'Connor, asked to see both legal teams. Two and half hours later, the court returned to hear Bowsher state, 'I have been instructed by the plaintiff to apply for leave to discontinue this action. I am instructed to say that the plaintiff withdraws all allegations made against Willie Morgan and Granada during the course of this action.'

Docherty was left facing the payment of Morgan's £30,000 costs and his own of £20,000, while newspaper opinion leaned heavily towards the view that he should resign or be fired from his job at Derby. The club's response was to suspend him for a week while they considered their position.* Hardy, whom Docherty liked but thought was not tough enough to be chairman, wanted him to stay, while president and ex-chairman Sam Longson, Brian Clough's nemesis, felt that an admission of lying under oath was enough to have him fired.

After their thinking time elapsed, Hardy declared the board's continued support. 'The whole thing is regrettable from the club's point of view,' he stated, but concluded, 'We hired him in the first place for his abrasive qualities and that is what he has given us. The matter is now closed.'

In fact, it was far from it.

While Docherty took to opening his speaking engagements with the line, 'You'll never believe this,' the Director of Public Prosecutions' office took a more serious view and ordered Scotland Yard to pursue charges of perjury. 'I don't know whether to be surprised or shocked until I know officially what is happening,' Docherty said when the investigation was announced in March 1979.

Around the same time came news that Derby were under scrutiny for an alleged illegal approach to Dundee United defender David Narey, who was said to have been 'tapped up' by Blunstone at Brussels airport after his team played a European tie at Standard

---

* In the meantime, Docherty appeared at a dinner where fellow guest Bobby Charlton described him as 'a great friend who never told me a lie' and Brian Clough declared, 'I've told thousands of lies and so have those who employed me.'

Liège the previous September. At the time, Dundee United manager Jim McLean was reported to rate Narey at £325,000, which Docherty described as 'the best joke to come out of Scotland since the Loch Ness monster'.

The unrest kept coming. In April, Daly was suspended by Docherty for the second time in the season, for staying out late on the night before a game at Aston Villa. Two months earlier he'd been banned for two weeks for his comments after being dropped for a game against Southampton.

With Derby having barely retained their place in the First Division, Docherty realised that it was time to escape the strain and squabbles. 'I could see only another season of struggle ahead. I might have stayed and worked to put it right had it not been for the directors.'

A surprise escape route was offered by a phone call from QPR chairman Jim Gregory, who had just fired manager Steve Burtenshaw after his team's relegation from Division One was confirmed. The man with whom Docherty had been able to work for only 28 days in 1968 told him, 'I've changed since the last time we worked together. Little wiser, lot older. Neither of us gave it a chance last time round.'

Docherty recalls, 'It never crossed my mind that I would ever go back there. But he said, "Tom, I know we had differences before, but I am looking for a manager. I'll double the salary you were getting at Derby. And I will give you a few quid for yourself." In that situation he was the best. If he wanted someone, money was no object. When I wanted to sign Tony Currie, he said, "How much do you want him?" I said, "Badly," and he made sure I got him. I didn't think things would be any different this time, but I thought, "I'll get the money now and see what happens later on." I knew something would.'

And that was the truth.

18

DOC IN THE DOCK

'I remember going into the Old Bailey and people were piling into a lift. Someone said, "Going down?" and I said, "I hope not!"'

It was around 8 a.m. on Thursday, 4 October in the Kensington Hilton hotel. Tommy Docherty's mind was occupied with Queens Park Rangers' upcoming game at Watford, where a win would take their unbeaten run to five games and possibly lift them into the top three of the Second Division. That would be a pretty satisfactory situation after losing three of their first four matches.

There had been numerous knocks on the door since he began using this as his weekday base after leaving Derby for QPR. This one, however, was different. Instead of room service or housekeeping, it was a pair of detectives. Instead of heading to the Rangers training ground, Docherty found himself spending nine hours in a Derby police station.

He was informed by the officers, led by Detective Superintendent Jim Reddington, that they were questioning him under the terms of the Prevention of Corruption Act about transfer dealings at Derby County. Docherty had read newspaper reports of such an investigation but had never expected to face an interrogation focusing on the free transfer he had given to Irish defender Don O'Riordan after he'd played only a handful of games for the club.

Asked why he'd allowed O'Riordan to join American club Tulsa Roughnecks for no fee, he was forced to explain that free transfers were often given to players in whom there was little interest to allow them to make a fresh start or, in the case of older players, to reward them by allowing them to accept a signing-on bonus from a club not burdened by a transfer fee.

'So how do you explain that Tulsa then sold him to Preston for £30,000?' Docherty was asked.

'You'd better ask them,' he responded. Detecting the inference that he had somehow colluded with Tulsa to make a few thousand pounds, he pointed out that O'Riordan had been free to join any club he desired.

'He obviously thought I wasn't good enough to play regular first-team football at that level,' O'Riordan explains. 'After I went to Doncaster for a month there was talk of Tulsa being interested and he said, "How about going for a look?" I have heard one or two stories and I don't know the goings on behind the scenes, but he put no pressure on me. The Doc had done everything in his power to help me at Derby. He arrived while the government had put a ban on pay rises, but he would take me to away games as part of the squad, which meant you would get some bonus.'

Docherty, who would write in his autobiography, 'Never at any time in my career as a manager did I ever get anything out of a transfer deal,' was also asked by police what he knew of Derby's commercial activities, to which he replied, 'Nothing.'

With one court case already hanging over his head, Docherty was relieved to be released, with DS Reddington announcing, 'No charges have been made.' A call to the newspapers clearly had, though. Like a convicted criminal, Docherty was huddled under a blanket on the back seat of Mary Brown's car as he drove past a posse of photographers and awoke to find his ordeal all over the front pages. It was another example of how his life seemed to have spiralled uncontrollably into a series of mishaps and misadventures since the day he'd informed Manchester United of his love for Mary.

Sometimes, though, the headlines were of his own making.

He had arrived at Loftus Road just in time to see QPR lose the final game of their relegation campaign 4–0 to Ipswich. A summer tour to Nigeria at least proved to him that he had a strike force to be reckoned with in teenagers Paul Goddard and Clive Allen, whose father, Les, had succeeded him as Rangers manager after his brief stint in 1968.

'He spoke to me and Paul and said we would be starting the season, even though it was still five weeks away,' says Allen. 'We had a number of international players who were coming to the end of their QPR careers and it was quite a move to tell us that he was going with the young players – a fantastic boost for us.'

Docherty's confidence would be justified by Allen's 28 League goals in the ensuing season and Goddard's 16, but other areas clearly needed strengthening. Chris Woods, understudy to Peter Shilton at Nottingham Forest, was bought for £250,000 before Jim Gregory's largesse allowed Docherty to bring ex-Sheffield United midfielder Tony Currie from Leeds. At last, he managed to prise David McCreery away from Manchester United for £200,000.

England youth international Steve Burke was signed for £150,000 from Nottingham Forest to add some width to the attack, while Bob Hazell, from Wolves, and Steve Wicks, from Derby, formed a new central defensive partnership, forcing Docherty's club captain Glenn Roeder forward into midfield. 'That's it for a bit,' Docherty said after paying £275,000 for Wicks. Yet in late November another familiar face arrived when he spent £175,000 to bring Gordon Hill from the Baseball Ground.

'I'd been out for nearly a year with a severe knee injury,' Hill recalls. 'They took all the cartilage out and the ACL [anterior cruciate ligament] was ruptured. In those days you were lucky to come back from that. I was absolutely scared to death. I trained hard and I got fit, but psychologically I wasn't right. I was wondering whether that knee would open up again. Ipswich wanted to buy me, even injured, but then the Boss said to me, "Come on, I am going to give you a chance," and I chose QPR. He believed in me and believed that maybe the injury wasn't as severe as it was. I had been at QPR as a kid, but it wasn't as nice this time.'

Ian Gillard, one of the few established players to maintain his place under Docherty, who had given him his first-team debut in 1968, recalls the unrest that the numerous changes created. 'The problem was that there were so many,' he says. 'In a football club there are rumours, and players come in and say they are on this and that, and it causes turmoil. If you're on a contract and have been in the team, and all of a sudden he is putting kids on double what you are earning, that is a problem.'

Any rifts between different groups within the squad were masked by results and performances. Allen continues, 'The Doc made sure he had players who could fit into the QPR way, which was the same attacking style as his other teams. He had an experienced side when he first came, but it needed to be changed. We started the season pretty well and we were scoring goals pretty freely. As a forward, you knew he was looking for the team to create chances for you. Paul and I had come through the youth team together and he saw the best way to get something out of us. We were never negative.'

Away from the field, Docherty's broken marriage had been the source of plenty of negativity and animosity, with a lot of the unseemly squabbling over money that surrounds many such cases. It took more than two years of legal back and forth before the case came to court in October 1979, at which point, Agnes recalled, Docherty's lawyers' offer of a one-off £25,000 settlement was rejected. She considered such a deal 'derisory'. Instead, the court ruled that Docherty must pay her £9,000 annually, plus another £1,000 in respect of their youngest son, Paul. The family home would be sold and the profits split.

Docherty's reputation and credibility might have been compromised by the events of the past two years, notably the Willie Morgan libel trial, but his outspokenness still made him an ideal choice to address a football writers' lunch in mid-November. The audience of journalists were not disappointed by what he delivered.

'Any manager who says he has not cheated or lied is not being honest,' was his headline-grabbing proposition. 'The morals in football are very different from other jobs. It is the law of life and sometimes the only way to survive is to tell lies. There are lots of times when managers are honest . . . but there are lots of other times when they are cheats. We all cheat, we all tell lies, we all con people.'

These were hardly the most advisable comments from a man waiting for the date of his perjury trial, but the intention was to convey the game of bluff that sport in the modern age had become. Besides, experience had led Docherty to the point in his life where he felt that he was likely to be damned whichever side of the honesty fence he came down upon. Eamon Dunphy argues, 'He learned a bitter lesson and decided to conform to football's perverse notion of integrity, and being the impulsive fellow he was – and fundamentally honest – he was less inclined, as the years went on, to conceal his roguishness.'

The mock-shocked reaction of some reporters belied their own knowledge that this was exactly how the football world operated.

Many would frequently have been complicit, gratefully accepting scoops about transfer targets or contract negotiations in the full knowledge that this was all part of the sport's drama of deceit.

The acknowledgement of the existence of such an underworld – an action that for a while raised the possibility of his expulsion from the Secretaries, Managers and Coaches' Association – was considered a lack of 'loyalty' towards his profession by the likes of writer David Miller, who said, 'Docherty has attempted to drag everyone down to the level of his own tattered reputation.' Yet he also conceded that there was 'an element of truth' in his comments. As usual, Docherty was provoking conflicting responses.

Meanwhile, another contradiction could be found in his relationship with Stan Bowles. 'Currie and Bowles were tremendously gifted individuals, but for me they were also great team players,' Docherty recalled. He even explained that he allowed Bowles, an inveterate gambler, to go dog racing on Friday evenings as long as he was back at the team hotel by 11 p.m. Never did he suspect his player of having a drink while he was at the track. Yet Bowles had responded to Docherty's promise that 'you can trust me, Stan', by responding, 'I'd rather trust my chickens with Colonel Sanders.' While continuing to play an important role in the first team, Bowles spent most of his time training with the reserves. He filled the role of chief provider for the Allen–Goddard partnership, not scoring his first goal of the season until a 4–0 win against Charlton late in November, a result that took Rangers to the top of the table after fourteen games with only one defeat.

A couple of weeks later Bowles was gone, Rangers finding an offer of £250,000 from Nottingham Forest too good to resist. Docherty had conducted negotiations from a hospital bed after the latest bizarre turn of events in his life.

Ever since taking the job at Derby in the weeks following the revelations about his love life, Docherty had heard the chants. Wherever his team played, opposition fans were quick to greet his appearance by striking up, 'Who's up Mary Brown?' to the tune of 'Knees Up Mother Brown'.

It would lead him to say, 'As a manager I am used to jibes and snide cracks. I can take them and give them. But for Mary I realise it must sometimes have been almost unbearable.' In the heat of a game, Docherty was able to grit his teeth and block it out. But on the evening of Saturday, 8 December, he was heading north after a home draw against Wrexham when a small group of youths, reported to be Manchester City fans, boarded the train. Discovering the identity of their fellow passenger, they settled into his carriage and burst into song.

At the end of a painful week in which he'd been forced to return to Scotland to bury his mother, it was all he needed. 'The worst day of my life was when she died, at the age of 82,' he says. 'When she died, all the money I'd sent her from my army days and throughout my career came back to me. She never spent it.'

Also on the train that evening was James Ferry of Stockport, who said, 'A group of about six men were in the buffet. They told me they had been to watch City play at Ipswich and knew the Doc was on the train. He had been sitting in the restaurant and they had been singing filthy songs.' Confronted by the familiar refrain at such close quarters and embarrassed for himself and fellow passengers, Docherty asked the choristers to desist, which, grudgingly and intermittently, they did. Yet when he stepped off the train at Stockport, members of the group followed and attacked him with kicks to the head and body, leaving him unconscious and bloodied. 'I was on the ground and they were kicking the hell out of me,' he said. After arriving at Stockport Royal Infirmary he was treated for concussion, ruptured tendons in his leg, which required surgery, bruised ribs and various cuts and grazes.

Released from hospital after six days with his leg in plaster and head bandaged, Docherty was reluctant to press charges. One of the men responsible for the attack had even phoned him in hospital to apologise, to which Docherty had responded, 'Don't worry about me. Let's call it a draw.' Even that gesture attracted criticism, with political columnist George Gale reminding Docherty in print that he 'is not the law of the land . . . public disorder is the public's concern'. But another courtroom was the last thing he wanted; nor did he wish to have Mary dragged into the headlines again. He wanted instead to turn his attention to getting back to work before the end of the two-month break he'd been ordered to take.

In the end, charges were brought and fines ranging from £25 to £250 handed out. 'A cheap price to pay for all my injuries,' noted Docherty, who was accused by one of those found guilty to have thrown the first punch. The defendant's solicitor, Rodney Taylor, even attempted to use Docherty's ill-fated libel trial to his client's benefit. 'Docherty has admitted lying under oath in widely publicised civil proceedings, but the defendant is a witness of truth.' The Stockport magistrates thought otherwise.

Docherty made it back to Loftus Road after five weeks, but in the meantime Rangers' promotion bid had suffered a fatal slump, with only one point gained from five games in his absence. Allen recalls Docherty calling a meeting where the players had a chance to identify any problems.

'He wanted us to give our opinion on what had happened and why results had dropped off,' Allen explains. 'It was a typical meeting where the defenders said it was down to the forwards, or the midfield players said we were letting in too many goals. When it came to the strikers I remember him saying, "If the front boys had not scored the goals they have, we wouldn't be in the position we are in." It was difficult, as a 17-year-old, having to speak up, but he did it for us, protected us.'

Allen saw it as a sign of Docherty's loyalty to those players in whom he believed: 'He did have disagreements with players and they were always played out in the papers, but if he liked you he stuck by you. You might not always play well, but if you were a player for him he would give you every chance and every confidence.'

Only two matches out of eighteen were lost following Docherty's return, but Rangers could finish only fifth, four points behind third-placed Birmingham. After a defeat at Shrewsbury, Docherty met the press with a piece of sticking tape over his mouth and told them, 'You write what you like. If I said what I thought, I'd be shot.'

Gregory was already loading his bullets, and in May he told Docherty he was terminating his contract. Not only had promotion been missed, the chairman was unhappy that his manager had still not bought a home in London and had even turned down an offer to live in one that Gregory owned. 'Not for one moment did I think the fact I lived in a hotel during the week affected my ability as a manager,' said Docherty, who insisted that his squad was primed for a promotion push in 1980–81. Gregory disagreed, and a brief statement saying that Docherty had left 'by mutual consent' was released.

Players and fans were reported to be equally disappointed at the developments. One unnamed player was quoted as saying, 'We're gutted. There is a real feeling of hostility about what's happened. The boss has been a great players' man. The spirit at the club has been unbelievable. I think some of the players might ask to see the chairman.'

They did exactly that. 'We told the chairman that the boss hadn't done anything wrong,' said skipper Roeder. 'If anything we had let him down by dropping silly points.'

Gillard offers further detail: 'Players like David McCreery, Steve Wicks and Chris Woods all wanted him to stay. We had a meeting and Gregory wanted the senior pros there. I spoke to him on the phone and he told me to get there and told me what players he wanted there. We went to his office and he basically said that Tommy was taking the piss out of him. He showed us his expense sheet, which was absolutely phenomenal, and said he'd offered him a house to stay in. But as a player you don't know the ins and outs; you only get all this from one source.'

Ken Shellito, a faithful servant from back in the Chelsea days, had gone to QPR as Docherty's coach, having had a spell as manager at Stamford Bridge in 1977–78. He recalls, 'We had a very good team at Rangers and we had just missed out on promotion. They were good players and good lads and they loved working for Tom.'

He remembers that they even put up with his attempted mind games. 'We played at Oldham one day, a hell of a good game, and we won 3–1. I was in the dugout and Tom came down for the last two minutes and said, "You sit there. When the players come in I am going to give them a right bollocking." I said he couldn't do that because they had played brilliantly, but he said, "I know. You sit here for five minutes." He went in there and he really battered them. I walked in the dressing-room and the lads looked around and said, "What's up with him?" So I had to think of something and I said, "I think he's had a row with the missus. I think he thinks you played quite well and deserved to win." He liked me and him to play against each other. Other times when I thought they were useless he'd say, "That wasn't that bad. One or two mistakes, but we'll sort it out Monday." The players responded to it.'

Despite his reservations, Gregory listened to the players, and a week later Docherty was back in a job, committing himself to a move south, which he said had been 'our intention all along'.

As well as receiving the official summons to appear in court later in the year on two perjury charges, Docherty's summer involved the bizarre sale of Clive Allen for £1.2 million to Arsenal. Before he'd played a game, the Gunners sent him to the club that really wanted him, Crystal Palace, from whom they acquired left-back Kenny Sansom in exchange. Rangers also accepted an £850,000 offer from West Ham for Paul Goddard. In his desperate search to replace their goals, Docherty found himself opening the season with Hazell up front alongside Mickey Walsh, the £400,000 purchase of Chelsea's Tommy Langley having gone through just too late. Everton midfielder Andy King arrived for the same amount in September, but results could hardly have gone worse for a manager who'd been reprieved on the promise that things were about to get better.

After ten League games, QPR had won only twice and were in 18th place. They'd had the satisfaction beating Docherty's old club, Derby, on penalties after two legs in the League Cup, only to crash 4–1 to Notts County in the third round.

Shellito says he saw little change in Docherty's character over the years, despite the setbacks. 'He was exactly the same all the way through. The same as he was when he first came to Chelsea: bubbly and bouncy. You think how terrific he is to have around.'

Yet after that Notts County game Docherty sounded like a man who'd had enough. 'If the game gets any worse I will pack it in,' he said. 'Football has lost a lot of enjoyment. I never thought I would see the day when I got fed up with football. It's all happened in the past year.'

While intended as a comment on the state of the game, it gives an insight into Docherty's own state of mind at that point. Having greeted each bad result with assurances that he was under no pressure, this sounded like a man struggling to keep up the cheerful facade after all that had gone on in his life and with a criminal case looming.

Hill, who knew Docherty's moods as well as anyone, says, 'He used his humour. He could be serious and then have a laugh, which you need when you are under pressure.' But he also recognised that Docherty was deeper than the comedian he was mostly portrayed as. 'To me, it was a front. It was the same thing as people calling me cocky. The Boss would try to laugh things off. But deep down we all have feelings, and we all have our own way of letting it out.'

Docherty looks back on that period of his life with thoughts first and foremost for Mary: 'My biggest regret about everything at that time was not for me, but for what it put her through. All the stuff with the court cases, she needed that like a hole in the head. I tried not to ever lose my sense of humour. There were lots of times when I would come home and feel down, but I tried to get on with it. After we got through those first few years, we knew nothing could be as tough as that.'

Things had still to reach their worst, though. On 8 October, the day after a goalless home draw against Orient, Docherty drove from his Berkshire cottage to see Gregory once more. According to Docherty's after-dinner speeches over the past three decades, Gregory announced, 'Tom, I think I'm going to call it a day,' to which he replied, 'Don't do that, Mr Chairman, you're doing a great job.'

Having made clear his intentions, Gregory asked, 'How much do we owe you?'

'Thirty thousand quid,' Docherty answered.

'I'll give you fifteen.'

'I'll take it.'

'Why,' Gregory continued, 'are you taking fifteen if we owe you thirty?'

'Because if I hold out for thirty I'll end up with nothing.'

'You're right. Tom, you could have been a great salesman.'

Writing Docherty a cheque for the agreed amount, Gregory added, 'How did you get here today?'

'The club car,' Docherty answered, indicating his Mercedes keys, which were swiftly snatched from his grasp. 'How am I going to get home?' he asked, nonplussed.

'You've got fifteen grand,' Gregory growled, 'Get a taxi.'

Shellito has his own recollection of Docherty's departure. 'We played Orient at home on a freezing-cold day – pitch bone-hard, lousy game,' he explains. 'Doc went up to have a drink with the chairman afterwards and Terry Venables was in there talking to him.* Mr Gregory phoned me later and said, "I have just sacked

---

* Venables would be named as Rangers' manager soon after Docherty's dismissal, leading them to the FA Cup final the following season. Incidentally, the firing of Docherty came in the same week that Malcolm Allison, so often bracketed with him in public perception, was fired from his second spell at Manchester

Tom. Come and see me." As simple as that. I didn't have a clue what went on.'

Docherty told reporters that he had not been sacked because of results, adding cryptically, 'I do know what cost me my job, but I am not prepared to say.'

According to Hill, 'The Boss was trying his hardest, but he found it a little bit tough. We heard he'd got the sack because he was wheeling and dealing on his expenses. The chairman was a street boy, and you can't diddle your expenses with somebody like that. I can imagine the meetings with them both sitting there wondering which ace the other has got up his sleeve.'

Shellito recalls, 'The players were devastated. Tom created enjoyment. Even when you were working hard, people enjoyed it. He had this magic touch.' Yet this time there was no reprieve, no deputation from the players, one of whom said, 'We are sorry to see Tom go, but working with him was like working with a time bomb. There's a little bit of calm, then wallop!'

Gillard, meanwhile, offers a damning assessment of Docherty's second spell at the club. 'For him to come back, I think it was just pure desperation from Gregory at the time,' he suggests. 'Tommy should never have taken the job. The club was absolutely in bits. He had his personal problems and problems with the chairman and I don't think he was the right man. I don't think his mind was on the job.' Echoing Blunstone's earlier suggestion, Gillard adds, 'I think he had a drink problem at that time.'

Docherty's name has never turned up in the kind of binge-drinking escapades that dogged his buddy Allison, or been linked to the chronic problem that eventually undermined the career of Clough. He himself says that he 'would always describe my drinking as being far less than even moderate' and once said that after Chelsea's promotion he got drunk on a single gin and bitter lemon given to him by the chairman. 'Since then I suppose I've made up for that abstinence,' he added.

Yet even Tom Finney noted that 'Tom was many things, but not a teetotaller and not interested in learning how to become one', and

---

City. Journalists mourned the simultaneous loss of two of the most quotable figures in the game. Allison, though, was soon installed to replace Venables at Palace.

it is interesting that at two different clubs it has been suggested that drink might have been his way of coping with the turmoil in his life at that time.

Gillard also recalls being surprised at his tolerance of others' alcohol intake. 'When we were travelling up north on Friday and staying in a hotel, he'd let the younger lads have a drink, and they thought it was great. I thought it was completely wrong. You are preparing for a game. He was a great character and would tell great stories, but the last part of his term at QPR was a complete disaster.'

Docherty had been pondering his future for only a couple of days when an old friend told him of an opportunity to manage Australian side Sydney Olympic. He needed little persuading, although first he had a date in late December at the Old Bailey. Representing Docherty, Barry Singleton stated his client was not prepared for the perjury trial because he would not have the necessary funds until fulfilling his contract in Sydney. 'He did not want to run up fees at a time when he could not possibly pay them,' Singleton stated. An adjournment of the case from March to October was reluctantly accepted by Judge Michael Argyle, who complained that 'the matter has been hanging around too long'.

Sydney club president John Constantine clearly felt that any baggage that came with Docherty was worth it, as was the £30,000 the club was reported to be paying him for a season. 'We are not concerned by his controversial record,' he said. 'He is a man whose vast experience can be used.'

Docherty landed with the view that he could 'contribute to Australian soccer if I stay here five or ten years'. But what he discovered at his club, which had a traditionally Greek fan base, hardly met with his immediate approval. Olympic trained at primitive facilities in the suburb of Croydon, where there were no goalposts, and within a week of arrival Docherty had released six of the players, saying, 'I don't want a team of bloody geriatrics.'

The club's ground, however, was 'neat and tidy', according to Docherty, who quickly developed a routine around the players' Tuesday and Thursday training sessions and his own media, promotional and speaking commitments. 'I loved life in Sydney,' he said.

Docherty signed a couple of players who had been on the fringes at Old Trafford, Martyn Rogers and Steve Paterson, yet the first game of the Phillips Soccer League season ended in a 3–1 defeat at Wollongong Wolves, setting the tone for a season in which Olympic would finish ninth out of sixteen teams. In the end, Docherty barely spent five months with the club, let alone five years.

In June, he was announced as the new manager of the first English club to have employed him, Preston North End, newly relegated to the Third Division. Preston director Howard McCann said that it was clear that Sydney wanted to keep Docherty, but the call of home proved irresistible and a fee of £30,000 paid by North End to Olympic secured his release.

Docherty left with a parting shot at the 'petty politics and bigotry' of Australian football, not realising that he would soon be returning: 'People in the state federations don't seem to be interested in Australian soccer. All they are interested in is being big bosses in their little own domains. I've got no time for these little people.' He also expressed disappointment that national team coach Rudi Gutendorf had not asked for his help during the qualifying campaign for the 1982 World Cup.

Australia, for its part, seemed sorry to see Docherty leave. Despite mediocre results, Constantine said he would have tripled his salary to keep him, while Tom Hammond of the *Sydney Morning Herald* said, 'He took a bunch of ordinary players and some talented youngsters and moulded them into the most attractive team in the PSL.' The paper also noted, 'At least when the master coach was in charge they lost with style. They would go out to give spectators value for money . . . they were exciting.'

Docherty, with typical hyperbole, stated, 'I think that was the best coaching job I have ever done. I didn't have the unlimited money I had in English football; I had to make do with what we had.' He was particularly pleased with having turned an ordinary club defender, Jim Zoras, into one of the country's leading sweepers and said of midfielder Peter Katholos, 'This boy could become a million-pound player in England. He has everything.'

Docherty announced his return to Deepdale with his similar bluster. 'Preston will be great again,' he declared. 'Tom Finney phoned to say that they had been inundated with requests for season tickets after my appointment. That will pay my wages. This is a football town waiting to reawaken. The fans will come back if we play entertaining football.'

Once again, he summoned Shellito to work with him. 'He called and said, "What are you doing? I have got a job for you,"' Shellito recalls. 'I never asked the club or salary or anything. My wife said, "Where are you going? How much? Have you got a car or a contract?" I said, "I don't know. Tom is sorting it out." I just enjoyed working with him.'

Perhaps Shellito should have waited before rushing to Docherty's side. His friend's tenure at Deepdale began with a 2–1 loss at Millwall, and after Alex Bruce got the only goal of the opening home game against Portsmouth it was not until ten games later that Preston achieved their second victory.

Goalkeeper Roy Tunks, a teenager under Docherty at Rotherham almost a decade and a half earlier, was now in the veteran category, which, as so often, meant he was surplus to the Doc's requirements. Having been Preston's regular number one for seven years, he never played a game under Docherty before being transferred to Wigan in November. 'The best thing about Tommy was that you knew exactly where you stood with him,' Tunks explains. 'The first time under him I was a yes and the second time I was a definite no. He hadn't changed a great deal. The experienced players, about 11 of us, were cut off straight away and were changing in the away team dressing-room. We called ourselves the "leper colony". But if he didn't want you he would help you get away. My move to Wigan suited both of us. Tommy made sure I picked up some of the money that was due to me in loyalty bonuses.

'I got the impression that he liked the youngsters because they gave him the energy he needed and they weren't the cynical old pros who knew what was going on as far as coaching was concerned. They were easier for Tommy to motivate and stimulate.'

Back from America, Docherty's former Derby player Don O'Riordan had feared for his future after learning the identity of his new boss. 'The Doc's reputation was that if he got rid of a player at one club he would get rid of you again,' he recalls. 'I was very committed that pre-season, and after a month he called me in, offered me a new contract, a rise and made me captain."

---

* O'Riordan remained close enough to Docherty to invite him to help raise funds for Galway United when manager of the Irish side in the late '90s. Having arranged for the club's supporters to play brief games on every Premier League

But O'Riordan soon became aware that Docherty was struggling to give the job his full attention. 'At that time he seemed to be away a lot. He had a book out and there was his legal situation. I don't think we got the best out of him. He was a very good manager, tactically very astute, but I felt he took the job at a time when his personal life was very busy, and it didn't help. His Manchester United team played really fantastic football, and to win games at that level you have to have a bit of magic. When he came to Preston his life was probably different and he must have been under a lot of pressure. Being a football manager is tough enough when everything is hunky-dory in your life.'

Docherty admits that he was distracted during this period by his looming court case. The initial feeling of comfort from his return to his first English professional home was quickly replaced by a growing fear of what might happen under further cross-examination in the witness box. 'I felt I was in danger of saying something I did not mean,' he admitted.

Meanwhile, the club was losing more than £300,000 per year and had no funds available for strengthening the team or rebuilding crumbling terraces. When promising centre-half Mick Baxter was sold to Middlesbrough for a reported £425,000, very little of that windfall found its way into the transfer budget. It was hardly a template for success.

Docherty's case came to the Central Criminal Court at the Old Bailey on Tuesday, 12 October. Presenting the prosecution, Paul Purnell outlined that Docherty had lied to a jury to protect his reputation and gave details of the two charges he now faced. The first related to his account of the Denis Law free transfer and his claim that Law was unsurprised and undisturbed by it. The second charge related to his assertion during the libel trial that he had been unaware of an agreement whereby United would owe a further £25,000 when Ted MacDougall reached 20 goals for them. According to Purnell, Doherty's stated ignorance of this was a 'deliberate lie'.

On the second day of the trial, Law told the jury of his

---

ground, O'Riordan asked Docherty to manage one of the sides. 'He travelled with us and every night he would tell different stories to all these guys who were football fanatics,' he recalled. 'I have nothing but praise for the way he conducted himself.'

'considerable shock' at hearing of his transfer on television. When Docherty came to offer a defence, he claimed to have been harrassed by the legal team for Willie Morgan and Granada TV. 'I was in such a state I didn't know what I was doing,' he told the court. 'I felt intimidated and bullied and I just didn't know where I was.' Docherty's barrister, Richard DuCann QC, told the court that his client was 'knocked all over the field' and asked him if he had intended to deliberately lie under oath. 'No way,' Docherty responded. 'Never in a million years. I would not do that.'

Throughout the proceedings, Docherty kept wondering how he had got himself into such a mess, how he had come to the point where his liberty was at risk. 'I thanked God I had Mary and her support, also that of family members and close friends,' he said.

A week after the case opened, the jury delivered their verdict. Having deliberated for only two hours, they returned a unanimous decision: not guilty. Having resisted the urge to celebrate as though he had just seen a goal go in, Docherty struggled to fight back tears. As he left the court he simply said, 'Thank God, I'm clear,' and kissed Mary, who had spent every day of the case in court. His freedom still cost him around £20,000, though, when the judge ruled that it had been appropriate for the case to be brought and therefore he could not claim costs, even though the jury had agreed that he'd not set out deliberately to lie during the libel case. He could also not escape the feeling that his reputation had been damaged to the point where no other major job opportunities were likely to come his way.

One positive aspect of the traumatic experience was the support he received from so many members of the public, some of them United fans, others with no obvious affiliation. 'They had been wonderful to me throughout it all,' he wrote not long after the case. 'I knew that many who had reservations about me figure now I may not be such a bad chap after all.'

Even Law would declare himself 'honestly delighted' at the verdict, saying, 'I didn't want to be involved in sending Tommy Docherty to jail,' and concluding, 'I don't bear him a grudge on a personal level, although it's hard to forgive him for what he put my family through.'

Back at Deepdale, preparation had been made for the jury's decision. 'I can remember going into the treatment room on the day of the verdict,' says Tunks. 'We used to have an ice machine and in it were a couple of bottles of champagne. The joke among the players was that Tommy had admitted perjury, but the judge wouldn't believe him.'

Docherty might not have been 'going down' after all, but Preston couldn't stop playing like a team about to do exactly that. Attempts to strengthen the team by buying Derby winger Paul Emson and making loan signings such as transfer-listed Ipswich forward Robin Turner had come to nothing, and on 3 December, with the team third from bottom after winning only three games and dumped out of the FA Cup 4–1 at Chesterfield, Docherty was fired.

His meeting with chairman Alan Jones quickly became the subject of another of his famous jokes: 'The chairman said, "We'll give you £10,000 to settle this amicably." I said, "You'll have to be a lot more amicable than that."' In the end, Docherty ended up getting a reported £15,000 pay-off the following July.

Club president Finney was sad to see his old teammate kicked out. 'The North End sickness was terminal and way beyond any cure the Doc could prescribe,' he would recall, adding that he was 'unable to stimulate players who fell well below his standards'.

As Docherty waited for the next job offer, he kept himself busy with media activity, such as a *Call the Doc* show on Manchester's Piccadilly Radio and being featured on BBC Radio 2's *The World Of . . .*

He was linked with Wolves, battling the drop to Division Two, and then publicly expressed an interest in the vacancy at Bristol City, although he pointed out that he never applied for any jobs – to which club chairman Archie Gooch replied, 'If Tommy Docherty has not applied he will not be considered.' Meanwhile, Northampton, bottom of Division Four and without a manager, reported they had turned down an offer from Docherty to work for them for expenses only.

In May 1982, he announced that he was returning to Australia to join a South Melbourne Hellas team that had not won a game in seven weeks. Initially, club president Sam Papasavas stated that Docherty would work alongside current coach John Margaritis under manager Lee Anazakis, yet Margaritis quit within hours of introducing Docherty to the players.

Scottish-born Melbourne defender Steve Blair recalls, 'It was huge for the club and for Australian soccer, given the name Tommy had in world football. We had mostly Greek support, but even they were excited. The night he arrived, John was training us and this big limousine arrived and the Doc got out. He had that character, that aura. John could see the writing on the wall and he left the club.'

Splitting his time between Melbourne and Sydney, where he was conducting coaching clinics, Docherty led the team to two wins and a draw in his first three games. It prompted the *Melbourne Age* to note their newfound commitment and remark upon the improved form of former Wolves, Liverpool and Aston Villa forward Alun Evans. Within weeks of Docherty's arrival, however, Evans had fallen out with his new coach and been placed on the transfer list.

'He had high expectations of us, even though we were part-time,' Blair continues. 'He could be pretty cut-throat if you didn't do what he wanted. He trained us hard. As well as Alun Evans, we had Bertie Lutton from Wolves and others where he knew their professional background. It was a lot different to what we'd had before because we'd just had local coaches.

'He created an excitement and expectation. The press were interested in him and there was a huge buzz. He wanted us to be attacking, to go at other teams and not be nervous. Mind you, he wasn't there for every training session. He would let somebody else do a lot of it. I think he enjoyed it. He was wined and dined, and I think he fell on his feet.'

A poor run of results halted the Hallas revival, but could not douse Docherty's outspokenness as he proceeded to criticise the standard of Australian coaches and described one rival team, Preston Makedonia, as 'worse than a pub team'.

Docherty would soon be returning to Sydney Olympic, although not before he came close enough to being given the job of coach of the Austrian national team to have newspapers speculating about how he would tackle the challenge of qualifying for the 1984 European Championship finals. Docherty had even stated, 'After being manager of Scotland I don't see why I can't be successful in this job.'

Instead, shortly before Australian football's end-of-season presentation evening, rumours of his return to Olympic on a two-year contract were confirmed, replacing the fired former Burnley midfielder Doug Collins.

Despite the aggravations, Docherty had enjoyed his return to Australia, sensing that the game was moving forward thanks to a greater sense of cooperation between teams and increased sponsorship and funding. Of course, this didn't stop him getting up the noses of his opponents. At a pre-season tournament in January 1983, St George coach Frank Arok warned, 'Tommy Docherty seems to be making a fair amount of noise about this and that. We'll soon see if his words have any bite. I want to put Docherty in his place early in the season. He has been bragging about the players he has brought in and that his team will win this and that.'

Docherty's signings were notable among those for whom Australian football was something more than a list of team names on a summer pools coupon. They included New Zealand international Ricki Herbert and highly rated Australian players Jim Patikas and Marshall Soper. This being Docherty, however, things did not quite run to plan. Olympic achieved only mid-table status, although there were plenty of incidents to keep Docherty in the headlines.

During one home defeat he took to the field to protest to the referee about the tough tackling of the Adelaide Giants players. Later in the year he fined Soper a week's wages for picking up a needless booking that led to a suspension. Docherty had even made him captain in the hope that he would react positively to the responsibility. 'I asked him to be careful, but instead he ended up chasing the referee,' he complained.

As the season progressed, Olympic's fans became increasingly disgruntled. Groups of hecklers began turning up at training sessions, with things coming to a head at a game against Brisbane City. Docherty had fruit thrown at him before kick-off and 40 fans stayed behind after the 3–0 defeat to shout abuse at him. Docherty's response was to warn the *Sydney Morning Herald*, 'I just won't put up with that sort of behaviour – spitting and throwing things. Some of them are just animals. They don't deserve a team.'

Olympic's English striker Steve Paterson, who had to be persuaded to stay on the field at half-time, added, 'Not even in England is it like this. There they acknowledge when you try; here they just spit at you.'

It was no surprise when club president Jim Petinellis announced at the start of September, 'After a long meeting with Tommy we have mutually agreed that he should be released.' The local paper spoke of the 'widening rift between him and club management over crowd behaviour'.

Before he returned to England, Docherty also claimed that finances had played a part in his departure, suggesting that he and his players had had to fight to receive their salaries. Petinellis denied such allegations, which, he said, 'cast serious aspersion on the good name of the club'. According to Petinellis, Docherty 'was always paid his very generous wages on time' and had received the A$6,000 that had been agreed when he left the club. Docherty's radio comments were being examined by the club's solicitors, he warned.

Back in England, Docherty was reported in October to be close to being given the vacant Bournemouth job by managing director Brian Tiler, his former player, following the resignation of Don Megson and the appointment of Harry Redknapp as caretaker manager. 'I was offered the job and accepted, but have heard nothing since,' he claimed more than a week after the speculation began.

When Docherty did return to the game, it was with one of the teams to have dominated English football during his playing days. As he was to discover, however, Wolverhampton Wanderers was a very different place three decades later.

19

GAME OVER

'My doctor told me to stay away from football for a while, so I took the job at Wolves.'

When Tommy Docherty arrived in the manager's office at Wolverhampton Wanderers in June 1984, it was only four years since the club had lifted their most recent trophy, beating Nottingham Forest to win the League Cup, yet a lot had happened to them in the meantime – nearly all of it bad. The Doc's last season in full-time professional football was to be his most miserable.

By 1982, Wolves were facing an increasing struggle against the debt incurred by the new Molineux Stand. The club almost went out of business in the summer, saved by a new team of owners taking over minutes before the Football League's deadline for extinction. At the forefront of the group – who beat off Aston Villa chairman Doug Ellis's bid to take control – was Wolves legend Derek Dougan. Appointed chief executive, the colourful former centre-forward was the front man for a consortium pieced together largely by club director Doug Hope and backed by Mahmud and Akbar Bhatti, the principals of a company called Allied Properties. The brothers initially insisted on keeping their identities hidden from the public and it took several months of journalistic digging to uncover Wolves' mysterious saviours. Yet, as Hope admits, 'We didn't do sufficient due diligence in relation to the Bhattis and a lot was taken on trust.'

Even while the team was gaining promotion in 1982–83 under new manager Graham Hawkins, it became apparent that the Bhattis did not have the money they had suggested. They had borrowed heavily against Wolves' assets, and the club's failure to secure planning permission for a superstore development left them facing a bleak financial future. 'The funding wasn't there from the Bhattis,' says Hope. 'They were reluctant to fund it even if they were in a position to do so.'

Without the money to maintain a playing staff capable of surviving in Division One, Wolves were instantly relegated, with Hawkins failing to see out the season. Enter Docherty, whose appointment took most observers by surprise. He'd not even been a universal choice at the club. Dougan was outvoted, having preferred one of the other candidates, who included former Wolves players Mike Bailey and John McAlle and other experienced managers in Alan Mullery and Alan Durban. Docherty hardly endeared himself to his boss by stating, 'Derek Dougan is to football what King Herod is to babysitting.'

Hope recalls, 'Doog wasn't keen on having Docherty, but we felt he was an experienced manager, a character, and felt he could lift the club. Derek and Tommy had crossed swords in the past, but I don't think there was any problem.'

Docherty confirms, 'Doog was all right; he didn't interfere with what I was doing. But I only met the Bhatti brothers twice – when they hired me and when they fired me.'

Offered a one-year contract, Docherty's long-term prospects were so uncertain that the club advised him not to move from his Derbyshire home, an hour and a quarter's drive away. Instead he commuted every day, stopping for a bacon roll with the lorry drivers at a roadside café trailer. 'There are a lot of people waiting for me to fail again,' he said on the day he arrived at Molineux for the first time. 'Most of them are other managers. I've said things about people who still bear a grudge. This is a difficult job, but I am loving it.'

If Docherty's credentials had been fading, then Molineux at this time was hardly the place to re-establish himself. At one stage the Professional Footballers' Association had to intervene to ensure the players were paid. Tim Flowers, a youngster who would go on to keep goal for England, recalled cockroaches among the peeling paint of the dressing-rooms. Boots had to be borrowed, the milkman stopped delivering and the local garage cut off the club's petrol supply.

For the opening match, at home to Sheffield United, Docherty selected the untested Flowers, not yet signed as a professional, and

18-year-old midfielder Paul Daugherty, who had played five games the previous season. 'Young players help to keep you young,' was his philosophy. Experience was provided by former Blackpool and Birmingham midfielder Alan Ainscow, who had signed for the club after returning from a spell with Eastern AA, in Hong Kong. 'The ground was dropping to bits and there wasn't enough quality in the side,' he recalled.

A 3–2 reverse at Leeds was the only game Wolves lost in the first five, but the next five all ended in defeat. 'The Wolves directors are the most honest men I have ever worked with,' Docherty said during the season. 'When I started they said I would have no money for new players and they have kept their word.'

He was forced to search for free transfers, such as Ipswich full-back David Barnes and Chester defender Peter Zelem, or those he could obtain on loan. Some familiar names were acquired for a few weeks at a time: former Wolves centre-forward Peter Eastoe, who arrived from West Brom, Derby forward Steve Biggins, and ex-Burnley and Leeds striker Ray Hankin, sacked by Peterborough after a string of dismissals. Ex-Everton and QPR midfielder Andy King was signed only after he agreed to pay his own £6,000 transfer fee to Dutch club Cambuur Leeuwarden as a way of getting back to England. Another late-season arrival was New Zealander Ricki Herbert, who had played for Docherty in Sydney. The two sons of chief scout Sammy Chapman, 17-year-old forward Cavan and 21-year-old defender Campbell, were each given a handful of games.

One summer signing, former Leicester midfielder Neville Hamilton, never made it into a Wolves shirt, forced to retire after a heart attack during pre-season training. Alongside him on the pitch that day had been 19-year-old midfielder Ian Cartwright. 'He collapsed right next to me,' says Cartwright, who, while sympathising with the financial restrictions Docherty faced, believes that he proved to be a poor choice as manager. 'I thought he was a good appointment at first, but he thought about himself more than the others. He brought in some people who weren't good enough. It was like friends and family, and it didn't work. Sammy Chapman's sons weren't good enough.'

Unusually, Docherty is accused by Cartwright of not persevering with the more talented youngsters at the club. Cartwright stresses, 'I don't want to talk badly about anyone because he is probably a great bloke,' yet he can't hide his contempt for the way he felt he was treated. 'I was injured and it finished me. He had me training on my bad ankle to get me right, and it just got worse and worse. There were other players who would fanny about and not put a foot in, so I would come in and play injured. They pumped me full of cortisone injections to get me to play. It finished my career in the end. At one point he fined me two weeks' wages and said I wasn't trying because other teams were tapping me up. He dropped me to the reserves and he said that I threatened someone, which I would never have done.'

Things got so bad that Cartwright's father, Fred, went to see Docherty, who told him, 'Your son is angling to get away. Birmingham are interested. He wants a two-year contract instead of one.'

Cartwright explains, 'I wanted two years instead of one because I was injured and I wanted some security. I was already on £20 a week less than a year earlier. The Doc offered my dad his hand and my dad refused to shake it. Docherty said, "You are not a man, Mr Cartwright," and my dad went mad. He was chasing him around the table and Doc was screaming the place down. I had to get my dad off him. He was like a big ape and would have shaken the Doc all over the place if he'd got him.'

Struggling to make changes that would have an impact on the field – despite fielding 30 players in the course of the campaign – Docherty tinkered with the backroom staff, firing assistant manager Jim Barron and youth coach Frank Upton, his old Chelsea player, and adding son Michael and former Aston Villa player Greg Fellows to his staff. 'Getting rid of Frank was the sort of thing I did throughout my career,' he says. 'I did what I had to do. But it made no difference.'

Cartwright believes it made things worse. 'Jim Barron was brilliant, but Greg had done little coaching at that time and Michael wasn't popular. I remember he had upset one of the apprentices, who then put a poo in the bath with him! Tommy was getting on. He was an old man, like a little pot-bellied pig. You sensed he was coming to the end. He was just gobby. Someone like Harry Redknapp is a motivator, but Tommy at that time was just a bullshitter.'

Instead of inspiring a revival, Docherty's personnel changes left him facing an industrial tribunal ruling four months later that he had acted unfairly in dismissing his coaches. He told the court that he had simply decided that they did not have the ability he required. His actions were hardly unusual practice in the world of football, but out of step with a more enlightened age of industrial relations.

Meanwhile, an attempt to sign veteran former England striker Frank Worthington on loan fell down when Docherty claimed Brighton wanted a fee. 'That's no way to do business,' he complained.

A 1–0 win at Portsmouth at the end of October, courtesy of a goal by on-loan Celtic forward Jim Melrose, was the club's first in sixteen away games and one of the season's few high spots. More typical were the failure to raise the £40,000 needed to sign Melrose permanently and the Football League's November ultimatum to pay the money they owed to four former players. In January 1985, with gates dropping to around 6,000, Dougan resigned, frustrated by the increasing remoteness of the Bhatti brothers and thwarted in his attempts to source funding for a takeover. 'It was an acrimonious departure,' says Hope.

As Wolves went four months and twenty-one matches without a win, Docherty resorted to gallows humour. He said of his back four, 'I am glad I didn't have you defending me in my court case. The judge would have put his black cap on.' And his attackers were also on the receiving end: 'We're allergic to opponents' penalty areas. When we score, they declare a public holiday.'

The inevitable relegation was confirmed – barring a mathematical miracle – with two games still to play when Wolves lost 5–1 at Brighton. Ainscow, who appeared in every game, recalled the trip to the south coast being the perfect summing-up of the season. 'We drove past all these lovely hotels on the sea front. Then we disappeared up one of the back streets and realised we were staying in a guest house.'

The travelling Wolves fans' generous reception for Docherty showed that most didn't hold him responsible, although in another of his after-dinner stories he recounts meeting a group compiling a petition for his dismissal, which he promptly offered to sign himself.

In that morning's papers he had warned, 'The Bhattis need to decide whether to finance the club or sell it. I will carry on next season, but I don't know whether the club can continue this way. I am trying to build a team, but it's impossible.' And after defeat he added, 'What has happened to Wolves is the result of 15 years' bad directorship.' The season concluded with a home win against Huddersfield in front of a pitiful crowd of 4,422 and a defeat at Blackburn that left them bottom of the table.

Docherty had been wrong in one respect. He wouldn't be back. On 4 July, he was given his independence, sacked by the club. 'They wanted to get rid of me and I couldn't wait to go,' he says. The impossible task he'd faced was evidenced by Wolves suffering their third consecutive relegation the following season under two different managers, including, briefly, the returning Bill McGarry.

Docherty's own misfortune, added to events that befell football that spring at Bradford and the Heysel Stadium – tragedies killing 91 people – left him ready to turn his back on the sport that had been his life. 'Managed-out' is how he describes himself at that time.

Unwilling to start applying for jobs at his time of life, he received a few offers that appeared to promise only the same trauma he'd been through at Preston and Wolves. Such positions, he felt, were better left to someone with fewer than almost 57 years on the clock. Media work and after-dinner speaking offered a way to put his experience and personality to good use without the aggravation.

The headlines continued to trail in his wake, however, whether for a two-year driving ban in the summer of 1985 after being found to have been three times over the legal alcohol limit as he drove home from a dinner in Liverpool, or being connected with the Republic of Ireland job early in 1986 before Jack Charlton began his famous reign.

And his domestic situation continued to hold a fascination for the tabloids. In April 1986, Agnes told the newspapers that she was suing Docherty for £5,000 in maintenance arrears, claiming that she was living off the goodwill of her bank manager while her estranged husband, although out of football, was earning a living from his public appearances. 'My information is that he is in demand and can earn a lucrative living from after-dinner speaking,' she said. 'I really do wish it had not come to this. I didn't want to have to advertise to find out what Tommy is doing.' Agnes claimed that she had not received her monthly money from Docherty since he had been fired by Wolves.

When the case came to court several months later, by which time the amount owed had risen to more than £9,000, Docherty's lawyers argued that Agnes had been infringing the terms of the maintenance settlement by continuing to refuse her husband the divorce he desired, which she had said was down to her Catholic beliefs. The divorce duly became final in February 1987 and the following month saw the conclusion of the financial row. With the arrears now at £10,500, Agnes was offered a final settlement of £15,000. When Docherty claimed he was bankrupt, she felt obliged to agree to the payment. 'Not only had he left me,' she would say later, 'he had also left me virtually destitute.'

Like the old heavyweight who decides he has one more tilt at the title in him, a combination of financial expediency and the restless desire to test himself a final time drove Docherty back into the football ring late in 1987. This, however, was the equivalent of being on the undercard at a municipal town hall.

Altrincham were one of the biggest clubs at their level in the country, and Docherty's description of them as 'the Manchester United of non-League football' was one of his less extravagant claims. Yet it was still a long way from where he'd been a decade earlier. 'You have something in your blood and it's hard to get it out even after all these years,' he said on becoming their manager. But, looking back at the job for which he broke his retirement, he admits, 'I shouldn't have done it.'

The GM Vauxhall Conference side's approach came during September from chairman Gerry Burman, following the resignation of John Williams ten games into the campaign. Former Norwich and Manchester City boss John Bond had also been considered, with Burman stating, 'Our aim is to get into the Fourth Division as quickly as possible.'

The club had won the Conference – formed in 1979 as the Alliance Premier League – in the first two years of its existence and as recently as two years earlier had won the FA Trophy and reached the fourth round of the FA Cup. Yet they'd had to settle for fifth the previous season and had not won in their last seven games when Burman, willing to work around Docherty's other commitments, introduced his new manager.

Jean Rook, one of Docherty's biggest critics a decade earlier, felt bound to have a dig at his latest job in her *Daily Express* column. 'It takes valour to pick up your life and run with it,' she noted with a tone of sarcasm, 'even when nobody's cheering.'

There were 2,328 – more than double the previous home attendance – cheering at Altrincham's Moss Lane ground when Docherty marked his arrival by ending the club's disappointing run with a 2–0 win against Runcorn. Former First Division centre-forward David Cross, who was coaching at the club, commented, 'You could see the lift the Doc gave the lads tonight. Of course he still means something.'

Docherty confessed, 'It's going to be tough dealing with my own expectations. I might want a standard of football that is just not possible, so I'll have to adjust.' Although several divisions from the highest level of the game, he was not averse to using his new position to having a dig at the long-ball style of play that had seen a series of less fashionable teams challenging the traditional glamour clubs. 'I won't have my players kicking the ball as if they hate it,' he affirmed. 'I tell them that the ball is to be caressed, possessed, not just booted. I won't tolerate the Wimbledon, Watford, Sheffield Wednesday stuff, even at this level. Football wasn't meant to be run by two linesmen and air traffic control.'

Over the next few weeks, Docherty made his customary wholesale changes. Results were solid yet unspectacular: eight wins, seven losses and two draws by the following February. One of those defeats had represented Docherty's final encounter with the competition that had played such an important part in his story. Wigan Athletic put paid to his hopes of a money-spinning and headline-making run in the FA Cup with a 2–0 win at Moss Lane in the first round.

In spite of unremarkable results, Docherty enjoyed a good relationship with Burman but grew tired of the other directors constantly questioning him about team affairs. When Burman was replaced as chairman by Geoff Lloyd in February 1988, Docherty was gone within 24 hours. 'I had a chat with Tommy and it became evident we didn't see eye to eye on the way the club should be run,' said Lloyd. 'It was best that we parted company.'

Describing Lloyd as a 'babe in the wood', Docherty added, 'He has been in the game for three years and I have been in it for forty. I couldn't work with him.'

When Lloyd concluded, 'It's down to a clash of personalities,' Docherty responded with another of his favourite put-downs. 'It can't have been a clash of personalities; he didn't have one.' He has used the line about many others since, including Sir Alex Ferguson.

But he would never again need to use the line with which he departed Altrincham: 'I know I have said it before, but this is definitely the end.'

And this time it was.

There were no more matches for Docherty, but there was one important date circled in his diary. On 28 May 1988, 11 years after the world became aware of their commitment to each other, he and Mary were married at Chorley Register Office. Liverpool manager Kenny Dalglish, whom Docherty had given his first Scotland cap, was among those who attended the celebrations.

Mary told journalists, 'We have been very, very happy together,' while some newspaper reports of the event still referred to 'lovestruck Tommy Docherty'. According to broadcaster James H. Reeve, who was about to get to know Docherty through a long broadcasting partnership, he meets that description even now. 'He and Mary are still like a couple of teenagers,' he says. 'Tommy and I went somewhere to do a gig and he insisted on stopping on the way back to buy her a little gift even though he'd only been away 24 hours.'

Football has, of course, continued to be as central to Docherty's life as Mary, their daughters and grandchildren. In 1989, he even played a cameo role in a BBC Scotland play, *The Gift*, about a pair of aspiring young professional footballers. When told that his part as a manager would keep him occupied for about ten days, he is said to have replied, 'That's about par for the course.'

For eight years, from 1986 to 1994, Docherty was a regular voice as Reeve's radio partner, most notably on Manchester station Piccadilly. 'I was put on anchoring the Saturday afternoon sports show,' Reeve recalls. 'I was comparatively well known for being a City fan and they decided they wanted someone to balance it out. After his fall-out with United, Tommy had done a couple of phone-ins and they had gone well. I had never met him. The only time I had ever seen him was when he used to live in Sale and a few of us gave him the V-sign as he drove past. They stuck us together and it evolved into something a lot of people found entertaining. We would have an hour with Tom in the studio talking about the prospects for the day and then he would go to whoever was playing at home – United, City or sometimes

Oldham – and would join us from the ground.'

According to Reeve, Docherty became a skilled broadcaster. 'He knew what he was talking about. But he knew how to play people, how to wind people up. One thing he learned to do on the radio was, every now and again, drop one in that he knew would get people furious. He'd say that "the boy cannae play" and you would see the switchboard light up.'

For the most part he was reliable, although Reeve explains, 'He did the occasional crafty one. Once, in the days when mobile phones were becoming popular, we managed to ring him to see where he was and he said, "I am in Dumfries. I rang in and told someone I wouldn't be there." He had got a big earner so he had fucked off there instead. But there were only a couple of those.'

Docherty and Malcolm Allison, in many ways kindred spirits, both found themselves out of football in the mid-'90s. It seemed natural, therefore, that they found a way to work together, even though Allison had not always been particularly complimentary about Docherty's achievements. At the conclusion of Docherty's career, Allison had said, 'Doc milked his image, but when you look at his career, what did he really achieve? He made a lot of people laugh, but you have to look hard to see how he built his reputation as a serious football man. As a coach and a manager I believe he destroyed more players than he made. His ego was destructive.'

Docherty would have recognised such comments as an example of giving his newspaper ghostwriter something to get his teeth into. He'd done it often enough himself. Allison, meanwhile, came to realise that Docherty's ability to make people laugh could be an asset, and the pair of them toured around small theatres in a show billed as 'The Doc and Big Mal – a frank and outspoken evening crammed with the stories they could not tell on TV'. *The Times* even sent Clement Freud along to critique the performance, but he confessed to leaving at the interval.

The double act disbanded quickly, but Docherty's has continued to be one of the first telephone numbers radio stations and newspaper men look up when needing a comment on a breaking news story, especially when it has something to do with Manchester United or Scotland. Barely a managerial change has occurred at his national team or a major transfer taken place at Old Trafford without someone asking Docherty's opinion, which he remains more than happy to offer. And if his views have wounded some people, well, he remains no more concerned about that than he was over upsetting players who fell out of favour at the clubs he managed.

Reeve continues, 'I think sometimes he would fail to give United the benefit of the doubt. He has got grudges against them because of the way they handled things with him, but I don't think it turned him into a United hater to the degree that it was detectable on air.'

Docherty admits he 'doesn't really know' Ferguson, but what he sees of him as a man he has not found appealing. He adds, however, 'Managerial-wise I wouldn't say a word against him. He has been fantastic and you can't argue with his record.'

His relationship with United is virtually non-existent. Whether or not it is related to the nature of his dismissal in 1977 he doesn't know, but it certainly does not compare to the way he is still greeted at Stamford Bridge or was welcomed to Aston Villa by former chairman Doug Ellis. 'Chelsea really look after you,' he says, 'and I have tickets there whenever I want. When it was my daughter's 21st birthday she wanted United tickets so I called them up and they arranged them for me. And then I got an invoice!'

What has meant more to Docherty in later life than freebies from Old Trafford are the laughs from audiences and the requests to keep rolling out his comedy routine. 'I work as much or as little as I want,' he says. 'I do the after-dinner speeches and the cruises. It's work. I am not the type of person who wants to sit in the house. You meet a lot of people and I enjoy the cruises. You do one performance, get a good fee and have a good time.'

And he retains a sense of childish delight that the sport he grew up loving can still help him pay the bills in the ninth decade of his life: 'I never thought I would make a living out of football. I just loved playing.'

As you might expect from someone whose first pay cheque from the professional game was £10, he believes there is no justification for the vast amounts paid to today's Premier League players, calling it 'crackpot stuff' and saying, 'We were players trying to become stars. Now they are stars trying to become players.' Although happy that his days of £20-per-week 'slavery' were abolished, he struggles to reconcile the lifestyle enjoyed by the journeymen of today with Tom Finney running a plumbing business to ensure a comfortable existence. The response he receives when he speaks about such issues convinces him there are many who feel the same.

The obvious question to ponder when Docherty discusses the modern game is how a man so symbolic of bygone times – the players-next-door of the '50s and the maverick managers of the '70s – would have fared in the Premier League. It is hard to imagine the self-important players and self-serving agents who litter the game standing for the kind of confrontation to which Docherty subjected his squad on a daily basis.

Bruce Rioch, who went from playing for Docherty to managing in the top flight, says, 'Players would be happy with him if they were in the side, but if you have players sitting on the sidelines on three-year contracts worth £50,000 a week, you aren't going to budge them the way Tommy liked to. In simple terms, the job is about getting good players, moulding them into a team, coaching and handling them well, getting the best out of them and supporting them in every single way – not hanging them out to dry in public. You wouldn't get away with that now. It happened in the past, but it's a different culture.'

It's difficult to pin Docherty down for a thoughtful answer on the subject, but when pushed he replies, 'On the field I would be no different today than I was back in the '60s and '70s. My principles would be the same: attacking football, playing 4–2–4 with two wingers. I have always believed in that. Away from the field, it is very different. My chairman at Chelsea always gave me a straight, honest answer and had patience. All these foreign owners, they have no patience. And if you leave a player out of the team now he goes running off to his agent.'

It is hard, then, to see the old Docherty thriving in the twenty-first century. Yet Steve Coppell is convinced that, cutting through the predictable bluster about overseas ownership and the lack of young British talent at top clubs, the old boss he admires so much would find a way. 'Doc is one of the brightest people I have met,' he insists. 'Sometimes he might appear rough and ready and sometimes he speaks before he engages his brain, but he is very sharp and calculating. He would have adapted to the demands of the modern game.'

And the likes of Sky Sports News would never have been away from his office. 'He would have been made for the interviews they do now,' Coppell continues. 'They would be replayed a hundred times. He would be provocative, he would be challenging and he would be on the back page more often than not. He was bright enough to change. He always had that quality.'

Of course, Docherty is right when he suggests that the modern Chelsea and Manchester United would be unlikely to tolerate a manager who suffered relegation, whatever flamboyance he brought to their clubs. Former player and colleague Ken Shellito says, 'I don't think Tom would have a cat in hell's chance of surviving in management now because the game and the people have changed completely. They don't want fun any more. How many footballers smile? That has all gone. There is so much pressure, and people like Tom and Ron Greenwood wouldn't last. It would destroy their personality.'

Perhaps the great Lionel Messi is one of the few who plays consistently with the sense of joy to which Shellito refers. And it is he who finally stands comparison, in Docherty's mind, to his former teammate. 'He reminds me of Finney with his attitude, the way he plays,' he says. 'You never see him involved in any unsavoury things, you never hear him criticising anyone. To me, Messi is Finney reborn.'

As Docherty goes through the roll call of his own teams and players, he names Chelsea's Peter Osgood as the greatest he ever managed. And he adds, 'I think my best days were at Chelsea. They were a fantastic club, I had a fantastic chairman and it was my first job as a manager, which makes it special.'

Recapping the second half of his managerial career, he reiterates, 'I should have stayed with Scotland. There was unfinished business. I had a great squad of players and we would have done well. But to go to United, where the politics was unbelievable, well . . . But I don't beat myself up about going there because if I hadn't I wouldn't have met Mary.'

Docherty spends little time analysing the decisions that have guided his life off the field and determined results on it, saying, 'Hindsight is a marvellous thing. It is easy to think of players you should not have bought and games you should have won. You do what you think is right at the time. I made some great moves and some bad ones.'

To his gratification, he discovers as he tours the clubs that however many trophies he may have won, or failed to win, those who saw his teams play retain fond memories. 'It is because of the type of football we played. I get a lot of people coming up to me saying that they had a great time at Old Trafford or Stamford Bridge, saying what a great team it was to watch, either winning 5–0 or losing 5–0.'

He prefers to take pride in that rather than debating the truth inherent in comments such as author Jeremy Novick's comparison with one of his old boys, George Graham. 'Graham thought that defence was the best form of defence. He also thought that defence was the best form of attack,' Novick writes. 'Tom won a couple of cups and picked up his Jack Nicklaus gag. George won everything and stayed at the Arsenal for a hundred years. There's a moral there somewhere.'

Regrets? Docherty has undeniably had a few. But too few to make him lose sleep over his own assessment that 'whatever charisma I have will always overshadow what I might have achieved in the game'.

Docherty is flawed. He is human. His misjudgements have been many: just count up the relegations and broken relationships alongside the trophies and tributes. The nature of his profession and his personality is that every turn he has taken in life has been scrutinised. With one notable exception – the disastrous libel case – he has accepted that people will say and think what they like and has tried, publicly at least, to retain an unconcerned air. Even after agreeing to participate in this book, he made no effort to influence its contents beyond what he chose to tell me in interview. He was even suggesting certain people I should contact, saying, 'They'll slag me off for you.'

Of course, a man who has happily built a post-football career upon the public's fascination for him is hardly in a position to complain when his life is dissected – although one of Britain's most eminent sports journalists, Patrick Collins, once suggested it was the media who were responsible for 'The Doc' in the first place. 'Had we left him alone, he might well have remained an adequate coach of impressionable youngsters,' he said. 'But we didn't. We nourished his ego, propagated his elderly jokes, publicised his dubious judgements and he became a "character".'

Which brings us back to our starting point: with Docherty running through his repertoire of anecdotes, put-downs and self-deprecation, each burst of laughter further immortalising the alter ego and pushing the achievements of the football man more completely into the wings.

On the day I am writing these words, Docherty is celebrating his 85th birthday. We last spoke a couple of weeks ago, when he was getting ready to watch the Manchester derby on television and was already looking forward to a summer that would feature three or four more cruises. I'd called to ask him to consider that question of how he would fare in the modern game, yet the mere knowledge that his words are being recorded seems to act as some kind of Pavlovian trigger. 'With all my sackings I would end up a millionaire,' he'd joked, as if unable to prevent himself slipping into wisecracking mode.

Finally, I'd asked how he would be marking his impending milestone, intending to follow up with something about thoughts of mortality. 'I'm not sure yet what I'll be doing,' he answered, before delivering the line I guessed was coming because I'd seen him use it before. 'If I'd known I was going to live this long I'd have taken better care of myself!'

You can be waiting a long time if you wait for Tommy Docherty to be serious and introspective; and you can strive for ever to determine if there is a point where the on-stage and on-field personas can be separated. Probably even he can no longer see the join. The merging of the two components are what make up 'The Doc' and without one or the other, his sport, over the course of several decades, would have been a duller place.

BIBLIOGRAPHY

Batty, Clive, *Kings of the King's Road: The Great Chelsea Team of the 60s and 70s* (Vision Sports Publishing, 2004).

Best, George, with Roy Collins, *Blessed: The Autobiography* (Ebury Press, 2001).

Burrowes, John, *Benny: The Life and Times of a Fighting Legend* (Mainstream, 1982).

Charlton, Sir Bobby, with James Lawton, *The Autobiography: My Manchester United Years* (Headline, 2007).

Clarke, Brian, *Docherty: Living Legend of Football* (Kingswood Press, 1991).

Clarke, Thurn, *By Blood and Fire: The Attack on the King David Hotel* (Hutchinson, 1981).

Coppell, Steve, with Bob Harris, *Touch and Go* (Willow Books, 1985).

Crerand, Paddy, *Never Turn the Other Cheek* (Harper Sport, 2007).

Dalglish, Kenny, with Henry Winter, *Dalglish: My Autobiography* (Hodder and Stoughton, 1996).

Dunphy, Eamon, *A Strange Kind of Glory: Sir Matt Busby & Manchester United* (William Heinemann, 1991).

Docherty, Agnes, with Tom Docherty, *Dear Tommy* (John Blake, 2009).

Docherty, Tommy, *Soccer from the Shoulder* (The Soccer Book Club, 1960).

—— *The Doc: My Story – Hallowed Be Thy Game* (Headline, 2006).

——, with Derek Henderson, *Call the Doc* (Hamlyn, 1981).

——, with Roy Peskett. *Tommy Docherty Speaks* (Pelham Books, 1967).

Egan, Sean, *The Doc's Devils: Manchester United 1972–1977* (Cherry Red Books, 2010).

BIBLIOGRAPHY

Falkner, David, *The Last Yankee: The Turbulent Life of Billy Martin* (Simon and Schuster, 1992).

Finney, Tom, *My Autobiography* (Headline, 2003).

Glanville, Brian, *The Story of the World Cup* (Faber and Faber, 2001).

Gordos, Steve, *Peter Broadbent: A Biography* (Breedon Books, 2007).

Graham, George, with Norman Giller, *The Glory and the Grief* (Andre Deutsch, 1995).

Grant, Michael and Rob Robertson, *The Management: Scotland's Great Football Bosses* (Birlinn, 2011).

Hale, Steve E., *Mr Tottenham Hotspur: Bill Nicholson OBE* (Football World, 2005).

Keith, John, *Billy Liddell: The Legend Who Carried the Kop* (Robson Books, 2004).

Kingsley-Long H. and A. McArthur, *No Mean City* (Corgi Books edition, 1978).

Kurt, Richard and Chris Nickeas, *The Red Army Years: Manchester United in the 1970s* (Headline, 1997).

Law, Denis, with Bob Harris, *The King: My Autobiography* (Bantam Press, 2003).

Lorimer, Peter and Phil Rostron, *Peter Lorimer: Leeds and Scotland Hero* (Mainstream, 2002).

Macari, Lou, *United: We Shall Not Be Moved* (Souvenir Press, 1976).

Macari, Lou, *Football: My Life* (Bantam Press, 2008).

McIlroy, Sammy, *Manchester United: My Team* (Souvenir Press, 1980).

Mears, Brian, with Ian MacLeay, *Chelsea: Football Under the Blue Flag* (Mainstream, 2001).

Meek, David (ed.), *The Manchester United Football Book* (Stanley Paul, various years).

Mitten, Andy, *United! United! Old Trafford in the '70s: The Players' Stories* (Vision Sports Publishing, 2011).

Motson, John, *Match of the Day: The Complete Record since 1964* (BBC Sport, 1992).

Neill, Terry, *Revelations of a Football Manager* (Sidgwick and Jackson, 1985).

Novick, Jeremy, *In a League of their Own: Football's Maverick Managers* (Mainstream, 1995).

O'Farrell, Frank, with Jeff Welch, *All Change at Old Trafford: The Frank O'Farrell Story* (Backpass, 2011).

Osgood, Peter, with Martin King and Martin Knight, *Ossie: King of Stamford Bridge* (Mainstream, 2002).

Pawson, Tony, *The Football Managers* (Eyre Methuen, 1973).

Puskás, Ferenc, *Captain of Hungary* (Cassell, 1955).

Sandbrook, Dominic, *State of Emergency: The Way We Were – Britain 1970–74* (Allen Lane, 2010).

Soar, Phil and Martin Tyler, *Arsenal: The Official Centenary History of Arsenal Football Club* (Book Club Associates, 1986).

Stepney, Alex, *Alex Stepney* (Arthur Baker, 1978).

Tossell, David, *Big Mal: The High Life and Hard Times of Malcolm Allison, Football Legend* (Mainstream, 2008).

Venables, Terry and Neil Hanson, *Venables: The Autobiography* (Michael Joseph, 1994).

White, Jim, *Manchester United: The Biography* (Sphere, 2008).

Whitehead, Richard, *Children of the Revolution: Aston Villa in the 1970s* (Sports Projects Ltd, 2001).

The following annuals, periodicals and other publications have also been particularly valuable reference sources: *Rothman's Football Yearbook* (Macdonald and Jane's/Queen Anne Press, various years); *News of the World Football Annual* (various years); *Shoot!*, *Goal*, *Charles Buchan's Football Monthly*, *Football Pictorial*, *World Soccer*, *Barnet Press*, *Birmingham Mail*, *Derby Evening Telegraph*, *Glasgow Herald*, *Lancashire Evening Post*, *Manchester Evening News*, *Melbourne Age*, *Sheffield Star*, *Sydney Morning Herald*, *Wolverhampton Express* and *Star* and multiple UK national newspapers.